# CONFRONTING
# RACISM

# CONFRONTING RACISM

## The Problem
## and the Response

Jennifer L. Eberhardt &
Susan T. Fiske *Editors*

**SAGE** Publications
*International Educational and Professional Publisher*
Thousand Oaks   London   New Delhi

*For information:*

SAGE Publications, Inc.
2455 Teller Road
Thousand Oaks, California 91320
E-mail: order@sagepub.com

SAGE Publications Ltd.
6 Bonhill Street
London EC2A 4PU
United Kingdom

SAGE Publications India Pvt. Ltd.
M-32 Market
Greater Kailash I
New Delhi 110 048 India

Printed in the United States of America

*Library of Congress Cataloging-in-Publication Data*

Main entry under title:

Confronting racism: The problem and the response / edited by
    Jennifer L. Eberhardt and Susan T. Fiske.
        p.  cm.
    Includes bibliographical references and index.
    ISBN 0-7619-0367-4 (cloth : alk. paper).—ISBN 0-7619-0368-2 (pbk. : alk. paper)
    1. United States—Race relations.  2. Racism—United States.
    I. Eberhardt, Jennifer Lynn.  II. Fiske, Susan T.
    E185.615.R2145  1998
    305.8'00973—dc21                                                97-45337

98  99  00  01  02  03  04  10  9  8  7  6  5  4  3  2  1

| | |
|---|---|
| *Acquiring Editor:* | Jim Nageotte |
| *Editorial Assistant:* | Fiona Lyon |
| *Production Editor:* | Sanford Robinson |
| *Production Assistant:* | Denise Santoyo |
| *Typesetter/Designer:* | Marion Warren |
| *Indexer:* | Teri Greenberg |
| *Cover Designer:* | Ravi Balasuriya |
| *Print Buyer:* | Anna Chin |

# Contents

## PART 2: The Response

# Preface

Racism is today's news. Some would have you believe that it's yesterday's news. Or that it never was news, only a figment of paranoid imagination, or self-interest—playing the race card to gain unfair advantage. Others would have you believe that you can ignore race in today's society by being color-blind, not noticing whether people are black, white, yellow, red, or brown. This book provides plenty of evidence that racism is a serious, current problem, and that ignoring race will not make it go away.

Racism is a problem for Americans—today. Look at the newspaper; listen to the talk shows; listen to the casual comments people make to each other. The controversy regarding affirmative action, crime debates laced with racial images, the latest racially tinged trial and the riots that may come in its wake, and other public controversies of the past decade all highlight the need for a new and thorough examination of racism and racial relations in the United States. Public discourse is replete with racially linked attitudes or concerns. Race plays a fundamental role in many of the most contentious political and social issues: violence, welfare, taxes, budgets, education, and health. Race remains a part of the debate relating to almost any government program or institution. Race and racism are everywhere in our country.

What have been your own responses to racism? Maybe you went to a fairly segregated high school or work in a fairly segregated organization and wonder why it remains so homogeneous. Maybe you went to an ethnically varied high school or work in an ethnically varied organization and wonder why people still seem to cluster by ethnicity. Or, maybe you went to an ethnically varied high school or work in an ethnically varied organization, where people all mix randomly without regard to race, but wonder why the outside world remains racially divided.

Whatever your experiences, *Confronting Racism: The Problem and the Response* should convince you to consider the *problem* of racism—whether

- racism indeed is a problem;
- racism has fundamentally changed;
- racism inevitably involves power and dominance;
- race is socially constructed to serve society;
- racial threat is a worldwide problem;
- white American racism toward black Americans is unique.

Whether you are considered white, black, partly, either, both, or neither, the book should also compel you to ponder your own *response:*

- How do potential victims respond to racism?
- On the other hand, how do potential perpetrators of racism respond to racism?
- Does racism destroy the self-esteem of its victims?
- How do Americans who are perceived as black buy into that identity?
- What effect does black racial identification carry for inclusion in "mainstream" American life?
- How can white and black Americans be comfortable together?
- Do we feel angry, awkward, or self-confident in interracial encounters?
- How can institutions encourage tolerance and enthusiasm between people of different ethnicities?
- What long-term effects will interracial contact have on people?

*Confronting Racism: The Problem and the Response* provides a contemporary, systematic treatment of the changing racial dynamics of U.S. society, linking social scientific insights and the practical problems of our society. The discipline of social psychology, bolstered by recent theoretical and methodological advances, is uniquely suited to answer some of the most perplexing questions about contemporary race relations. This collection of writings by distinguished experts on race accomplishes a comprehensive and systematic social psychological analysis of the role of race in U.S. society. The work presented here employs a wide range of theoretical approaches—and empirical methods that range from the minute measurement of subliminal responses to international demographic trends. The book identifies critical cognitive and motivational influences on the intrapersonal, interpersonal, and intergroup processes that lead to racism. These social scientists collectively account for the variety of racial outcomes and dynamics that result from the complex and multifaceted nature of contemporary racism and racial relations.

The book links public discourse on race and social scientific analysis in a way that few other books have. The reader will come to understand how racial attitudes both affect and reflect trends in public discourse. The authors introduce the reader to general social psychological principles through the analysis of specific racial issues. Their approach not only connects race with broader social psychological processes but also deepens the reader's appreciation of the interdependence of the individual and the social environment.

This book explores the experiences of those forgotten actors in the racial drama: the targets of race prejudice and stereotyping. Whereas much social psychological research during the past five decades has been inspired by the need to reduce the negative impact felt by the targets of racism, those same targets of racism, until recently, have rarely been the focus of research. Although central to our understanding of contemporary racial dynamics, responses of the targets have not been systematically examined in any introductory text such as this one.

Finally, the book connects theory and practice in the diverse social domains within which race prejudice and stereotyping operate. What are the policy implications of social psychological research on race in the areas of education, employment, law, crime, and politics? What individual interventions might be successful in ameliorating some of the most harmful effects of racism in a particular area? *Confronting Racism: The Problem and the Response* tries to answer these questions.

## ■ How This Book Came to Be What It Is

Eberhardt and Fiske have in common a Harvard doctorate, but 15 years apart. We met in the spring of 1993, brought together by James Jones (the commentator on this volume), and commenced a research collaboration and friendship that has spanned the continent and the subsequent years. Both of us teach courses in the psychology of racism, and both of us were dissatisfied with then available texts. Both of us talk to concerned citizens and policymakers, and both of us wanted to recommend a volume that collected social psychology's major race scholars in an accessible form. This book resulted from those shared discontents.

Some of the chapters in this book are based on talks delivered at a 1994 conference titled "Racism: The Problem and the Response," held at the University of Massachusetts at Amherst. We are grateful to the 1993-1994 Chancellor's Multicultural Advisory Board for funding that conference, and to Christine McGroarty, Beth Morling, and Don Operario, for helping organize it. Prominent social psychologists presented research related to racism with special attention given to its impact on college campuses. Other distinguished social psychologists have provided chapters that broaden the focus beyond the academy to other societal domains. Besides presenting applicable theory and empirical findings, the authors outline anti-racism strategies that emerge from their research, discuss how these strategies might be implemented, and analyze how much change is possible and how quickly this change is likely to take place. We are especially pleased that about half the authors of these chapters identify as black, and about half as white (and some as neither); in 1990s academia, we feel fortunate to have assembled such a fine roster of minds.

## ■ Two Notes

A note about terminology—for the most part, we use the terms *black* and *white* to refer to people racially categorized or racially identified. We considered terms such as African American, European American, Caribbean American, but felt that the crucial cultural distinction these days places people into black or white, regardless of their most recent or historical family origins. Except in an explicit international context, we have encouraged our authors to do the same. We have also opted to lower case black and white, so as not to unduly dignify these terms, for they are fraught with cultural baggage.

Another note about inclusion: We deliberately focused this book on white racism toward black targets. For one thing, most extant social psychological research focuses on this particular case. For another, several chapters defend the idea that this constitutes a unique case—of legalized slavery, problematic persistence, power dynamics, and institutional intransigence. We agree, but we in no way prioritize this one form of oppression over other forms. Each has its own historical, cultural, and social psychological dynamics. Nevertheless, the principles of white-on-black racism provide important insights about other target groups, other perpetrators, and their various combinations; the authors note many of these, and we hope these insights spark more research on neglected issues.

## ■ Who Should Read This Book

This book is ideal for college undergraduates, beginning graduate students, college administrators, organizational managers, and concerned citizens everywhere. Racial tension has become a problem on many college campuses and in many workplaces, but has not been addressed by any systematic presentation of writings such as this.

*Confronting Racism: The Problem and the Response* fits well in diversity courses, which are increasingly common in colleges, universities, and organizations. It deals with racism at the face-to-face level so important to individuals in any kind of organization. This book offers insightful analysis of the factors producing and contributing to negative racial attitudes and problematic interracial relations.

The book is also for those committed to combating racism in the workplace. Like colleges and universities, organizations are increasingly concerned with creating healthy and productive environments for individuals from diverse groups. This book could be a useful supplement to many such diversity courses, workshops, or instructional formats.

Finally, the book is for those involved in creating social policy. The authors not only present their research, but discuss effective strategies for reducing racial problems and suggest specific methods of intervention that bridge the gap between theory and practice.

Whoever you are, gentle reader, you need to know more about racism. We all do.

—JENNIFER L. EBERHARDT
SUSAN T. FISKE

*To my mother, Mary, and the memory of my father, Harlan*
*—JLE*

*To my parents, Barbara and Donald*
*—STF*

*For their inspiration*

# PART 1

---

# The Problem

# 1

# On the Nature of Contemporary Prejudice

## The Causes, Consequences, and Challenges of Aversive Racism

*John F. Dovidio*
*Samuel L. Gaertner*

ace relations in the United States are better now than ever before. Or are they? On one hand, the dramatic positive impact of the civil rights legislation of the 1960s is undeniable. Before this legislation, in many parts of the country, it was customary for whites to limit the freedom of blacks (e.g., limiting blacks to the back of buses), to demand deference from blacks (e.g., requiring blacks to give up their seats to whites on buses), and to restrict residential, educational, and employment opportunities for blacks. Under the civil rights legislation, discrimination and segregation became no longer simply immoral, but also illegal. As a consequence, black Americans currently have greater access to political, social, and economic opportunities than ever before in our history. On the other hand, there are new signals of deteriorating race relations. Symptoms of racial tension, which emerged in the 1960s, are reappearing. As the 1990s began, riots in Miami, Tampa, New Jersey, Washington, D.C., and Los Angeles reflected large-scale and violent racial unrest. Over the past 5 years, over 300 colleges have reported significant racial incidents and protests. In the first 6 months of 1996, there were 27 suspicious

AUTHORS' NOTE: The work presented in this chapter was supported by NIMH Grant MH-48721. We express our appreciation to Jennifer Eberhardt and Susan Fiske for their thoughtful comments on earlier versions of the chapter. Correspondence regarding this chapter should be addressed to John F. Dovidio, Department of Psychology, Colgate University, Hamilton, NY 13346.

3

fires, presumed to be racially motivated arson, across the South (Morganthau, 1996). The majority of blacks in the United States today have a profound distrust of the police and the legal system, and about a third are overtly distrustful of whites in general (Anderson, 1996). Middle-class blacks are very worried about the future for blacks and for the nation (Hochschild, 1995). This chapter examines one factor that contributes to the current frustrations of black Americans: the operation of a subtle form of racism among individuals that is less overt but just as insidious as old-fashioned racism.

## ■ Racial Attitudes in the United States

Across time, the attitudes of whites toward minorities, in general, and blacks, in particular, are becoming less negative and more accepting. Negative stereotypes are declining. For example, in 1933, 75% of white respondents described blacks as lazy; in 1993, that figure declined to just 5% (Dovidio, Brigham, Johnson, & Gaertner, 1996). White America is also becoming more accepting of black leaders. In 1958, the majority of whites reported that they would not be willing to vote for a well-qualified black presidential candidate; in 1994, over 90% said that they would (Davis & Smith, 1994). In addition, the increase in tolerance of white Americans extends beyond blacks to other racial and ethnic minority groups as well (American National Election Survey, 1995).

Despite these encouraging trends in the intergroup attitudes of white Americans, there are still reasons for concern. One reason is that, across a variety of surveys and polls, 10%-15% of the white population still expresses the old-fashioned, overt form of bigotry. These respondents consistently describe blacks as innately less intelligent than whites, say that they will not vote for a well-qualified presidential candidate simply because of that person's race, and oppose programs designed to ensure full integration and equal opportunity. Another reason for concern is that a substantial portion of the white population expresses merely racial tolerance but not true openness to or enthusiasm for full racial equality. A third reason for concern, which is our current focus, is that there is also evidence that many of the people who are part of the 85%-90% of the white population who say and probably believe that they are not prejudiced may nonetheless be practicing a modern, subtle form of bias.

We believe that the existence of this subtle form of bias helps to account, in part, for the persistence of racism in our society. In a 1988 nationwide poll

(Gelman, 1988), 25% of the black respondents said that they believed that white people "want to hold" black people down; 44% of all respondents said that they believed that society is holding blacks down. In a more recent poll, 32% of blacks reported that discrimination is the primary obstacle to achieving equality in the United States (Anderson, 1996). Furthermore, despite dramatic improvements in whites' expressed racial attitudes over time, racial disparities persist in the United States. Gaps between black and white Americans in physiological areas (e.g., infant mortality, life expectancy) and economic areas (e.g., employment, income, poverty) have continued to exist; and, in many cases, these disparities have actually increased over the past 30 years (Hacker, 1995).

## ■ Aversive Racism

Over the past 20 years, we, with a number of our colleagues, have investigated a prevalent type of modern racial bias, called *aversive racism* (Dovidio & Gaertner, 1991; Gaertner & Dovidio, 1986; Gaertner et al., 1997; Kovel, 1970). In contrast to "old-fashioned" racism, which is expressed directly and openly, aversive racism represents a subtle, often unintentional, form of bias that characterizes many white Americans who possess strong egalitarian values and who believe that they are nonprejudiced. Aversive racists also possess negative racial feelings and beliefs of which they are unaware or that they try to dissociate from their nonprejudiced self-images. The negative feelings that aversive racists have for blacks do not reflect open hostility or hate. Instead, their reactions involve discomfort, uneasiness, disgust, and sometimes fear. That is, they find blacks "aversive," while, at the same time, they find any suggestion that they might be prejudiced aversive as well.

In contrast to traditional approaches that emphasize the psychopathology of prejudice, we propose that the negative feelings that aversive racists harbor toward blacks are rooted in three types of normal, often adaptive, psychological processes. The first process is cognitive and involves the way that people think of others. For example, people inherently categorize others into groups, typically in terms that delineate one's own group from other groups (Hamilton & Trolier, 1986). This classification, in turn, initiates bias: Once categorized, people begin to value others in their own group more and may often devalue others belonging to different groups (Brewer, 1979; Tajfel & Turner, 1979; Turner, 1987). Categorization can occur spontaneously and automatically based on what people see (Campbell, 1958). Because race is one of the first aspects of another person that is noticed, racial categorization can form a foundation from which prejudice develops.

A second type of normal process that can contribute to the development of prejudice is motivation. Motivational processes relate to the desire of people to satisfy basic needs. People have needs—the need for power, the need for control—not only for themselves personally but also for their group (Tajfel & Turner, 1979; see also Chapter 2, this volume). In a world of limited resources, one of the ways that people maintain their control or power is by resisting the progress of competing groups.

The third type of process, which relates to sociocultural influences, involves the fact that people internalize the values and beliefs of society, often automatically (Devine, 1989; see also Chapter 10, this volume). Many of these values reflect racist traditions. Despite the nation's commitment at its inception to the principle that "all men [sic] are created equal," it took the United States almost 200 years to pass legislation guaranteeing that blacks would be equal to whites. Even in contemporary society, subtle messages persist (Dovidio & Gaertner, 1986b, 1991). White males continue to possess a disproportionate amount of political, economic, and social power (Hacker, 1995). This sends a strong message regarding what is valued, whether intentional or not, to people of all colors.

Because of current cultural values, however, most whites also have convictions concerning fairness, justice, and racial equality. The existence of both almost unavoidable racial biases and the desire to be nonprejudiced form the basis of an ambivalence that aversive racists experience (cf. Katz & Hass, 1988; Katz, Wackenhut, & Hass, 1986). We recognize that all racists are not aversive or subtle, that old-fashioned racism still exists, that there are individual differences in aversive racism, and that some whites may not be racist at all. Nevertheless, we propose that aversive racism generally characterizes the racial attitudes of a large proportion of whites who express apparently nonprejudiced views.

The aversive racism framework helps to identify when discrimination against blacks and other minority groups will or will not occur. The ambivalence involving both positive and negative feelings that aversive racists experience creates psychological tension that leads to behavioral instability. Thus, unlike the consistent and overt pattern of discrimination that might be expected from old-fashioned racists, aversive racists sometimes discriminate (manifesting their negative feelings) and sometimes do not (reflecting their egalitarian beliefs). Our research has provided a framework for understanding this pattern of discrimination.

Because aversive racists consciously recognize and endorse egalitarian values—they truly want to be fair and just people—they will not discriminate in situations in which they recognize that discrimination would be obvious to others and themselves. Specifically, we propose that when people are presented with a situation in which the appropriate response is clear, in which right and wrong is clearly defined, aversive racists will not discriminate against blacks. Wrongdoing, which would directly threaten their nonprejudiced self-image, would be too obvious. Because aversive racists still possess negative feelings, however, these negative feelings will eventually be expressed, but they will be expressed in subtle, indirect, and rationalizable ways. For instance, discrimination will occur when appropriate (and thus inappropriate) behavior is not obvious or when an aversive racist can justify or rationalize a negative response on the basis of some factor other than race. Under these circumstances, aversive racists may discriminate, but in a way that insulates them from ever having to believe that their behavior was racially motivated.

Aversive racists may be identified by a constellation of characteristic responses to racial issues and interracial situations. First, aversive racists, in contrast to old-fashioned racists, endorse fair and just treatment of all groups. Second, despite their conscious good intentions, aversive racists unconsciously harbor negative feelings toward blacks, and thus try to avoid interracial interaction. Third, when interracial interaction is unavoidable, aversive racists experience anxiety and discomfort, and consequently they try to disengage from the interaction as quickly as possible. As we noted earlier, the negative feelings that aversive racists have toward blacks involve discomfort rather than hostility or hatred. Fourth, because part of the discomfort that aversive racists experience is due to a concern about acting inappropriately and appearing prejudiced, aversive racists strictly adhere to established rules and codes of behavior in the interracial situations that they cannot avoid. They also frequently assert that they are color-blind; if they do not see race, then it follows that no one can accuse them of being racist. Finally, their negative feelings will get expressed, but in subtle, rationalizable ways that may ultimately disadvantage minorities or unfairly benefit the majority group.

Consistent with the aversive racism perspective, other theories of contemporary racism also hypothesize that bias is currently expressed more subtly than in the past. One such approach is symbolic racism theory (Sears, 1988; Sears, Citrin, & van Laar, 1995; see also Chapter 4, this volume) or a closely related derivation called modern racism theory (McConahay, 1986). According to symbolic racism theory, negative feelings toward blacks that whites acquire early in life persist into adulthood but are expressed indirectly and symbolically, as opposition to busing or resistance to affirmative action, rather than directly or overtly, as in support for segregation. McConahay (1986) further proposes that because modern racism involves the rejection of traditional racist beliefs and the displacement of antiblack feelings onto more abstract social and political issues, modern racists, like aversive racists, are relatively unaware of their racist feelings. Whereas symbolic and modern racism are subtle forms of contemporary racism that seem to exist among political conservatives, aversive racism seems to be more strongly associated with liberals.

We have found consistent support for the aversive racism framework across a broad range of situations (see Gaertner & Dovidio, 1986). In this chapter, we consider four implications of our framework: (a) The bias of aversive racists is expressed in more subtle ways than that of old-fashioned racists; (b) Despite their conscious rejection by aversive racists, unconscious negative feelings linger; (c) Aversive racists express more bias toward higher-status than toward lower-status minorities; and, relatedly, (d) Aversive racists will oppose programs designed to improve the status of blacks, but ostensibly on the basis of factors other than race. We conclude the chapter by briefly reviewing ways of combating subtle bias.

## ■ Subtle, Rationalizable Bias

Because of the ambivalence that characterizes their attitudes toward blacks, aversive racists' interracial behavior is more variable than that of old-fashioned racists. In this section, we illustrate support for our framework concerning how aversive racism operates. We first examine spontaneous reactions to blacks, and then we compare the effects of aversive racism to old-fashioned racism in more deliberative decisions.

*Reactions in an Emergency.* In one of the early tests of our framework (Gaertner & Dovidio, 1977), we tried to take advantage of a naturally occurring event and model it in the laboratory. The event was the Kitty Genovese incident, which occurred in New York City in 1964. Kitty Genovese was returning home one evening. As she entered the parking lot of her building, a man drove up, jumped out of his car, and began to stab her. She screamed. Lights went on in her building. The brutal attack continued for 45 minutes, but no one intervened or even called the police. After he was sure she was dead, the assailant calmly got into his car and drove away.

We know so much about this case because when the police arrived a short time later, they found that there were 38 witnesses who watched the event from beginning to end. How could it happen that none of these people helped, either directly or indirectly? One explanation that psychologists have developed concerns the bystander's sense of responsibility (Darley & Latané, 1968). When a person is the only witness to an emergency, that bystander bears 100% of the responsibility for helping and 100% of the guilt and blame for not helping. The appropriate behavior in this situation, helping, is clearly defined. If, however, a person witnesses an emergency but believes that somebody else is around who can help or will help, then that bystander's personal responsibility is less clearly defined. Under these circumstances, the bystander could rationalize not helping by coming to believe that someone else will intervene. Of course, if everyone believes that someone else will help, no one will intervene. That presumably was what occurred in the Kitty Genovese incident.

To test our hypotheses about subtle discrimination, we modeled a situation in the laboratory after a classic experiment by Darley and Latané (1968). The situation we created was a serious accident, not a stabbing, in which the victim screamed for help. Like Darley and Latané (1968), we led some of our subjects to believe that they would be the only witness to this emergency, while we led others to believe that there would be two other people present in this situation who heard the emergency as well. As a second dimension, we varied the race of the victim. In half of the cases the victim was white; in the other half of the cases the victim was an African American. The participants in the study were white, as were the other two people who were sometimes presumed to be present.

We predicted that when people were the only witness to the emergency, aversive racists would not discriminate against the black victim. In this situation, appropriate behavior is clearly defined. Not to help a black victim could easily be interpreted, by oneself or others, as racial bias. We predicted, however, that because aversive racists have unconscious negative feelings toward blacks, they would discriminate when they could justify their behavior on the basis of some factor other than race—such as the belief that someone else would help the victim. Specifically, we expected that blacks would be helped less than whites only when white bystanders believed that there were other witnesses to the emergency.

The results of the study supported our predictions. When white bystanders were the only witnesses to the emergency, they helped very frequently and equivalently for black and white victims. In fact, they even helped black victims somewhat more often than white victims (95% vs. 83%, respectively). There was no evidence of old-fashioned racism. In contrast, when white bystanders were given an opportunity to rationalize not helping on the basis of the belief that one of the two other witnesses could intervene, they were less likely to help, particularly when the victim was African American. When participants believed that there were two other bystanders, they helped the black victim half as often as they helped the white victim (38% vs. 75%). If this situation were real, the white victim would have died 25% of the time; the black victim would have died 62% of the time. As we hypothesized, the nature of the situation determines whether discrimination does or does not occur. This principle applies in more considered decision-making situations, often with equally severe consequences for blacks. Next we consider the roles of subtle and overt biases in juridic decisions.

*Is Justice Color-Blind?* Traditionally, blacks and whites have not been treated equally under the law (see also Chapter 6, this volume). Across time and locations in the United States, blacks have been more likely to be convicted of crimes, and, if convicted, sentenced to longer terms for similar crimes, particularly if the victim is white (see Johnson, 1985; Nickerson, Mayo, & Smith, 1986). In addition, blacks are more likely to receive the death penalty (General Accounting Office, 1990). Baldus, Woodsworth, and Pulaski (1990) examined over 2,000 murder cases in Georgia and found that a death sentence was returned in 22% of the cases in which black defendants were convicted of killing a white victim, but in only 8% of the cases in which the defendant and the victim were white. Although differences in judicial outcomes have tended to persist, paralleling the trends in overt expressions of bias, racial disparities in sentencing are declining over time, and the effects are becoming more indirect (Nickerson et al., 1986).

Although the influence of old-fashioned racism in juridic judgments may be waning, aversive racism appears to have a continuing, subtle influence. That is, bias does occur, but mainly when it can be justified on the basis of some other—ostensibly nonrace-related—basis. For example, in a laboratory simulation study, Johnson, Whitestone, Jackson, and Gatto (1995) examined the effect of the introduction of inadmissible evidence, which was damaging to a defendant's case, on whites' judgments of a black or white defendant's guilt. No differences in judgments of guilt occurred as a function of defendant race when all the evidence presented was admissible. Consistent with the aversive racism framework, however, the presentation of inadmissible evidence increased judgment of guilt when the defendant was black, but not when the defendant was white. Furthermore, suggesting the unconscious or unintentional nature of the bias, participants' self-reports indicated that they believed that the inadmissible evidence had less effect on their decisions when the defendant was black than when the defendant was white. Johnson et al. (1995) conclude that these results "are clearly consistent with the modern racism perspective, which suggests that discriminatory behavior will occur only when it can be justified on nonracial grounds" (p. 896).

Another study of simulated juridic decisions by Faranda and Gaertner (1979) demonstrated how traditional and aversive forms of racism can combine to shape perceptions of a defendant's guilt. Specifically, this study investigated the hypothesis that, whereas the racial biases of those who are likely to have traditionally racist attitudes (high authoritarians) would reflect primarily antiblack biases, the racial biases of those who are likely to exhibit aversive racism (low authoritarianism) would mainly represent pro-white biases. Thus, complementing the work of Johnson et al. (1995), this experiment examined the extent to which high- and low-authoritarian-scoring white college students playing the role of jurors would follow a judge's instruction to ignore inadmissible prosecution testimony that was damaging to a black or white defendant.

As predicted, both high- and low-authoritarian participants displayed racial biases in their reactions to the inadmissible evidence, but they did so in different ways. In their ratings of certainty of guilt, high authoritarians did not ignore the inadmissible testimony when the victim was black: They were more certain of the black defendant's guilt when they were exposed to the inadmissible evidence than when they were not presented with this testimony. For the white defendant, however, high authoritarians followed the judge's instructions appropriately. Low-authoritarian participants, in contrast, followed the judge's instructions about ignoring the inadmissible testimony when the defendant was black. They were, however, biased in favor of the white defendant when the inadmissible evidence was presented. That is, low authoritarians were less certain of the white defendant's guilt when the inadmissible evidence was presented than when it was omitted. Thus, low-authoritarian participants demonstrated a pro-in-group bias. It is important to note that the anti-out-group bias of high authoritarians and the pro-in-group bias of low authoritarians both disadvantage blacks relative to whites, but in fundamentally different ways.

Recently, we have also found laboratory evidence of direct and indirect patterns of racial discrimination among whites scoring high and low in self-reported prejudice in recommending the death penalty (Dovidio, Smith,

Donnella, & Gaertner, 1997). High- and low-prejudice-scoring white college students read a summary of facts associated with a case in which the offender was found guilty of murdering a white police officer following a robbery. The race of the defendant, black or white, was systematically varied. After reading the case and before making a decision, participants viewed five other jurors on videotape individually presenting their decisions to vote for the death penalty in the case. In half of the conditions, all of these jurors were white; in the other half of the conditions, the second juror presenting a decision was a black male student. The main measure of interest was how strongly the participant subsequently recommended the death penalty.

It was hypothesized on the basis of the archival research on racial disparities in death sentencing and on social psychological research on racial biases that black defendants would be discriminated against relative to white defendants. The aversive racism framework, however, suggested that the patterns of discrimination displayed by participants high and low in self-reported racial prejudice would be different. In particular, whereas the bias of highly prejudiced participants would be direct and overt, reflecting generally stronger recommendations for the death penalty for black defendants than for white defendants, the pattern for participants scoring low in prejudice would be more indirect and subtle. Specifically, it was hypothesized that participants scoring low in prejudice would discriminate against the black defendant primarily when they could avoid attributions of racial bias for their recommendations for the death penalty for a black offender, such as when one of the jurors recommending the death penalty was black. To the extent that an aversive racist is complying with the judgment of a black person about a black defendant, attributions of racial bias can be avoided.

As predicted, high-prejudice-scoring whites showed a straightforward pattern of bias against black defendants: Regardless of the other jurors, they gave generally stronger recommendations for the death penalty for black defendants than for white defendants. Low-prejudice-scoring white participants, in contrast, demonstrated a more complicated pattern of responses. Their strongest recommendations for the death penalty occurred when the defendant was black and a black juror advocated the death penalty. Under these conditions, in which their response could not necessarily be interpreted as racial bias, low-prejudice whites were as discriminating as high-prejudice whites. When, however, all of the jurors were white and thus their responses could potentially be attributed to racial antipathy, low-prejudice scoring whites exhibited the strongest recommendations *against* the death penalty when the defendant was black. Consistent with the aversive racism framework, aversive racism is expressed subtly, indirectly, and in rationalizable ways. Although the bias may be subtle, the consequences may still be of great consequence, potentially influencing life or death decisions. In the next section of the chapter, we examine how aversive racism is reflected in the conscious and nonconscious manifestations of attitudes and beliefs about blacks.

## ■ Bias in Words and Thought

We believe that aversive racism has relevance to the way that whites express their racial attitudes. When we ask people directly, as in surveys, "Do you support integration?" "Would you vote for a well-qualified black presidential candidate?" the socially acceptable answer is very obvious to people. To say anything but "yes" could be interpreted by other people and oneself as racial bias. As a consequence, we believe that many of the nationwide surveys overrepresent the racially tolerant response.

*Blacks Are Not Worse Than Whites, But. . . .* To examine how aversive racism relates to questionnaire or survey responses, we conducted an experiment in which we asked people on 1 to 7 scales (e.g., good to bad) to describe blacks and whites (Dovidio & Gaertner, 1991). These white respondents demonstrated no racial difference in their evaluative ratings. A biased response (e.g., "bad") is obvious, and respondents consistently rated both blacks and whites on the positive ends of the scales. When, however, we varied the instrument slightly by placing positive and negative characteristics in separate scales (e.g., bad, from *not at all* to *extremely*), we found that bias does exist, but in a subtle form. Although the ratings of blacks and whites on the negative scales showed no racial bias, the ratings on the positive scales did reveal a significant difference. Whereas blacks were not rated more negatively than whites, whites were evaluated more positively than blacks. Apparently, aversive racists resist believing that blacks are bad or even that they are worse than whites, remarks easily interpreted as racial bias. Subtle bias is displayed, however, in respondents' willingness to believe that whites are better than blacks. Again, this is not the old-fashioned, overt type of bias associated with the belief about black inferiority. Instead, it is a modern, subtle form of bias that reflects a belief about white superiority.

There are several limitations to self-report measures, even subtle ones such as those we have developed. For example, self-reports are susceptible to attempts to manage impressions. Respondents can identify the socially appropriate position and respond accordingly. In addition, self-reports are better measures of what people say than what they actually do. Thus, in subsequent research, we tried to learn what people actually think and how these thoughts affect split-second decision making. Important decisions often have to be made in a split second; we wanted to know if split-second racial decisions reflect subtle bias.

Our tests of decision making have involved response latency methods (Dovidio, Evans, & Tyler, 1986; Gaertner & McLaughlin, 1983; see also Wittenbrink, Judd, & Park, 1995). Cognitive psychologists have found that the more associated thoughts are in person's mind, the faster the person can make a decision relating to them. For example, participants in one study of natural categories were asked to think about the category "bird," and then to decide whether the next two words belonged to that category (Rosch, 1975). As expected, participants responded more quickly when the two words were typical of the category (e.g., robin-sparrow) than when they were unusual (e.g., ostrich-pelican). Our studies examined whites' beliefs about the typical characteristics of blacks and whites. For example, in one study (Dovidio & Gaertner, 1991), we presented participants with the social categories "blacks" and "whites" on a computer screen and asked them to respond as quickly as possible whether the word that followed could ever describe a member of that category. These words included the positive and negative characteristics that we used in our self-report study. Faster reaction times are presumed to reflect greater category association. It is also important to note that participants were making truly split-second decisions—responses typically in less than a second.

The results of this study converged with those of our self-report study. As illustrated in Figure 1.1, in which faster response times (i.e., lower numbers) indicate stronger associations, participants were not more likely to associate negative characteristics with blacks than with whites. They did, however, associate more positive characteristics with whites than with blacks. Again, it is not that blacks are bad (i.e., black inferiority); it is that whites are better (white superiority). Apparently, whites are currently more successful at suppressing (or avoiding developing) relatively negative feelings about blacks than they are about suppressing relatively positive feelings about whites.

*Lingering Negative Feelings.* One of our basic assumptions is that, because of virtually unavoidable cognitive, motivational, and sociocultural processes, aversive racists do develop negative feelings about blacks. Be-

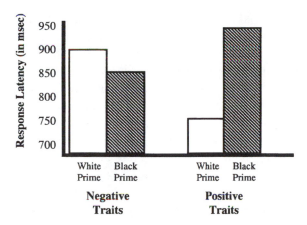

**Figure 1.1.** Associations of Positive and Negative Traits With Whites and Blacks

cause, however, they consciously hold egalitarian values and believe that they are not prejudiced, they suppress these negative feelings. These negative feelings linger unconsciously.

To test this hypothesis, we had to devise a way of assessing what people may be thinking and feeling unconsciously. Recently, we have developed such a procedure. The procedure is similar to our earlier reaction-time study, but also has important differences. In this technique, we do not mention race, which might prepare our participants to censor negative feelings. Instead, we presented black and white primes subliminally. On each of the key experimental trials, we first presented a sketch of a black or white person very rapidly on a computer screen, and then we covered up ("masked") the sketch with the large letter "P" in the same area of the computer screen so that participants are unaware that the sketch even appeared. Thus, participants were not aware that we were assessing their racial beliefs and feelings. The letter "P" was clearly visible to participants, and they were informed that this symbol indicated that they should make a decision about whether the next word that appears can ever describe a person (i.e., P for person). Next, we displayed a characteristic, for example "good" or "bad," and recorded how long participants took to make the decision. As in our previous work of this type, faster response times are assumed to reflect greater association. This time, we wanted to know whether the subliminal sketch of a black or white person would affect their decision-making times.

Using this subliminal procedure, we again found that our white participants had more positive associations with whites than with blacks, even
though they were not aware of the schematic faces or that the study tested their
racial attitudes. Furthermore, when we go below the level of consciousness,
we now find that there are negative feelings. Not only do whites have more
positive feelings about whites than about blacks, but unconsciously they also
have more negative associations about blacks than about whites. In addition,
we found that these biased associations were only weakly associated with
participants' self-reported racial attitudes (see also Dovidio & Fazio, 1992;
Fazio, Jackson, Dunton, & Williams, 1995). There were a considerable number of participants who appeared low in prejudice on the self-report measure
but who were racially biased on the measure of unconscious attitudes—a
pattern reflecting aversive racism.

The identification of aversive racists who say that they are not prejudiced,
but who have these unconscious negative associations, is important to our
understanding of contemporary racism (see also Chapter 10, this volume). For
example, in a recent study (Dovidio, 1995), unconscious racial attitudes were
used to predict and understand the development of conflict in interracial
communication. The study examined the possibility that whites and blacks
attend to different aspects in social interactions. A black person and a white
person first interacted and then completed questionnaires that asked how
friendly they felt they behaved during the conversation and how friendly their
partner acted. In general, whites' perceptions of their own friendliness corre-
lated with their self-reported prejudice scores: Those who said they were less
prejudiced said that they behaved in a more friendly manner with the black
partner in the subsequent interaction. These perceptions were apparently
guided by the conscious attitudes of whites; at this level, they seemed to be
behaving consistently. In contrast, the perceptions of black partners about the
friendliness of these same white participants were more strongly associated
with the whites' response latency measure of bias (see also Fazio et al., 1995).
That is, in assessing how friendly the white person was, blacks may have been
considering not only the overt, consciously controlled behavior of the partner,
but also concentrating on the nonconscious behaviors (such as eye contact,
nonverbal expression of discomfort) that whites were unable to monitor or
control. These findings suggest that although whites may intend to convey a
positive and friendly attitude to their black partner and believe that they have
succeeded, in the same interaction the black partner may be attuned to the
negative or mixed messages inadvertently sent by whites (see Devine, Evett,

& Vasquez-Suson, 1996). These unintended messages can produce a very different, potentially conflicting, perspective that can contribute to racial tension and distrust.

Earlier we presented the idea that bias can be based on normal processes. One of the normal processes we implicated in aversive racism was the categorization of people into in-groups, "we," or out-groups, "they." To understand how these normal processes can account for some of our results, we ran the same study over again, except that instead of presenting black and white primes subliminally, we used the words "we" and "they" (Perdue, Dovidio, Gurtman, & Tyler, 1990). The results were very similar. Participants associated more positive characteristics with "we" than with "they"; participants also associated more negative characteristics with "they" than with "we." We are not trying to argue that the we-they distinction explains all of racism or bias. Racism is much more complicated. But we do want to emphasize the point that normal processes may contribute to subtle, unintentional forms of racial bias.

What does all this have to do with behavior? If the decisions that people make are biased in systematic ways, they will have biased outcomes for minorities and nonminorities. Attitudes translate into the way people think, and the way people think translates into the way people behave, sometimes as discrimination. In the next section we consider a relatively unique prediction of the aversive racism framework—that more bias is expressed toward higher status blacks. Regarding discrimination, it may also be that it is not that blacks are worse than whites, but that whites are better than blacks.

## ■ Higher Status, Greater Bias

We investigated the relationship between status and bias in the context of an important decision for our participants (Kline & Dovidio, 1982). We recruited participants to help us make admissions decisions for their university. Because students believed that their decisions would have direct implications for them, partially determining who would attend their college, we hypothesized that bias against blacks would be expressed, but in subtle ways (Dovidio & Mullen, 1992). Participants were presented with information about an applicant whose qualifications were systematically varied. Some participants evaluated a poorly qualified applicant, some rated a moderately qualified candidate, and others judged a highly qualified applicant. In addition, the race of the applicant was manipulated by a photograph attached to the file. The central question concerned how this picture would affect students' admissions decisions.

Discrimination against the black applicant occurred, but, as expected, it did not occur equally in all conditions (see Figure 1.2). Participants rated the poorly qualified black and white applicants equally low. They showed some bias when they evaluated the moderately qualified white applicant slightly higher than comparable black candidate. Discrimination against the black applicant was most apparent, however, when the applicants were highly qualified. Consistent with our other studies, there was no bias on the "low" end: Poorly qualified black applicants were not rated worse than poorly qualified white applicants. As in the previous studies, discrimination occurred at the "high" end. Although white participants evaluated the highly qualified black applicant very positively, they judged the highly qualified white applicant, with exactly the same credentials, as even better.

This study also included individual items that contributed to the overall evaluative score, scaled according to how directly they related to the information presented in the applicant's transcript. The less directly related the item was to the transcript information, the greater the bias. These results are consistent with the findings in organizational settings that whites tend to evaluate blacks less favorably than whites on subjective dimensions of work performance (Kraiger & Ford, 1985) and support Goddard's (1986) observation in applied settings that "vague, ill-defined, subjective criteria lend themselves to all kinds of biased judgments" (p. 34).

Once again, it is important to note that although the expression of aversive racism may be subtle, the consequences are not subtle. Aversive racism, like more blatant forms, may contribute to the restriction of opportunity for blacks and other minorities. Affirmative action, for example, is a federal policy originally designed to ensure fair treatment to historically disadvantaged minorities. Affirmative action is commonly erroneously assumed to involve quotas or other forms of "reverse discrimination," even though quotas are neither legal nor part of affirmative action policies (see Crosby, 1994). Consistent with the aversive racism framework, resistance to affirmative action is not commonly expressed directly but rather mainly as concerns about individual freedom or about unfair and biased distribution of rewards. Although a central principle in affirmative action is that the candidate must first qualify for the position to benefit from the policy, common protests by whites regarding affirmative action seem to express mainly the concern that qualified whites will be disadvantaged relative to less qualified blacks. It is possible,

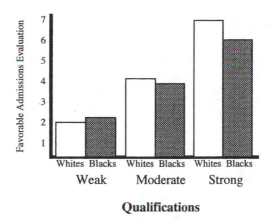

**Figure 1.2.** Evaluations of Black and White Applicants With Weak, Moderate, and Strong Qualifications

however, that this response represents a nonrace-related justification to op-pose affirmative action, although it is the reversal of the traditional role relationship, in which whites have occupied positions of superior status, that represents the primary threat to whites (see also Chapter 6, this volume). Thus, the purpose of another study was to investigate the possibility that the generally articulated issue of relative competence is a rationalization in which a nonracial factor, competence, is used by whites to object to affirmative action programs, which increases the likelihood that they will be subordinated to minority groups (Dovidio & Gaertner, 1981).

White male undergraduates were introduced to a black or white male confederate who was presented as either the participant's supervisor or sub-ordinate. In addition, the confederate was described as being higher or lower than the participant in an intellectual ability that was relevant to the dyad's task. The dependent measure was an incidental helping task, picking up pencils that the confederate "accidentally" knocked to the floor.

Overall, participants helped black partners more than white partners. The effect of race, however, was moderated by status and ability. Specifically, the results indicated that relative status, rather than relative ability was the primary determinant of helping behavior toward blacks. Black supervisors were helped less than black subordinates, whereas white supervisors were helped somewhat more than white subordinates. Relative ability, in contrast, did not affect prosocial behavior toward blacks. In general, high- and low-ability blacks were helped equally often, whereas high-ability white partners were helped more frequently than were low-ability white partners. Thus, ability, not status, was instrumental in determining helping toward whites, but status, not ability, was the major factor influencing prosocial behavior toward blacks. Given that there were no significant effects involving participants' self-reports of prejudice, it seems that even well-intentioned whites will respond negatively to a black supervisor compared to a black subordinate, regardless of apparent qualifications.

How could people in this experiment rationalize not responding positively to competent blacks? Subjects' postexperimental evaluations of their partners revealed that their behaviors may have been mediated by perceptions of relative intelligence (competence). Although participants' ratings indicated that they accepted high-ability white partners as being somewhat more intelligent than themselves, the ratings revealed that participants described even high-ability black partners as significantly less intelligent than themselves. Blacks may be regarded as intelligent, but not as intelligent as whites. It therefore appears that although whites may accept that a black person is intelligent on an absolute dimension, white participants are reluctant to believe that a black person is higher or equal in intelligence compared to themselves.

We have described a considerable amount of research to illustrate how aversive racism operates at the personal level. Under the controlled conditions of the laboratory, we can isolate the subtle but systematic influence of aversive racism. Organizations are complex, however. There are many different factors involving decisions that occur in organizations. As a consequence, we can never say that because disparities exist, racism is the cause. But, where racism exists, disparities will exist. Thus, we have attempted to apply our model to data from a range of organizations. We recognize the obvious limitations of this approach, but the results are nevertheless provocative.

Across organizations as diverse as the armed forces, federal government, and Fortune 1000 companies, we find data consistent with our prediction of greater racial disparities at higher-status levels. In addition, these patterns persist over the past decade. Within the Navy, for example, blacks represent 13% of the force, but only 5% of the officers and 1.5% of the admirals. Furthermore, these differences cannot be accounted for by vastly different backgrounds. A recent study by the General Accounting Office (1995) found that, over a recent 5-year period, the success rate of blacks who qualified for promotions was systematically below the rate of whites across all of the military services. Consistent with our model, the disparities in promotion rates tended to increase with higher ranks for enlisted personnel and up through ranks equivalent to Major for officers (Hudson, 1995). We have also examined patterns of disparities for various segments of federal employees and found evidence consistent with our model: Blacks are generally less well represented in higher grades (e.g., GS 16-18) than in lower grades. Furthermore, these disparities have remained relatively stable across time. A study of industry provides independent evidence of the "glass ceiling effect" for minorities (Federal Glass Ceiling Commission, 1995). Representations of minorities consistently decline with higher occupational status. Fewer than 1% of the top-level executives in Fortune 1000 industrial and Fortune 500 service firms are black. Independent research reveals that not only are blacks promoted less frequently than whites, they have less access to training and development opportunities (Greenhaus, Parasuraman, & Wormley, 1990).

A U.S. Bureau of the Census study (Bennett, 1992) further confirmed substantial income disparities between black and white men. In 1990, black men with a high school education earned $5,828 less per year than white men with comparable education ($16,554 vs. $22,382). The gap was even larger ($7,940) between college-educated black and white men ($30,766 vs. $38,706). These gaps did not occur between black and white women. With a high school degree, black women made only $333 less than their white counterparts, and with a college degree they made $3,210 more. Still today, black males must work about 16 months to earn a salary equivalent to what a white male earns in one year (Murrell, in press). A recent report by the Economic Policy Institute concluded that the wage gap in recent years "interestingly . . . grew faster for those black males with more education" (McClain, 1995, p. A11).

Thus, across a range of settings we see consistent patterns of disparities in occupational advancement and income. Disparities between blacks and whites, particularly for men, in representation and compensation increase with higher levels of status. We acknowledge that the glass ceiling effect can occur for a wide range of reasons and that the leap from laboratory to organizations is a large one. Nevertheless, the pattern of disparities that we see in organizations conforms to our predictions. Furthermore, we suggest that by understanding some of the fundamental causes of these disparities, individuals and organizations will be better equipped to combat bias and to understand resistance to programs designed to address the consequences of racism. In the next section, we further examine the potential role of aversive racism in opposition to affirmative action.

## ■ Resistance to Progress

Whereas blatant racial and ethnic prejudices relate to support for policies that unconditionally restrict the rights and opportunities of minority groups, subtle racism is associated with support for the status quo or for restrictions when other justifications (e.g., lack of credentials) are available (Pettigrew & Meertens, 1995). Thus, aversive racism may be influential in resistance to affirmative action programs. White Americans, for example, appear deeply ambivalent about affirmative action. On one hand, surveys have shown that over 75% of whites support the principle of affirmative action programs that help blacks and other minorities get ahead. On the other hand, typically about three quarters of whites oppose the implementation of specific affirmative action programs (Dovidio, Mann, & Gaertner, 1989). Like Kluegel and Smith (1986), we argue that "opposition to equal opportunity programs stems from the threat these programs present to an economic order that is believed to be just in principle and to work well in fact" (Kluegel & Smith, 1986, p. 212). Thus, although racist traditions may have initially produced social inequalities, many whites, truly believing that they are nonprejudiced and nondiscriminating, may presently be participating in the continued restriction of opportunities for blacks and other minorities by opposing programs that threaten their own advantaged status.

As we noted earlier, one popular criticism of affirmative action centers on the selection procedures. The protest expressed by many whites concerning the *Regents of the University of California v. Bakke* (1978) decision illustrates this point. In the *Bakke* case, many people objected to the admissions procedure of the medical school because it was seen as a form of "reverse discrimination" that violated their fundamental beliefs about procedural fairness or justice. That is, the commonly articulated reason for challenging the admissions procedure that involved preferential treatment for blacks was that this policy was discriminatory and negated individual selection, evaluation, and advancement based on merit. Thus, resistance to affirmative action may occur, in part, because individuals believe that category membership (e.g., race or sex) should not be a relevant criterion used in merit-based decisions (Nacoste, 1994).

If perceptions of fairness are a key factor in reactions to affirmative action, then how a specific policy is framed can substantially influence an individual's response. Whereas many people may initially feel that affirmative action policies are unfair when characteristics such as race or sex are weighed in individual decisions, they may come to see the procedure as fair if, at a broader level, they recognize the value of diversity, "that individuals bring with them into the organization not merely different amounts of the same things, but also different kinds of things that make them valuable to an organization" (Clayton & Tangri, 1989, p. 180). Similarly, whereas affirmative action may be seen as unfair in a specific case, the same action may be perceived as more fair if it is presented as a compensatory response to redress historical inequities.

Racism may also motivate resistance to affirmative action, either directly or indirectly. The connection between opposition to affirmative action, on one hand, and racism, on the other, has been empirically verified (e.g., Jacobson, 1985; Kravitz, 1995). For example, Sears et al. (1995), using data from four representative surveys, recently found that symbolic negative attitudes toward blacks predicted opposition not only to policies specifically presented as benefiting blacks (affirmative action for blacks, open housing for blacks) but also to policies designed to benefit all racial and ethnic groups but that are stereotypically associated with blacks (e.g., welfare support). Thus, although there may be a number of predictors of who will oppose affirmative action, racism appears to be among the strongest.

Our framework suggests that racism may also manifest itself more subtly and indirectly in opposition to affirmative action, when this resistance can be justified on the basis of some factor other than race, such as unfair procedures. We predict that negative reactions to affirmative action among whites will be most pronounced when its benefits to groups associated with negative feelings and beliefs (e.g., blacks) are emphasized and the procedures are framed in ways that can be perceived of as unfair (e.g., preferential treatment). A study by Murrell, Dietz-Uhler, Dovidio, Gaertner, and Drout (1994) illustrates this process.

In this study, respondents were questioned about their perceptions of fairness and support of four common ways of presenting affirmative action policies. Two of these policies focused on nonmerit-based factors to address disparities that may readily be perceived as unfair: preferential treatment and reverse discrimination. The other two policies provided societal justification of the fairness of these approaches by achieving diversity or remedying historical injustices. To evaluate the possibility that resistance to affirmative action may be an expression of racial bias, we assessed respondents' reactions to affirmative action policies involving three target groups that respondents were not members of: blacks, elderly persons, and physically handicapped persons. To the extent that racial bias is a key factor in reactions to affirmative action, respondents would be expected to exhibit more negative responses to policies targeted at blacks than at other groups, particularly when these reactions could be justified on the basis of some factor other than race, such as violations of normal standards of fairness.

The findings supported the predictions. Our results underscore the importance of how a policy is framed: Programs that were framed to remedy historical injustice (past discrimination) or increase cultural diversity were more acceptable to respondents than those that focused on specific implementations that are often incorrectly assumed to characterize affirmative action (i.e., preferential treatment and reverse discrimination). In addition, consistent with the hypothesis that racism contributes to resistance to affirmative action, policies directed at benefiting blacks were responded to more negatively than were policies for persons with physical handicaps or elderly persons. Moreover, consistent with the specific predictions of the aversive racism framework, whites' responses to affirmative action were particularly negative when the group described as benefiting was blacks (vs. handicapped or elderly persons) and when the goal of the policy was presented as involving "preferential treatment" or "reverse discrimination" (vs. as achieving cultural diversity or compensating for past discrimination). If, as egalitarian values would suggest, race was truly an irrelevant factor, attitudes toward "reverse discrimination" polices would be uniformly negative, regardless of the specific target group involved. We found, however, that, whereas giving preference based on nonmerit factors is reacted to negatively, giving such preference to blacks produces a significantly stronger negative reaction.

Resistance to affirmative action motivated by aversive racism can significantly undermine the effectiveness of the beneficiaries of these programs and help to create a self-fulfilling prophecy. When people are perceived to benefit unfairly from affirmative action, others judge them as less competent and effective compared to when their selection or advancement was viewed as based on their personal merits (Garcia, Erskine, Hawn, & Casmay, 1981). Furthermore, people's self-evaluations of competence and task performance can be adversely affected by programs that provide help that is unnecessary or unwanted (Schneider, Major, Luhtanen, & Crocker, 1996) or is perceived to unfairly benefit them (see Major & Crocker, 1993; Turner & Pratkanis, 1994). Thus, when selection procedures are perceived to be unfair, members of the benefiting groups may become stigmatized. Consistent with the aversive racism framework, however, these procedures are more likely to be perceived as unfair when the beneficiaries are black.

## ■ Combating Subtle Bias

Like a virus that has mutated, racism has also evolved into different forms that are more difficult not only to recognize but also to combat. This subtle process underlying discrimination can be identified and isolated under the controlled conditions of the laboratory. In organizational decision making, however, in which the controlled conditions of an experiment are rarely possible, this process presents a substantial challenge to the equitable treatment of members of disadvantaged groups. Krieger (1995), in the *Stanford Law Review,* notes that this aspect of contemporary bias poses a particular problem for society and the legal system: "Herein lies the practical problem. . . . Validating subjective decision-making systems is neither empirically nor economically feasible, especially for jobs where intangible qualities, such as interpersonal skills, creativity, and ability to make sound judgments under conditions of uncertainty are critical" (p. 1232). In addition, to the extent that legal proof of discrimination requires the demonstration that race is *the* determining factor and that the actions were intentional, the biases of aversive racists are immune to legal prosecution. Aversive racists discriminate only when other, nonrace-related factors can justify their negative treatment of blacks, and their biases are normally unconscious and unintentional, factors that may disqualify many employment discrimination suits from successful outcomes (Krieger, 1995).

Because of its pervasiveness, subtlety, and complexity, the traditional techniques for eliminating bias that emphasized the immorality of prejudice and illegality of discrimination are not effective for combating aversive racism. Aversive racists recognize that prejudice is bad, but they do not recognize that they are prejudiced. Thus, aversive racism must be addressed at multiple levels, at the societal and intergroup level, as well as the personal level.

*Societal and Organizational Norms.* Recently, we began to consider the possibility that aversive racism may largely reflect in-group favoritism rather than out-group devaluation (Gaertner et al., 1997). As a consequence, social norms that emphasize primarily the avoidance of negative behavior toward blacks and other people of color are not effective for addressing manifestations of aversive racism. Aversive racists have already internalized these norms and are very guarded about overtly or intentionally discriminating against people of color. Instead, Pettigrew (1994) has argued that to address the motivations underlying contemporary forms of bias, it is as important to establish positive norms for proactively pursuing equality as it is to strengthen existing norms against discrimination. These norms may be internalized as an important aspect of organizational citizenship and, at the very least, can produce significant compliance. For instance, across a number of years in the U.S. Army, among candidates identified as qualified, the officer promotion rates of minorities were consistently lower than rates for whites. Concerned about these disparities, the Army set as an explicit goal for promotion boards in 1991 and 1992 that women and minorities be promoted at a rate no lower than the overall service rate. The promotion boards achieved these objectives in a way that was unprecedented in any previous year.

In addition, corporate research has revealed that the recognition of the value of diversity by top management and higher administration is a key factor for successfully achieving corporate equality (Hitt & Keats, 1984; Marino, 1980). Allstate Insurance, for example, made corporate diversity a high priority in 1976, initiating a voluntary diversity program that exceeded federal affirmative action requirements. From 1975 to 1995, it increased its representation of black white-collar workers from 9.5% to 14.8%, a rate of increase that is more than double the rate of increase for all other corporations (Fineman, 1995). Thus, the engineering of positive social norms is essential for eliminating the impact of aversive racism. Conversely, allowing the development of norms within groups that encourage, or simply permit discrimination, can create a climate in which aversive and old-fashioned racists more closely resemble each other.

*Intergroup Perceptions.* We have argued in this chapter that aversive racism may be rooted, in part, in fundamental, normal psychological processes. One such process is the categorization of people into in-groups and out-groups, "we's" and "they's." People respond systematically more favorably to others whom they perceive to belong to their group than to different groups. Thus, changing the basis of categorization from race to an alternative dimension can alter who is a "we" and who is a "they," undermining a contributing force to aversive racism.

In recent years, we have attempted to reduce intergroup bias by changing group members' cognitive representations from different groups to one group (Gaertner, Dovidio, Anastasio, Bachman, & Rust, 1993; Gaertner, Rust, Dovidio, Bachman, & Anastasio, 1994). In application, recategorization from different, potentially competing groups to one group can be achieved by calling attention to existing common superordinate group memberships (e.g., their common university identity) or by introducing new factors (e.g., common goals or fate) that are perceived to be shared by members. We have found that evaluations of former out-group members significantly improve as these individuals become identified with the superordinate, more inclusive in-group (Gaertner et al., 1993).

We view the recategorization of different groups into one group as a particularly powerful and pragmatic strategy for combating subtle forms of bias. Creating the perception of a common in-group identity not only reduces the likelihood of discrimination based on race but also increases the likelihood of positive interracial behaviors. People are more helpful toward in-group members (Kramer & Brewer, 1984; Piliavin, Dovidio, Gaertner, & Clark, 1981) and apply different and more generous standards of morality, justice, and fairness to in-group members than to out-group members (Opotow, 1990).

In one test of the hypothesis that out-group members will be treated more favorably in the context of a common in-group identity than they would be if they were regarded only as out-group members, we conducted a field experiment (Gaertner et al., 1997) at the University of Delaware football stadium before a football game between the University of Delaware and Westchester State University. Black and white student experimenters, wearing signature hats to indicate their apparent university affiliation, approached white fans whose clothing similarly revealed school symbols, colors, or names. The experimenters asked these fans to participate in an interview of "food preferences." The dependent measure was whether the fan agreed to participate in the interview. We predicted that potential bias against black experimenters would be eliminated when the fan and the experimenter shared a common group identity—the same university affiliation.

The results were generally consistent with the hypotheses, but not exactly what we expected. Although the presence or absence of common university identity did not affect compliance with a white interviewer (43% vs. 40%) and white fans did not significantly discriminate against blacks when they did not share a common identity (36% vs. 40%), they did comply significantly more frequently with a black interviewer when they shared common university identity than when they had different university affiliations (59% vs. 36%). Thus, as expected, making an alternative, common identity salient produced more positive and helpful behavior by whites toward blacks.

The development of a common in-group identity does not necessarily require people to forsake their subgroup identity. Indeed, it is often undesirable or impossible for people to relinquish their ethnic or racial subgroup identities (see Chapter 8, this volume). This may, however, have beneficial rather than detrimental effects on the reduction of intergroup prejudice. It is possible for people to conceive of two groups (for example, parents and children) as operating interdependently with the context of a superordinate (family) entity. The dual identity in which members' subgroup and superordinate group identities are salient simultaneously (e.g., African American) may be particularly likely to permit the positive benefits of contact to generalize to out-group members not present in the contact situation. In contrast to a purely one-group representation, the dual identity maintains the associative link to these additional out-group members (see Anastasio, Bachman, Gaertner, & Dovidio, 1997). Consistent with this reasoning, we have found that in a multiethnic high school those students who reported a dual identity (e.g., Korean Americans) had more positive intergroup attitudes than those who reported a separate group identity (e.g., Koreans; Gaertner et al., 1994). The simultaneous recognition of distinct and common aspects of identity may provide the effective balance for producing favorable and generalizable intergroup attitudes.

*Personal Commitment.* Finally, because aversive racism involves a fundamental conflict between a conscious commitment to egalitarian principles and unconscious, perhaps automatic, negative feelings and beliefs about blacks, aversive racism must also be combated at the personal level. As we have demonstrated in a number of studies, such as the emergency intervention study presented earlier in this chapter, when aversive racists accept personal responsibility for the welfare of blacks (as when they are the only bystander), they behave as positively toward blacks as toward whites. Thus, individuals must assume personal responsibility for change to occur. For the disparities in well-being between blacks and whites that we described, it is easy to react with explanations that do not directly involve race. In fact, people often automatically adopt these other explanations and dismiss the possibility of racial biases entirely. For example, people might attribute the differences in the status within organizations presented earlier in this chapter entirely to differences in educational background and fail to consider at all the barriers created by overt and subtle discrimination. Where disparities in social outcomes or personal treatment do exist, it is important that people recognize that bias may indeed be a factor, examine and challenge other explanations, and consider the ultimate impact of these various possibilities.

As we have noted throughout this chapter, however, aversive racists are not only generally unaware of their prejudice, but also they are motivated to remain unaware. Not recognizing their own biases insulates aversive racists from having to confront negative aspects of their racial attitudes. How then can aversive racists productively be made aware of their potential biases? One possibility is to confront aversive racists with direct evidence of the negative aspects of their racial attitudes. Public confrontations, though, are likely to arouse defensiveness and reactance: From all of the information that they are consciously aware of, aversive racists "know" that they are not prejudiced. Presenting feedback in a more impersonal and objective form, such as through information about their physiological reactions, also has only a limited effect. Dutton and his colleagues (Dutton & Lake, 1973; Dutton & Lennox, 1974) found that providing whites with false physiological feedback indicating that they were racially prejudiced did produce more positive responses to blacks, enough to reinforce their nonprejudiced self-image, but these responses were short lived and represented token behaviors rather than a more fundamental change in orientation.

Alternatively, more indirect strategies that benefit from aversive racists' genuine motivation to be nonprejudiced and are less publicly threatening may have longer term, deeper effects. Simply educating aversive racists about the existence of subtle forms of racial bias and demonstrating how these biases operate may sensitize them to alternative understandings of their race-related feelings and behaviors. This information may allow aversive racists to recognize and combat their potential for bias more effectively. For example, educating people about how groups can inhibit bystander intervention in emergencies (the phenomenon we described earlier in this chapter) increases the likelihood that people will subsequently take personal responsibility for helping another person in distress (Beaman, Barnes, Klentz, & McQuork, 1978). Furthermore, techniques that lead aversive racists to discover, apparently without much external pressure, inconsistencies among their self-images, values, and behaviors may arouse cognitive dissonance (Leippe & Eisenstadt, 1994) or other negative emotional states (Rokeach, 1973) that can produce more favorable attitudes toward specific race-related issues and toward blacks in general. In Rokeach's (1973) value confrontation procedure, for example, whites are guided to recognize contradictions between their core value of equality and other core values (e.g., freedom), and the potential impact of this conflict on their racial attitudes. This discovery of contradictions among self-conceptions, values, and attitudes arouses a state of dissatisfaction that motivates participants to increase the importance of equality as a core value and to behave in ways that are more consistent with their nonprejudiced self-concept (Grube, Mayton, & Ball-Rokeach, 1994). These effects may be quite enduring and influence even subtle interracial behaviors.

Penner (1971), for instance, demonstrated increases in eye contact among participants with a black confederate 3 months after the procedure.

Research by Devine and Monteith (1993) further illustrates how awareness of inconsistency between one's interracial behavior and one's egalitarian standards produces a negative emotional reaction and a genuine motivation to behave in a more egalitarian fashion in the future. Specifically, they found that people who indicated that they were relatively nonprejudiced exhibited feelings of guilt and compunction when they became aware of discrepancies between their potential behavior toward minorities (i.e., what they would do) and their personal standards (i.e. what they should do). These emotional reactions, in turn, can motivate people to control subsequent spontaneous stereotypical responses and behave more favorably in the future (Monteith, 1993). Recently, Blair and Banaji (1996) demonstrated that conscious efforts to suppress stereotypically biased reactions can inhibit even the immediate activation of normally automatic associations. Although the negative beliefs and feelings of aversive racists may be unconscious and automatic, these responses are not inevitable.

From our perspective, an alternative strategy would be to accentuate positive behaviors toward blacks, which could be motivated (among other ways) by the recognition of common in-group identity, without specifically attempting to inhibit negative reactions. The well-intentioned attitudes of aversive racists may be used to increase their recognition of a common group identity with blacks and other minorities that may be more problematic for other whites. The emphasis on positive rather than negative behavior eliminates potential problems arising from attempts to suppress negative thoughts and feelings. Trying to inhibit negative reactions not only produces primarily perfunctory and tokenistic behaviors, but it also can result in rebound effects (Macrae, Bodenhausen, Milne, & Jetten, 1994), which subsequently amplify the negative reactions that were initially suppressed.

The well-intentioned attitudes of aversive racists may thus be harnessed productively to eliminate the prejudicial aspects of their attitudes and behavior. The genuine commitment to equality may provide the motivation for people to confront their own potential for bias. Actual interracial interaction, however, is also critical. Aversive racists may possess the knowledge and desire to change but, because race relations involve the reciprocal behaviors of whites and blacks, they also need the experience to learn how to translate their intentions into effective actions. This experience can also help to alleviate the anxiety that aversive racists experience in interracial situations. Understanding in the abstract how one's own subtle bias may operate is not sufficient to relieve interracial anxiety any more than learning about how airplanes fly is sufficient to eliminate a person's fear of flying. Thus, personal commitment and personal experience are essential. Devine and Monteith (1993) proposed an analogy between prejudice reduction of this type and breaking a habit: "Breaking any habit requires effort, practice, and time. In breaking the prejudice habit, people must first make a decision to eliminate the habit (i.e., renounce prejudice). They must then *learn* to inhibit the habitual . . . responses and to generate responses that are consistent with their beliefs and standards" (p. 320, emphasis in the original). If recognized and managed appropriately, aversive racism may therefore be a transitional stage toward creating a society in which there is greater consistency between the reality and the principles of equality on which our country was founded.

## ■ Conclusion

In summary, despite apparent consistent improvements in expressed racial attitudes over time, aversive racism continues to exert a subtle but pervasive influence on the lives of black Americans. This bias is expressed in indirect and rationalizable ways that restrict opportunities for blacks while insulating aversive racists from ever having to confront their prejudices. It is an elusive phenomenon: When aversive racists monitor their interracial behaviors, they do not discriminate. In fact, they may respond even more favorably to blacks than to whites as a way of reaffirming their nonprejudiced self-images. When they are not conscious of their actions, however, bias is subtlety expressed, usually in ways that can be justified on the basis of some factor other than race. Although the expression of bias may be more subtle, the consequences of aversive racism are comparable to that of old-fashioned racism—the restriction of opportunity to other groups and support for a system that is believed to be fair in principle but that perpetuates the social and economic advantages of the majority group over minority groups.

Even though these negative feelings, which aversive racists harbor toward blacks, may be unconscious and rooted in normal processes, this does not imply that this bias is either excusable or immutable. Having the potential for bias is not an acceptable excuse for being biased. In addition, what is unconscious can, with increased awareness and commitment, be made conscious and replaced by truly egalitarian beliefs and feelings. Racial bias, whether subtle or blatant, is inconsistent with standards of fairness and justice. The unfulfilled potential of human lives as well as the expense of violence and other crimes that arise out of disaffection with the system and personal despair, makes racism costly to both blacks and whites. Thus, recognition of this subtle racism may be an essential step in moving a significant segment of white America from feeling nonprejudiced to actually being nonprejudiced.

# 2

# Racism Equals Power Plus Prejudice

## A Social Psychological Equation for Racial Oppression

*Don Operario*
*Susan T. Fiske*

> If beliefs, per se, could subjugate a people, the beliefs which Negroes
> hold about whites should be as effective as those that whites hold
> about Negroes.
>
> *Cox, 1948, p. 531*

Fifty years ago, social theorist Oliver Cox foreshadowed an important
variable missing from social psychology's quest to understand racism.
Cox suggested that cognitive thought processes and affective biases, discussed
in the previous chapter, cannot alone explain the oppression of entire groups
of people. He implied that a truly societal variable, one that extends beyond
the scope of internal processes, underlies racism. We suggest that this variable
is power.

Most social psychological approaches to racism have not directly examined
the role of power. Instead, the empirical focus has relied almost exclusively
on person-level, internal processes such as affect (emotion) and cognition

AUTHORS' NOTE: The authors thank Michael Berg, Lucy Burns, Jennifer Eberhardt, Monica
Lin, Paul Norris, and Darren Spielman for thoughtful comments on earlier drafts of this chapter.
Manuscript preparation was supported by NIMH Research Training Grant MH15742 (administered by the American Psychological Association) to the first author, and both NIMH Grant MH
41801 and NSF Grant SBR 9421480 to the second author.

(thought). For example, the authoritarian personality theory (Adorno, Frenkel-Brunswik, Levinson, & Sanford, 1950) suggests that racist attitudes stem from people's early childhood experiences, particularly their relationship with their parents; modern racism theory (McConahay, 1986) explores how racism articulates through people's ideological and political values (see also Chapter 4, this volume); aversive racism theory (Gaertner & Dovidio, 1986) describes how well-intentioned people can express racist tendencies (see also Chapter 1, this volume); and, the prejudice dissociation model (Devine, 1989) offers a process whereby people can inhibit or control their personal racist tendencies (see also Chapter 10, this volume). Scientific research addressing the nature of stereotyping and prejudice has indeed proliferated in the past few decades, resulting in the publication of several thousand articles, many of which offer remedies for racial tension (for reviews, see Eberhardt & Fiske, 1996; Fiske, 1998; Hamilton & Trolier, 1986; Hilton & Von Hippel, 1996; Mackie, Hamilton, Susskind, & Rosselli, 1996; and this volume). Most of this research, however, does not explicitly consider the societal and contextual dynamics that distinguish stereotyping and prejudice in general from racism in particular.

Collectively, social psychological research on stereotyping and prejudice converges on two consistent themes: (a) All people are prone to perceive others based on their social category memberships, and (b) all individuals tend to display affective and evaluative biases in favor of their in-group and, concomitantly, against out-groups. In other words, stereotyping (a) and prejudice (b) are basic, perhaps universal, human tendencies (see Fiske, 1998). As we will review, the research also indicates that these biases are functional and adaptive strategies that people depend on to simplify a complex social world (cf., Allport, 1954; Lippmann, 1922).

The universality of in-group bias presents a paradox for understanding racism: If all people display in-group bias, then what drives the enduring oppression of some, but not all, human groups—specifically, minority racial groups? A resolution to this paradox lies in Cox's allusion to forces beyond the individual level of analysis that determine how people think and feel in intergroup situations.

Throughout this chapter, we argue that power supplements the cognitive and affective biases common to all individuals (see Chapter 1, this volume), conferring on those who hold power a disproportionate ability to exercise their biases. *Power,* which we define as the ability to control the outcomes of others (Dépret & Fiske, 1993; for similar definitions see Jones, 1972; Thibault & Kelley, 1959; Wilson, 1973), engenders stereotypic thinking, encourages in-group favoritism, and enhances perceived intergroup differences. The central thesis of this discussion is that individuals and groups who hold power over others are more prone to act on, and benefit from, racial stereotypes and prejudices.

This chapter examines the role of power in sustaining all aspects of racism. Five core ideas will guide this argument: (a) Societal power directs the construction of racial categories; (b) cognitive consequences of racial categories, such as stereotyping, underlie people's perception that these arbitrary categories are real and meaningful; (c) affective and evaluative consequences of racial categories, such as in-group favoritism, underlie people's biases against different categories; (d) power plus prejudice transforms universal psychological processes into asymmetrical societal processes; and, thus, (e) racism is a personal and societal challenge.

In the sections that follow, we will consider each core issue. The discussion draws most heavily from basic social psychology research, but also briefly reviews some important messages from other disciplines such as sociology, anthropology, and history. Racism and race relations are indeed complex issues, perhaps too complex for one course or one discipline to adequately address. Social psychology's insight into this persistent human problem is a good place to start.

## ■ Societal Power Directs the Construction of Racial Categories

Before examining the psychological processes that sustain racism, the discussion opens by considering the concept of race—where it comes from, what it means, why it exists. People rarely question the reality of racial categories; most people accept race as a fundamental truth (Eberhardt & Randall, 1997; see also Chapter 3, this volume, for more discussion). In this section, we concur that race is indeed a reality. But this reality is a subjective one, rather than an objective, absolute one. Racial categories exist because people and societies believe them to be true; they derive from psychological and societal processes, rather than from biological or evolutionary processes.

## ■ The Meaning of Race

Almost everyone seems to know the meaning of race, until asked to provide a definition. Some people define race based on apparent physical differences between groups; other people define race by geographic or national origins, whereas others' definition relies on abstract concepts such as cultural practices or values. The elusive nature of race has frustrated theorists throughout history. Even over 100 years ago, anthropologist Topinard stated that "races exist; it is undeniable; our intelligence comprehends them; our minds see them; our labors separate them out. . . . But nowhere can we put our fingers on them" (cited in Scheidt, 1924, p. 389).

This confusion over a singular definition of race strikes even the most dedicated scholars. Some of the earliest scientific studies of race relied exclusively on people's salient physical features to draw lines between human groups. Physical qualities such as hair color and texture, height, body shape, and facial characteristics thus provided initial criteria for labeling different races. The growth of science, specifically biology and genetics, allowed more technological definitions of race. These molecular and genetic approaches to studying race used differential gene frequencies, blood composition, and metabolic activity to distinguish between races. As the social sciences developed in strength and stature, some researchers adopted macrolevel approaches to classify people into races. In this tradition, race-defining variables included ethnicity (e.g., the German "race"), religion and language (e.g., the Jewish "race"), and geography (e.g., the Mediterranean "race"). Psychologists have also contributed their own perspectives to the discourse on race. Classic psychological approaches to labeling and understanding race were based on traits and personality differences between human groups, such as intelligence, aggression, passivity, and promiscuity (see Yee, Fairchild, Weizmann, & Wyatt, 1993; Zuckerman, 1990, for more discussion).

Perhaps the only overarching conclusion from these differing academic views is that scholars cannot agree on the scientific basis of race. One distinguished anthropologist reflected on the disparity between academic perspectives, saying that "in all modern science there is no field where authorities differ more than in the classification of human races" (Benedict, 1959, p. 22). Perplexed by the inability to understand and define race, some theorists have advocated abandoning the concept altogether (see Marger, 1994).

The lack of academic consensus does not mean that races do not exist. The prevalence of racism in U.S. society attests to the undeniable social reality and importance of this concept. But thus far, scientists have not discovered or isolated the "essence" of race (Eberhardt & Randall, 1997). Indeed, several researchers argue that no simple race-defining variables allow scientists to pinpoint biological, genetic, physical, cultural, or psychological criteria. A different perspective that many scholars now advocate, which we will also advance shortly, is that race is an invention of human history (Omi & Winant, 1986). That is, race is a human-made schema, developed over time and history, for delineating human group boundaries.

## ■ The Invention of Race

Although most people cannot agree on a singular definition of race, most members of U.S. society can easily generate a list of races. Many standard lists commonly include Asians, blacks, whites, and Latinos. Some lists might also include native Caribbeans, Australian aborigines, Arabs, and Malay or Pacific Islanders. Yet others might refer to Mediteranneans, South Asians or Indians, and Jews as distinct races. The categories on any particular list are likely to depend on one's cultural context, one's prior experiences with out-group members, and one's own racial identity. Indeed, the lack of a singular definition of race contributes to the inconsistency between people's ideas of racial categories.

This confusion exists because racial categories are human inventions with weak scientific validity. Individuals with their own biases created the taxonomies that we call racial categories; over time, societies have accepted these human-made taxonomies as fundamental truth. But the arbitrary and fallible nature of racial taxonomies is evident throughout history, as racial criteria change constantly over time, and different cultural contexts invent their own racial categories (Omi & Winant, 1986).

In U.S. society, the four most commonly accepted racial categories roughly correspond to a typology developed by Linnaeus, who in 1735 classified humans into four groups: Homo europaeus, Homo asiaticus, Homo africanus, and Homo americanus. Historically speaking, these categories are quite recent. His classification scheme developed out of Europe's Renaissance-era expansion, which involved the "discovery" of non-European groups. The four initial categories were based largely on apparent physical differences between previously unacquainted groups (Marger, 1994; Stepan, 1982). This scheme persists in many Western societies even today. A look at almost any U.S. demographic questionnaire reveals the acceptance of Linnaeus's four races: European (white), Asian, African (black), and Native American.

But these categories are not fixed or permanent. A glance back at U.S. history reveals the evolving nature of racial categories within this society (see also Chapter 3, this volume; Gossett, 1963; Smedley, 1993). These categories often have shifted and changed because of the United States' social or political interests. For example, immigrants from Ireland and Italy were once considered racially distinct from Americans of northern European descent; these minority groups received discriminatory treatment in immigration, housing, and employment (Alba, 1990). Ironically, in the face of contemporary immigration trends, many Irish and Italian Americans now simply identify themselves as "white."

Consider also society's shifting definition of "black." Prior to the Civil War, one's race was determined by one's mother; children born to black women were categorized as black. In effect, this policy restricted the people born to white fathers and black mothers—or slaveholders who procreated with slaves—from claiming themselves as free whites. After slavery was abolished, many states adjusted their criterion for who was black, applying the "one-drop" rule to label those with any trace of black lineage. Again, this revised criterion had a policy-based nature, because it kept almost all Americans of African descent from sharing postslavery white privileges (Davis, 1991).

Japanese Americans have similarly faced changing standards of their racial status. During the Jim Crow era, Japanese in the U.S. South were regarded as "honorary whites," and hence allowed to use the "white-only" drinking fountains and restrooms, and to sit in the front seats of buses (Hosokawa, 1969). This treatment contrasts sharply with the incarceration of Japanese Americans during the World War II "yellow peril" scare.

Some social scientists argue that race undergoes constant evolution and reinvention, particularly within the U.S. context (Hirschfeld, 1996; Omi & Winant, 1986). The racial categories that Americans currently acknowledge reflect the history and development of their society. Guiding the categorization of races throughout U.S. history (and indeed world history) is *power:* the power to classify and categorize via (changing) scientific standards, the power to enact race-based laws via political dominance, the power to subordinate via social and economic control (see also Chapter 3, this volume). Thus, societal power provides the impetus for creating racial categories, as well as the force for sustaining their validity.

## ■ The Reification of Race

Although arbitrary in nature, racial classifications have become very real. The process by which abstract, arbitrary notions (such as race) become unquestioned and even legitimate concepts is called reification. Because of history, society, and power, race has become reified from an imprecise classification scheme to a meaningful reality.

Linnaeus's initial racial categories, based on physical differences, did not presage the strong ideological assumptions that people now associate with race. In many societies, particularly U.S. society, people attribute social hierarchy, personality, merit, and overall human potential to race. And according to some recent data, race in the United States correlates with mortality, socioeconomic status, professional advancement, and psychological well-being (see Taylor, Repetti, & Seeman, 1997, for a review). These findings do not suggest that races are scientifically discrete entities. Rather, they suggest that societal and psychological processes legitimize and perpetuate racial classifications. Power is perhaps the strongest societal and psychological variable that drives the reification of race.

Power provides the justification for, and meaning behind, racial differences. Power has guided social history, allowing some groups control over others. The racial categories commonly accepted in contemporary U.S. society were developed by those holding the most economic and military power centuries ago—namely, western Europeans (Marger, 1994). U.S. history has continually favored those of western European descent, granting them the power to develop, and benefit from, race-based hierarchies and ideologies (Smedley, 1993; see also Chapter 6, this volume). Over time, powerful groups have legitimized race via self-fulfilling prophecies, self-justifying ideologies, and self-perpetuating systems.

## ■ The Legacy of Race

The concept of race is deeply embedded within all aspects of U.S. society, whence derives the reality and legacy of race. Racial categories exist because people and societies believe them to be true. As we will review, psychological processes uphold racial categories: People perceive racial differences, people identify with their racial category, and people act based on their racial assumptions.

The discussion thus far reminds us that racial categories proceed from historical events and power differentials, not from essential classifications. In other words, racial categories are human inventions; racial categories have no inherently natural basis. But as discussed shortly, social categories provide a useful basis for making sense of the world. Thus we posit a social psychological definition of *race* as a socially constructed categorization scheme for inferring human group differences (biological, psychological, cultural, and ideological) from superficial, usually physical, criteria.

The discussion now considers the empirical social psychological literature to clarify the processes by which arbitrary categories develop into meaningful social realities. In this next section, we will review findings from social cognition research to understand the internal thought processes guiding the perception of race. This discussion will provide further evidence for the adage that once "people define situations as real, they are real in their consequences" (Thomas & Thomas, 1928).

## ■ Cognitive Consequences of Racial Categories

> Open-mindedness is considered to be a virtue. But, strictly speaking, it cannot occur. A new experience must be redacted into old categories. We cannot handle each event freshly in its own right. (Allport, 1954, p. 19)

As Gordon Allport (1954) noted in his groundbreaking psychological treatise on prejudice, social categories are neither inherently dangerous nor inherently demeaning. Rather, they are vital to human cognitive functioning. Even the most open-minded people depend on social categories to understand the people, objects, and stimuli filling their environments. All human perceivers categorize other people to simplify the complex, often confusing, social world (see Lippmann, 1922).

## ■ Stereotypes Are Everywhere

The mere classification of people into social groups allows people to understand others with regard to one or a few main characteristics, such as their age, gender, social role, physical appearance, or relation to the self. One should not confuse the process of categorization, which facilitates the ability to think clearly, with the "cultural baggage" associated with these categories. The former is essential for people's psychological functioning; the latter is constructed by society, history, and power.

The cultural baggage associated with social categories resides within the content of our *stereotypes*. A stereotype can be defined as "a cognitive structure that contains the perceiver's knowledge, beliefs, and expectancies about some human group" (Hamilton & Trolier, 1986, p. 133). One is hard-pressed to imagine any significant social category not associated with a stereotype—for example, lawyers as ambitious and slick, professors as intelligent and socially awkward, and athletes as dull-witted and aggressive. Stereotypes are vital for simplifying the process of social perception; they provide perceivers with just enough information (albeit of questionable validity) to understand, predict, and structure their social environments. Thus stereotypes, like the social categories they represent, are not the source of social oppression, nor do they sufficiently explain racism.

Imagine what life would be like without stereotypes: Each person would have to perceive every other person by attending to all diagnostic perceptual cues available (e.g., appearance, mood, personality traits, speech qualities, social setting, and so on) to form an impression. Rather than use such an exhausting cognitive strategy, perceivers can instead rely on broader social cues, such as social categories, to form quick, good-enough impressions and understand the environment. Stereotypes give people some amount of predictive insight into others, based on information associated with their social categories. Thus, stereotypes can be pragmatic psychological adaptations for perceiving the world.

## ■ Not All Stereotypes Are Equal

Although the psychological tendency to use stereotypes is universal, stereotypes differ in potency and negativity, depending on the group they describe. Stereotypes are unequal to the extent that the groups they describe are unequal. Some stereotypes can provide the ideological justification for the oppression of entire groups, whereas others are relatively innocuous. Stereotypes that maintain or augment hierarchy between social groups are exceptionally insidious (Jost & Banaji, 1994). We argue that stereotypes based on power differentials between groups have the most potential to harm.

Because of their history of powerlessness, U.S. racial minority groups carry particularly insidious stereotypes. Cognitive representations of Asian, African, Latino, and Native Americans have strong negative connotations that reflect the history of these groups in relation to Anglo Americans. This history includes institutionalized slavery, antimiscegenation laws, selective nonimmigratory status, mass internment, wars over boundaries, and the forced expulsion of natives from their homeland. Many non-U.S. societies are stratified by criteria other than race, such as the caste systems of India or Japan. In those societies, the relatively powerless groups are associated with pejorative stereotypes, much like the case for U.S. minority groups (see Chapter 5, this volume).

Thus, power and history make some stereotypes worse than others. Stereotypes that perpetuate the status quo typically associate low-power groups with insulting, derisive characteristics (e.g., Asians are asocial, blacks are violent, Latinos are lazy). These historically based negative stereotypes underlie societal beliefs that hinder intergroup relations and racial equality (see also Chapter 6, this volume).

## ■ Racial Stereotyping Is Practically Inevitable

Derogatory racial stereotypes are an inescapable facet of life in the United States. People do not have to endorse historically defined stereotypes to be influenced by them (Devine, 1989). Moreover, most people are not consciously aware of the influence that stereotypes have over their thought processes (Banaji & Greenwald, 1994).

All members of U.S. culture have some knowledge of existing racial stereotypes, regardless of whether they personally accept or reject the stereotypes. Exposure to these stereotypes starts early in life, and pervades one's entire lifespan across all aspects of society (Hirschfeld, 1996). Culture transmits racial stereotypes to people via several vehicles, including history books, media depictions of out-groups, family networks, community organizations, and other everyday interactions (see Ashmore & Del Boca, 1981; Mackie et al., 1996, for reviews).

Because racial stereotypes are so strongly socialized within U.S. culture, most people are not conscious of the control they exert over personal thoughts, feelings, and behaviors. Research suggests that as soon as people categorize others, stereotypes instantaneously become activated (Bargh, 1996; see Chapter 1, this volume). Once activated, stereotypes can unconsciously bias people's perceptions, judgments, and intentions (see Fiske, 1998, for a review). For example, perceivers tend to encode information that fits with previous knowledge more readily than information that does not match prior knowledge (Johnson & Macrae, 1994). As mentioned, expectancy-confirmation bias can be relatively benign in most scenarios. But when these expectancies concern historically powerless racial categories, they tend to carry harmful implications. Hence, people can and often do stereotype others without direct awareness of doing so. This usually occurs automatically, as soon as perceivers can place others within a category, as well as unintentionally, even to the most well-intentioned and egalitarian people.

Stereotypic information becomes reinforced throughout one's life, providing an unconscious belief system for perceiving the world. The socially ingrained, yet often unconscious, racial stereotypes of the "cunning Asian," "illegal Latino immigrant," and "aggressive black male" can serve not only as cognitive shortcuts for perceiving others, but as ideological or symbolic grounds for behavior (see also McConahay, 1986; Chapter 4, this volume). Recent news events attest to the power of racial stereotypes operating more or less unconsciously on people's behavior; these include the Vincent Chin murder, in which a Chinese American man was killed by unemployed Detroit auto workers who thought he was Japanese; the passage of Proposition 187 in California, which dismantled the state's affirmative action initiatives; and the Rodney King incident, in which police officers brutally beat King, a black man, after a high-speed car chase.

Indeed, racial stereotypes are ubiquitous features of U.S. society. Racial stereotypes pervade U.S. culture because people rely on cognitive shortcuts to simplify the world, and the qualities associated with racial minority groups in particular have historically negative connotations. Insofar as these automatic and unconscious stereotypes stay uninhibited, smooth race relations remain a difficult objective.

## ■ Racial Stereotyping Can Be Controlled

Although racial stereotypes automatically ensue from racial categorization, people can control the impact of stereotypes on their thoughts, feelings, and behaviors. Social psychologists have spent considerable effort studying the variables that inhibit stereotypes once they become activated. Research indicates that controlling the influence of automatic stereotypes is arduous, but not impossible (see also Chapter 10, this volume).

As mentioned, stereotypes activate instantaneously. Research indicates that people can categorize others within microseconds after first seeing them (Zárate & Smith, 1990). People's first thoughts and impressions of others start from categorization, whereby insight into others comes mainly from beliefs about their social group. Racial categories are among the most noticeable social tags that people constantly carry (along with their sex and age), and are difficult to ignore completely. Thus, one of the first pieces of information that we have about another person is race, as well as all the cultural baggage associated with that category. Many perceivers do not look any further beyond the categorical level before forming impressions; stereotypes hence provide the only source of information about others.

With motivation, effort, and attention, these initial thoughts and impressions can evolve into more complex and individuated (as opposed to category-based) ones (Brewer, 1988; Fiske & Neuberg, 1990). Perceivers can disarm the power of racial stereotypes by employing high-effort cognitive strategies, attending to specific details about the other person, especially details that disconfirm categorical expectancies. But again, this takes effort. In many situations, people are not particularly motivated to expend cognitive energy to think about others; category-based perceptions can satisfy people's casual, good-enough standards of judgment. Racial stereotypes thus direct people's thoughts by default because they cannot, or do not want to, think with effort (Macrae, Milne, & Bodenhausen, 1994).

People with internalized standards to expend extra cognitive effort can override the default tendency to stereotype (Monteith, 1993). These perceivers are more likely to control the impact of automatically activated stereotypes, paying attention to details about the person rather than the person's category. With motivation and attention, people can disconfirm stereotype-based expectancies, forming information-based impressions instead.

## ■ Summary

Social cognition research suggests that stereotyping is a perfectly natural way of thinking, although not always the best or most accurate way. People use stereotypes by necessity; it is impossible to think effortfully during every second of consciousness. Stereotypes simplify the world by providing information based on social categories. Racial stereotypes are thus unavoidable because people's racial categories tend to be one of the first things we notice. The stereotypes associated with minority racial categories carry much more negative baggage than those associated with majority or high-power categories. Although stereotypes occur automatically, people can control the impact of stereotypic information. People who have internalized nonbiased standards of judgment have the most success at encoding stereotype-inconsistent information, forming less biased impressions. But as reviewed shortly, power muddles the motivation to think effortfully. Sometimes, power motivates people to stereotype even more.

## ■ Affective and Evaluative Consequences of Racial Categories

In addition to influencing people's cognitive processes (thought), social categories impact people's affective feelings and evaluations about others. The distinction between cognition, reviewed previously, and affect, to which we now turn, is an important one. Many social psychologists regard cognitive processes as relatively cold and mechanistic, in comparison with affective processes, which tend to be more heated or, at least, personally involving. Roughly, racial stereotyping represents the cognitive component of racism, whereas racial prejudice represents the emotional and evaluative components of racism. Cognition (stereotyping) and affect (prejudice) are undeniably interconnected (Fiske, 1982; Smith & Ellsworth, 1985), but they do not overlap completely. As we will discuss, people's feelings and evaluations do not always match their cognitions and perceptions (e.g., Zajonc, 1980), particularly regarding racial categories.

## ■ Minimal Requirements for Prejudice

In some early studies of prejudice, social psychologists encountered a startling phenomenon. Researchers found that participants assigned to one of two random groups, for example, after the flip of a coin, displayed significant bias in favor of their group and against the other group (see Hogg & Abrams, 1988, for a review). Social psychologists refer to this experimental technique as the "minimal group paradigm." The mere existence of social groups in the laboratory, even arbitrary and meaningless ("minimal") ones, led participants to prejudge other participants based on their assigned group membership. Similar to the case for stereotyping, researchers have found that in-group favoritism occurs automatically and unconsciously; people display bias in favor of their group without knowledge of doing so (Perdue, Dovidio, Gurtman, & Tyler, 1990; see also Chapter 1, this volume).

Dozens of the minimal group studies indicate that people tend to evaluate members of their (randomly assigned) in-group more positively, allocate more resources to their in-group, and evaluate the performance of their in-group more positively (see Brewer & Brown, 1998, for a review). The minimal group paradigm thus offers a glimpse into the social psychological prerequisites for prejudice. One variable alone can elicit emotional and evaluative bias among participants in the laboratory—dividing people into an in-group ("us") and an out-group ("them"). No other situational variables need to be present to elicit baseline bias effects. That is, a cognitive component, in the form of stereotypes, need not accompany these evaluative biases; prejudice reflects a gut-level reaction often devoid of cognitive rationale.

Prejudice outside the laboratory, especially with regard to historically defined social groups, is much more complex. Real-world groups often have long histories of antagonism and power hierarchy. These variables exacerbate the baseline effects obtained in minimal group studies (Mullen, Brown, & Smith, 1992; Mullen & Hu, 1989; Ostrom & Sedikides, 1992). Most definitions of prejudice presuppose the existence of more complex intergroup relations than those created in minimal group laboratory scenarios. For example, Jones (1972) defined prejudice as "the prior negative judgment of the members of a . . . *significant social role;* . . . an affective, categorical mode of mental functioning involving rigid prejudgment and misjudgment of human groups" (p. 61, emphasis added).

Social prejudice in general, and racial prejudice in particular, ensues from more significant conditions than experimenters can create in the laboratory. Psychology studies using minimal groups indicate that some bias even occurs in the absence of complex intergroup conditions, but these experiments can only partially explain racism. As discussed shortly, racism reflects in part the universal tendency to favor the in-group. Societal variables, however, transform this basic process into a more systemic, insidious phenomenon.

## ■ Group Identity and Self-Regard

Psychologists have developed several theories to explain prejudice and in-group bias. One of the most influential theories emerged from Europe, referred to as social identity theory (Tajfel & Turner, 1979). According to social identity theory, people have a fundamental need to feel positively about themselves, and often satisfy this need through bolstering their group or social identities.

Group identity refers to the part of one's self-concept that comes from belonging to a collective social unit, such as one's country, gender, club affiliation, political party, or race. People who derive personal and emotional value from their group membership are likely to express bias in favor of that particular collective identity. Hence, as the minimal group paradigm demonstrates, people evaluate their in-group more positively than the out-group, allocate more rewards to other members of the in-group, and sometimes derogate out-group members (see Brewer & Brown, 1998, for a review; Tajfel & Turner, 1986). In doing so, people can elevate their self-esteem by heightening the position of their in-group relative to the out-group (see also Chapter 8, this volume).

Much like the cognitive processes that drive stereotyping, social identity theorists argue that people display in-group favoritism almost automatically after categorizing themselves within some social unit ("us"), that is distinctive from another unit ("them"). After categorizing themselves as a group member, people tend to amplify the perceived differences between groups. Thus, the mere acknowledgment of in-groups and out-groups leads to the perception that they are discrete, nonoverlapping entities (e.g., "they" are different from "us"). This in turn leads to prejudice, because people tend to associate feelings and values with the supposed differences between groups (e.g., "they" differ from "us" because "we" are better than "them").

A more recent theory extends social identity theory's initial argument, by detailing the cognitive basis for group identification and prejudice. Self-categorization theory (Turner, Hogg, Oakes, Reicher, & Wetherell, 1987) suggests that individuals psychologically create (or perceive) group categories based on the variation among people within a given social context. That is, individuals "carve up" their environments by clustering similar elements (people) together, and differentiating them from dissimilar elements (people). The criteria for clustering people into groups include (a) the range of human diversity within the situation, (b) the situational importance of any particular attribute or quality, and (c) the personal importance placed on any particular attribute or quality (see Turner, Oakes, Haslam, & McGarty, 1994, for more discussion). According to this perspective, people's social identities can shift depending on how they perceptually carve up their environment, which determines how they designate "us" as opposed to "them."

The point behind self-categorization theory is that these groups often are not static entities. Groups usually are perceived, subjective entities with fuzzy, undefined boundaries. Such is the case for race, as discussed earlier. Racial categories have fuzzy distinctions, yet people perceive them as fixed, rigid divisions. Thus, racial prejudice can result simply by accepting race as a valid social category, and categorizing oneself within racial parameters. As mentioned, prejudice involves gut-level reactions to group distinctions; it does not need to involve elaborate stereotypes.

Social identity and self-categorization theories suggest that prejudice occurs naturally and automatically, as a function of basic psychological mechanisms. But despite its almost universal nature, not all social categories benefit equally from, or suffer equally from, in-group bias and racial prejudice. When groups' power and resources enter the equation for intergroup relations, the scenario changes drastically.

## ■ Threat to Group Resources

Another important theory for understanding prejudice and intergroup relations is realistic group conflict theory (Levine & Campbell, 1972). This theory examines how competition for resources contributes to intergroup bias.

Realistic conflict suggests that real-world groups outside of the laboratory exist in states of conflict over scarce resources. Prejudice results from implicit competition over incompatible intergroup goals (see also Fiske & Ruscher, 1993).

Research from a number of disciplines, including anthropology, political science, and sociology, support realistic conflict theory by stressing the roles of competition and resource scarcity. For example, violence between groups increases under conditions of overpopulation and food shortage, when groups must compete for scarce resources (Divale & Harris, 1976; Gleick, 1993; Homer-Dixon, 1991, 1994; Wilson, 1973). Intergroup conflict can erupt even in times of resource abundance, as groups compete for resource control and allocation (Cummings, 1980).

Real-world dilemmas provoke group categorization and differentiation, thereby contributing to social prejudice. Macrolevel phenomena such as economic threat, land disputes, and environmental disasters exacerbate people's basic tendency to identify with a group and enhance their group's status.

## ■ Prejudice Inhibition

Like stereotyping, prejudice can be controlled. People with internalized egalitarian values can regulate their emotional and evaluative responses to out-group members (Monteith, 1993). Overcoming prejudice is a long process, perhaps more difficult than inhibiting stereotypes. This takes practice, patience, and constant self-monitoring, but is very possible (see Chapter 10, this volume). But, like stereotyping, we will argue that power hinders this process.

## ■ Summary

Racial prejudice represents the combination of fundamental psychological processes, such as the need to belong (Baumeister & Leary, 1995), along with perceived or actual competition between groups. The mere classification of people into racial categories engenders and encourages the tendency to differentiate one's in-group as superior to the out-group. The perception of resource scarcity contributes to feelings of intergroup competition and threat. Racial prejudice thus follows from the social and historical forces that have rendered intergroup boundaries meaningful and conflictual.

## ■ Power Plus Prejudice

Thus far, the chapter has noted the implications of arbitrary social (racial) categories for people's thoughts and feelings. The mere presence and acceptance of race leads people to simplify others through cognitive mechanisms, as well as prefer similar others (the in-group) over dissimilar others (the out-group) through affective and evaluative mechanisms. Nevertheless, as Cox informed us in his opening quote, these factors alone cannot explain the insidious, asymmetrical nature of racism. Something more must be operating.

The psychological basis of racism stems from asymmetrical social power. Members of social groups holding the most control over valued resources are prone to stereotype others and favor their own members, particularly when motivated to maintain dominance, privilege, and status (see also Fiske, 1993). In turn, members of low-power groups are vulnerable to subordination and exploitation by those who control resources.

Racial oppression thus derives from (a) power—the disproportionate ability of some individuals or groups to control other people's outcomes; and (b) prejudice—the universal tendency to favor the in-group over the out-group. Racism functions additively from asymmetrical power and racial prejudice. Without both essential variables, racism could not manifest itself as individual-, institutional-, and cultural-level phenomena.

This argument is not new. Theorists from several disciplines argue that power is central to racism (e.g., Blauner, 1968; Jones, 1972, 1997; Schermerhorn, 1970; Wilson, 1973). Prejudice alone does not determine racism; everyone has prejudices, because all people prefer their group over others. History and society confer power to certain groups, granting them excessive ability to exercise their prejudice. According to one social psychologist, "Ethnocentrism is transformed to cultural racism by the accumulation of POWER. The ability to control, through the exercise of power, the lives and destinies of black people becomes cultural racism when those destinies are chained to white ethnocentric standards" (Jones, 1972, p. 154; see also Chapter 12, this volume).

Power plus racial prejudice can thwart people's ability or willingness to suppress racial bias. Powerlessness, or outcome dependency, can have a converse effect on people, motivating acquiescence to others' biases. Thus, power is not just a sociological or political construct. Power operates at the individual level and is the sine qua non (without which, nothing) to the psychology of racism.

## ■ Control Motivates Bias

Power can increase people's tendency to stereotype and discriminate against others for two main reasons. First, powerful individuals or members of powerful groups often lack the motivation to inhibit stereotyping and prejudice. In this case, bias results by default, because powerful people rest on their automatic, uninhibited assumptions about others. Power reinforces spontaneous, categorical assumptions about others simply because powerful people lack contingency on those they control (Fiske, 1993); they can get away with stereotyping and prejudice with relative impunity. This explanation provides a relatively innocuous depiction of power, suggesting that added motivation can wipe away the default tendency to display bias. Indeed, motivation in the forms of internalized values, situational norms, and public policies can inhibit racial stereotyping and prejudice somewhat (see also Chapter 10 and Chapter 11, this volume).

A second reason why power facilitates bias is that powerful individuals or members of powerful groups often want to maintain, or even increase, the disparity between groups. In this case, bias results by design, because power-ful people exert extra energy to categorize others and discriminate against out-group members (Goodwin & Fiske, 1996). Powerful people, by virtue of their roles or group identities, can be motivated to preserve their position in the status quo and bolster their perception of control over others (Jost & Banaji, 1994). Such individuals use stereotypes, typically negative ones, to rationalize and justify existing power differentials. This depiction of power is much more insidious compared to the previous one.

In short, power (or control) motivates racial bias because powerful people (a) lack the inherent need to inhibit stereotypes and prejudice (not the case for low-power people, discussed shortly), or else (b) strategically use stereotypes and prejudice to legitimize group differences.

## ■ Dependency Motivates Acquiescence

Research suggests two psychological links between outcome dependency and acquiescence to the status quo. First, outcome dependency motivates people to pay extra attention to those who control their outcomes. People must be able to predict the behavior of those who control their resources or destinies. Low-power perceivers cannot rely on simple stereotypes as high-power people can; their low-status position motivates the need to predict the behavior of those higher up. In effect, they take in more useful information, forming less category-based impressions of the powerful (Erber & Fiske, 1984; Neuberg, 1989; Neuberg & Fiske, 1987; Ruscher & Fiske, 1990). Even when motivated to stereotype the powerful (e.g., as villains or despots; Dépret & Fiske, 1996), low-power people lack the essential resources to enact their biases and influence those higher up (Sachdev & Bourhis, 1985, 1991). In some cases, dependency motivates positive biases, whereby low-power people perceive the powerful in flattering ways (Stevens & Fiske, 1996), or else ally themselves with those in control (Dépret & Fiske, 1996).

Second, outcome dependency motivates people to adjust their behavior to comply with top-down standards or norms. By definition, they depend on the powerful for valued resources, so they must appear agreeable or competent. In the course of satisfying top-down standards or norms, outcome-dependent people can unintentionally confirm stereotypes about their groups (Copeland, 1994). Social psychologists refer to this phenomenon as behavioral confirmation (Snyder, 1992, provides an overview).

Behavioral confirmation is not inevitable, especially if the powerless are aware of the biases against them (Hilton & Darley, 1985), and motivated to improve their relative standing within the status hierarchy (see Eberhardt & Fiske, 1996). Individuals who present themselves positively in accordance with general social standards (e.g., appearing competent), rather than accede to others' biases against their group, are likely to disconfirm negative expectations (Operario & Fiske, 1997). In addition, people with strong self-concepts are unlikely to conform to expectations about their group (Swann & Ely, 1984). But again, the powerless have a hard disconfirming biases against their group when perceivers hold high levels of power (Copeland, 1994; Operario & Fiske, 1997), or else have dominant personalities, whereby they simply prefer controlling others' outcomes (Operario & Fiske, 1997).

To conclude, outcome dependency motivates low-power people to think attentively, perceive optimistically, and behave correspondingly with powerful people's standards. The psychological effects of dependency drive acquiescence, thereby reinforcing power differentials from the bottom up.

## ■ Summary

Power has converse implications for high-power versus low-power people. Individuals who control others (or who belong to groups that control other groups) have less motivation to inhibit stereotyping and prejudice. They may even desire to derogate others to elevate self-esteem or maintain their status. In contrast, individuals who depend on others have ample motivation to

predict and to think accurately, or at least optimistically. Dependency motivates acquiescence to gain important resources—jobs, promotion, education,
praise. Thus, power underlies the psychological discrepancy between those
who control and those who are controlled. For the former, stereotypes and
prejudices of others can become intensified, whereas for the latter, stereotypes
and prejudices of self can be perpetuated due to motivated compliance.

## ■ Racism Is a Personal and Societal Challenge

Racism transcends levels of analysis, presenting a multifaceted problem
that individuals, institutions, and societies must address (Jones, 1972). Although social psychology focuses on individual-level responses to racism,
these responses build on one another, contributing to societal phenomena.

For example, sociological data indicate that well-intentioned employers
often hesitate before selecting black job applicants (Braddock & McPartland,
1987; Kirschenman & Neckerman, 1991; see also Chapter 1, this volume).
Over time, each individual decision adds up, denying employment to large
numbers of black candidates. These aggregated, racially biased decisions
widen the socioeconomic gap between racial groups (these trends also underlie employment discrimination against women, see Martell, Lane, & Emrich,
1996).

In a similar vein, cultural beliefs about Asian Americans as individually
passive, obedient, hardworking, and socially inept encourage employers to
hire them, but not promote them to upper levels of management. The combined effect of these racial beliefs produces a glass ceiling: Asians are hired
and encouraged to fulfill their categorical stereotype of diligence and acquiescence, but often denied access to higher levels of responsibility (Duleep &
Sanders, 1992).

Individual-level thoughts, feelings, and behaviors do matter in the societal sense. Each personal decision to hire, include, support, or simply befriend
a member of a racial out-group has implications for the well-being of a
multicultural society. But, of course, power obstructs this goal. Without
increased motivation, high-power individuals and members of high-power
groups are unlikely to shoulder their part. Societal structure does not motivate
many members of high-power groups to look beyond racial categories before
making judgments; in some cases, that motivation has actually diminished in
recent years.

Institutions and societies must reinforce the desire to inhibit stereotyping and prejudice. Social norms and policies must express enthusiasm for multicultural values (see Chapter 11, this volume). The equation for racism, power plus prejudice, cannot work at one level alone. All units of analysis, from people to communities to cultures, must value egalitarianism and racial impartiality. If not, the automatic tendency to favor the in-group and maintain status quo will persist.

## ■ A Glimmer of Hope

We foresee a potentially optimistic future for race relations in this country. This depends on recognizing first the arbitrary nature of race, and second, the centrality of power in sustaining racial categories and motivating racial thoughts and behaviors.

The task is not an easy one. Challenging the concept of race and racial dominance may threaten people's fundamental assumptions about how the world operates. Contrary to arguments in other academic fields, this chapter does not advise ridding society of the concept of race altogether. Race has taken on enormous social meaning and, as a result, is integral to the identity and self-concept of many people (see Cross, 1991; Phinney, 1990b; Porter & Washington, 1993; Chapter 8, this volume). What this chapter does advocate, however, is invalidating the power hierarchies and negative connotations associated with race that limit the thoughts, feelings, and behaviors of all individuals.

# 3

# Social Psychological
# Processes and the Legal
# Bases of Racial Categorization

*R. Richard Banks*
*Jennifer L. Eberhardt*

**M**ost studies in social psychology presuppose the existence of racial groups. Rather than investigate the origin of racial groupings or the processes of racial categorization, social psychological studies examine the views that perceivers hold about members of a particular racial group, how perceivers' behavior or attributions differ based on a target's race, the link between racial attitudes and beliefs about other issues, and (to a lesser extent) the negative consequences that targets of racial stereotypes and prejudice experience as a result of being stigmatized (Dovidio & Gaertner 1986a; Macrae, Stangor, & Hewstone, 1996).

Yet, race is not a naturally occurring phenomenon. The belief in race as a biological concept cannot withstand scrutiny on at least two bases. First, genetic differences between population groups cannot support the claim that there are genetic differences that justify racial groups (Nei & Roychoudhury, 1983). There are genetic differences among groups of people but these population groupings are not the same as racial groupings. The genetic distinctiveness of population groups is a function of geography (Lewontin, Rose, & Kamin, 1984). But racial categorization is not and could not be based

AUTHORS' NOTE: Special thanks to Susan Fiske for her comments on a previous version of this chapter and to Mina Kim for research assistance that helped to make this chapter possible.

strictly on geography. Population groups that "belong" to different racial groups may be very similar genetically, whereas population groups that "belong" to the same racial group may be relatively dissimilar genetically.

Second, physical differences among racial groups do not reflect genetic differences (Nei & Roychoudhury, 1983). Genotypic differences are not reliably mirrored by the phenotypic differences on which racial group membership is largely based. The physical differences that signify race do not correlate with the genetic differences on which the biological claim for racial categorization must rest. Even if genetic variation justified a concept of race, our demarcation of racial groupings based on physical features fails to correspond to the underlying genetic differences.

In sum, racial categories do not track genetic variation among population groups. Even if there were an underlying genetic justification for the designation of racial, as opposed to population groupings, genetic differences are not reliably reflected in the physical characteristics that are taken to signify race. As we discuss in this chapter, the "existence" of commonly recognized racial groups is a matter of social, political, and historical contingency, rather than transhistorical biological necessity.

Race is a social construction. A century ago, belief in the biological basis of racial categorization obscured this fact. Now, however, the biological bases of race have been widely discredited (Cavalli-Sforza & Feldman, 1973; Lewontin et al., 1984; Nei & Roychoudhury, 1983). From the standpoint of biology, there are no races. Yet, race continues to be among the most meaningful of social categories. From the standpoint of social psychology, race is among the most interesting and important of social phenomena.

This chapter applies cognitive and social psychological categorization processes to the phenomenon of race. Even though its experimental studies rarely examine the socially constructed nature of race, cognitive social psychology does provide the categorization principles through which racial categorization can be understood. For instance, no matter what is being judged, people typically use a similarity principle in deciding which people or objects fall into the same category. Racial categorization is but one example of the general categorization processes through which the social world is created and ordered. Examining the racial categorization process is the first goal of this chapter.

The second goal of this chapter is to delineate the relation between legal rules and judicial decision making and the social construction of race. Legal norms and decision making are deeply implicated in racial categorization. Psychologists have uncovered the cognitive mechanisms of categorization.

Yet neither legal scholars nor psychological researchers have linked basic psychological principles to the process of racial categorization promoted by legal rules and judicial decisions. Law identifies the physical characteristics and internal essences that constrain the similarity judgments essential to everyday racial categorization. As this chapter will argue, law provides the raw materials through which the mechanisms of social categorization act.

Just as law fortifies the bases of racial categorization, so too do prevalent beliefs about race find expression in legal reasoning. Law has shaped race and changing notions of race have shaped law. During the past century, the recognition that race is a socially created rather than naturally occurring phenomenon has altered the form of legal reasoning about issues that implicate race. Now, both attitudes about race—that it is socially constructed and that it is naturally occurring—are evident in legal reasoning and judicial decision making. Judges and policymakers are deeply divided about the meaning of race in U.S. society.

## ■ Categorization and Race

Categorization is fundamental and essential to human cognition. Were it not for our propensity to categorize, life would appear overwhelmingly complex and unmanageable. Categories serve as organizational units that save time and energy. They "engender meaning upon the world" and "give order to our life-space" (Allport, 1954, p. 176). Psychologists have thus conducted decades of research on how people categorize and why they chose to construct the particular categories that they do.

In the traditional view of category formation (referred to as the classical view in psychology), objects belong in a particular category if they simply possess the features considered necessary and sufficient for category membership. This classical view "assumes that mental representations of categories consist of summary lists of features or properties that individually are necessary for category membership and collectively are sufficient to determine category membership" (Medin, 1989, p. 1470).

This traditional view has now been rejected as not adequately explaining either the structure of categories or the placement of objects in one category rather than another. Many categories, for example, contain members that do not have necessary and sufficient features. According to the traditional view, people will classify an object as a bird if it has wings and feathers and if it can fly, sing, and lay eggs. But relying on some or all of these features to determine category membership poses problems. Penguins and ostriches do not share all of these features yet are categorized as birds. Airplanes, pillows, mosquitoes, opera performers, and spiders possess one or many of these features yet are not categorized as birds. Contrary to the classical view (and to people's common sense notion of category construction), category members do not possess essential properties that bind them together.

In place of the classical view, psychologists turned to a probabilistic view of category formation that rejects the idea of necessary and sufficient features. According to this view, category membership is a matter of degree—some objects are more typical or more representative of a category than others. For example, a robin may be thought a better or more typical example of the category bird than an ostrich. People use probabilistic similarity rules to determine whether an object is a "good fit" for a category. These probabilistic rules form the basis for two models of categorization. The prototype model proposes that people judge objects against a category prototype that represents a summary of features likely to be found in the category. In the exemplar model, people decide on category membership by comparing an object to specific and vivid examples from the category. Both models have been applied to social categorization and stereotyping, and both have empirical support (see Fiske & Taylor, 1991, for distinctions between prototype and exemplar models for social categories).

Nonetheless, probabilistic models beg the central questions of categorization: First, why, of the infinite possible categories, do particular categories become constructed? Second, how are similarity judgments made among objects with different characteristics? Given that objects may share some characteristics (but not others) with other members of a category, what determines whether a particular object belongs in a particular category? How do categories and the objects placed within them define each other?

A number of researchers currently believe that similarity judgments are shaped by an implicit belief in essentialism (see Medin, 1989, for example). Although categories do not have necessary and sufficient features, people form similarity judgments as if categories have essential properties (Medin, 1989). People follow particular theories of category construction that determine not only which features are relevant, but how these features are related to one another. According to this theoretical model, a bird's feathers and wings, for example, are significant surface characteristics which might indicate or point to the presence of some deeper properties (e.g., genetic material) that people consider the essence of birdhood.

This "psychological essentialism" stabilizes categories by providing an implicit theory that links surface characteristics to each other and to the (sometimes unapparent) core of the category itself. The concept of the category's essence serves to "embody or provide causal linkages from deeper properties to more superficial or surface properties" (Medin, 1989, p. 1477). Because "the basis for category membership rests on deep underlying non-obvious structure, it is possible to ignore violations of the usual appearance of a category member" (Rothbart & Taylor, 1992, p. 14). For instance, when an object lacks the typical surface characteristics (e.g., when a bird does not possess feathers or is unable to fly), an object can remain in the category if the deeper properties are thought to be present. People believe that it is the deeper properties that are necessary and sufficient for category membership, not the surface characteristics.

Psychological essentialism is adhered to even in the face of serious ambiguities and enormous conflictual evidence. People's "belief in essentialism is not disturbed by an inability to specify the exact nature of an essence. . . . Although the essence of a . . . category is only vaguely understood, people may not be deterred from assuming it exists" (Rothbart & Taylor, 1992, pp. 18-19) even if this essence cannot be precisely defined or located.

Thus, similarity judgments are constrained by essentialistic theories. However, the fact that similarity judgments are constrained by essentialistic theories begs another question: If theories constrain similarity judgments, what constrains theories?

We argue that theories of race, in particular, are developed from and become perpetuated through legal norms and mechanisms. The law, then, works to constrain our theories of racial categories. Legal norms and practices determine which characteristics, both superficial and deep, constitute either the markers or essence of race. The law, therefore, participates in how and which racial categories get constructed.


■ Race as a Social Category

Race is a social category that was created historically to serve particular interests. "Racial categories did not emerge simply as the products of energy- and time-saving cognitive devices, but as functional entities constructed in the service of social power and cultural domination" (Eberhardt & Randall, 1997). The idea of race did not exist in its present form before the Atlantic slave trade; it only gradually took hold in U.S. society as it became necessary to rationalize slavery (Fields, 1990). If there were races, and if one was inferior to the other, then the democratic principles of liberty and equality were not threatened or undermined by the existence of slavery.

Specific definitions of race were also developed to fulfill particular goals of the system of slavery. The general principle that "one drop" of "black blood" made someone black, for example, combined with the principle that a child took his or her mother's race to ensure the maintenance of the slave population in spite of widespread miscegenation between white men and black slave women.

Historically, appearance has been the identifiable, surface characteristic on which racial categorization has been based. Physical features such as complexion, hair, nose, lips, and body type have been central to determinations of race. Ancestry, although not a "physical" feature, may be best viewed as a surface characteristic that points toward the essence of the category more than it constitutes it. Ancestry and appearance are linked through the metaphor of "blood," whose physicality suggests physical features and whose biological character symbolizes the transmission of race through lines of descent.

The deeper properties of race are thought to be comprised not only of a biological essence (DNA, for example), but also of psychological and social status characteristics as well. Beliefs about these deeper properties constitute the essence of racial categories. The psychological characteristics of race include factors such as racial sentiments, instincts, affinities, proclivities, and moral character. The social status characteristics include the general (e.g., dominant vs. subordinate) and specific (e.g., master vs. slave) roles that racial groups occupy in society relative to one another. Biological conceptions of race often, but not always, underpin beliefs in race-based psychological and social status characteristics.

Although both psychological and social status characteristics can be thought of as the deep properties of race (and therefore as a part of the essence of the categories), social status characteristics (i.e., which roles particular racial groups occupy in society) may be believed to naturally follow from psychological characteristics (for further evidence on this point see Hoffman & Hurst, 1990; Jost & Banaji, 1994; or Yzerbyt, Rocher, & Schadron, 1997). Black Americans' low status in contemporary times, for example, can be thought to result from their aversion to hard work.

Disparate physical features such as hair, complexion, and bone structure become understood, through the prism of racial essence, as similar. Some features but not others become salient because they are taken to signify race. Relatedly, surface features such as skin color and hair texture, in this view, signify internal qualities of an individual. As Allport (1954) has suggested, "[dark] skin implies more than pigmentation, it implies social inferiority"

(p. 136). Far from merely contributing to appearance, surface features point toward the unseen moral, intellectual, or psychological properties of race.

Law works to connect surface characteristics and deep properties into a coherent theory. By providing and enforcing a unifying racial theory, the law eases the tension that would otherwise result from the inevitable conflicts of the external indicators of ancestry and appearance. The law makes it possible that individuals of wildly varying backgrounds and appearance can be thought to belong to the same race. Race may not have created the need for legal mechanisms to keep the categories stable and coherent, so much as legal norms and decision making have created race.

### ■ The Role of the Legal System in Defining Racial Categories

Law has made race matter. For most of U.S. history, law has distributed burdens and benefits, rights and lack of rights on the basis of race. For more than 150 years, the only immigrants to the United States who could become citizens were those who were white. Because rights have so coincided with race, determinations of race have been immensely important. The assignment of an individual to a racial category often meant the difference between freedom and slavery. The Jim Crow regime, in the North as well as the South, left no area of life untouched. Separate churches, schools, bathrooms, trains, and hotels all were required. Even the most intimate of decisions yielded to the demands of race law. Whom one could marry, where one could live, how one could work all turned on race.

The legal system has been integral to both the defining of racial categories and the sorting of individuals into the "appropriate" categories. Furthermore, law has stabilized the social psychological basis of racial categories through its reinforcement of ideas of racial essence.

> The voluminous record before us contains fascinating evidence of race as a matter of physical appearance, heredity, self-perception, community recognition, and cultural bias. The record includes trial testimony, depositions of elderly relatives and neighbors, testimony of state employees who register and maintain vital statistics, and expert testimony of genealogists and a geneticist. Also in evidence are detailed genealogical charts supported by official and unofficial records spanning some 200 years, along with photographs of scores of . . . family members. The intriguing historical, social, and anthropological issues raised by this evidence belie the simple legal ques-

tions—the only questions courts of law are authorized, or indeed able, to answer. (*Jane Doe v. State of Louisiana,* 1985)

Law has developed a body of definitions and procedures for assigning racial group membership. The case quoted here concerned a family's effort to have their deceased parents' racial designation in official state records changed from black to white. The quote is ironic in that the court recognizes the complexity of racial categorization yet futilely attempts to separate the legal determination of race from that complex social process. Contrary to the court's suggestion, legal rules and decision-making processes are deeply implicated in the maintenance of racial categories. The often contradictory nature of the hereditary and morphological elements of race is no less confounding in legal than social judgments. Even as the court emphasized the "simple legal questions" with which it was confronted, it could not avoid delving into a morass of evidence that complicates rather than simplifies determinations of race. Ultimately, the court rejected the plaintiffs' demand that their parents' racial designation be changed. Although declining to rule that the parents were black, the court held that the plaintiffs failed to prove that the parents were white.

As expected, the court focused in part on the centrality of physical appearance in the determination of racial group membership. Although the link between physical features and race has not been embodied in any federal or state statutes, judges in numerous cases have relied on physical features to determine race.

One case from 1938 required the court to determine whether a woman was black to settle an alimony dispute. After his former wife filed a claim for alimony, the ex-husband sued to annul the marriage and thus negate the possibility of alimony. His basis for annulment was that his former wife was in fact a Negro. If the wife was a Negro, their marriage would be legally void because the man was white. The former husband attempted to prove his claim by evidence that his former wife's great-great-grandmother was a Negro. He produced a document from the early 19th century that identified the great-great-grandmother as a "free woman of color." But this raised more questions than it answered. The court observed that prior to the Civil War the phrase "people of color" may have referred to people who were neither black nor white, or alternatively to anyone who was not white, including Indians. The wife claimed that her great-great grandmother was Indian, not Negro (Indian-white marriage was not illegal).

Inevitably, the court turned to evidence as to the physical appearance of the great-great-grandmother. One defense witness who saw her said "she was copper colored and had long straight black hair." A witness for the plaintiff testified "that he could not remember whether [the great-great grandmother's] hair was 'straight or kinky' but that he knew 'she had tolerable fair hair hanging down on her [fore]head'; that her hair was long, and that it was black in color." Further complicating matters, the great-great-grandmother's daughter (the great-grandmother of the defendant wife) was found to be "of fair complexion, with blue eyes and long straight hair."

Law has more formally specified the role of ancestry in racial categorization. Most states at one time or another had statutes that defined racial categories. Statutes varied, but each generally defined race based on the proportion of one's black ancestors. Some states required only 1/32 of "black blood" to make one black, whereas others declared "one eighth Negro blood" (Stephenson, 1969, p. 15) sufficient; still other states required as much as "one fourth Negro blood" to be classed with that race (Stephenson, 1969, p. 15). In all states, a small amount of black "blood" made one black, whereas white racial status depended on nearly 100% white ancestry. This asymmetry has been termed the hypodescent rule (it has also been termed the "one-drop rule"). As one early 20th-century commentator described the implications of this rule, "miscegenation has never been a bridge on which one might cross from the Negro race to the Caucasian, though it has been a thoroughfare from the Caucasian to the Negro" (Stephenson, 1969, p. 19).

Racial categorization, by both appearance and ancestry, is a matter of social context. Historically, who is white, for example, has not remained static. Immigrants who were not white on their arrival in the United States eventually became white. Sociologists and historians have traced the path that Irish immigrants, in particular, have taken to become white (Ignatiev, 1995; Roediger, 1991). Even Chinese immigrants, who were classed along with blacks in one period, assimilated into the concept of white at later periods (Loewen, 1971), only to be reclassed as "people of color" in contemporary times. In some areas, black Americans were identified as "Negro," "Afro-American," "Colored," or some other term that applied only to them. In other periods and places, black Americans were referred to mostly by the term "people of color," which included other nonwhite groups as well.

The changing content of racial categories has also posed challenges for courts. In a pair of cases during the 1980s, for example, the Supreme Court confronted the question of whether Arabs and Jews, respectively, could state claims for racial discrimination under 19th-century statutes (*Shaare Tefila*

*Congregation v. Cobb,* 1987; *Saint Francis College v. Al-Khazraji,* 1987). Is discrimination against an Arab or a Jew on the basis of being an Arab or a Jew a case of racial discrimination? In both cases, the Supreme Court ruled that it is. Acknowledging the changing content of racial categories, the Court observed that "the question before us is not whether Jews are considered to be a separate race by today's standards" (*Shaare Tefila Congregation v. Cobb,* 1986, p. 617). The Court concluded that during the time of the passage of the relevant statute during the Reconstruction Era "Jews and Arabs were among the peoples then considered to be distinct races and hence within the protection of the statute" (*Shaare Tefila Congregation v. Cobb,* 1987, pp. 617-618).

In contemporary society, the legal system may seem to be much less implicated in the maintenance of racial categories than in generations past—in that rights are no longer formally allocated on the basis of race. But race remains an important legal concept. As recently as 1970, the state of Louisiana passed a statute (later repealed in 1983) that prohibited "a person having 1/32 or less of Negro blood [from being] deemed, described, or designated by any public official in the state of Louisiana as 'colored,' a 'mulatto,' a 'black,' a 'Negro,' a 'griffe,' an 'Afro-American,' a 'quardroon' [sic], a 'mestizo,' a 'colored person,' or a 'person of color'" (*State of Louisiana ex. rel. Frank Plaia v. Louisiana State Board of Health,* 1974).

Currently, a variety of laws either explicitly or tacitly require the determination of individuals' race. Race thus permeates not only societal consciousness, but legal rules and public policy as well. The administration and enforcement of the nation's antidiscrimination laws, most obviously, necessitates the maintenance of racial categories and the placement of individuals in one category rather than another. The racial discrimination claims made by Arabs and Jews in the two cases discussed here, for example, could not be ruled on without deciding whether Arabs and Jews, for purposes of the applicable statute, are white or not. Under the terms of the statute, if Arabs and Jews were determined to be white, their claims for racial discrimination would have been rejected because the 19th century statute upon which their claim was based guaranteed all persons the same rights "enjoyed by white citizens."

To administer antidiscrimination laws, governmental officials and private organizations regularly must ascertain race based on physical appearance. Private employers and public schools, for example, must report to the federal government the racial group membership of their employees and students, respectively. Mortgage lenders must track loan applications, denials, and approvals by race.

Unlike past eras, much contemporary racial designation is self-reported. Census data on race, for example, reflect individuals' self-identification. Applications to government programs or educational institutions often rely on self-reports of racial group membership. This trend toward self-reporting represents a momentous change in the means of ascertaining race. Interestingly, this momentous change in the method of obtaining racial designations has produced almost no change in the racial demographics for some groups. For example, regardless of the racial designation method, the size of the black population has not changed at all (remaining at about 12% of the U.S. population; Davis, 1991). Some researchers view this as indicative of the extent to which racial designations have been individually internalized, so that we all know what we are (e.g., Davis, 1991).

Historically, racial group determination could not be left to self-reporting because many slaves would no doubt have freed themselves by becoming white. Racial designations were a matter of external imposition. Courts developed a variety of evidentiary considerations that bore on racial categorization. One primary evidentiary consideration was the race of one's associates. In the alimony case discussed previously, for example, the wife's claim that she was not Negro was bolstered by the fact that "in railroad cars, street cars, and busses [sic] [the wife and her mother] ride in the seats reserved for white persons. They attend theatres [sic] and patronize hotels and restaurants as white persons. Their friends and associates are apparently exclusively of the white race" (*Sunseri v. Cassagne,* 1938, pp. 220-221).

Courts' propensity to rely on such evidence can be understood as a belief in racial essence in the form of racial instincts or sentiments that would "naturally" bond together those of the same race. Courts presupposed racial affinities that would reveal one's true race when the evidence based on ancestry and physical features left the matter in doubt.

## ■ The Role of Legal Rules in Maintaining Racial Categories

In at least three interrelated ways, the law has reinforced the idea of racial essence. Historically, the law has created and preserved status differences based on race, has given deference to racial sentiments (which are one expression of psychological characteristics), and has relied on notions of racial difference, which today we would refer to as stereotypes.

## ■ Status Differences

Social status has been central to racial categorization and the law is a fundamental mechanism through which social status has been allocated on the basis of race. For most of U.S. history, formal legal rights were assigned on the basis of race. De jure segregation mandated racial separation in nearly every facet of public life. Blacks were excluded from political, social, and legal institutions.

The legal allocation of status based on race resulted in many rules and outcomes that would be comical were they not aspects of a societal tragedy. For many years, for example, it was libelous to call a white person a Negro. The charge was deemed so pernicious that its damage to the reputation of the aggrieved party was presumed as a matter of law, making it unnecessary to show that one had been harmed, financially or otherwise (Stephenson, 1969). As one court stated, "under the social habits, customs, and prejudices prevailing in Louisiana, it cannot be disputed that charging a white man with being a negro [*sic*] is calculated to inflict injury and damage" (*Louis Spotorno v. August Fourichon,* 1888, p. 423).

In one case that dramatically illustrates the extent to which law and legal officials enforced racial status differences, a judge held a black man in contempt of court for using improper language. His error: He insisted on referring to another black man, also a party to the case, as "sir" (Stephenson, 1969).

## ■ Racial Sentiments

Well into the 20th century, racial sentiments occupied an important place in the law. Far from being frowned on as unenlightened thinking, racial attitudes among our 19th-century forebears, for example, were treated more as the natural outgrowths of racial differences. If hostility existed between the races, it was because the races, in fact, were different. Reflecting the Darwinian thinking prevalent during the late 19th century, the idea was that just as different species of animals struggled for survival and competed for superiority, so too did human races.

The law has incorporated the idea of racial sentiments in two ways. Lawmakers and judges have premised laws on the notion of racial sentiments or affinities. First, judges have created exceptions to legal rules for private social judgments premised on beliefs in racial affinities. With regard to the claim of libel for calling a white person a Negro, for example, such a spurious accusation would not subject one to liability if one had previously seen the person in the company of Negroes. Relatedly, during the Jim Crow era, railroad conductors who could be liable for improperly placing a white passenger in the Negro car were exempted from liability if they had a reasonable basis for believing the person to be black, such as having seen the person in the company of Negroes. In both cases, races were thought, as if by magnetism, to cohere. Those perceived to share a common bond were assumed to be of the same racial group.

Perhaps the most common defense for segregation laws was that they were required by the "natural" affinities and repulsions races were bound to feel. Speaking of the social practices of segregation, one court in 1889 noted that "when public sentiment demands a [racial] separation of the passengers, it must be gratified to some extent" (*McGuinn v. Forbes,* 1889, p. 639). Another court, in 1870, noted the railroads' responsibility "to seat passengers so as to preserve order and decorum, and prevent contacts and collisions arising from well-known repugnances" (*Chicago & Northwestern Railway Company v. Anna Williams,* 1870). The Pennsylvania Supreme Court observed, in an 1870 case, that the "danger to the peace engendered by the feeling of aversion between individuals of the different races cannot be denied. It is a fact with which the [railroad] company must deal. If a negro [*sic*] take his seat beside a white man or his wife or daughter, the law cannot repress the anger, or conquer the aversion that some will feel" (*West Chester & Philadelphia Railroad Co v. Miles,* 1867, pp. 212-213).

Evidence of judicial deference to racial sentiments can be found among the most well known Supreme Court cases. *Plessy v. Ferguson* (1896) is perhaps the most widely recognized case of the late 19th century. In *Plessy,* as in countless lower federal court and state court decisions as well as other Supreme Court cases, the justices' views of race reflected societal attitudes characteristic of the time. In *Plessy,* the U.S. Supreme Court gave constitutional protection to de jure racial segregation, commonly known as "separate but equal."

Homer Plessy, a Louisiana Creole, was prosecuted for the crime of violating the state's separate but equal statute by insisting on sitting in the white passenger coach of a railroad rather than the passenger compartment set aside for colored passengers. Plessy challenged his prosecution by arguing that the separate but equal law was invalid, and the case eventually reached the U.S. Supreme Court, where the Court upheld the law.

In *Plessy,* as in scores of other segregation cases both before and after, judicial reasoning relied on assumptions about the reality of race and the inevitability of racial sentiments. Racial differences were thought to naturally give rise to racial sentiments. Writing for the Supreme Court majority in the case, Justice Brown described the social "distinction that is founded in the color of the two races [as one], which must always exist so long as white men are distinguished from the other race by color" (p. 543). The difference between the races, in Justice Brown's view, had little to do with contingent social beliefs, attitudes, or stereotypes. Rather, racial difference represented a natural difference "which must always exist." Implicitly analogizing racial group membership to the natural groupings of animals, Justice Brown declared that "legislation is powerless to eradicate racial instincts or to abolish distinctions based on physical differences" (p. 551).

The *Plessy* Court allowed the law to be validly based on racial difference and racial sentiments. Railroad law that embodied common racial sentiments would lead "to the promotion of [passengers'] comfort, and the preservation of the public peace and good order" (p. 550). In embracing such a rationale, the *Plessy* Court was no different than lower courts, both before and after *Plessy*.

## ■ 19th-Century Racial Difference and 20th-Century Racial Stereotypes

The Supreme Court's decision in *Plessy v. Ferguson* (1896) also embodies the widespread 19th-century belief in racial differences, along with the notion of race as some internal essence or underlying quality that physical appearance merely signified. Although Homer Plessy was admitted to be "seven eighths Caucasian and one eighth African blood" (p. 541), Justice Brown declined to suggest that Homer Plessy was not colored. Rather, he deferred to state law "on the question of the proportion of colored blood necessary to constitute a colored person, as distinguished from a white person" (p. 552). The Court never disputed that Homer Plessy did not visibly appear to be a member of the colored race. If his racial group membership was not a matter of appearance, then it must have been some quality within him—a primordial, immutable trait—that external characteristics sometimes fail to signify. In the Court's eyes, Homer Plessy's blackness was not his color and morphology, but rather the deeper qualities to which these external characteristics typically pointed. Along with most judges of his time, Justice Brown would not have thought to question the nature of the racial categories whose existence the law presumed, even when difficulties of categorization suggested the arbitrariness of the entire project.

The Supreme Court's ruling in *Plessy* was not unanimous. Justice Harlan wrote a famous dissent in which he announced the principle that "our constitution is color-blind." In spite of his vigorous and forceful disagreement with the majority, Justice Harlan similarly accepted the naturalness of the racial categories on which the law relied. Justice Harlan argued that the separate but equal law should have been held unconstitutional as unduly infringing individual liberty on the basis of race. Rather than merely allowing whites and blacks to occupy separate passenger compartments, or granting the railroad the authority to make such determinations, the law mandated separate facilities based on race.

Although Justice Harlan is rightly celebrated for his argument that the constitution should prohibit laws that take account of race to subordinate a particular group, he did not reach that conclusion due to any rejection of the naturalness of racial groupings. Indeed, to illustrate the pernicious nature of the separate but equal law for blacks, Harlan noted that

> there is a race so different from our own that we do not permit those belonging to it to become citizens of the United States. Persons belonging to it are, with few exceptions, absolutely excluded from our country. I allude to the Chinese race. But by the statute in question, a Chinaman can ride in the same passenger coach with white citizens of the United States, while citizens of the black race in Louisiana . . . are yet declared to be criminals, liable to imprisonment, if they ride in a public coach occupied by citizens of the white race. (*Plessy v. Ferguson,* 1896, p. 561)

The irony of Harlan's opinion is that even in arguing against the separate passenger law, he provided support for the ideas of ingrained, natural, unchanging racial essence that fueled and justified de jure segregation. Although Harlan sharply differed with the majority as to the constitutionality of the particular law in question, he shared their view of the reality of the racial groups such laws regulated.

Other courts were often more forthright than the *Plessy* Court in their discussion of racial differences. The Pennsylvania Supreme Court in 1867 had this to say:

> The question remaining to be considered is, whether there is such a difference between the white and black races within this state, resulting from nature, law and custom, as makes it a reasonable ground of separation [in railroad seating]. The question is one of difference, not of superiority or inferiority . . . the races [are] distinct, each producing its own kind, and following

the peculiar law of its constitution . . . human authority ought not to compel these widely separated races to intermix. The right of such to be free from social contact is as clear as to be free from intermarriage. . . . When, therefore, we declare a right to maintain separate relations . . . it is not prejudice, nor caste, nor injustice of any kind, but simply to suffer men to follow the law of races . . . and not to compel them to intermix contrary to their instincts. (*West Chester & Philadelphia Railroad Co v. Miles,* 1867, pp. 213-214).

In many instances, the law was interpreted and enforced to promote specific formulations of racial essence, what we would refer to today as racial stereotypes. Ideas of a particular racial essence, of course, were dependent on the more general ideas of racial difference evident in the *Plessy* case and the *Miles* case quoted previously.

During the mid-19th century, prior to the spread of de jure racial segregation, legal consideration of black women's claims for access to public facilities often reflected implicit beliefs about black women. Many cases involved railroad travel. During this period, much Southern transportation was not formally segregated by race. Instead, accommodations were segregated by gender. The best railroad accommodations were the "ladies' car" and the worst the "smoking car," which was much dirtier, more raucous, and more cramped than the ladies' car.

A woman could gain access to the nicer accommodations provided that she was a "lady." As one railroad described its seating practices in one case, "a certain car in the defendant's passenger train, commonly called the ladies' car, was set apart to be exclusively used and occupied by persons of good character, and genteel and modest deportment, from which said car [were] exclude[d] all persons of improper character, or addicted to deportment offensive to modesty and decorum" (*Brown v. Memphis & C. R. Co.,* 1880, p. 38). Prostitutes and women of dubious reputation were not admitted to the ladies' car. Nor, frequently, were black women. But many black women refused to be excluded. So they sued. Because there was no explicitly racial basis of seating, they had a right to be seated in the ladies' car, provided they were, indeed, ladies. In one case, the lawyer for the defendant railroad argued that the railroad had excluded a black woman from the ladies' car because she was "a notorious courtesan, addicted to lascivious [*sic*] and profane conversation and immodest deportment in public places" (*Brown v. Memphis & C.R. Co.,* 1880, p. 38).

In courts' efforts to determine whether a black woman was a lady, they frequently emphasized aspects of the woman's appearance and ancestry or background. Lawyers for the railroads often highlighted aspects of the woman's background that might predispose the jury or judge not to consider the woman a lady. As one historian notes with respect to this line of cases, "where railroad lawyers knew a woman had been a slave, they made a point of asking her the question before the jury. The question was always deemed relevant" (Welke, 1995, p. 454). Women who had not been slaves and many whose ancestors were white stood a better chance of being regarded as a lady. For example, one black woman argued that she was a lady because she was "seven eighths white," and another because she was "of light complexion" (Welke, 1995, p. 508).

Appearance was made an issue in nearly every case brought by a black woman in response to being denied entry to the ladies' car (Welke, 1995). In one 1859 Ohio case in which the black woman was found to be a lady, the judge noted that "she appears on the stand and seems to be about as much of the white as African race—in fact a mulatto, and apparently one of the better portion of her class" (*State v. Kimber*, 1859, p. 198). In ruling for the black woman plaintiff, a Texas judge described the plaintiff as "a young married woman with some degree of negro [*sic*] blood in her veins, [but] that casually looking at her or her husband it would be difficult to distinguish either of them from white persons" (*Houck v. Southern Pacific Railway*, 1888). A Philadelphia trial judge described a black woman plaintiff as "a very respectable woman, almost white" (*Derry v. Lowry*, 1865). In yet another case, the judge observed that the black woman plaintiff had, at the time she was denied entry to the ladies' car, been "clad in plain and decent apparel" (*Chicago & Northwestern Railway Company v. Anna Williams*, 1870).

Often, matters of appearance and ancestry coalesced in the judge's mind. As one trial court judge described a black woman plaintiff:

> The plaintiff in this case is a lady of color, genteel in her manners, modest in her deport, neat in her appearance, and quite fair [even] for one of mixed blood. Her features are rather delicate, with a nose that indicates a decided preponderance of Caucasian and Indian blood. The blackness and length of the hair, which is straight, confirm this idea. She was never a slave, nor a descendant of a slave. Her ancestors were always as free as herself. (Welke, 1995, p. 518)

In a few cases, however, the light complexion of a black woman's family worked against her. Sallie Robinson, a light-skinned black woman, traveling at night with her equally light-skinned nephew, was shunted into the smoking car in spite of her appearance and deportment. The conductor who had forced them out of the ladies' car described her as a "young, good-looking mulatto woman about 28 years old." The problem was that her nephew was similarly light; in fact, he was not only of "light complexion [but he had] light hair and light blue eyes." This caused the conductor, based on his years of experience, to conclude that the nephew was a white man traveling with a mulatto woman for "illicit purposes," which would most certainly have disqualified them from the ladies' car (Welke, 1995, pp. 461-462).

These cases provide interesting evidence of the links between appearance, ancestry, and racial essence. The whiter one appeared, the less "black" one was and the more likely one would be found to be a lady. To prove themselves ladies, these black women were forced to negate or distance themselves from the racial essence that stood between them and ladyhood. Their attempts to prove they were ladies necessarily turned on their proximity to whiteness, both as a matter of appearance and ancestry.

Laws have also been enforced against black men in ways that both relied on and promoted racial stereotypes. During the late 19th and early 20th century, for example, laws against domestic violence were disproportionately enforced against black men as compared to white men (Siegel, 1996). The relative lack of prosecution of white men for domestic violence promoted the belief that they were nonviolent, that aggression was antithetical to their nature. In contrast, the vigilant enforcement of such laws against black men suggested that they were habitually violent, law breaking, and uncivilized. This disparate pattern of the enforcement of formally neutral laws suggested that racial groupings were inherently meaningful and provided "evidence" that racial stereotypes were merely accurate summaries of "racial" propensities, all the more justification to believe in the naturalness of race.

The entire system of de jure segregation could be said to embody an essentialist view of black men as sexual predators in search of white women. A primary motivation of racially exclusionary laws and practices was to keep black men from white women. In the ladies' car cases discussed previously, for example, the ladies' car was available for ladies as well as any gentlemen traveling with the lady. Even when a black lady was allowed into the car, however, black men were usually banished to the smoking car. In his defense of one railroad's racially segregated seating policy, the Pennsylvania Supreme Court Justice in the *Miles* case discussed previously claimed that the "tendency to intimate social intermixture is to amalgamation, contrary to the law of races. . . . From social amalgamation it is but a step to illicit intercourse, and but another to intermarriage" (p. 213).

In some cases the motive of racially biased legislation was nearly undeniable, as when the Atlanta city council in 1905 passed an ordinance that
prohibited black barbers from cutting the hair of white women and white girls.
So deeply ingrained and so potent were such sentiments that a group of black
barbers who challenged the ordinance did not even contest the prohibition on
cutting white women's hair. Instead, they focused their energies on another
section of the ordinance that limited the hours during which black barber
shops could remain open (*R. C. Chaires et al. v. City of Atlanta,* 1905).

Law has been indispensable to the perpetuation of racial categories.
Judges and legislators have continually made determinations of race. Law has
reflected beliefs in racial essence that are fundamental to the categorization
process. Perhaps most important, the confluence of race and rights has made
race such a significant social, political, and legal category that no one could
ignore it.

## ■ The Effect of Social Conceptions of Race on the Law

As law creates and perpetuates race, so does it draw on prevalent social
conceptions of race. In the late 19th century, race was seen as a natural reality.
Now, the emergence of the idea of race as a social construction has expanded
the vocabulary, so to speak, of legal reasoning. The ascendant notion that race
is not "real" has opened up an entirely new set of arguments about the validity
and role of racial distinctions in the law. This "new" way of thinking has not
predetermined legal outcomes, but it has transformed the nature of the arguments and the reasoning on which judges are likely to rely in cases that directly
or indirectly implicate race.

The belief in the biological, or otherwise natural, basis of racial groupings
has, of course, not disappeared. But now it is not the only view that informs
judicial attitudes toward race. So, contemporary judges' attitudes toward race
are beset by a sense of ambivalence, contradiction, and equivocation.

The impact of the changing conception of race can be seen in the change
in the judicial stance toward two race-related concepts: racial differences and
racial sentiments. The Court's changing stance toward these two concepts
reflects the society's changing belief about the reality of race. When race was
thought of as biological, racial differences were primordial and racial sentiments inevitably arose from them. Now, neither biological racial differences
nor racial sentiments are readily accepted. Most people no longer believe in
innate racial differences. The innate racial "differences" of the late 19th

century are now referred to as stereotypes. Racial sentiments, whether in the form of affinities or repulsions, are generally accorded no deference by the law. Two relatively recent Supreme Court cases—*Shaw v. Reno* (1993) and *Palmore v. Sidoti* (1984)—illustrate these changes.

*Palmore v. Sidoti* (1984) is the Supreme Court's most forceful enunciation of the principle that the law cannot give respect to racial sentiments. The background facts of the case are as follows: Linda and Anthony Sidoti were both white. They married, had a daughter, and then divorced. The mother was granted custody of the child. When the mother remarried, the father sued for custody on the basis that his former wife's new husband was black and that being raised in a biracial home would subject the child to social stigmatization and, hence, psychological difficulties. Other children would taunt and ridicule her due to her biracial parents.

The Florida judge applied a best-interests-of-the-child analysis, as he was required by law to do. Under this approach, the court's disposition of the controversy should be determined by what would best serve the child. Based on the factual finding that the child would suffer in a biracial family due to the racial views of others, the judge awarded custody to the father.

In a unanimous opinion, the U.S. Supreme Court reversed the Florida court. The Court did not question the lower court's factual conclusion that racial hostilities meant that the child would suffer in a biracial family. Rather, the Court reasoned that the law cannot give effect to societal biases. In contradiction of widely accepted judicial reasoning of a century earlier, the Court concluded that societal racial biases could not be a justification for legislative or judicial action. Racial sentiments, which once justified law, could not now be accorded any deference by law.

In *Shaw v. Reno* (1993), a well-known voting rights case, the justices' divergent views of race are particularly salient. In *Shaw,* the plaintiffs challenged the creation of a majority black legislative district by the State of North Carolina in conjunction with the U.S. attorney general, pursuant to the Voting Rights Act of 1965. Although the case formally concerned the constitutional validity of race-conscious legislative districting, embedded within the justices' reasoning were varied ideas about the meaning and reality of race.

Writing for the majority, Justice O'Connor invalidated the newly created majority black district. She described the redistricting scheme as grouping together individuals "who may have little in common with one another but the color of their skin [and] reinforcing the perception that members of the same racial group . . . think alike, share the same political interests, and will prefer the same candidates at the polls" (p. 2827). Such reasoning relied on what O'Connor termed "impermissible racial stereotypes" (p. 2827). In describing race-based districting in this way, Justice O'Connor puts forth a vision in which race is not real, not natural, not significant. This is not a view that existed to any meaningful extent in late 19th-century America.

Justice Souter, in his dissenting opinion, presented an alternative view of race, which suggested a notion of racial essence. In contrast to O'Connor, Souter argued that the race-based legislative district at issue should have been upheld in part because "members of racial groups have [a] commonality of interest" (*Shaw v. Reno,* 1993, p. 2845). Indeed, for any of the variety of justifications offered in support of race-based districting to be coherent, one must accept such a view. Otherwise, there is no rationale for drawing legislative districts based in part on race.

## ■ Conclusion

U.S. society, as reflected in judicial decision making, is divided about the meaning and the reality of race. Because race is not a natural reality does not mean it has ceased to be an important social phenomenon.

The fact that race is socially constructed means that law is unavoidably implicated in the maintenance and meaning of racial categories. Insofar as legal rules and decision making channel behavior, influence preferences, and thereby shape identity, no legal decision can simply reflect social reality.

It is partly because determination of race would require the legal system to do what it does not want to do that in U.S. society, racial categorization is mostly ad hoc and unsystematic. To have explicit principles and procedures for racial categorization that were intentionally implemented would expose the undeniably political nature of racial determinations and of racial categories themselves.

Racial determinations, of course, have always been political. But a century ago, courts and legislators who promulgated race-conscious law hid behind claims of the reality of race. In contemporary society, we can take no such convenient refuge.

Rather than take race as a given or ignore it, courts would do well to consider how their actions or inactions shape the meaning of race. Courts may not simply ignore race, for ceasing to give legal effect to race would not necessarily diminish its social significance. In face, race is so much a part of everyday life, so deeply ingrained in our societal fabric, that its social significance might continue even in the absence of legal recognition. On the other hand, courts cannot simply accept race as a given, when many decisions that recognize race may simultaneously create it. Descriptive choices may conceal normative judgments.

Ultimately, courts, and society, must decide what role race should play in our national life as well as our personal identities. There is no easy, generalizable answer to this question. Rather, the inquiry is necessarily a matter of context. In some circumstances, we may want race to matter and be willing to allow law to promote that function of race. In other circumstances, we may determine that race should have no role. The problem of race in American society is not so much that race has mattered, but how it has mattered.

Whatever our determination about the ultimate place of race in any particular context, we must consider the vital question of means: What is the best way to get from here to there?

While the answers are not easy, focusing on the right questions is the best place to start. At the very least, we should all become more conscious of the ways in which we promote one meaning of race rather than another.

# 4

# Racism and Politics in the United States

*David O. Sears*

thnocentrism and nativism have been strong streaks in the American psyche since the founding of the nation, resulting in prejudice at one time or another against virtually every ethnic group. Many have tried to turn such ethnic divisions to partisan political advantage, whether against Catholics or Jews, Germans or Italians, African Americans or Latinos.

But throughout, African Americans have had a unique political role among all of the United States' many ethnic and racial groups. They lived under slavery for most of U.S. history, and then were emancipated, only to be condemned to the lower-caste existence known as Jim Crow. They finally achieved formal equality in U.S. life, but only within the past three decades. All other immigrant minorities have undergone substantial integration and assimilation with time; only blacks have remained significantly and persistently segregated. It is that experience that has given rise to the oldest, most intractable and socially costly vein of racism in U.S. society.

Since the 1960s, controversies stemming from the lasting inegalitarian effects of this history have been central to U.S. politics. Considerable dispute (both political and academic) has revolved around the origins of opposition to such racially redistributive policies as fair housing, busing, and affirmative action. The purpose of this chapter is to analyze how racial conflict in the United States has been played out in mass politics during this era. It will focus primarily on the majority whites' reactions to racial conflicts in this country, rather than on the dynamics of minorities' political attitudes and behavior.

That latter subject is a complex one, and deserves extensive treatment in its own right. The analysis presented here assesses the value of such motives as "symbolic racism," "principled conservatism," self-interest, and group interest in explaining whites' attitudes.

Considerable progress has been made in the search for racial equality. But numerous obstacles, distractions, and complications remain. Those discussed here include (a) the Democratic and Republican parties' positions on racial issues; (b) the ease of using racial themes in symbolic politics; (c) continuing economic inequality between the races; (d) increasing ethnic diversity, resulting in new conflicts; (e) the numerous claims on the civil rights movement as a model for other groups' striving for equality, and the new ideology of "multiculturalism"; and (f) a weakened institutional capacity for collective action within U.S. society.

## ■ A Brief History

The distinctive historical experience of African Americans can be divided conveniently into six historical periods. The first goes back over three centuries, to the beginnings of the slave trade. African Americans are the only group in U.S. history ever systematically subjected to slave treatment. The period of their slavery lasted over two centuries, about two thirds of our nation's history. White indentured servants were relatively quickly assimilated into the mainstream of the society, as were other immigrant groups such as Catholics and Quakers, Germans, French, Spaniards, and the Dutch. Africans were not. Indeed, at the pivotal moment of nation building, in the late 18th century, only African Americans were singled out in the constitution as counting for less than one human being each. Article I, Section 2 of the U.S. Constitution specified that free persons were to be counted as whole persons, whereas slaves (almost all of African descent) were to be counted as three fifths of a person each.

A second period began in the 1830s, with the forceful protests of the treatment of the African American slaves by the abolitionists. After three decades of ever-increasing and vicious political conflict, the Civil War broke out, the most deadly war in our history. It led to the emancipation of the slaves, and then to the numerous but brief revolutionary experiments that now go under the name of Reconstruction.

Soon, however, the Compromise of 1877 ended all that, and restored the system of white supremacy to the South. This third period, described simply as the Jim Crow system of racial supremacy, kept most African Americans in a lower social caste (because most then lived in the South), subject to omnipresent racial discrimination. The system of Jim Crow extended beyond the South in some respects: Many national U.S. institutions were formally racially segregated, such as the armed forces and all professional sports. This period lasted for nearly a century.

The aftermath of World War II marked the beginning of a fourth period, a surge of progress in U.S. race relations. In *Brown v. Board of Education* in 1954, the Supreme Court unanimously decided that racial segregation in the schools was unconstitutional. The nonviolent civil disobedience movement in the South in the 1950s and 1960s, with pivotal leadership by Martin Luther King Jr., gradually became an effective force for provoking change. Landmark civil rights legislation was passed in 1964 and 1965 ending official racial discrimination. Over a period of 25 years, the entire system of white racial supremacy and legally enforced segregation, dominant for over three centuries, had effectively been dismantled.

A fifth period followed almost immediately, one of greatly rising racial tensions. The segregationist Alabama governor, George Wallace, ran strong insurgency presidential campaigns from 1964 to 1972, a populist mixture of racial backlash and antigovernment feeling. An increasingly demanding black movement grew in strength and visibility throughout the nation. Blacks' frustration and impatience over years of delay escalated into large-scale ghetto rebellions in almost every city in the country in the mid-1960s. No comparably violent uprisings have ever been instigated by any other ethnic group in the United States. A series of such riots in 1967, especially those in Newark and Detroit, led President Johnson to appoint the National Advisory Commission on Civil Disorders (the "Kerner Commission"), which warned that "our nation is moving toward two societies, one black, one white—separate and unequal" (*Report of the National Advisory Commission on Civil Disorders*, 1968, p. 1). To continue present policies, they said, was "to make permanent the division of our country into two societies; one, largely Negro and poor, located in the central cities; the other, predominantly white and affluent, located in the suburbs" (p. 22).

That was the context in which the present period began. Starting in 1971, court judgments mandated the busing of school children to promote school desegregation in northern as well as southern school districts. These busing plans became increasingly unpopular. Affirmative action programs were broadly implemented, and with time also became increasingly controversial. Crime increased in urban areas throughout the country, and "law and order" began to appear prominently on politicians' agendas, with many suspecting that it was merely a codeword for race. America's industrial base fell and the black underclass grew, spotlighting "welfare" as another political target with racial overtones.

Put together, the periods of slavery and Jim Crow forced African Americans, unlike any other ethnic group, into a legalized second-class citizenship for over 300 years. This has had two crucial effects. First, African Americans have always been the most ill-treated ethnic group in U.S. society. Before the Civil War, they were housed in ramshackle slave quarters and denied any formal education, denied the right to choose the best job available, and often denied the right to marry. In the late 20th century, widespread prejudice and discrimination still condemns most blacks to life in the oldest, most run-down, and most crime-ridden housing in our aging cities, and the poorest quality schooling, without access to the family financial advantage that helps support college for many young whites. As a result, African Americans have, as a group, always inhabited the bottom of the economic ladder in jobs, wages, educational level, housing, and family financial assets (Jaynes & Williams, 1989; Massey & Denton, 1993; Oliver & Shapiro, 1995). They are more at risk than any other group in almost every respect one can think of—for educational failure, hypertension and heart disease, murder, imprisonment, teenage pregnancy, alcoholism, drug addiction, racial discrimination, and police mistreatment.[1]

This is not to say that all blacks are poor or on welfare—most are not. It is not to say that blacks are only passive victims of a racist society; as with any other peoples, the story is more complex than that. But, the large black underclass today deflects our society from attaining many of our ideals, and much of that is the result of blocked opportunity in the past and continuing racial segregation and discrimination today.

This long history has also profoundly influenced the ordinary white voter's thinking about race. As will be seen, most people first learn their attitudes about race as preadults, and these early-learned attitudes are among the most stable of all the political attitudes Americans possess. This is not to say that our racial attitudes are set in concrete before we ever reach adulthood, but that early learning has a strong, persistent, and pervasive influence on how we appraise political issues later in life.

With that in mind, we must remember that virtually every generation of white Americans has grown up in a society in which African Americans were, by law, formally unequal to whites. Most of today's white voters grew up in an era of considerable formal racial discrimination and strong overt racial prejudice. The current era, of formal racial equality, began only about 30 years ago, within the memory of most living U.S. voters; this period of liberalizing change is a very brief one in the totality of U.S. history. Let us keep this in mind, and perhaps not expect that U.S. whites will have fully replaced their historic racial prejudice with sympathetic support for true equality.

### ■ Whites' Racial Attitudes: Change and Resistance

Let us then begin by sketching out what has changed, and what has not changed, in whites' political attitudes about race since World War II.

*Progress.* First, there has been very real progress in race relations in the United States, incorporating blacks much more thoroughly as equals into U.S. society. There has been much successful integration of the workplace, higher education, and political life.

Whites' attitudes have changed enormously. Before World War II, most white Americans believed in whites' racial superiority, in the legitimacy of white racial supremacy, and supported legalized segregation and discrimination. This has been described as "old-fashioned racism" (McConahay, 1986) or opposition to "general principles of equality" (Schuman, Steeth, & Bobo, 1985). There is a general consensus that it has largely disappeared. The doctrine of racial superiority is no longer widely regarded as a legitimate position, and support for segregation and racial discrimination has largely evaporated. This is a major change and an important one.

In politics, black candidates enjoy a considerable advantage among members of their own group, as is generally the case among ethnic groups. They have historically had great difficulty winning votes from white voters, so that blacks have rarely won in such predominantly white jurisdictions as statewide office or majority-white legislative districts. That has been changing in recent years. Being black continues to provide a significant obstacle with white voters, but no longer such a profound obstacle that it limits black candidates' success to majority-black districts. Rather, today there are black congressmen in mostly white districts, and blacks have even been competitive in occasional gubernatorial or mayoral races in which blacks are a district minority, such as California, Virginia, New York City, or Los Angeles.

*Polarization.* A second point, however, is that there is continuing indication of severe racial polarization over racial issues. The two races perceive the quality of race relations very differently. Most whites believe that discrimination has been greatly reduced and that equal opportunity does in fact exist. In contrast, most blacks believe that discrimination remains at high levels, that opportunities are not equal, and that things are not especially getting better for blacks. For example, in a May 1991 national survey reported on a television news broadcast, 79% of whites thought blacks were better off compared to 10 years earlier, whereas only 48% of blacks thought so. In a 1992 Los Angeles survey, 80% of the black respondents, compared to 39% of the whites, felt that blacks do not receive "fair treatment in the courts and criminal justice system" (Bobo, Zubrinsky, Johnson, & Oliver, 1994).

*Continuing White Antagonism.* In four areas there is evidence of significant continuing racial antagonism among white Americans. First, there obviously remain pockets of old-fashioned racism. Examples include the recorded conversations between Los Angeles police officers during and immediately after the Rodney King beating in 1991, in the 1992 campaign for Senate by David Duke in Louisiana (Kuzenski, Bullock, & Gaddie, 1995), or the old-fashioned overt racism commonly expressed by white supremacist and "skinhead" groups. Surveys detect some residual traditional racial prejudice in the general public, although mainly limited to those over the age of 50 (Kluegel, 1990).

Second, racial stereotypes remain. Whites continue, on average, to perceive blacks as poorer, lazier, more dependent on welfare, less intelligent, and more violence prone than whites (Sears, Citrin, & van Laar, 1995). Over time, whites' beliefs in these stereotypes have diminished. Today, such stereotypes are not universal or categorical, but they are there (also see Sniderman & Piazza, 1993). Even those who do not subscribe to such conventional racial stereotypes are usually familiar with them (Devine & Elliott, 1995).

Third, despite their broad support for the general principles of racial equality, whites resist redistributional government policies that would promote that equality. Most whites are opposed to government policies that would implement equality, such as busing children for school integration, affirmative action, actively enforced fair housing legislation, or placing public housing projects in suburban areas. Schuman et al. (1985) call this the "principle-implementation gap."

Fourth, black candidates do better these days, but still frequently have a rough ride, due in part to racial antagonism. In most elections involving black candidates, the races split quite sharply, and relatively few whites vote for the black candidate. This was most obvious in the divisive Harold Washington campaigns for mayor of Chicago and the Jesse Jackson presidential campaigns in the 1980s (Kleppner, 1985; Sears, Citrin, & Kosterman, 1987). Even the successful races run by David Dinkins for mayor of New York City or Douglas Wilder for governor of Virginia were marked by relatively weak support among whites, compared to the strength of comparable white candidates. A possible exception is Tom Bradley's nearly successful 1982 run for the California gubernatorial office (Citrin, Green, & Sears, 1990). And, in all these cases, racial prejudice was a strong factor distinguishing which whites opposed these black candidates, and which supported them, indicating that race is an important factor.

## ■ Opposition to Racial Policies and Black Candidates

How can old-fashioned racism have largely disappeared while white opposition to racially egalitarian policies and black candidates runs rampant? This is a puzzle that has attracted the attention of many researchers. There are a number of conflicting theories, and not all who research the question are agreed (to say the least). Nevertheless, I think some things can be said with confidence.

Does racism continue to contribute to such resistance? To address this question, I will define *racism* fairly narrowly, as a categorical hostility or antagonism toward African Americans because of their race. That is, racism is present when, everything else being equal, whites feel or act more negatively toward blacks than toward other groups or individuals from other groups. I do not intend any important distinction between racism and prejudice for the purposes of this chapter.

Racism, defined in such terms, and measured explicitly, does contribute centrally to whites' opposition to racial policies and black candidates. Racism plays a major role in issues such as busing or affirmative action or opposition to Jesse Jackson, all attitude objects referring explicitly to race. This direct association of racial attitudes with opposition toward racial policies has been quite thoroughly documented, with controls for other variables (see Sears, 1988; Sears et al., 1987; Sears, Hensler, & Speer, 1979; Sears, van Laar, Carrillo, & Kosterman, 1997).

But the political effects of racism go beyond policies like affirmative action that explicitly target blacks in particular. Racism is also central to attitudes toward law and order and welfare. These issues usually are not posed explicitly in racial terms, but they drew on widely understood underlying racial stereotypes. Thus, racism contributes to such law-and-order attitudes as opposition to "permissive judges" and support for the death penalty (Sears, Lau, Tyler, & Allen, 1980), and to stronger opposition to spending on welfare programs (Gilens, 1995; Smith, 1984). And the effects of racism extend even into campaigns that neither mention race explicitly nor draw on any obvious underlying racial stereotypes, such as campaigns to cut government spending and taxation in general (Sears & Citrin, 1985).

## ■ Old-Fashioned Versus Symbolic Racism

Although still politically powerful, the nature of racism has changed. This has led us to propose a distinction between two kinds of racism. As indicated here, old-fashioned racism is characterized by a belief in blacks' inherent racial inferiority and support for racial segregation. This has gradually been replaced by *symbolic racism* (Kinder & Sears, 1981; McConahay & Hough, 1976; Sears, 1988; Sears & Kinder, 1971), a blend of antagonism to blacks with attachment to traditional American values that have nothing to do with race (such as the work ethic, traditional morality, and respect for traditional authority). It fits our definition of racism because it focuses on violations of such traditional values by blacks in particular, rather than by just anyone. Symbolic racism is measured by agreement with such views as that blacks are pushing too hard for equality, that they are making unfair and illegitimate demands, that they get too much attention and sympathy from elites, that their gains are therefore often undeserved, and that racial discrimination is a thing of the past. It is called "symbolic" because it is phrased in terms that are abstract and ideological, reflecting the white person's moral code and sense of how society should be organized rather than having any direct bearing on the person's own private life, and because it is focused on blacks as a group rather than on any specific individual.

Symbolic racism is plainly different from old-fashioned racism, focusing on contemporary resentments of blacks rather than those of a bygone era. The two are associated because they share common roots in antagonism toward blacks. But symbolic racism is much more common, and it is a considerably stronger determinant of opposition to racial policies and black candidates today than old-fashioned racism, racial stereotypes, or even simple antiblack antagonism (McConahay, 1982, 1986; Sears et al., 1997).

Three sets of alternatives to the symbolic racism approach have been proposed. Numerous researchers have observed that the most powerful political impact of race in U.S. society today mixes racism with nonracial values.

But symbolic racism is only one way to conceptualize it. Other related concepts include *subtle racism* (involving a defense of traditional values, exaggeration of cultural differences, and denial of positive emotions; see Pettigrew & Meertens, 1995); *aversive racism* (a combination of negative racial affect that distances whites from blacks, and a commitment to the principle of equality that argues for equal treatment; see Dovidio & Gaertner, 1986b); *ambivalent racism* (a combination of sympathy for blacks' plight with the belief that they have contributed significantly to it; see Katz, Wackenhut, & Hass, 1986); *stratification ideology* (attributions of blacks' disadvantage to internal factors such as lack of motivation; see Kluegel, 1990); and *economic individualism,* the interpretation of blacks' economic disadvantage as due to their lack of work ethic (Carmines & Merriman, 1993; Sniderman & Piazza, 1993).

These all share a portrait of a *new racism,* which combines old-fashioned racial prejudice with nonracial values and attitudes. They probably all capture much the same phenomenon, differing mainly in the terms used to describe it. This phenomenon has considerable generality, applicable to intergroup relations in Europe as well as in the United States. Pettigrew and Meertens (1995) have shown that British attitudes toward West Indians and Asians, Dutch attitudes toward Turks and Surinamers, French attitudes toward North Africans and Asians, and Germans' attitudes toward Turks all predict support for extremist racist political movements in those countries.

A second alternative is that such analyses of a new racism underestimate the prevalence of simple, old-fashioned racism (Sniderman & Piazza, 1993). This viewpoint agrees that prevailing social norms about expressing overt racism have changed dramatically, in that it is no longer socially acceptable in most social contexts to express old-fashioned racism directly. But it argues that there may be more crude, old-fashioned racism out there than is openly expressed in public or in survey interviews, just because people try so hard to disguise how they really feel. To be sure, we need to remember some hard-core racists do remain in our society, and a little old-fashioned racism remains in many whites. Nevertheless, most available evidence indicates that the amount of old-fashioned racism has dropped a great deal.

A third alternative might be called a "principled conservatism" theory. It views opposition to racial policies as stemming primarily from racially neutral values and attitudes, such as opposition to excessive government power, individualistic values of self-reliance, authoritarian values, or ideological conservatism (perhaps especially among the better educated). In this view, racial prejudices are no longer major factors in whites' thinking about public policy (Sniderman & Piazza, 1993). Indeed, several studies have found that nonracial values all by themselves, with little or no connection to racism, do significantly increase white opposition to policies that give special treatment to blacks, such as affirmative action or busing (Bobo & Kluegel, 1993; Carmines & Merriman, 1993; Sears et al., 1979; Sniderman & Piazza, 1993).

In these same studies, however, racial prejudices and stereotypes prove also to be involved, and often play an even stronger role. Moreover, numerous other studies have shown that racism strongly affects racial policy preferences even holding race-neutral ideology constant. For example, prejudice contributes to opposition to affirmative action among liberals and conservatives alike. Table 4.1 shows that in a national sample of white adults in 1992, political conservatives were more likely than liberals, by a 72% to 59% margin, to strongly oppose giving preferences to blacks in hiring and promotion. But symbolic racism had a much larger effect: 81% of those high in symbolic racism strongly opposed it, whereas only 41% of those low in symbolic racism did so. Most important, symbolic racism increased opposition to affirmative action to a highly significant degree among both conservatives and liberals alike. Race-neutral values and attitudes do contribute to opposition to racial policies, but racism is usually an even more powerful influence (Sears, 1988; Sears et al., 1997).

## ■ Origins of Racism

But this account is plainly incomplete. Symbolic racism is a central factor in generating opposition to racial policies, but so far we have said little about where that racism itself comes from. Before the civil rights movement and the end of Jim Crow, the origins of old-fashioned racism were widely understood: it was most common in the South, and among older, less educated whites. What can we say about the origins of newer forms of racism? There have been several different approaches to this question.

## ■ Socialization

The symbolic racism theory assumes that basic racial prejudices mostly stem from socialization in early life. We know that attitudes toward salient social groups are among the earliest products of a child's learning of his or her culture (e.g., Aboud, 1988). We know also that racial attitudes are among

**Table 4.1**  Symbolic Racism and Political Conservatism: Two Determinants of
White Opposition to Affirmative Action

|  | Symbolic Racism | | | |
|  | High | Low | All | n |
| --- | --- | --- | --- | --- |
| Conservative | 80 | 63 | 72 | 962 |
| Liberal | 83 | 45 | 59 | 558 |
| All | 81 | 41 | 61 | 1,520 |
| n | 758 | 762 | 1,520 | |

SOURCE: 1992 American National Election Studies.
NOTE: The entry is the percentage of white adults *strongly opposed* to the idea that "because of past discrimination, blacks should be given preference in hiring and promotion." The *n* refers to the number of cases. The symbolic racism measure is based on six items; here it is simply divided at the median.

the most durable, and unchanging, of Americans' political attitudes, across their lifetimes (Converse & Markus, 1979; Sears, 1983). The key to understanding the origins of racism would seem to lie in what we are taught, and what we passively learn from observation, as we are growing up.

For many years, social scientists were hopeful that the effects of racial prejudice would simply disappear with time, as the practices of slavery and segregation receded into history, and children were brought up in a less racist society. For years, each successive generation of whites was indeed less prejudiced than its predecessors (Firebaugh & Davis, 1988; Schuman et al., 1985). As indicated earlier, support for the key tenets of old-fashioned racism is common today only in the oldest generation, those born before the Great Depression of the 1930s.

Can we expect continuing decreases in white racism in the future? That depends, according to this theory, on how young people are socialized. That socialization depends on what issues are salient as they are growing up, and the dominant sympathies of people around them concerning those issues. Sometimes the most salient issues draw quite unprejudiced reactions from white adults. For example, white children growing up in the early 1960s heard a great deal about the civil rights movement's struggles in the South. But those struggles often involved conflicts between blacks asking for simple access to equal opportunity, such as being allowed to attend state universities. Their opponents were often flagrantly bigoted, unpleasant officials trying to maintain the obviously unfair Jim Crow system. In that climate of opinion, white children's socialization often tended to be favorable to racial equality.

In recent years, however, the most salient racial issues have been those that draw more opposition from whites, such as mandatory busing, ghetto-based crime, affirmative action, and welfare abuse. Blacks do not always receive the same sympathetic treatment in young whites' socialization on such issues. As a result, younger adults do not support such contemporary racial policies much more than do older generations (Steeth & Schuman, 1991). Indeed, in some isolated cases, it appears that today's young whites are even more prejudiced than their elders, such as in the striking level of prejudice among young British adults against black West Indians (Pettigrew & Meertens, 1995).

## ■ Interests

A major theoretical alternative to the socialization approach begins with the assumption that people's political attitudes stem in some more or less rational manner from their interests in adulthood. These might reflect self-interest, such as the fear that the jobs one wants will go instead to minorities, or that affirmative action might prevent our own admission to the college of our choice, that busing might harm the education of one's own children, that we might be personally victimized by black crime, and so on. Or they might reflect a sense of group interest, such as whites' opposing racial policies because of a fear that their group (whites in general) might be disadvantaged, even if they do not think they will be personally affected.

There is now a good bit of evidence that self-interest is not a major factor in whites' attitudes toward racial policies. Relatively few whites perceive such policies as affecting their own lives very much, and among those who do, such presumed personal impact has little political effect (Sears & Funk, 1991). For example, opposition to busing for school integration might be thought to result from the realistic threat introduced to the personal lives of white parents and their children. But relatively few whites are personally affected by busing, and the personal impact of busing generally does not have a significant effect on opposition to it; parents of children in public schools where busing is under way or planned are not more opposed to it than nonparents. Rather, busing seems to have become a highly symbolic issue, and opposition to it is generated most strongly by racial prejudice (Sears et al., 1979).

Self-interest does play a role in some places, at some times, on some issues, however. Self-interest did have a substantial impact on whites' opposition to busing in Los Angeles just as that city's busing plan unfolded in 1976

(Sears & Allen, 1984). It would not be surprising to see the personal impact of racial issues play an important role in the future. Admissions standards at many universities vary a good bit across ethnic and racial groups, and there is rising resentment about impaired opportunities for nonminorities. But the personal impact of racial issues is not at the moment the main force driving whites' resistance to policies intended to increase racial equality.

Group interest is another matter. An issue can affect the group as a whole, even when the individual group member in question is not much affected. For example, an Asian American businessman might be very concerned about educational opportunities for young Asian immigrants, and therefore might strongly oppose affirmative action in college admissions for blacks and Latinos out of a spirit of group interest, because he thinks it may deprive Asian youths from access to college. But it does not affect his own life, so it is not in any simple sense a matter of self-interest for him.

Several theories predict strong effects of group interest on whites' political preferences. Realistic group conflict theory would view whites as responding negatively when racial policies threaten to redistribute scarce resources from whites and blacks (Bobo, 1983). Theories that emphasize a "sense of group position" (Blumer, 1958; Bobo, Kluegel, & Smith, 1997) or "social dominance orientation" (Sidanius, Pratto, & Bobo, 1996) hold that whites are mainly interested in maintaining their privileged positions in society, and claim that one gets ahead by ability and by individual striving only to legitimize that superior position.

Consistent with the group interest hypothesis, whites' opposition to racial policies has been increased by perceptions that blacks' gains will come at the expense of whites' (Bobo & Hutchings, 1996; Sears & Jessor, 1996) and by a sense that racial policies or black officeholders harm the interests of whites (Vanneman & Pettigrew, 1972). Similarly, opposition to racial policies is greater among whites who are high in "social dominance orientation," believing in the legitimacy of an inegalitarian society, and therefore presumably protecting whites' relatively privileged position (Sidanius et al., 1996).

Group interest is, however, not always an easy factor to pin down in detail. One possible implication of the group interest view is that whites' identification with other whites as a common racial category should be a key factor. This would be a central implication of social identity theory (Tajfel, 1981), realistic group conflict theory (Bobo, 1983), the sense of group position theory (Bobo & Hutchings, 1996), social dominance theory (Sidanius et al., 1996), and fraternal deprivation theory (Vanneman & Pettigrew, 1972). But so far there is not much evidence of that. Whites' perceived closeness toward other whites does not influence their attitudes toward racial policies and black candidates. Nor do feelings toward other whites influence attitudes toward white presidential candidates (Sears & Jessor, 1996; Sears et al., 1997).

On the other hand, there has as yet been little research on attitudes toward white candidates who aggressively and explicitly advocate white supremacy, white solidarity, or both, such as the early George Wallace, the segregationist governor of Alabama in the 1960s, or the Louisiana politician David Duke (the founder of the National Association for the Advancement of White People; see Kuzenski et al., 1995). We probably have not heard the last of the strain of white resentment that they, and to some extent Pat Buchanan, in his recent presidential candidacies, have tapped into. That white resentment may partly arise from a feeling that whites as a group are being shortchanged.

In short, it is tempting to conclude that much of whites' resistance to legislation implementing racial equality is due to a sense of either self-interest or group-interest—that blacks' gains will come at my own expense, or at the expense of whites like me. We need to be cautious, however, about the theory that such resistance is due to whites' perceived interests, especially those that have an explicitly selfish basis; the evidence is not always very strongly in its favor.

## ■ Partisan Polarization Over Race

Long before and after the Civil War, the Democratic party was dominant among southern whites. It defended slavery from the abolitionists right up to the eve of the shelling of Fort Sumter, and it staunchly defended Jim Crow. The "solid South" gave almost unanimous support to Democratic presidential and congressional candidates for nearly a century. But the Democratic administrations of Franklin D. Roosevelt and Harry S. Truman, in the 1930s and 1940s, began some far-reaching civil rights initiatives, with strong northern Democratic support. By the late 1950s, the Democratic party was increasingly torn internally over race, between an aggressive northern civil rights faction and the need to pacify the racially conservative southern wing of the party. The Republicans tended to be split as well between a relatively liberal northeastern faction and more conservative midwesterners. As a result, at the outset of the 1960s, the two political parties were not widely seen as differing very much on the issues relevant to race.

But through the early 1960s, the Democratic administration of President John F. Kennedy increasingly supported a strong civil rights agenda. Immediately after JFK's assassination, President Lyndon B. Johnson strengthened the Democrats' commitment to civil rights still further, whereas his Republican opponent, Barry Goldwater, explicitly opposed federal civil rights legislation. Johnson's sweeping victory in the 1964 presidential election led to the passage of landmark legislation in a brief window of opportunity, under the leadership of a Democratic party with unusually great political powers owing to sympathy for a fallen popular president. This legislation has set the course for racial policy in the United States ever since.

As a result, the early 1960s sharply polarized the two parties over the question of race for the first time in nearly a century (Converse, Clausen, & Miller, 1965). In 1968, the Republicans nearly lost the presidential election because George Wallace ran a strong third-party race centered on animosity toward civil rights. The Republicans then resolved not to be outflanked again on the issue of race. By 1972, racial issues had an increasingly central place in the public's perceptions of differences between the two parties, with the Republicans regularly seen as more conservative (Carmines & Stimson, 1989). The Democratic candidacies of Jesse Jackson in the 1980s increased this racially polarized perception of the two parties (Sears et al., 1987).

## ■ The Democrats' Achilles Heel and the Republican Tightrope

This partisan polarization over race was not necessarily a losing proposition for the Democrats in the early 1960s. Old-fashioned racism quickly became discredited, even in the South, as the civil rights movement won the day. Being against segregation became a bit like being against sin. But the same cannot be said for the racial policies that have been at the heart of U.S. political controversies in the past two decades. Since the 1960s, most whites have supported the general principle of racially integrated schools, but most have opposed busing. Affirmative action has become more controversial, and when framed as "quotas" or "reverse discrimination," as its opponents prefer to do, is opposed by most whites. The relatively high welfare dependency and crime rates among African Americans have also been given a great deal of publicity, and, of course, stimulate antagonism among whites.

For a variety of reasons, the Democratic party has been saddled with the losing side of all these issues. The Republicans have won most of the presidential elections since that time. For most of that period, the Democrats still retained control of Congress. But since the passage of major civil rights legislation, in 1964 and 1965, the South, once solidly Democratic, has gradually shifted to the Republican side. This shift is due entirely to change among white southerners, because blacks have been reliable Democrats throughout. In 1952, almost 80% of the white southerners were Democrats, whereas in 1994, slightly over 40% were. The result has been that as of the mid-1990s, Republicans increasingly dominate both presidential and congressional voting in the South. Racial issues are central to southern Republican conservatism (Edsall & Edsall, 1992; Petrocik, 1987; Sears et al., 1987). Indeed, race and ideology have become inextricably linked, threatening the viability of liberalism within the Democratic party (Edsall & Edsall, 1991). In 1996, Bill Clinton ran for a second term claiming to have disowned the "liberal" label.

But the nature of racial issues involved in the conservatism of southern Republicans is not the old-fashioned racism that targets blacks as a whole. Rather, it focuses in particular on the black underclass, which, therefore, as Edsall and Edsall (1992, p. 235) perceptively observe, has become the Achilles heel of the modern Democratic party. Why? Because the black underclass symbolizes much of the black population to many whites. Moreover, much of the political debate that swirls around issues such as crime and welfare has an underlying racial bias. Black criminals symbolize the crime problem, and the black welfare mother symbolizes the welfare problem. And, as they say, "Race will remain an exceptionally divisive force in politics as long as the debate is couched in covert language and in coded symbols" (p. 281).

So, on racial issues the political dialogue has been dominated by the Republican party. But they walk a tightrope. They regularly appeal to latent racism by opposing quotas and welfare and supporting law and order. At the same time, they try to steer clear of positions that could be denounced as sympathetic to old-fashioned racism, so they do not oppose all forms of affirmative action, or support David Duke, or restrict the Supreme Court to white justices only.

Liberals frequently decry the tendency of such conservatives as George Bush, Jesse Helms, and David Duke to "play the race card"—to interject racial themes into campaigns to get white support. The paradigmatic case is the 1988 Willie Horton commercial, used in George Bush's campaign for president. Bush attacked his Democratic opponent, Michael Dukakis, for having an "ultraliberal, ultralenient approach to crime," reciting the case of Willie Horton, a black, convicted first-degree murderer, who, while on weekend furlough from prison, raped a white Maryland woman and assaulted her husband. A visual commercial, used many times in the Bush campaign, showed "revolving door justice," with prisoners of ambiguous skin color being released from prison as soon as they were admitted. Similarly, the Republican Jesse Helms, in his North Carolina reelection campaign for the

Senate in 1990, running against a black mayor, Harvey Gantt, showed ads opposing affirmative action, featuring a white man said to have lost his job to a black man.

Mendelberg (1997) hypothesized that candidates have turned in recent years to commercials that are implicitly concerned with racial minorities, which can prime racial attitudes in a way that either explicitly racist or nonracial ads cannot. To test this, she conducted an experiment in which students were shown news broadcasts that discussed either the Willie Horton ad or pollution in Boston Harbor. Symbolic racism predicted opposition to government aid for blacks especially strongly among those who had seen the Willie Horton ad. In other words, the racial cues in the news broadcast did prime or stimulate racial predispositions, and cause them to have greater political impact.

A considerable line of recent research has demonstrated the "agenda-setting" power of the political media (especially television), determining which issues are perceived as most important, and which ones get used as yardsticks in evaluating candidates (Iyengar & Kinder, 1987). Presumably political candidates can therefore emphasize whatever issues they think will be most advantageous to their side. This might imply that "playing the race card" is completely arbitrary and wholly cynical. There is certainly some truth to that view, but playing it is probably not completely arbitrary. Contemporary racism centers on things that in part reflect reality: violent crime in the ghetto, high rates of unemployment and welfare dependency, black mothers as single heads of households, gang fights, drug usage, the high percentage of young black males in prison and the low percentage in college, and the like. A Willie Horton ad or Jesse Helms's antiaffirmative action ad is not completely arbitrarily or randomly selected; in part it reflects a harsh reality of modern life, and one that is well ingrained in the popular mind.

The "race card" is more than purely arbitrary, then; it does reflect a reality out there. We must bear in mind, however, that it is an exaggerated, selective, and distorted reality. Most blacks are not criminal, on welfare, poor, or jobless. In that sense, there is clearly something to the agenda-setting argument.

### ■ Are All Politics Therefore Racial?

The view of the journalist Tom Edsall (Edsall & Edsall, 1992) and others is that "when the official subject is presidential politics, taxes, welfare, crime, rights, or values . . . the real subject is race." "All political issues have become racial." Can that be true?

As indicated earlier, symbolic racism does play a significant role in whites' attitudes toward explicitly racial issues, such as affirmative action or school integration, as well as implicitly racial issues such as welfare and law and order, and attitudes toward black candidates such as Jesse Jackson. On the other hand, there seems to be no major direct effect of old-fashioned racism on such core political attitudes as ideology or party identification (Abramowitz, 1994; Sears et al., 1997) or even on attitudes toward Ronald Reagan. There are limits to the direct effects of racism.

But when race is considered in conjunction with nonracial conservatism, it does get to the very heart of U.S. politics. A black man named Willie Horton by himself is not politically evocative; a black man who has raped a white woman and is then released from jail via a permissive liberal penal policy is. A TV commercial about a white man who loses his job does not evoke racial attitudes, but one about a white man who loses it because of a racial quota system does. Race is central in both cases; neither event has great political punch without the racial element. It is the mixture of antiblack affect with nonracial values represented in symbolic racism that is explosive, generates polarization over the domestic issues just cited, and therefore has become central to partisan debate in our time.

# For the Future

Where do we stand for the future, then? Let me make four points by way of summary.

# Economic Problems

An important backdrop for the analysis of race in politics as we move into a new century is the dramatic economic change facing Western societies. The United States and Western Europe are in many ways "postindustrial" societies, in which much large industry, employing skilled and unskilled blue-collar workers, has fled to less developed nations with lower wages. This is a national economic problem, but it is compounded by race. It has hurt blacks, in particular, because continuing housing segregation has often meant they have had lower-quality education, and have limited mobility to seek new jobs (Massey & Denton, 1993; Wilson, 1987). This economic change has therefore magnified the already difficult problems of the urban underclass that are devastatingly costly to African Americans, breeding social problems too numerous to count (Farley, 1984; Oliver & Shapiro, 1995). Most African Americans are not poor, violent, or rejected—not all, not always, not everywhere, nor in every context. Yet it is a powerful truth that African Americans are, as a group, more vulnerable to such harsh economic changes than any other group. The social problems thus caused are enormously costly to the society as a whole, and affect the quality of all our lives.

## ■ Increasing Ethnic Diversity

The rising tide of immigration into the United States, especially from Asia and Latin America, is creating some startling changes. In California as a whole, our most populous state, minorities will soon be the majority. "Diversity" has become a buzzword. No longer do we have the Kerner Commission's black and white world, but one with many voices. This has led to a difficult political dynamic.

Ethnic and racial hostilities show up with respect to these other ethnic groups, and issues that affect them, as well. Perceptions that Asian and Hispanic immigration is having a negative effect on the country contribute to support for English as an official language, and to opposition to voting rights for non-English speakers and to bilingual education. Whites are more likely to support such monolingual policies than are Asians or Hispanics (Citrin, Sears, Muste, & Wong, 1996). Both symbolic racism and antagonism against Hispanics contribute to opposition to bilingual education, especially when bilingual education is justified as helping to maintain immigrants' original cultures (Sears & Huddy, 1992).

One of African Americans' great successes in this century was the overthrow of Jim Crow segregationism in the South in the 1950s and 1960s. This came not long after World War II, a time of great American patriotism, and the early stages of the Cold War, when McCarthyite zealots tended to denounce as "communists" anyone with a critical word to say about America. After the suppression of critical examination of our society in these eras, the civil rights movement triggered renewed soul searching about social injustice.

One of the side effects of the success of the civil rights movement, then, and to some extent black militancy of the late 1960s, was that other disadvantaged groups began to model their pleas or demands for better treatment on those of the black movement. The African American experience served as the model for such groups as feminists, gays and lesbians, the disabled, the homeless, Chicanos, Asian Americans, and AIDS victims.

This heightened awareness of the problems faced by other groups has had three general effects. First, it has meant less focused attention on the very real long-term problems of the black population. For example, many more minority children must be considered in school integration, and many more people claim entitlement to affirmative action, which then makes any such social policies much more costly.

Second, in many quarters, blacks became thought of as just another special interest group that was demanding special treatment rather than just working hard. But blacks are not just another special interest group. As indicated earlier, blacks were the only ethnic group singled out at the time of the nation's founding as assigned to a lower status, separate caste. They were at the heart of the nation's most wrenching political conflict, the Civil War. They remain our most distinctive political class; prejudice toward blacks has more far-reaching effects than that toward any other group (Sears et al., 1995).

And third, the claims by other disadvantaged groups to the same level of redress as blacks, often supported by the Democratic party, have helped label it as the party of "special interests." The original claims of the black population had some special persuasive appeal because of the uniquely disadvantaging impact of slavery and Jim Crow. The same message has less appeal when made on behalf of today's immigrant groups. Although they are often needy and disadvantaged, they are not perceived as facing any obvious barriers greater than those of previous immigrant groups who have come to the United States. For example, there is less concern about Hispanics or Asians than about blacks, and they are less negatively stereotyped (Sears et al., 1995). The descendants of previous immigrant groups, who now regard themselves as having largely assimilated by their own efforts into the larger society, often look with skepticism at pleas for special attention on their behalf.

## ■ Multiculturalism

One spin-off of this broad claim to group-based redistribution of resources is the "multiculturalism" movement. This, in some of its extreme forms, advocates more attention to and special treatment of ethnic groups as groups, overturning the traditional individualistic view that each individual is treated on his or her own merits. Our surveys on attitudes toward multiculturalism among whites, blacks, and Latinos in Los Angeles County and the nation as a whole can help us describe public response to this movement (see

Citrin et al., 1996; Sears, Citrin, Cheleden, & van Laar, 1997); let us briefly summarize the most important points.

There is some appreciation for the value of cultural diversity; ethnic groups should not only try to "blend in." But, given a choice, the great majority of respondents in every ethnic group prefer to identify themselves foremost as "just an American" rather than as members of some racial, ethnic, or religious group. The majority in all groups similarly believes that people in general should think of themselves more as Americans than as members of ethnic groups. Most think that ethnic organizations tend to promote separatism. Nor is there majority support for three of the more controversial policy elements of the multicultural agenda: ethnic preferences in hiring and promotion; ethnic quotas of officeholders, public employees, or teachers that match the sizes of various ethnic groups; or liberalized immigration policies.

In most of these areas Anglos, African Americans, and Hispanics alike oppose such official multiculturalism. In three areas, however, Hispanics depart: They generally are more supportive than the other groups of official multilingualism (such as bilingual education and printing ballots in languages other than English) and they are more opposed to severe restrictions on social services for immigrants and to severe border control and deportation policies. But even they would prefer to reduce the overall flow of immigration.

There is no unified ethnic support for multiculturalism, contrary to the notion of a "rainbow coalition," beyond some temporary alliances in local circumstances. Indeed, there is evidence of black-Latino polarization over language and immigration policy based on divergent ethnic group interests. For example, Hispanics generally are more supportive of multilingual policies and liberal treatment of immigrants, whereas African Americans are not. This resistance among blacks is based in part on their perceptions that added immigration will come at the expense of blacks' well-being (Vidanage & Sears, 1995; also see Bobo & Hutchings, 1996).

It would appear that the notion of group-based entitlements reflected in the multiculturalist agenda does not have much popular resonance at this point, even in the ethnic and immigrant groups intended to receive its benefits. But we do see the budding signs of ethnic polarization in policy areas that tap into group interests, such as language and immigration. This opens up the possibility that ethnic divisions once again will become central to much of U.S. politics. These tensions are sure to play themselves out more vigorously in the next few years, as the effects of massive immigration increasingly make themselves felt in numerous areas of the country. What will happen remains to be seen. The nation may begin to polarize along ethnic lines, as so many other nations have. It may polarize between the defenders of traditional Americanism and the proponents of some new multiculturalism. Or the new immigrants may for the most part assimilate to traditional U.S. culture, perhaps isolating African Americans again.

## ■ National Disarray

Any effort to deal head-on with America's racial problems confronts a time of some national disarray, in several respects. There are anxieties about U.S. ability to compete internationally. There is much individual insecurity about the future; most parents do not think their children will be as affluent as they have been. The debt structure, private and public, makes it difficult to mount new national initiatives. Institutions that helped lead the fight for equality a generation ago have backed off. The U.S. Supreme Court, the leader among government institutions in assuring blacks' rights in the 1950s and 1960s, has turned more conservative, becoming more skeptical about affirmative action and redistricting efforts to increase blacks' legislative representation.

The political parties are declining in influence. The U.S. electorate (like that in other Western democracies) is in a long process of gradually lessened loyalty to the political parties, a process called *dealignment.* Declining numbers of people identity themselves as Democrats or Republicans, with increasing numbers calling themselves "Independents." Furthermore, people are more inclined now to split their presidential and congressional votes between the parties. Decades of partisan political gridlock, a host of scandals, and years of political apathy in the general public have reduced respect for politicians and political institutions.

One generalization that most political scientists agree with is that collective goods tend to get underproduced. That is, actions that benefit everyone tend to be performed less often than actions that benefit the self. "Social capital" consists of relations among persons, such as trust in other people, social networks, or participation in voluntary organizations (Putnam, 1995). It provides the social glue that keeps a democratic society together, and helps to improve the efficiency of society by facilitating cooperative, coordinated actions (as opposed to competition between people). For example, participating in a civic organization such as the United Way can help to ease the life of the poor and needy, even though it may not benefit the participator very much.

Putnam (1995) has suggested that the supply of "social capital" has become depleted in recent years in the United States. People trust each other less, and they engage less in collective civic activities. Participation in civic organizations, such as the PTA or hobby clubs or church-affiliated groups, has declined; voter turnout has declined; trust in other people has declined; and confidence in institutions, whether in government (such as Congress or the president or the courts) or not, has declined. This represents one additional possible resource that is of declining value for any collective action to address the problems of the black population.

## ■ Conclusions

There is good news and bad news in this account. The good news is that white Americans have by and large renounced their old claim to racial superiority and any moral justification for officially sustained inequality. To be sure, there are some who continue to believe in the inherent superiority or inferiority of various racial groups, and many who believe that group inequalities are inevitable in the nature of human life. But that is a far cry from turn-of-the-century (turn of that earlier century!), Jim Crow, old-fashioned racism.

Our societal discourse about racial groups has been substantially cleaned up. Overt racist talk, in the form of derogatory racial terms or demeaning stereotypes, is much less common than it used to be. The media rarely show minority groups in the old stereotyped roles: One rarely sees the Negro butler, the Aunt Jemima cook, or the Amos and Andy of years gone by, or the savage Indians (or drunken Indians). These changes are not merely the result of some oppressive political correctness; there is more widespread understanding of the hurtful and unfair impact of such derogation and stereotyping.

In politics, there are many advances. Many African Americans have been elected to Congress in recent decades, and have served in central roles. A black man, Colin Powell, would surely have garnered a great deal of support for a run at the presidency in 1996 had he chosen to run. Black candidates have won elective office in a number of predominantly white political jurisdictions throughout the United States. Perhaps another impressive sign of progress is that conservative Republican blacks have attained high office as well.

The bad news is that African Americans are still seriously disadvantaged in the areas of income, employment, educational attainment, crime rates, and most health indicators. Although much progress was made in closing these gaps in the 1960s and 1970s, it is not clear that the gap is being closed any more, and by most indicators, blacks are still at the bottom of the heap. There are indications of some very serious social pathologies in certain areas: Many too many young black men reside in prison; racial segregation in housing closes off too many opportunities for blacks; a shortage of stable families dooms too many black women to poverty and welfare dependency, and too many black children to less attention than they need for an optimal start in life.

The nation as a whole seems unwilling or incapable of taking the steps that are required to deal with such problems. Much of that unwillingness can be traced back to antagonism toward (or at least lack of sympathy for) poor blacks, a central feature of U.S. politics since colonial days. In the contemporary world, this antagonism pivots on symbolic racism, as indicated previously. The claimants for group entitlements are proliferating, and ethnic tensions seem to be rising. It seems to me unlikely that a nativist backlash will dominate the country, but it will be heard loudly, and we will see various elements of it enacted into law.

U.S. society continues to reap the diseased harvest of decisions made in the 17th and 18th century. We have on our hands a very longstanding, very difficult, and terribly costly social problem. The society at large has played a large role in creating the problem and continues to play a large role in nurturing it, in many and complex ways. Society at large should take an equally large role in trying at least to ameliorate its worst effects. We should be realistic enough to know that there is no single magic wand that we can wave. There are many obstacles.

It is tempting to become impatient with America, and even to denounce it as a racist nation with a racist people. This impatience might be tempered by a realization of how far the nation has come in the past 40 years, as well as by the parallel difficulties that can be seen in so many other nations. Perhaps in the complexities and difficulties of the moment, it is well to remember one of our greatest strengths as a people is the fundamental belief almost all share, expressed so eloquently in the Declaration of Independence, that "all men are created equal, that they are endowed by their Creator with certain inalienable rights, that among these are the rights to life, liberty, and the pursuit of happiness." This is an ideal that the nation can never completely fulfill. It also is a moral commitment that Americans are unlikely to go back on, and so, it represents a beacon that should, in the long run, guide us toward greater social justice.

■ **Note**

1. This discussion ignores the plight of Native Americans, which is often equally grievous. This is a much smaller group, however—in 1990, less than 2 million, against 29 million blacks—and for various other reasons much less politically central as well.

# International Perspectives
# on Prejudice and Racism

*James S. Jackson*
*Kendrick T. Brown*
*Daria C. Kirby*

In 1988, we conducted national household surveys among citizens in four major Western European countries, France, Great Britain, Germany, and The Netherlands, regarding intergroup attitudes, beliefs, and reported behaviors toward specific, ethnic immigrant groups (Jackson, Kirby, Barnes, & Shepard, 1993; Pettigrew et al., in press). A subset of the questions asked in these surveys replicated part of the intergroup questions included by researchers in the 1986 National Election Survey in the United States (Kinder & Sanders, 1986). The surveys in these countries form a unique set of parallel, cross-national data on factors related to expressions of prejudice and discrimination by dominant groups toward selected subordinate immigrant and national ethnic-racial groups. Based on the findings of this project, we have concluded that understanding the nature of prejudice and racism, and the psychological and social consequences in any given country, can be accomplished only by studying similarities and differences in the relationships between dominant and subordinate groups across countries (Jackson, Lemaine, Ben Brika, & Kirby, 1993; Kohn, 1987; Pettigrew et al., in press).

AUTHORS' NOTE: The work presented in this chapter was supported by NIMH Grant MH 47182-06. We express our appreciation to Marita Inglehart and the members of the Michigan and International Working Groups on Racism for their support in the work reported in this chapter. We also thank Jennifer Eberhardt and Susan Fiske for their helpful comments on an earlier version of this chapter. Correspondence regarding this chapter should be addressed to James S. Jackson, 5006 Institute for Social Research, University of Michigan, P.O. Box 1248, Ann Arbor, MI 48106-1248.

For the most part, research on prejudice and racism has been largely target-group specific. Researchers have focused on understanding prejudiced reactions toward one specific group, such as whites' reactions to blacks in the United States (Pettigrew & Meertens, 1995). We attempted to go beyond this narrow focus in two ways. First, we studied the responses of randomly selected dominant group members in five different nations and compared reactions toward different, specific, target groups within these countries. Second, we also asked general questions of respondents about reactions toward persons from other nationalities, religions, races, cultures, and social classes (Inglehart & Yeakley, 1993). This allowed us to investigate the question of the contexts of stereotypes and prejudiced reactions. Social scientists want to understand the processes underlying prejudiced reactions; they study these processes at many different levels of analysis: on a biological level (e.g., Lopreato, 1984; van den Berghe, 1981), on a basic cognitive process level (e.g., Allport, 1954; Macrae, Stangor, & Hewstone, 1996; Tajfel, 1982), on the person level (e.g., Adorno, Frenkel-Brunswik, Levinson, & Sanford, 1950—authoritarian personality), or on the group level (Sherif & Sherif, 1953—real group competition and conflict). Rarely, however, does research focus on questions concerning the context of prejudiced reactions (Holmes & Inglehart, 1994): Why are certain groups targets of prejudiced practices? Why is it, for example, that obese persons are stigmatized in the United States today (Zebrowitz, 1996) but were not in the past, or are not as stigmatized in other countries where overweight men are often viewed as "strong"? Why do stereotypes about the elderly differ by country and national origin, whereas maintaining a consistent negativity over time in the United States (Snyder & Miene, 1994)? Why do prejudiced reactions toward specific groups change over time and others do not? For example, Japanese American stereotypes during and after World War II and today are distinctly different, whereas stereotypical beliefs about African Americans are largely unchanged over several centuries (Jones, 1997).

Cross-cultural and cross-national studies permit us to examine a range of contextual factors that might influence prejudiced reactions (Triandis, 1990). Specifically, the cross-national design allows us to study (a) the influence that different norms have on the expression of prejudiced reactions; (b) the influence that differences in value orientations and other moderating variables (e.g., control beliefs) have; and (c) the influence of different structural factors, for example, nature of work opportunities, unemployment (Kohn, 1987), or different social welfare systems.

Comparative cross-national studies and analyses on dominant and subordinate groups are necessary to understand those aspects of social psychological intergroup relations (discrimination and racism) that are nation-state and target-group specific, as well as those components that are common across national boundaries and groups (Pettigrew et al., in press). In general, we believe that a very broad cross-national comparative framework is required. For example, in South American countries the sociocultural history and contemporary relationships among dominant and subordinate groups differ greatly from those in contemporary South Africa, the Caribbean, Eastern Europe, or New Zealand. To arrive at valid and useful theory, larger and more explicitly comparative research on these intergroup relationships in different nation-states is needed (Kohn, 1987). We suggest that one source of the confusion in theoretical accounts of intergroup conflict has been the lack of comparable data in these different national contexts.

In this chapter, we address commonalities and differences in the relationships among dominant group members' racial attitudes and out-group rejection across four member states of the European Union (EU) and the United States. We recognize that broader international comparisons than our initial focus on industrialized Western countries are needed (Pettigrew et al., in press). Initial comparisons, however, between the United States and Western Europe provide a useful starting point for larger and more comprehensive studies in other parts of the world (Bowser, 1995; Pettigrew et al., in press).

We also address the nature of inequality, racism, and injustice by examining dominant group attitudes and the potential linkages to subordinate group responses. The remainder of the chapter is divided into four sections. In the first, we present arguments for the importance of studying contemporary prejudice, racism, and discrimination in Western Europe and the United States. In the second, we briefly discuss commonalities among intergroup-relations theories that are relevant to this examination. Given the large number of these theoretical models, it is not our intent to provide a thorough review. We are interested in pointing out the possible commonalities across these different theoretical accounts. For interested readers, some of the most important theoretical frameworks are presented in greater detail elsewhere in the volume (Chapter 1 and Chapter 4, this volume). Similarly, Jones (1997) recently completed a thorough review of theories of prejudice and racism. In the next section, we describe empirical analyses and findings on our studies of out-group rejection among dominant group members across nation-states in the EU and the United States. And finally, we offer conclusions and possible directions for future research.

## ■ Prejudice and Racism in the United States and Western Europe

Recent studies in the United States have reported a decrease in prejudice and racial intolerance over the past few decades, but no concomitant increase in support for policies oriented toward assistance for racial out-groups (e.g., Schuman, Steeth, & Bobo, 1985). Some researchers have argued that this is due to the fact that racism has taken a new form today, that it has become more subtle and intertwined with conservative orientations (Chapter 1 and Chapter 4, this volume; Pettigrew et al., 1997). Others (e.g., Sniderman & Tetlock, 1986) have argued that conservative ideology is not necessarily related to racism or discrimination. Still other researchers have suggested that real and perceived group conflict exerts significant influence on support for government policies designed to assist out-groups and on specific government actions designed to overcome discrimination (e.g., Bobo, 1987).

In the United States, there seems to be little question that prejudice, racism, and discrimination continue to adversely affect the social, economic, and political statuses of African Americans and other racial-ethnic groups (see Chapter 1, this volume; Pincus & Ehrlich, 1994). There have, however, been few systematic attempts to empirically assess the influence of racism or racial discrimination and to explore the consequences, if any, for the psychological and physical well-being of these discriminated against groups (Jackson et al., 1996). We recognize that many other groups in all parts of the world, including the United States, share similar subordinate statuses. African Americans, however, are a prototypical exemplar of subordinate groups. Substantial proportions of the African American population live in environments where they are likely to be exposed to a relatively high number of stressors (Jackson et al., 1996). Low socioeconomic status is related to a stressful lifestyle that may include poor nutrition, poor education, crime, traffic hazards, substandard and overcrowded housing, low-paying jobs, unemployment and underemployment, and a lack of health insurance and access to basic health services. It is frequently suggested that these factors contribute to the development of a wide range of economic, social, and health problems in the black community.

Researchers uniformly note that racism and discrimination must be an important factor in understanding African American social, economic, and health statuses. Recent research (e.g., Anderson, McNeily, Armstead, Clark, & Pieper, 1993) found strong signs of persistent and chronic stress, with both psychological and physical outcomes, as a result of unfair and discriminatory treatment. Thus, there is little question that African Americans, and other groups around the world, stand in low positions on social-, economic-, and political-status hierarchies. This poor standing may be linked to experiences of racism and discrimination, which appear to result in negative individual and group physical, social, and psychological consequences.

Over the past decade, unprecedented historical changes have occurred in the political, social, cultural, and economic arrangements among nation-states across the globe. During this same period, expressions and acts of overt discrimination and racism have increased both in Europe and the United States, and ethnic armed conflict is on the rise worldwide. In Europe, the collapse of communism has revealed that ethnic group antipathies lie just below the surface and can be easily aroused (Solomos & Wrench, 1993). In the eyes of many, immigrant and refugee groups have less rightful claims to the resources of European nations (Small, 1994). Thus, it has become apparent that the social, political, and economic statuses of these groups may actually diminish over the coming years. Domestic unrest and attacks on immigrants and guest workers in countries such as Great Britain and Germany have already provided unfortunate examples. Ongoing ethnic wars in the former Soviet Republics and Yugoslavia and anti-Semitic tensions in Poland and other Eastern European countries demonstrate the power of ethnic-group boundaries in contributing to armed conflict, bloodshed, and human atrocities. The enduring and virulent religious conflicts in the Middle East, Rwanda, and Northern Ireland reinforce the fact that neither simple nor short-term solutions are readily available in any part of the globe.

Rioting and open conflict with ethnic minorities and immigrant groups have escalated over the past 5 years in the EU. In the United Kingdom, there has been a strong public outcry from several segments of the population against immigrants. For example, a conservative member of British Parliament in a recent speech called for a halt to the "relentless flow of immigrants lest the traditions of English life be lost" (Stevenson, 1993). Similarly, a member of the neo-Nazi party won a local council seat in London with a campaign message stating "that if Britain is to be great again, it must deport all nonwhites" (Stevenson, 1993). Certainly, these expressions of antiethnic-racial sentiments are not attributable solely to England. Similar events have occurred in Germany, France, and The Netherlands (Pettigrew et al., in press). These racist acts are also evident in employment settings. Racial discrimination plays a significant role in the underemployment of racial-ethnic minorities, especially in recruitment and selection procedures. For instance, it has been found that half of the Dutch personnel officers interviewed admitted to using negative stereotypes when making employment decisions (Forbes & Mead, 1992). Thus, it is clear that social problems related to the politics of identity, racism, ethnocentrism, and overt hostility predicated on group memberships will be of continuing critical import for the foreseeable future.

The governing bodies of the EU have taken several steps to address this rise in outward expressions of racism. For example, the member states of the EU have proclaimed 1997 to be the "European Year Against Racism." The objectives are to highlight the threat posed by racism, xenophobia, and anti-Semitism, to encourage reflection and discussion on ways to combat them, and to promote the exchange of experience and good practice. The resolution suggests achieving these aims by means of conferences, seminars on specific aspects of racism, information campaigns, and the exchange of experience between competent bodies. In addition, to signal to the EU the necessity of a communitywide policy against racial discrimination, an independent group of race relations experts developed the Starting Line, a proposal for a council directive concerning the elimination of racial discrimination. The authors of this document present two key arguments in support of communitywide legislation. First, they assert that although national legislation in the member states has a vital role to play, due to extreme variations in the racial discrimination policies, it has not succeeded in tackling the problems (Starting Line, 1993). Second, they argue that community action against racism and xenophobia is now necessary because unjust discrimination interferes with the free movement of persons, and that variations between national levels of protection will discourage persons likely to suffer discrimination from moving to those states where protection is minimal or nonexistent (Starting Line, 1993). Although needed, these actions are still in the beginning stages of eradicating the presence of racism and xenophobia throughout the EU. Our research on the nature of prejudice and racism takes a conceptual step back by examining the attitudes, beliefs, and values that may be related to these overt actions.

In sum, increased immigration and swelling numbers of economic and political refugees will continue, especially in Western Europe. These changes in demographic composition may portend many "hot summers," as experienced in the United States in the late 1960s and 1970s, as well as more recently in the 1980s in Great Britain (Small, 1994). Many European countries have closed their borders to general immigration. This is an option that may not be politically feasible in EU countries. Many of these nations have colonial ties and political arrangements with immigrant sending countries (e.g., Great Britain and Hong Kong), relationships that place domestic immigration and minority rights policies in a larger international diplomatic context. This is a problem that the United States avoided in its conflicts and legal struggles with Americans of African descent, but will itself increasingly face as immigration accelerates from Asia, Mexico, and Central and South America (Sassen, 1994). One vivid example is the international furor over recent changes in United States' national, and individual states' immigration legislation.

Many of the causes of current ethnic conflicts in varied parts of the world are deeply rooted in long histories of prior conflict and bloodshed. The potential danger of these conflicts is much greater today than earlier in this century. The wide distribution and availability of weapons of mass destruction demands the undivided attention of all nations to address the root causes of racism and intergroup conflict: Problems that may threaten the peace and security of future generations. Indeed, finding workable solutions for reducing ethnic and racial conflict may be the major problem facing the world community today (Jackson & Tull, 1996).

■ **Prejudice and Racism: Conceptual and Methodological Considerations**

Based on our research over the past decade or so (Jackson, Kirby, et al., 1993; Pettigrew et al., in press), we suggest that a synthesis may be emerging in the intergroup relations area regarding the importance of individual-level threat based on (a) the perceptions of basic value differences among dominant and subordinate groups; (b) perceived threats to individual and family stability; and (c) the threats to the social, political, and economic status of the in-group (Pettigrew et al., in press). Several theoretical models of intergroup relations and research are couched in these terms, for example, symbolic racism, aversive racism, relative deprivation, belief congruity, scapegoating, real group conflict, and social identity theories. Examining these different frameworks in a cross-national context may provide the opportunity for comparisons among cultures that share many commonalties in values and goals but enough dissimilarities to permit comparisons among different theoretical frameworks of individual out-group rejection within and across national boundaries (Kinder, 1986; Kohn, 1987; Meyers, 1984).

Many of the intergroup theories have a great deal to offer, but the lack of a multidisciplinary focus and paucity of empirical research on a range of alternative explanations for observed effects have hampered efforts to develop robust theoretical models. In this we agree with Kinder (1986), who suggested that there has been too little confrontation among different theoretical perspectives on out-group rejection, and that what is needed is greater empirical tests of different theoretical predictions (Rex & Mason, 1986).

A review of the literature reveals a recurrent emphasis on values. This emphasis includes the historical importance of values, ideology, and beliefs among scholars of ethnicity, largely sociologists (Meyers, 1984; Nielsen, 1985; Taylor, 1979; Yancey, Ericksen, & Juliani, 1976; Yinger, 1985), a long-standing concern in social psychology and political science among a few researchers (Insko, Nacoste, & Moe, 1983; Jones, 1997; Rokeach, 1979), and an emergent focus on values, ideology, beliefs, and intergroup phenomena among all disciplines in recent years (Bobo, 1987; Kinder, 1986; Klugel & Smith, 1986; Sniderman & Hagen, 1985; Yinger, 1985). In addition, we note the growing theme of competition and perceptions of threat that seem to have shown a significant increase among individual-level theorists. This theme is of continuing concern to systems theorists and Marxist-oriented sociologists (Nielsen, 1985). At the individual level, however, the perception of threat is also important and research has focused on the examination of such perceptions within intergroup competition models (e.g., Giles & Evans, 1985; Stephan & Stephan, 1985).

Few studies, however, have been designed to investigate the issues of values and threat (Kinder, 1986), particularly in a cross-national context (Pettigrew, 1983). Insko et al. (1983), in their critique of value-incongruity theories and out-group rejection, suggested that research on out-group rejection could profit from comparative studies on different groups across different cultural contexts (Kohn, 1987). As a result, we have conceptualized our work within a framework that highlights the perception of threat to the dominant group as a major underlying characteristic of intergroup conflict models (Stephan & Stephan, 1985). Based on recent writing and analyses, we argue that for some outcomes the perception of threat should be interpreted in a stress theoretical framework (Jackson & Inglehart, 1995).

As indicated earlier, several studies in the United States have found a decrease in prejudice or racial intolerance over the years (e.g., Schuman et al., 1985). Three explanations of these findings have emerged. First, some researchers argue that this is due to the fact that racism has assumed new dimensions; that it has become more subtle and intertwined with political conservatism (Kinder, 1986; Sears, 1988). A second group argues that conservative ideology is not necessarily related to racism or discriminatory behaviors (Sniderman & Tetlock, 1986). A third group argues that real and perceived group conflict exerts significant influence on support for government policies designed to assist out-groups, and on specific government actions designed to overcome discrimination, even though U.S. society has become attitudinally and in some ways behaviorally (e.g., intermarriage) more tolerant (e.g., Bobo, 1987). Each of these perspectives furthers our understanding of racial attitudes, although none, to our knowledge, have investigated these issues outside of the United States, and few (Bobo, Johnson, Oliver, Sidanius, & Zubrinsky, 1992, is an exception) outside the confines of white-black intergroup relationships.

Theories of individual prejudice and racism range from interpersonal and psychodynamic models to economic conflict theories (e.g., Adorno et al., 1950; Allport, 1958). During the lengthy period of research on ethnicity, race, and intergroup relations, no one theoretical position has emerged as an accepted, encompassing explanatory system. The scientific controversy over the role of personality, position in the social structure (e.g., educational level), and situational factors (e.g., national and group norms) as proximal causes of racism and anti-Semitism has existed since the beginnings of this century. The rise of fascism in Europe during the 1920s and 1930s and the prevailing Freudian psychoanalytical viewpoint enticed many scholars to examine the individual psychological determinants of Fascist ideology. The writings of Reich, Fromm, and Maslow were prominent during this period. It was, however, the emergence of the Third Reich, culminating in the shocking events during World War II, that fully brought the issue to a head. Faced with the inexplicable horror of Nazi death camps, serious scholars pondered the possibility of whether individual personality factors, including psychopathology, could account for such deviant and widely shared behaviors.

Because individual psychopathology explanations seemed dubious in accounting for the extensive and mass adherence to Fascism and the repugnant actions of the Third Reich during World War II (as well as state-supported racism in the United States and South Africa), most scholars turned to some type of general personality factors that might account for these behaviors. Research has focused on various aspects of personality, such as susceptibility to frustration, low self-esteem, social dominance orientation, political and religious conservative beliefs, and cognitive rigidity, as correlates of prejudice, discrimination, and anti-Semitism. Adorno's research (Adorno et al., 1950) became the most persuasive of these scientific efforts, although by no means the only serious scholarly work.

No one explanation produced the outpouring of research and criticism as did the work of Adorno and his associates on the authoritarian personality and the Fascism Scale (Adorno et al., 1950). Their research attempted to operationalize the authoritarian personality as a response to a set of questionnaire items labeled the F (Fascism) Scale (and to a lesser extent, the Ethnocentrism and Anti-Semitism scales as well). The problems that Adorno's work addressed have not dissipated over the decades, and questions regarding the role of national character and individual personality factors in ethnocentric beliefs and behaviors remain unanswered (Altemeyer, 1988; Duckitt, 1992a).

It is as true today as it was nearly 40 years ago, when Allport (1958) completed his famous monograph on *The Nature of Prejudice,* that the field lacks an ordered system of underlying theory to guide research, especially in a cross-national and cross-cultural context. *Prejudice* is generally considered as an attitude or set of attitudes held toward a group, encompassing a set of negative feelings (affect), beliefs (stereotypes), and intentions (behavioral dispositions) to act unfavorably toward groups or members of groups (Duckitt, 1992a). These attitudes are considered to have been formed as part of a person's early social development and normally are thought to arise from direct parental socialization as well as indirect social learning from other family members, peers, and increasingly, the mass media (Duckitt, 1992a). *Ethnocentrism* refers to both generally held positive attitudes about one's own group, as well as negative views of a wide variety of other groups, groups that differ ethnically and racially from one's own group (Yinger, 1985).

*Discrimination* denotes intentional acts that draw unfair or injurious distinctions, that are based solely on ethnic or racial bases, and that have effects favorable to in-groups and negative to out-groups. Normally, discrimination is the set of observable behaviors that might ensue from ethnocentrism, prejudice, or racism.

The term *racism* is usually reserved for negative beliefs and behaviors toward racially categorized groups or members of groups, involving elements of power differentials between dominant and subordinate groups, including strongly held beliefs about the racial or ethnic superiority of one's own group (Jones, 1997). At least three different forms of racism, all including strong beliefs about ethnic or racial inferiority, have been identified (Jones, 1997). *Individual racism* is most directly linked to the concept of prejudice and refers to individually held out-group hatred, combined with ethnocentric views and beliefs of racial inferiority of the target groups. *Cultural racism,* linked to the concept of ethnocentrism, refers to the beliefs in the inferiority or nonexistence of cultural traditions, implements, and values of the target group. And *institutional racism* refers to the system of laws; policies; and political, economic, and institutional arrangements that perpetuate and maintain subordinate and dominant group positions in a society. In addition to issues of definition, some of the general problems with existing theories of prejudice and racism are (a) confusion among process, content, and outcomes; (b) the lack of interdisciplinary perspectives; and, (c) a disproportionate focus on either the perpetrators of prejudice or their victims, and not enough attention to the nature of intergroup interaction.

Literally dozens of theories concerned with prejudice and discrimination have been published in the past half century (Jones, 1997). They have emphasized historical, sociocultural, situational, or psychodynamic factors (Duckitt, 1992a). There are many suggestions for ways to categorize them (Insko et al., 1983; Kinder, 1986). Some of the oldest theories of prejudice can be subsumed under personality or individual difference models. In these models (Allport, 1958), frustration and deprivation within individuals, if uncontrolled, are likely to be discharged against ethnic minorities. For the most part, these theories (e.g., Adorno et al., 1950; Dollard, Doob, Miller, Mowrer, & Sears, 1939) view problems of prejudice and discrimination as residing within the person.

A second set of theories identifies value, belief, and ideological differences among in-group and out-groups as motivation for out-group rejection behaviors (Insko et al., 1983; Kinder, 1986; Rokeach, 1979; Chapter 4, this volume; Sears & Kinder, 1985; Weigel & Howes, 1985). Many of the models within this category have been viewed as antagonistic (Pettigrew, 1985; Weigel & Howes, 1985). An underlying theme, however, is an emphasis on perceived or actual ideological differences and a deemphasis of "irrational" motives, for example, prejudice, as immediate causes of negative reactions to out-groups.

A third group of intergroup conflict theories can be loosely labeled as social-conflict theories. These models hold that it is actual conflict in group interests that lead the dominant group to engage in negative out-group behaviors toward the subordinate group(s) (Bobo, 1983, 1988; Giles & Evans, 1985; Jackman & Muha, 1984). These models are closely tied to basic Marxist analyses as well as ethnic theories of social movements (e.g., Nielsen, 1985). These theories also encompass some of the concerns regarding out-group threats to personal and familial interests (Kinder, 1986; Weigel & Howes,

1985). A fourth set of theories in this domain views interpersonal anxiety regarding interaction with ethnic and racial out-groups, and perceived individual threat, as leading to out-group rejection (e.g., Stephan & Stephan, 1985).

Finally, a fifth category of theories is based on evolutionary theories, building on the principle of inclusive fitness (Wilson, 1978). From this perspective, positive biases about one's own group and negative biases about other racial and ethnic groups, are extensions of sentiments derived from family and kin relationships (e.g., Sidanius, Pratto, & Bobo, 1994; van den Berghe, 1981).

As shown in Figure 5.1, we propose that the bulk of the theories described can be ordered within three major areas: (a) person-centered prejudice models of out-group rejection; (b) group-conflict models; and, (c) value-congruity models. In person-centered prejudice models, the conflicts are internal and become cathected on external objects, resulting in out-group rejection and conflict. According to these models, the perceived threat is related to a sense of personal integrity. In the group-conflict models, perceptions of conflict and threat are tied to social, economic, or political group status, and these conflicts over valued goods form the basis of out-group rejection behaviors. Finally, in the value-differences models, perceived disparities between one's own group and the out-group in the extent of adherence to cherished values, beliefs, or ideologies, and the perceived threat to one's own ideological position results in out-group rejection behaviors.

The underlying theme in all of these models is conflict and perceptions of threat, although the kind of perceived threat differs dramatically. Threat to self-identity (Allport, 1958; Chapter 1, this volume; Stephan & Stephan, 1985) in person-centered models, threat to position dominance (Bobo, 1987; Giles & Evans, 1985; Nielsen, 1985; Sidanius et al., 1994; Yinger, 1985) in group conflict models, and threat to group identity (Milner, 1981; Tajfel & Turner, 1979) in value-congruity models provide the motivation for overt out-group reactions. Some recent work by Walter Stephan and his colleagues (Stephan, Ybarra, & Bachman, 1996; Stephan, Ybarra, Martinez, Schwarzwald, & Tur-Kaspa, 1996; Ybarra & Stephan, 1994) has reached similar conclusions about the central importance of intergroup anxiety and perceived threat. We suggest that all of the numerous theories of intergroup conflict have some currency, dependent on historical circumstances, cultural considerations, and the economic, social, and political contexts, and thus may serve to highlight the operation of factors unique to each model or set of models. Under circumstances of constrained resources, real group conflict may be operative (Sherif & Sherif, 1953), resulting in perceived threat (e.g., Britain). Under

| Traditional Classification | Threat-Based Classification |
|---|---|
| • Personality or individual difference models (i.e., frustration-aggression theory, authoritarian personality)<br>• Perceived individual threat<br>• Social-conflict theories (i.e., realistic group conflict theory)<br>• Evolutionary theories<br>• Value, belief, and ideological differences (i.e., symbolic racism, aversive racism) | • Personal threat models (sense of personal integrity or self-identity is threatened)<br>• Group threat models (sense of group's social, economic, or political status is threatened)<br>• Value threat models (cherished value, belief, or ideological position is threatened) |

**Figure 5.1.** Classifications of Theories of Prejudice and Discrimination

conditions of relatively rich resources and a relatively tight status hierarchy among different racial and ethnic groups (e.g., The Netherlands), social identity may be more salient, resulting in threat and group anxiety (Tajfel, 1982). Under conditions in which long-term ethnic and racial divisions and conflict demarcate the status hierarchy among some groups (e.g., France and the United States), then socialization theories, symbolic concerns, and basic value differences may provide a more parsimonious explanation of group conflict (Chapter 1 and Chapter 4, this volume). On the other hand, we argue that regardless of the specific theoretical model, threat (and stress), especially to the hierarchically dominant group and individual, is what accounts for the proximate immediate orientation, feelings about, and actions toward individuals in the groups lower in the status hierarchy (Jackson & Inglehart, 1995).

Understanding the nature of racism, and its psychological and social consequences in the United States, can be accomplished only by studying similarities and differences between dominant and subordinate groups in a comparative, cross-national, multiple out-group context (Pettigrew et al., in press). In the next section, we detail the empirical approach used to examine the link between threat to the dominant group and intergroup conflict in the member states of the EU and the United States.

## ■ Empirical Approach to Western Europe and United States Comparisons

The type of theoretical approach that is needed for examining intergroup relations is amenable to empirical examination. Although laboratory methods have been often used often in such studies (see Chapter 1, this volume), we were interested in investigating this phenomenon among community-dwelling adults, not college students. For this reason, we approached the problem using sample household surveys in the respective countries. As indicated earlier, in 1988 an extensive survey of intergroup attitudes, beliefs, and values was conducted in four EU countries: France, Great Britain, Germany, and The Netherlands. The surveys of the EU, called Eurobarometers, are a long-running set of opinion polls that are conducted twice yearly in the spring and fall on nationally representative samples of the EU countries. These surveys have been conducted in varied form since 1970. Although the themes of the surveys have changed on each occasion, a central concern has been with the attitudes of the EU publics toward the common market, attitudes toward other European countries, and the priority of goals and values within each country.

In 1974, the Commission of the European Communities initiated the Eurobarometer series, a supplemental survey within the European Omnibus Survey designed to provide a regular monitoring of social and political attitudes of the publics within the EU. Over the years, Eurobarometers have focused on special topics such as public attitudes toward the role of women in economic, social, and political life; attitudes toward poverty and multinational corporations; public attitudes toward science, early retirement, environmental issues, guest workers, and a number of similar timely public concerns (Rabier, Riffault, & Inglehart, 1986).

Because of the interest in having salient populations of either immigrant workers or racial-ethnic out-groups for the study, and cost considerations, we limited our intensive research to samples of dominant groups in only four of the 12 EU countries: France ($N = 1,001$), Great Britain ($N = 1,017$), The Netherlands ($N = 1,006$), and (West) Germany ($N = 1,051$).[1]

The 1986 American National Election Study (ANES) data were used for comparison with the United States (Kinder, 1986). The American Election Studies are a long-running series of surveys conducted on representative samples of the U.S. population every 2 years. They are a pre- and postelection panel design. A special module of questions regarding race and racial attitudes was asked in the 1986 election study (Kinder, 1986).

Similar to racial attitudes research conducted in the United States, we preselected country-specific subordinate group(s) to which dominant-group respondents reacted. For example, in the United States blacks have been used as the major relevant out-group (Kinder, 1986; Kinder & Sanders, 1986). We did not have responsibility for the design and execution of the 1986 National Election Study. The principal researchers of this study used blacks as the only major target group (Kinder & Sanders, 1986). In the European surveys, we selected two out-groups within each country, except in (West) Germany. In this latter country, we decided to study only Turks, based on the advice of our collaborators there about the lack of broad national recognition of other potential target groups in 1988. North Africans and Southeast Asians were selected as the target groups in France; Turks and Surinamers were selected in The Netherlands; South Asians and West Indians were chosen in Great Britain. This procedure had the advantage of providing two randomly drawn samples within three of the four nations so that we could examine the relationships among the constructs, not only across countries but also within countries for different groups. For some purposes, the data for each group within each country may be combined to provide larger sample sizes. The selection of the relevant group(s) was done within each country with the assistance of co-investigators who were familiar and knowledgeable about the status and situations of these groups within their respective countries.

The use of specific groups within each country also makes the internal national analyses more meaningful and contributes to our major goal of evaluating and comparing the different theoretical frameworks of out-group rejection across the different countries. In each country, the selection of different groups captures some important aspects of the various sociohistorical relationships among different dominant and subordinate groups. Each dominant and subordinate target-group pairing entails a unique and nonduplicated social history. For purposes of our social psychological analyses, some significant part of this rich history is captured by having different subordinate group targets within and across each country.

Four major groups of analyses have been conducted by members of the research group (Pettigrew et al., in press). These analyses reflect our interest in the interrelated areas of psychological processes and behavioral intentions; the structure of racial attitudes; cognitive distortions and racial attitudes; and threat, stress, and racism.

## ■ Psychological Processes and Behavioral Intentions

One group of analyses focuses on the differences and similarities of psychological processes and their relationships to endorsement of government help and positive immigration policies among the different countries. Overall, the results of these analyses suggest some consistent differences among countries in the levels of affective, racial, and policy positions toward government action and immigration (Jackson, Lemaine, et al., 1993; Leach, 1995).

In addition, differences are observed in the reactions toward different groups within countries. The overall pattern of results suggests that policy orientations regarding government help and immigration policies toward out-groups can be accounted for largely by a combination of modern and traditional out-group prejudice (see Pettigrew & Meertens, 1995), perceived economic threat from out-groups, and negative feelings toward out-group members.

We used a variety of measures to assess dominant group members' racial attitudes toward out-groups and support for government policies aiding out-groups. Similar items were used in both European and U.S. samples. The Affective Thermometer, a feeling thermometer, was used to measure feelings toward the out-group(s) in each country. The specific question read: "I would like you to rate each (group) of them on a 0 to 100 scale. Ratings between 51 and 100 mean that you feel favorable toward that group. Ratings between 0 and 49 mean that you don't feel too favorable toward that group. A rating of 50 means that you don't feel particularly favorable or unfavorable toward that group." We reversed and converted the responses to a scale from 0 to 10, such that 0 to 4 was favorable, 5 represented neither favorable nor unfavorable, and 6 to 10 was an unfavorable feeling toward a group. The Modern Racism Index included four items that assessed beliefs about the out-group's need for welfare, being "pushy," needing to overcome adversity like other groups, and the amount of discrimination against the out-group. Overall, this average index had a response range from 1 to 4, with 4 representing a high level of modern racism toward an out-group. The Traditional Racism Index contained three items: willingness to have sexual relations with out-group, out-groups take jobs that majority should have, and majority can never really be comfortable with out-group. This average index was coded into a 4-point scale; higher scores represented higher traditional racism.

The Negative Ideology Beliefs Index encompassed four items about out-group members needing to try harder to be as well off as majority people, teaching their children values and skills different from those required for success, coming from less able races, and being from cultures less well developed than that of the majority group. The average index had a range from 1 to 4, with 4 signifying strong negative ideological beliefs about an out-group. Perceptions of economic competition from out-groups assessed respondents' perception of economic threat. The first item (economically worse: in-group) measured respondent's perception of personal economic misfortune. "Would you say that over the past 5 years you have been economically a lot better off, better off, the same, worse off, or a lot worse off than (nationality) people like yourself?" The second item (economically worse:

out-group) measured respondent's perception of group economic misfortune related to their out-group: "Would you say that over the past 5 years people like yourself in (country) have been economically a lot better off, better off, the same, worse off, or a lot worse off than most (out-group) people living here?" For each question, scores greater than 3 indicated that the respondent felt worse off and those below 3 indicated that the respondent felt better off than the respective comparison group.

Two policy-relevant indexes assessed behavioral intentions regarding the out-group. Government efforts on behalf of out-group, measured by a single item, addressed the extent of agreement to the statement: "The government should make every effort to improve the social and economic position of out-groups." Higher scores on a 4-point scale indicated greater opposition to government assistance for racial-ethnic out-groups. Immigration policy, assessed by a social-distance-like scale, focused on the extent of endorsement with varying stances regarding immigration policies toward specific out-group members. The most unfavorable position ("send all out-group members back whether born here or not") was assigned a score of 6 and agreement with the most favorable item (send back none of the out-group members) was assigned a score of 1.

## ■ Findings

Overall, the findings suggest that constructs and measures largely developed in the United States in the context of black-white relationships have currency in Western Europe. As shown in Figure 5.2a, the findings suggest consistent differences among countries in the levels of affective, racial, and policy positions toward government action and immigration. In addition, some slight differences can be observed in the reactions toward different groups within countries.

*Affective Thermometer.* As assessed by the feeling thermometer, blacks in the United States and Surinamers in The Netherlands are disliked the least in their respective countries. Generally, African Americans in the United States received a lower negative affective rating than immigrant groups in the European countries.

*Modern and Traditional Racism.* Overall differences among countries are small. There is a slight tendency for the Europeans to indicate lower mean levels of modern racism toward their respective out-groups than the U.S.

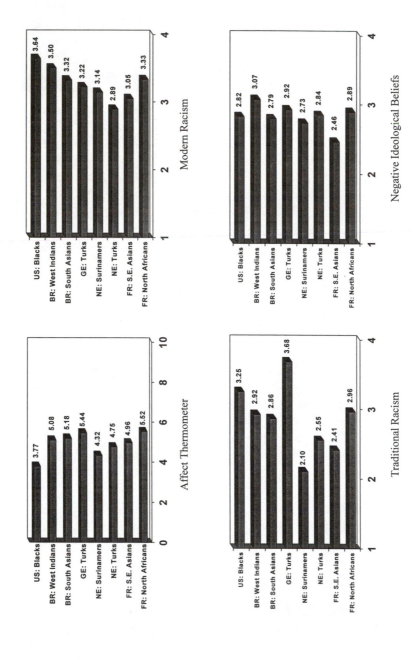

**Figure 5.2a.** Mean Ratings on Affect Thermometer, Racism, and Ideological Beliefs by Country and Out-Group

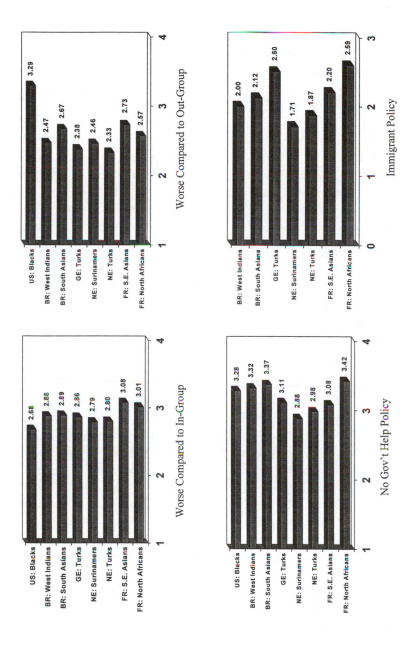

**Figure 5.2b.** Mean Ratings on Economic Comparisons and Government Out-Group Assistance by Country and Out-Group

majority expresses toward blacks. The Traditional Racism Index indicates a little more spread in attitudes.

*Negative Ideology Beliefs.* Similar to modern racism, the differences in negative ideology beliefs held about the out-groups between countries appears to be small. African Americans are the recipients of intermediate levels of negative ideological beliefs.

*Economic Competition.* As shown in Figure 5.2b, small but significant differences are found on the perceptions of personal economic misfortune. As expected, average differences are not found between individuals exposed to different target groups within countries.

On the related measure of group economic competition with an out-group, some commonalities were present. Turks, whether in The Netherlands or Germany, are not perceived as an economic threat. On the other hand, Asians, whether in France or Great Britain, are perceived to be more of a threat, as are African Americans in the United States.

*Government Efforts on Behalf of Out-Group and Immigration Policy.* When asked about whether the government should assist out-groups, a fairly similar pattern of means can be observed. Overall, Europeans are less likely to strongly endorse help for immigrant groups than are U.S. whites to endorse such help for blacks. In Europe, when asked about the endorsement of increasingly restrictive immigration policies, significant differences among countries are found.

Additional analyses reveal modern and traditional racism, perceived economic threat from out-groups, and negative affect toward out-group members are most strongly related to negative policy positions toward out-groups. In general, our findings strongly indicate the presence of negative racialized attitudes among dominant group members in the United States and our selected European countries, and more important, an impact of these attitudes on government and immigration policy positions related to out-group members (Jackson, Lemaine, et al., 1993; Pettigrew et al., in press).

The consistency of these findings across counties and out-groups is remarkable. In fact, the rank ordering of the most important factors is highly similar across all countries and target groups (Jackson, Lemaine, et al., 1993). It is this finding that leads us to consider the role of threat (Bobo & Hutchings, 1996; Blumer, 1958; Volckens, 1996), regardless of its source, as the proximal cause among dominant group members for prejudicial and discriminatory beliefs toward out-groups. Thus, although there may be vast differences in social, historical, economic, and political relations among dominant and subordinate groups across countries, the most immediate cause of negative beliefs, feelings, and behaviors is the perception of threat.

In addition to the findings that suggest similarities in proximal causes of public policy positions toward different target groups among dominant group members across the countries, we have also found instances of strong differential cultural influences. The 1988 study attempted to examine social cognitions (stereotypes, prejudices, and so forth) and affective reactions regarding persons from another nationality, religion, race, cultural, and social class. Holmes and Inglehart (1994) showed that although the overall level of prejudice in these different countries might be similar, there are clear differences in who will be chosen as a target of prejudice. We found that France and Britain are high in their negative reactions toward persons from another race, whereas Germans' reactions toward members of another race are comparatively the least negative. Germans, however, score highest with regard to religious intolerance. Holmes and Inglehart (1994) speculated that it may be the historical context of having experienced World War II that made Germans sensitive to race arguments and that has led to low scores on racial prejudice. France and Britain are highest on negative reactions. We do not interpret this finding as indicating that Germans are generally less bigoted than the French or English, but it may mean that due to their cultural background, they have different specific contents to which they attach their bigotry. Thus, it is necessary to consider that some cultures focus their out-group hostility and atrocities toward persons from another race (e.g., Britain and France), whereas other nations may focus it on persons from another nationality or religion (e.g., Turks in Germany) (Holmes & Inglehart, 1994). The results of these preliminary analyses among four of the major Western European publics indicate significant overall resistance to government interventions; a small but significant proportion in favor of removing immigrant groups; and, a small but significant proportion unequivocally opposed to any punitive action against out-groups. These findings strongly suggest that it is only by studying different dominant and subordinate groups in the different countries that we can understand how the contents of prejudice and psychological processes interact.

## ■ Structure of Prejudice and Racism

The second group of analyses focuses on understanding the structure of prejudice and racism. These studies have attempted to disentangle different forms of racism (Pettigrew & Meertens, 1995) and to understand how prejudice and racism might be embedded in a general worldview of values and beliefs about the world (Jackson & Inglehart, 1995). From 20 items traditionally associated with the measurement of racism, 5 groupings (or factors) emerged as cohesive scales: a four-item factor focusing on intimacy with an out-group; a six-item grouping pertaining to threat and rejection of the out-group; a four-item index of traditional values not to be violated by the out-group; a four-indicator cultural differences factor assessing the degree of difference between the majority and out-group; and a two-item grouping measuring negative emotions evoked by the out-group. These factors tap into various aspects of what have been conceived as subtle and blatant manifestation of racism (Pettigrew & Meertens, 1995). They have proven to be reliable across each of the target groups in each country with little variation (Brown, Crocker, Jackson, Lightborn, & Torres, 1996; Brown, Torres, & Jackson, 1996; Pettigrew & Meertens, 1995). Following in the vein of studying the more elusive and indirect forms of racism, for example, symbolic (Chapter 4, this volume) and aversive racism (Chapter 1, this volume), Pettigrew and his colleagues (Pettigrew, 1989; Pettigrew & Meertens, 1995; Pettigrew et al., in press) developed the two 10-item blatant-subtle prejudice scale. The blatant scale has two dimensions, four items measuring intimacy, and six threat and rejection items. The subtle scale contains thee dimensions, four items measuring traditional values, four cultural difference items, and two affective prejudice items. As with other work on the structure of racial attitudes, the dimensions of the blatant-subtle scale were stable with similar reliability across countries and target groups. In addition, research on the scales suggests that blatant and subtle prejudice are not simple polar opposites but instead represent different types of prejudicial reactions of dominant groups toward subordinate target groups.

In their research, Pettigrew & Meertens (1995) have found three major trends: (a) large differences in two nations, France and The Netherlands, indicating much greater French prejudice toward North Africans than Southeast Asians, and significantly greater Dutch prejudice against Turks than Surinamers; (b) a notable pattern in The Netherlands of lower blatant but higher subtle prejudice toward both groups; and (c) much higher subtle than blatant prejudice across all countries and target groups. Pettigrew and Meertens (1995) suggest that these findings indicate normative pressures, especially among the Dutch, to control blatant expressions of prejudice, but that these same normative pressures do not operate against the expression of more subtle forms of out-group prejudice. Pettigrew and Meertens (1995) refer to those individuals who score low on both scales as Equalitarians, those who score high on both as Bigots, and those who score low on the blatant and high on the subtle as Subtle racists. Those who score high on the blatant scale but low on the subtle scale were too few of the respondents to analyze (2%). One analysis of interest indicated that Bigots favor sending all immigrants home, regardless of their immigrant status; Equalitarians generally prefer to send none of the immigrants home regardless of their status; and Subtles favor sending immigrants home only when there is a seemingly nonprejudicial reason to do so, for example, they have committed crimes or do not have their documents (Pettigrew et al., in press). This latter finding is very similar to the aversive racist so aptly noted and described by Dovidio and Gaertner (Chapter 1, this volume).

## ■ Normative Analyses

Population-based attitudes and feelings may be related to public positions on institutionalized arrangements, for example, jobs and equal opportunity, and these attitudes and positions may be related to broad-based public support for government interventions and public policy changes. We would like to present one possible mechanism, pluralistic ignorance, that may contribute to continuing and perhaps increasing negative views by the dominant group toward government intervention in the plight of racial and ethnic groups in the United States and elsewhere (and especially in Europe in the increasing negative sentiments toward immigration policies).

*Pluralistic ignorance*, broadly construed, is the shared erroneous belief, either over- or underestimate, of the extent to which others in a given population hold the same views as the believer. Recent writings have emphasized errors of overestimation, but the general concept of pluralistic ignorance refers to any such errors. Prior work on this topic (e.g., Allport, 1958; Banton, 1986; Fields & Schuman, 1976; Katz, 1991; O'Gorman, 1986) has shown the tendency for dominant group members who are positive toward subordinate out-groups to overestimate the proportion in the dominant group population who hold negative views, and for those who are negative to overestimate the proportion in the majority population who are negative, even more so than those who are positive. It is possible that this phenomenon may play a role in contributing to and maintaining institutionalized forms of racism and anti-immigrant sentiments (Jones, 1997). It may also provide an assessment of the extent of support or lack of support for the upward mobility of out-groups.

The pluralistic ignorance variables were formed by crossing self-perceptions of willingness to have an out-group member as a boss (or out-group member as a close family member by marriage) with perceptions of the willingness of others, like themselves, in the country to do the same. In examining the descriptive differences among countries in the distribution (Figures 5.3-1 to 5.3-8) of the pluralistic ignorance beliefs, two major themes are found. First, the results substantially replicate the major findings of previous work, largely done in the United States and Great Britain (Leach, Kirby, & Jackson, 1995; Miller & McFarland, 1987), showing that people who are positive tend to overestimate the numbers in the population who are negative; and, that those who are negative overestimate even more than the positive individuals the numbers in the population who are negative. As shown in these figures, in nearly every country and for every group, those individuals who are personally positive toward working with an out-group as a boss, or marriage to an out-group member, tend to overestimate the degree to which other citizens of their countries like themselves are negative. The effect is present regardless of the average level of personal negativity expressed within each country. Similarly, in all cases except one, those members who are personally negative toward an out-group member as a boss or marriage to an out-group member, tend to overestimate even more than those who are positive, the extent to which others like themselves are negative.

In general, the findings in Table 5.1 indicate that marriage to out-group members is viewed much more negatively than is being supervised by out-groups in work settings, and that the magnitude of these differences vary by country and out-group targets. Overall, the (West) Germans are much more negative toward Turks in their country than any other country by group combination. The French are especially negative toward North Africans in both employment and marriage domains in comparison to South East Asians, and the Dutch tend to be more negative toward Turks, especially in the marriage domain; whereas the British are slightly more negative toward South Asians in the marriage domain and slightly less negative toward this same group in the employment situation.

In examining the differences among countries and target groups in the distributions of the pluralistic ignorance measures, two major themes are found. First, the results substantially replicate the major findings of previous work, largely done in the United States and Great Britain. And second, there is one notable exception in the major trends, (West) Germany, where the full pluralistic ignorance effect is not found. Even in (West) Germany, however, some support for cognitive distortions is found among those who themselves are negative.

*(text continues on p. 128)*

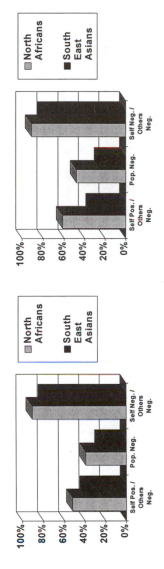

**Figure 5.3-1.** Pluralistic Ignorance: Out-Group as Boss—France: North African and Asian Out-Groups

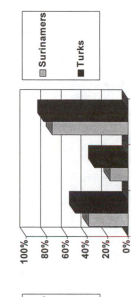

**Figure 5.3-2.** Pluralistic Ignorance: Marriage to Out-Group—France: North African and Asian Out-Groups

**Figure 5.3-3.** Pluralistic Ignorance: Out-Group as Boss—Netherlands: Surinamers and Turkish Out-Groups

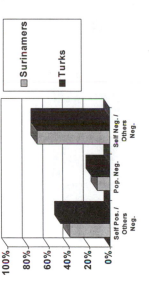

**Figure 5.3-4.** Pluralistic Ignorance: Marriage to Out-Group—Netherlands: Surinamers and Turkish Out-Groups

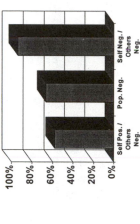

**Figure 5.3-5.** Pluralistic Ignorance: Out-Group as Boss—Germany (West): Turkish Out-Groups

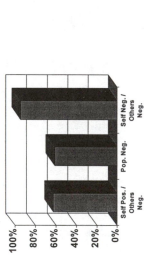

**Figure 5.3-7.** Pluralistic Ignorance: Out-Group as Boss—Britain: South Asian and West Indian Out-Groups

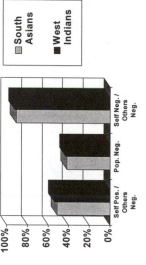

**Figure 5.3-6.** Pluralistic Ignorance: Marriage to Out-Group—Germany (West): Turkish Out-Groups

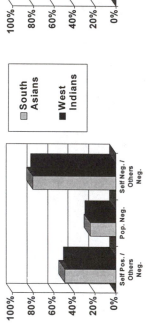

**Figure 5.3-8.** Pluralistic Ignorance: Marriage to Out-Group—Britain: South Asian and West Indian Out-Groups

**TABLE 5.1.** Distributions of Items Constituting Pluralistic Ignorance Measures

| Country: Out-Group | Most (NATIONALITY) People Would Not Mind If a Suitably Qualified (OUT-GROUP) Person Was Appointed as Their Boss | | | I Would Not Mind If a Suitably Qualified (OUT-GROUP) Person Was Appointed as My Boss | | | Most (NATIONALITY) People Would Not Mind If a (OUT-GROUP) Person With a Similar Economic Background Joined Their Family by Marriage | | | I Would Not Mind If a (OUT-GROUP) Person With a Similar Economic Background Joined My Family by Marriage | | |
|---|---|---|---|---|---|---|---|---|---|---|---|---|
| | Agree | Disagree | Do Not Know | Agree | Disagree | Do Not Know | Agree | Disagree | Do Not Know | Agree | Disagree | Do Not Know |
| Germany (West): Turkish | 16.0% (164) | 76.2% (778) | 7.6% (78) | 36.8% (376) | 54.3% (553) | 8.9% (86) | 17.3% (177) | 76.2% (778) | 8.4% (86) | 33.0% (336) | 58.6% (597) | 8.5% (87) |
| France: Southeast Asians | 45.6% (228) | 45.4% (227) | 9.0% (45) | 70.8% (354) | 21.6% (108) | 7.6% (38) | 48.8% (244) | 39.2% (196) | 12.0% (60) | 72.8% (359) | 22.0% (110) | 6.2% (31) |
| France: North Africans | 29.8% (138) | 64.8% (301) | 5.4% (25) | 59.7% (277) | 34.5% (160) | 5.8% (27) | 21.4% (99) | 69.2% (321) | 9.5% (44) | 51.8% (240) | 44.4% (206) | 3.9% (18) |
| Netherlands: Surinamers | 52.1% (252) | 38.6% (187) | 9.3% (45) | 80.8% (391) | 12.7% (61) | 6.6% (32) | 48.2% (233) | 38.9% (190) | 12.6% (61) | 76.5% (370) | 15.9% (77) | 7.6% (37) |
| Netherlands: Turkish | 42.6% (212) | 45.6% (227) | 11.8% (59) | 71.3% (355) | 17.4% (87) | 11.2% (56) | 32.7% (163) | 55.0% (274) | 12.2% (61) | 59.7% (297) | 29.4% (146) | 11.0% (55) |
| Britain: South Asians | 38.5% (192) | 53.4% (266) | 8.0% (40) | 70.9% (353) | 24.3% (121) | 4.8% (24) | 29.5% (147) | 59.6% (297) | 10.8% (54) | 55.4% (276) | 36.4% (181) | 37.5% (192) |
| Britain: West Indians | 43.7% (224) | 47.3% (242) | 9.0% (46) | 69.4% (355) | 20.5% (105) | 10.2% (52) | 24.8% (127) | 61.9% (317) | 13.3% (68) | 11.0% (55) | 8.2% (41) | 12.1% (62) |

These results replicate prior work on pluralistic ignorance in the United States and Great Britain, suggesting that the concept has cross-national validity. The lack of full effect in (West) Germany may suggest the presence of different socialization and environmental variables, leading to a operation of a divergent set of cognitive processes in that national context, as opposed to other countries (Brislin, 1990). The findings are provocative and suggest that pluralistic ignorance may be related to policy options about immigrant groups-guest workers held by dominant groups, over and beyond that accounted for by prejudice and negative feelings. Pluralistic ignorance may add to negative attitudes and broaden the negativity among citizens in a given country toward immigrant groups.

The cognitive distortions are related to the negative views held by dominant members toward the policy issues of relevance for immigrant groups. As we have found, even in the absence of personal antipathies toward immigrant groups, many Europeans, based on their distortions of the beliefs about the views of "others like themselves," may not support positive public immigration policies (Jackson, Kirby, et al., 1993). It may be that more than "simple" racism may be operating to influence the negative positions that many European citizens hold toward immigration policies.

Admittedly, the attitudes of the publics in the European countries are complex and thus probably determined by large numbers of factors. These results suggest, however, that cognitive distortions represented by the pluralistic ignorance phenomenon may contribute to maintaining negative ethnic attitudes and public support for negative immigration policies. This effect may differ only slightly by country and target out-group.

## ■ Threat, Racism, Stress, and Health

We have proposed (Jackson & Inglehart, 1995) that the concept of perceived threat (Stephan & Stephan, 1985) is theoretically related to the concept of stress. One common definition of *stress* relates to events in which environmental demands, internal demands, or both, tax or exceed the adaptive resources of an individual, social system, or tissue system. Stress is neither an environmental condition nor an individual's response, but rather an environment-person transaction. Recent work (Cohen, Kessler, & Gordon, 1995) points to the important psychological dimensions of the stress response. They suggested in relation to the psychological dimension of stress that "the perception of threat arises when the demands imposed on an individual are perceived to exceed his or her felt ability to cope with these demands." Perceiving members of other social groups as a threat can be stress-provoking (Stephan & Stephan, 1985) and negative for one's psychological and mental health.

We propose that (a) a person's basic beliefs, attitudes, and values will feed into the subjective appraisal process. We, however, also argue that (b) situational-structural factors will shape the subjective appraisal of social situations. For example, political, social, and economic changes in the "real" world might lead to high rates of unemployment and inflation, crime, and violence. These are structural factors that clearly cause stress both on a community and on an individual level, and might prime and enhance negative appraisals of social situations. For example, affirmative action provides a timely illustration of threat. In the United States, blacks constitute only 15% or so of the total population and an even lower proportion of those who are adult, able bodied, and capable of work. If all blacks were given jobs, it is not clear, given the size of the U.S. population and economy, whether this would pose a significant risk of preventing other Americans from obtaining gainful employment. Yet, the perceptions of threat to jobs among whites certainly revolve around opposition to affirmative action and stated fears of either loss of opportunity or blocked opportunities for advancement in careers and jobs (see Chapter 1, this volume; Chapter 6, this volume). Opinion poll results indicate that 60% of whites felt that affirmative action discriminated against whites (Painton, 1991). Additional opinion poll results indicate that 47% of women thought that whites' losing out because of affirmative action in the workplace was a bigger problem than blacks' facing discrimination (Alpern, 1995). Both of these results imply a perception that the job that respondents felt they were entitled to went to someone else because of affirmative action. We believe that this points to the importance of perceptual processes and the psychological nature of threats to hierarchical position.

Individual, cultural, and institutional racism can be, and are, interpreted as stressors for the targets of this discrimination, and can thus negatively affect social, economic, psychological, and health outcomes (Jackson et al., 1996; Ruggiero & Taylor, 1995). The significance, however, of understanding the effects of racism and intergroup conflict on the dominant groups' stress level and individual psychological and physical health status has been a neglected topic. By neglecting the fact that being a bigot can be "dangerous to one's health" (Jackson & Inglehart, 1995), a wide range of considerations have been excluded from empirical investigation and, as a result, an important area for initiating changes in social policies has been overlooked.

The relationship between (psychological) health and racism in the dominant group was traditionally seen as unidirectional, although not exclusively so. Psychologically unhealthy conditions, such as an authoritarian personality (Adorno et al., 1950), frustration (Dollard et al., 1939), or low self-esteem (Crocker, Thompson, McGraw, & Ingerman, 1987), were seen as causes of prejudiced reactions. In many scientific accounts (e.g., Adorno et al., 1950), prejudiced reactions were often interpreted as serving a positive function for the racist. For example, one might have argued that by scapegoating a certain out-group member, inner peace might have been reestablished (Duckitt, 1992a).

Reducing intergroup conflict and racist behavior will be beneficial for all groups and individuals in a hierarchically ordered society. For the racist, dominant group members, regardless of any positive tangible social or psychological gain, several detrimental psychological effects accompany bigoted behavior. First of all, if one agrees that hostility is one crucial component of racism, one recognizes the significance of research that shows a strong negative relationship between a person's degree of hostility and psychological and physical health outcomes. Hostility and anger are often invoked in stressful situations.

Everyone in a racially (or ethnically or religiously, and so on) stratified society suffers from racism; stress will affect racism and be affected by it; health outcomes are related to stress and racism among both dominant and subordinate group members. Whatever the theoretical intergroup model, threat is at the end of the story. Stress follows threat and whatever prejudice, racism, and discrimination may be, they are certainly hostile, aggressive, and mean-spirited beliefs and acts, just what we might expect from groups and individuals who are psychologically stressed. Recent research by Krause (1994) and work by Thoits (1991) point out the importance of stressors in salient life roles. This threat-racism-stress chain and its effect on persons' well-being is at the core of the argument that we are making (Jackson & Inglehart, 1995). These observations about stress, however, in no way relieve individuals or groups from responsibility in discriminatory acts.

## ■ The Reverberation Model of Stress, Racism, and Health

We have proposed that stressors, like unemployment and downturns in economic conditions, will influence the perceptions of both dominant and subordinate group members in a given community, country, or other defined geographic region. Among dominant group members, we suggest that stress will directly lower psychological well-being and increase racist sentiments toward subordinate groups. Among subordinate groups, these same negative macroeconomic conditions will contribute to the experiences of stress, which, in turn, will lower well-being. In addition, the racism directed toward subordinate groups by dominant groups will also be experienced as stressful and will contribute independently to lowering well-being even further. Thus, community-level stressors enhance individual-level stress among both dominant and subordinate group members. This stress contributes to dominant groups acting in racist ways toward subordinate groups, which adds even more stress to the lives of subordinate group members. Several causal mechanisms may account for the hypothesized threat-stress-racism relationships: (a) pure economic competition, that is, removal of potential competitors under stressful conditions; (b) cognitive explanation, for example, lowers cognitive ability to individuate under stress; (c) stress lowers psychological barriers against expressing racism; (d) stress heightens in-group bias; or (e) stress accentuates negative out-group feelings.

We hypothesized that (a) community-level stressors influence individuals in all dominant and subordinate groups; (b) stress contributes directly to increased racism in a hierarchical manner among relatively well-situated and poorly situated dominant and subordinate groups; (c) racism is stressful to both dominant and subordinate groups; and (d) the lower the subordinate group, the higher the stress and associated experienced group conflict and group and individual mental health-related disorders.

In a recent work (Jackson & Inglehart, 1995), we predicted that economic stress would lead to increased racism and simultaneously lower well-being among dominant groups. Similarly, we predicted that racism would lead to lowered well-being. Thus, there is a cost to being a racist and that cost is a lowering of one's own well-being. Although not immediately testable, we also predicted that the racism of the dominant group would be reflected in increased perceptions and experiences of racism among the subordinate groups. Similarly, we predicted that racism would also contribute, over and beyond that of community stressors, to the economic stress as perceived by the subordinate group.

Among the subordinate groups, we hypothesized that economic stress and perceived and experienced racism would lower well-being (Jackson & Inglehart, 1995). We also suggested that perceived and experienced racism would raise economic stress, while simultaneously, economic stress may lead to an increase in perceived and experienced racism. We tested these relationships among dominant (white) and subordinate (African Americans) groups in the

United States and among dominant groups (Europeans) in Western Europe. We lacked the data to test these predictions among subordinate groups in Western Europe. The data are from the National Panel Survey of Black Americans (1979-1980 and 1987-1988), the 1984 General Social Science Survey (GSS), and the 1988 Eurobarometer Survey using the selected countries of France, Great Britain, Germany, and The Netherlands. Details on the samples and measures are presented in Jackson and Inglehart (1995).

Overall, the results provided strong preliminary evidence for the Reverberation Model of Stress and Racism that we hypothesized. Increased stress, represented by perceived financial strain due to unemployment and poor job prospects, is associated with increased negative antipathy toward outgroup(s). These relationships were found in national samples from the United States among whites and also in combined national samples of Europeans across four major Western European countries. In addition, the same relationships were found in each of the four Western European countries.

Although perceived economic stress directly reduces well-being, racism also has direct effects. Thus, there are costs associated with holding racist beliefs. Whereas lower levels of well-being might lead to increased racism, the pattern of relationships and the direction of the stress effects argue against this interpretation.

Finally, although not directly testable, racism among the dominant groups might be related to the nature of perceived racism, experienced stress, and well-being among subordinate groups. A partial test of this hypothesis among a longitudinal sample of African Americans (in both 1979-1980 and in 1987-1988) showed that reports of experiences of both racism and stress are directly related to reduced well-being; and that economic stress may be more strongly related to experience of racism than experiences of racism are related to economic stress.

These results suggest that stressors, such as unemployment and poor economic conditions, are related to the nature of experienced stress and discriminatory responses among both dominant and subordinate groups. In most theoretical models of intergroup competition and conflict, the poor social, economic, and psychological outcomes of those lower in the hierarchy are acknowledged, that is, the cost of being a subordinate group member. In our model, we view racism as a potential community-institutional stressor, having chronic and pervasive characteristics similar to natural disasters and macroeconomic conditions (e.g., unemployment, recessions, and so on). The observed relationships are modest in comparison to the stress-producing potential of natural disasters, but given the millions of people involved worldwide in ethnically and racially stratified hierarchical communities, the social, psychological, and financial impact can be enormous. Racism and discrimination may create chronic psychological and physical health risks for both the perpetuator and victim.

## ■ Conclusions

As indicated earlier, all of the many theories of intergroup conflict may have value, dependent on historical circumstances, cultural considerations, and the economic, social, and political contexts, all of which may serve to highlight the operation of factors unique to each theory. Thus, under circumstances of constrained resources, real group conflict may be operative. Under conditions of rich resources and a relatively tight hierarchy among groups, social identity processes may be a more operative. Under conditions in which long-term ethnic and racial divisions and conflict demarcate the hierarchy, socialization theories, symbolic concerns, and basic value differences may provide a more parsimonious explanation of group conflict. We suggest that regardless of the theoretical model, threat and psychological stress, especially to the hierarchically dominant group and individual, is what accounts for the immediate orientation, feelings about, and actions toward individuals in the groups lower in the hierarchy (Blumer, 1958).

Our work, which began with the research in Western Europe and later moved to the United States, suggests that there are definite and obvious material, social, and psychological costs to being a subordinate group member in different nations, even for groups who have significantly different sociohistorical and current relationships to dominant groups in their respective countries (Pettigrew et al., in press). On the other hand, our cross-national research also reveals that whereas there may be immediate material and perhaps social gains for the dominant group member holding prejudicial and racist attitudes about immigrant and racial groups lower in the status hierarchy, there may also be psychological costs. Although the analyses reveal differences in the intensity of the attitudes and beliefs across countries, they also indicate that the relationships among these attitudes, beliefs, and policy options regarding different subordinate groups are relatively similar and robust across countries. These findings do not necessarily indicate that intergroup relationships are universal (Pettigrew et al., in press). The differences in levels of intergroup attitudes across groups within countries (e.g., South Asians and Caribbeans in Britain) and within groups across countries (e.g.,

Turks in The Netherlands and Turks in Germany) may reflect differences in the qualitative aspects of hierarchical relationships among dominant and subordinate groups within, and across, different countries. The similarities, however, in relationships of attitudes and beliefs to behavioral intentions, such as government assistance and immigration policy across countries, do suggest that the immediate influences of perceived threat may be a common feature to dominant-subordinate group relationships, regardless of country (Blumer, 1958; Stephan & Stephan, 1985).

Finally, based on our cross-national studies, we have proposed that dominant group attitudes and behaviors and subordinate group responses are inextricably linked. Yet, theoretical approaches to the study of dominant and subordinate group relationships have lacked clear articulation and conceptualization of these linkages. The possibly self-affirming processes of dominance maintenance on one hand, and the interrelated cognitive, affective, and behavioral responses of subordinate groups on the other, should be studied in tandem. In fact, this is why we have conceptualized much of our work within a framework that views the perception of threat to the dominant group (e.g., Stephan & Stephan, 1985) as the major underlying characteristic of intergroup conflict models (Jackson & Inglehart, 1995). Based on recent writing and analyses, we argue that the perception and experience of threat (Stephan & Stephan, 1985) will add to our understanding of hierarchical models of intergroup interaction. Comparative study and analyses done simultaneously on both dominant and subordinate groups in different national contexts, having different social, political, and economic histories, may contribute to understanding those social psychological dimensions of intergroup relations that are nation-state and target-group specific, as well as those components that are common across national boundaries and contending ethnic and racial groups.

### ■ Note

1. The studies through 1989 were conducted by the European Omnibus Survey organization, a conglomerate of Gallup, Inc.-related companies across the 12 EU countries. In the four countries of our particular focus, the work was conducted by the following organizations: France—Institut de Sondage Lavialle, Issy-Les-Moulineaux; Belgium—DIMARSO, Brussels; The Netherlands— Nederlands Institute Voor De Publieke Opinie en the Marktonderzoek B.V. (NIPO), Amsterdam; West Germany—EMNID-Institut für Markt- und Meinungsforschung, Bielefeld; Great Britain— Social Surveys (Gallup Poll) Ltd., London; and Spain—Gallup Spain. The field work in each country was coordinated from the Paris Gallup affiliate, Faits et Opinions, as well as the subsequent coding and building of the data tapes. Faits et Opinions constructed a French and English version

of the questionnaire, which was then sent to the affiliate organization within each country for translation. Within each of the four countries where our module of questions was asked, our co-investigators checked the translation for accuracy and made suggested changes. The actual sampling and field work was conducted by the Gallup affiliates in each EU country. Representative samples were drawn of the adult populations aged 15 years and older within each country. The sampling designs were a mixture of multistage national probability and national stratified quota procedures, similar to the Gallup polls conducted within the United States. Adjustments can be made to the samples in each country so that they are representative of the population in each country, and for the four Western European countries combined.

Because of cost considerations, we limited our 1988 research to studying only four of the 12 EEC countries more extensively with additional questions. These four countries were France, Great Britain, The Netherlands, and Germany. In each of these four countries, we identified relevant target groups facing dominant group hostility and asked the dominant group samples a set of specific questions concerned with perceptions of, and attitudes toward, members of these particular groups. These target groups were (a) Southeast Asians and North Africans in France, (b) West Indians (Caribbeans) and South Asians in Britain, (c) Surinamers and Turks in The Netherlands, and (d) Turks in (West) Germany. These group-specific data from these different countries provide an excellent basis for cross-national comparisons of the same groups in different countries (such as Turks in The Netherlands and Germany), as well as for comparisons of reactions toward different groups in the same and in different countries. We designed the 1988 research based on the belief that more comparisons among different groups and cultural contexts are needed to understand the nature of out-group rejection within any given national context. We used a random assignment of two different questionnaires within each country, except in what was then West Germany. This procedure had the advantage of providing two randomly drawn samples of dominant group members within each nation that reacted, respectively, to one of two preselected target groups. This made it possible to examine the relationships among the constructs, not only across countries, but also within countries for different groups. Many of the questions included on the fall 1988 Eurobarometer also appeared in the 1986 National Election Study in the United States. This has permitted some limited comparisons of dominant group perspectives between the United States and Western European countries.

# Hierarchical Group Relations, Institutional Terror, and the Dynamics of the Criminal Justice System

*Jim Sidanius*
*Shana Levin*
*Felicia Pratto*

L ooking at social systems around the world and throughout recorded human history, one of the things we notice is that societies tend to be stratified along at least one salient social dimension (e.g., along racial, ethnic, tribal, socioeconomic, religious lines), and members of subordinate groups tend to be imprisoned at significantly higher rates than members of dominant groups. The disproportionate imprisonment of low-status groups is quite ubiquitous and can be observed across a wide variety of cultures and nations, including the Maori of New Zealand (Older, 1984), Aborigines in Australia (Sanson-Fisher, 1978), Native Americans in the United States (Young, 1993), Native Americans in Canada (Moyer, 1992), Native Algerians under the French occupation (Fanon, 1963), Caribbean immigrants in England (Hood & Cordovil, 1992), foreign immigrants in The Netherlands (Junger & Polder, 1992), foreign immigrants in Sweden (Von Hofer & Tham, 1991), the Lapps of Finland (Poikalainen, Nayha, & Hassi, 1992), the Burakumin and Koreans of Japan (De Vos, 1992; Kristof, 1995), and the Arabs of Israel (Sherer, 1990).

Recent U.S. data demonstrate an extreme case of the overrepresentation of a subordinate group in the criminal justice system. In 1995, almost one

AUTHORS' NOTE: The authors would like to thank Colette van Laar, UCLA, for her help in collecting and processing some of the data and references used in this chapter.

136

third (32.2%) of all young African American males across the United States between the ages of 20 and 29 were under some form of criminal justice supervision, either in prison, in jail, on probation, or on parole (Mauer & Huling, 1995). Even more dramatically, a 1996 study of the California criminal justice system (see Schiraldi, Kuyper, & Hewitt, 1996) discovered that almost 40% of California's African American males in their 20s were either in prison, in jail, or on probation. The same study found that the rate of imprisonment for African Americans under California's "three-strikes" law[1] was 17 times the rate for European Americans in Los Angeles County. These findings are even more astounding when one considers the fact that the incarceration rate for black males in the United States is four times the rate of incarceration for black males in South Africa under the Apartheid regime (i.e., 3,109 prisoners per 100,000 population vs. 729 prisoners per 100,000 population; Voigt, Thornton, Barrile, & Seaman, 1994).

There are two broad processes that produce the overrepresentation of subordinate groups within the criminal justice system. First, there is reason to believe that the criminal justice system actively discriminates against members of subordinate groups. All other factors being equal, members of subordinate groups are under more intense scrutiny by the legal authorities, are more readily charged with serious offenses, are more likely to be found guilty, and receive harsher legal sanctions than members of dominant groups. Second, there is also reason to believe that, everything else being equal, members of subordinate groups actually commit a disproportionate number of criminal offenses.

In this chapter, we discuss five different mechanisms of institutional discrimination and review empirical evidence illustrating each mechanism. We also discuss several different theoretical reasons for the higher levels of self-handicapping, criminal behavior on the part of members of subordinate groups. Using social dominance theory as a general framework, we shall argue that both institutional discrimination and self-handicapping criminality among members of subordinate groups are complementary mechanisms contributing to the establishment and maintenance of group-based systems of social hierarchy.

■ **Terror and Criminal Justice**

Introduced by Sidanius and Pratto in the early 1990s (Sidanius, 1993; see also Pratto, Sidanius, Stallworth, & Malle, 1994), social dominance theory

(SDT) argues that complex human societies appear predisposed to organize themselves as group-based social hierarchies with one or a small number of dominant social groups and at least one subordinate group. Such social hierarchies can be based on social class, "race,"[2] ethnicity, religion, nationality, or any other psychologically salient and socially constructed group distinction. Although the degree of group-based hierarchical organization seems to vary both across cultures and over historical time, the basic hierarchical nature of human social organization appears to be quite constant. Because of the ubiquitous nature of group-based human hierarchies, social dominance theorists assume that this form of social organization has probably served one or a number of adaptive functions in human evolutionary history (see Sidanius, 1993). After observing the hierarchical nature of human social organization, social dominance theory then goes on to identify the various processes that are believed to produce and maintain social hierarchy.

SDT is far from the first to observe the hierarchical and group-based nature of social organization (see, e.g., Gramsci, 1971; Lenski, 1984; Marx, 1972; Michels, 1991; Mosca, 1939; Pareto, 1979). Although many models of social stratification have made this basic observation, social dominance theory differs from standard models in that it considers both structural factors (i.e., institutional and societal factors) and psychological factors (i.e., attitudes), as well as their interplay. SDT primarily addresses how individual and group differences along psychological dimensions are influenced by and, in turn, influence structural differences between groups, resulting in the maintenance of group-based systems of social hierarchy. One important individual difference variable that is thought to facilitate social hierarchy is called *social dominance orientation* (SDO). SDO is defined as a very broad orientation expressing one's general support for group-based systems of social stratification (see the Appendix for the $SDO_6$ Scale).[3]

Although societies differ in the degree to which they are hierarchically organized and the basis for these social hierarchies, social dominance theory posits that the means by which group-based hierarchies are established and maintained are similar across social systems. We believe three primary mechanisms facilitate the development and maintenance of group-based social hierarchy: (a) *aggregated individual discrimination,* where individuals discriminate against members of subordinate groups and in favor of members of hegemonic groups; (b) *institutional discrimination,* where social institutions allocate more negative outcomes to members of subordinate groups than to members of dominant groups (e.g., customs, laws, and institutional practices); and (c) *behavioral asymmetry,* where individuals' social behaviors that contribute to the continued functioning of the group-based social hierarchy tend to vary as a function of the position of one's group within that social hierarchy (e.g., the disproportionate number of criminal offenses committed by members of subordinate groups). Here we will focus on the latter two mechanisms (see Chapter 2, this volume for a discussion of the first mechanism).

Like other group conflict models such as Marxism (Bonger, 1916) and pluralist conflict theory (Sellin, 1938; see also Quinney, 1977; Sutherland, 1940; Turk, 1969; Vold, 1979)—and opposed to value-consensus models (see, e.g., Parson, 1962)—SD-theory does not view the "law" and the criminal justice system as neutral and disinterested instruments in the maintenance of law and order (see also Chapter 3, this volume). Although keeping the peace is certainly part of the law's function, SDT and other group conflict models argue that the law also functions to maintain the relative privilege and power of dominant groups, thereby helping to preserve the hierarchical nature of group relations. In other words, the law and the criminal justice system function not only to maintain group-based social order, but to reproduce this social order as well (for similar arguments, see Chevigny, 1995; Ericson, 1982). One of the primary means by which the social hierarchy is maintained is through the use of terror.

Webster's electronic dictionary defines *terror* as "the use of violence and threats to intimidate or coerce, especially for political purposes." Terror not only is used by small groups of radicals, but is employed by states and governments as well. Because states are disproportionately controlled by dominant groups (e.g., races, ethnic groups, clans, tribes, and economic classes) rather than by subordinate groups, it is natural to expect that state terror will be disproportionately directed against members of subordinate groups rather than dominant groups. When terror is used disproportionately against members of subordinate groups to force them into submission, the inferior position of these groups in society is reinforced.

■ Institutional Discrimination and the Laws of Law

Using these assumptions about the hierarchy-enhancing function of the law and the criminal justice system, we can derive a number of hypotheses concerning the way the criminal justice system functions within hierarchically organized social systems. Because these principles are assumed to have broad transcultural and transhistorical generality, they take on the appearance of general laws, so we call them the "laws of law." Thus far, we have been able to derive five such laws or hypotheses, and have marshalled some empirical evidence in their support.[4]

### First Law of Law

*When society's laws are perceived to be violated, the expected level of negative sanction directed against members of subordinate groups will be greater than the expected level of negative sanction directed against members of dominant groups.*

There is a good deal of empirical evidence consistent with this first law of law. The bulk of this evidence indicates that, even after one controls for all other legally relevant factors such as type and severity of crime, prior criminal record, and so on, members of subordinate groups will still face more severe sanctions from the state than members of dominant groups. Although these differences will manifest themselves at all stages of the criminal justice process,[5] as we will see, this bias appears especially likely to occur at the earlier stages of the criminal justice process (e.g., the arrest stage, severity of charges leveled, likelihood of plea bargain offer) rather than at the later stages of the process (e.g., severity of penalty imposed by the court, likelihood of probation).[6]

The most dramatic example of the first law of law can be found in U.S. prosecutorial policy regarding drugs, in general, and crack cocaine in particular. As part of the "war on drugs," the U.S. Congress passed the Anti-Drug Abuse Act of 1986, which, among other things, set a 5-year mandatory federal prison sentence for anyone trafficking 5 grams or more of crack cocaine, and a 10-year term for anyone trafficking 50 grams or more. No such draconian laws were passed, however, for trafficking of powder cocaine. To receive a 5-year mandatory federal prison sentence for powder cocaine, one would have to be found trafficking 500 grams of cocaine, or 100 times the amount needed for crack cocaine (see Figure 6.1). In addition, under the Anti-Drug Abuse Act of 1988, whereas possession of more than 5 grams of crack cocaine demands a minimum sentence of 5 years in prison, simple possession of any quantity of any other illegal drug by a first-time offender, including powder cocaine, is still regarded as a misdemeanor offense, punishable by a maximum of one year in prison.

One might try to justify the differences in punishment severity for powder versus crack cocaine by reasoning that use of crack cocaine is associated with significantly higher levels of violence. There is, however, no empirical support

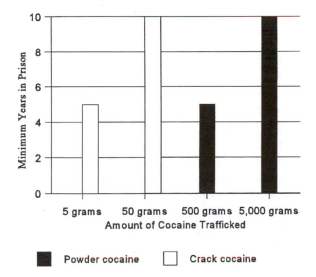

**Figure 6.1.** Mandatory Minimum Federal Sentences for First-Offense Powder and
Crack Cocaine Trafficking
SOURCE: U.S. Sentencing Commission (1995).

for this conclusion. A review of the empirical evidence by the U.S. Sentencing
Commission (1995) concluded the following:

> The Commission finds no research to suggest that powder cocaine users
> are any less likely to commit crimes to support their habits (than crack
> cocaine users). Studies report that neither powder nor crack cocaine excite or
> agitate users to commit criminal acts and that the stereotype of a drug-
> crazed addict committing heinous crimes is not true for either form of
> cocaine. (p. ix)[7]

Among other reasons, it was just this lack of support for a relationship between
crack and violence that led the U.S. Sentencing Commission, set up by the
U.S. Congress, to recommended to Congress that the 100-to-1 penalty ratio
between crack and powder cocaine sentencing be changed. Congress, however, decided to ignore this recommendation.

Besides lacking any defensible rationale from a criminal justice perspective, these antidrug laws are of interest to social dominance theorists for two
reasons. First, powder cocaine is disproportionately used by whites, whereas
crack cocaine is disproportionally used by blacks and Latinos.[8] Second,

because drug surveillance by the police is much more active and widespread in black and Latino residential neighborhoods than in white residential neighborhoods, the actual conviction and incarceration rates for cocaine use do not reflect the actual rate of drug usage by the different ethnic groups.

This fact is shown in Figure 6.2, where we see that the rate at which whites are convicted of powder cocaine possession is substantially lower than their actual use of powder cocaine, whereas the rate of conviction for possession among blacks and Latinos is greater than their actual use. Specifically, although 75% of those using powder cocaine in 1991 were white, only 58% of those convicted for simple possession of powder cocaine in 1993 were white. On the other hand, although 15% of powder cocaine users were black, 26.7% of those convicted for possession of the drug were black (U.S. Sentencing Commission, 1995, pp. xi, 156).

The disparity in the use and conviction rates for blacks is even more dramatic with respect to the use and possession of crack cocaine (see Figure 6.3). As Figure 6.3 shows, 52% of those using crack cocaine in 1991 were white, whereas only 10.3% of those convicted for simple possession of crack cocaine in 1993 were white. On the other hand, although 38% of crack users were black, fully 84.5% of those facing harsh federal convictions for crack possession were black (U.S. Sentencing Commission, 1995, pp. xi, 156).[9]

The dramatic and cumulative impact of these U.S. criminal justice policies on African Americans can be seen in Figure 6.4. This figure compares the rates of overall drug use, drug arrests, drug convictions, and prison sentences for drug possession. As can be seen, although only about 13% of monthly drug users are African American, African Americans constitute 35% of drug possession arrests, 55% of drug possession convictions, and 74% of prison sentences for drug possession (see Mauer & Huling, 1995).[10] Altogether, the two low-status groups of blacks and Latinos constitute almost 90% of all those sentenced to state prisons for drug possession in the United States (Mauer & Huling, 1995, p. 2).

There is evidence that this extreme disproportionality in the prosecution and conviction rates for drug offenses among blacks and Latinos in the United States, compared to those among whites is, in part, due to "discretionary differential targeting," or the fact that law enforcement is much more keen on enforcing antidrug laws within low-status communities (especially black and Latino) than within high-status communities (Lynch & Sabol, 1994).

For example, Hardt (1968) conducted a comparative study of police activity against juvenile offenders within three different socioeconomic communities: (a) low-income blacks, (b) low-income whites, and (c) middle-

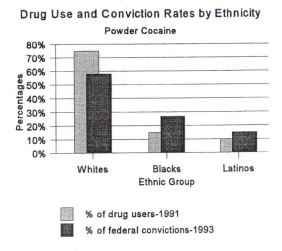

**Figure 6.2.** Use and Conviction Rates for Possession of Powder Cocaine
by Ethnic Group
SOURCE: U.S. Sentencing Commission (1995).

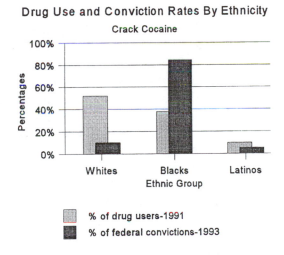

**Figure 6.3.** Use and Conviction Rates for Possession of Crack Cocaine
by Ethnic Group
SOURCE: U.S. Sentencing Commission (1995).

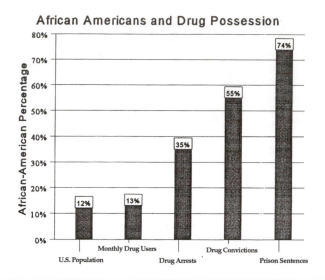

**Figure 6.4.** Criminal Justice Response to Drug Possession by African Americans
SOURCE: Mauer and Huling (1995). Reprinted with permission from The Sentencing Project.

income whites. He found that when rates of law violation were held constant, police apprehended a larger number of black boys than white boys (see also Fyfe, 1982; Heussenstamm, 1971). These discretionary targeting results suggest that the more discretion that is allowed in the enforcement of criminal laws, the more likely these laws are to be enforced in a discriminatory manner. As we shall see, law enforcement officers involved in arrest and prosecution (e.g., police officers and prosecutors) are more likely to endorse hierarchy-enhancing social attitudes. These social attitudes are more likely to be manifested in discriminatory behaviors when police officers and prosecutors are allowed more discretion in law enforcement.

Evidence supporting the notion of disproportionate sentencing as a function of social status is not limited to the United States. For example, Junger and Polder (1992) examined the degree of involvement in crime by Moroccan, Turkish, Surinamese, and Dutch boys (aged 12-17 years) in The Netherlands. The data showed that the arrest rates for boys from the three low-status, ethnic minorities were substantially higher than those among the comparable group of Dutch boys. Although the arrest rate was only 15% among Dutch boys, it was 23% among Surinamese boys, 22% among Turkish boys, and 34% among Moroccan boys (see also Mair, 1986). Other Dutch research has shown that

(a) criminal cases against foreigners were less likely to be dismissed than cases against native Dutch defendants (see Maas & Stuyling de Lange, 1989); (b) once charged with a crime, foreign citizens were more likely to be remanded to custody rather than released on bail (see Bosma, 1985); and (c) once found guilty, foreigners were sentenced to longer prison sentences than native Dutch citizens (see Timmerman, Bosma, & Jongman, 1986; however, for contradictory findings, see Beijers, Hille, & de Leng, 1994).

Likewise, data from Australia indicate that although Australian Aborigines (a low-status group in Australia) represent only 2% of the total population, they constitute more than 38.9% of the occupants of criminal institutions for juveniles. Once again, although a portion of this overrepresentation is due to higher rates of criminality among Aborigines, another portion of this overrepresentation is due to the discriminatory behavior of the Australian criminal justice system (Sanson-Fisher, 1978). Similarly, although Arab juveniles represent only 23% of Israel's juvenile population, they constitute 33% of those juveniles charged with criminal offenses (Sherer, 1990). Moreover, there is consistent evidence that Israeli police are more likely to arrest Arab juveniles than Jewish juveniles for similar offenses (Sherer, 1990). Furthermore, Israeli Arab adults receive disproportionately harsher sentences than their Jewish counterparts, and among Jews, Sephardic Jews (i.e., low-status Jews) receive disproportionately harsher sentences than Ashkenazic Jews (i.e., high-status Jews; Statistikah pelilit, 1992).

Evidence for the first law of law can even be found within the relatively egalitarian society of Sweden. Research shows that although foreign residents in Sweden (i.e., a low-status group in Sweden) constitute only 5% of the population, they constitute 17% of those convicted of crimes. In addition, once convicted of a crime, the average foreign resident receives a significantly longer prison sentence than the average Swede (7.7 months vs. 5.4 months). In line with the findings from other nations, even when one controls for factors such as type of crime, age, gender, and region of residence, foreign residents still run a higher risk of being convicted than native Swedes (Von Hofer & Tham, 1991).

The most comprehensive, non-U.S. study of the criminal justice system of which we are aware is a recent report prepared by the Commission for Racial Equality in Great Britain (Hood & Cordovil, 1992). In this study, the Hood Commission inspected a total of 2,884 criminal cases adjudicated by the Crown Court Centres covered by the West Midlands Police in 1989. These criminal cases involved white, black (Afro-Caribbean), and Asian (primarily East Indian) defendants. A rough inspection of incarceration data indicates that Asian males, and black males especially, occupy British prison cells at rates far exceeding their proportion in the general population. For blacks, the number of males imprisoned in Britain is between eight and nine times greater than their representation in the British population. Detailed analyses of the data indicate that these differences are due to both the fact that blacks commit a disproportionate number of crimes and the fact that racial discrimination exists within the British criminal justice system.

Similar to data from other nations, the data show evidence of racial discrimination at all stages of the criminal justice process, from arrest to length of prison sentence served. For example, the evidence suggests that blacks in Britain are more likely to be stopped, questioned, and searched by the English police than are whites (see also Skogan, 1990; Smith & Gray, 1985). Once arrested, blacks are more likely to be remanded to custody awaiting trial rather than released on bail, which has a major effect on the likelihood of receiving a prison sentence at trial, all other factors being equal. Moreover, this racial effect holds even after controlling for all other legally relevant variables (e.g., seriousness of crime, previous criminal record, intention to contest the case at trial).

Furthermore, once tried, blacks are more likely to be sentenced to prison terms than whites (after controlling for all other legally relevant factors), but only when the severity of the crime is at an intermediate level. At this level, the black imprisonment rate of 68% was significantly higher than the white imprisonment rate of 60%. It is also important to point out that, compared to very high and very low crime seriousness, it is within the intermediate range of crime seriousness that courts have the greatest degree of discretion in how to weigh factors such as previous convictions and seriousness of the offense. The fact that racial bias is strongest in the intermediate range of crime seriousness is consistent with other research in England, the United States, and Israel showing that racial bias is most likely to occur when court and police officials are allowed the greatest degree of discretion (see Hood & Sparks, 1970; Sherer, 1990; Unnerver & Hembroff, 1988).

Once sentenced to prison and after controlling for all legally relevant variables, black males in Britain and, even more so, Asian males, are sentenced to significantly more prison time than white males. This disparity is especially acute when the defendants plead not guilty. Finally, there are also significant differences in the use of alternatives to prison such as discharge, fines, probation, community service, and suspended sentences (especially within the intermediate level of crime severity), with ethnic minorities being more likely to receive harsher alternatives to prison than whites (e.g., more suspended sentences rather than probation or community service).

## Second Law of Law

*When members of low-status groups are accused of acts of violence against members of high-status groups, the accused faces a particularly high risk of being found guilty and of suffering a particularly severe punishment. This is called the "out-of-place" principle.*

There are two reasons why we should expect this principle to hold. First, within hierarchically organized social systems, the lives and well-being of people from high-status groups will be considered to be more valuable than the lives and well-being of people from low-status groups. Because the lives of people from high-status groups are perceived as being more valuable, crimes against these lives will be judged as more serious. Second, and perhaps even more fundamentally, acts of violence against members of high-status groups by members of low-status groups will be considered more serious because such violence reaches beyond mere criminality and can be considered an act of political insubordination. When such insubordination takes violent forms, it becomes intolerable because it threatens the stability and integrity of the group-based system of social hierarchy as a whole.

There is a great deal of empirical evidence consistent with this second law of law or out-of-place principle. Data from the United States show that the out-of-place principle is particularly applicable in capital murder and sexual assault cases. There has been a consistent line of research showing that blacks who murder whites are much more likely to face the death penalty than blacks who murder blacks, whites who murder blacks, or whites who murder whites (Arkin, 1980; Baldus, Pulaski, & Woodsworth, 1983; Baldus, Woodsworth, & Pulaski, 1985; Bowers & Pierce, 1980; Gross & Mauro, 1989; Keil & Vito, 1989; Paternoster, 1984; Radelet, 1981).

In a major review of death penalty research, the General Accounting Office (GAO, 1990) conducted a meta-analysis of studies concerning race and the application of the death penalty. This report seemed to indicate that the race-of-victim/race-of-defendant combination most likely to lead to a death sentence was the case of blacks accused of killing whites. This race-of-victim/race-of-defendant effect appeared to be most influential at the early stages of the criminal justice process, when prosecutors were more likely to bring capital charges and refuse to plea bargain in the case of blacks accused of murdering whites.

The magnitude of this early stage race-of-victim/race-of-defendant effect is clearly demonstrated in a death penalty study by Paternoster (1983). In this study of prosecutorial decisions in South Carolina, Paternoster found that when blacks were accused of killing whites, prosecutors were 40 times more likely to request the death penalty than when blacks were accused of killing other blacks.

The major role that early prosecutorial decisions play in the racial disparity for death penalty outcomes is further supported by more recent studies. In 1995, Sorensen and Wallace examined the issue of racial disparity in Missouri's capital punishment system between 1977 and 1991 using data from the Supplemental Homicide Reports and trial judge reports. Consistent with the bulk of data in this area, their findings suggested that when blacks were accused of killing whites, prosecutors were much more likely to charge black defendants with capital murder and to proceed to penalty trial in convicted cases. In addition, these racial disparities, which began at the earliest stage in the criminal justice process, were not rectified during sentencing (Sorensen & Wallace, 1995).

As alluded previously, the out-of-place principle also appears to apply to sexual assault cases as well. For example, LaFree (1989) found that black men who sexually assaulted white women were charged with more serious offenses and were sentenced to longer prison terms than all other race-of-victim/race-of-perpetrator combinations. It is also noteworthy that the least severe sanctions were applied in cases of black men sexually assaulting black women. These conclusions were further substantiated by Walsh (1987), who found that black males accused of sexual assault against white females received relatively severe sanctions, whereas males accused of sexual assault against black females received relatively mild sanctions. Spohn's (1994) more recent study confirmed these general findings, but her study also showed that, somewhat surprisingly, these interactive effects of victim-race/perpetrator-race appeared to be restricted to crimes involving homicide and sexual assault, and did not hold true for other felonies such as assault and robbery. This pattern of institutional discrimination in sexual assault cases is congruent with Pratto's (1996) social dominance theory analysis of the intersection between sexual inequality and group-based inequality.

Consistent with what social dominance theory and other group conflict models would expect, empirical evidence shows that the out-of-place principle is generalizable beyond the United States. For example, Sobral, Arce, and

Farina (1989) reviewed research conducted since 1952 on the psychosocial aspects of criminal sentencing in both Spain and the United States. This review found the same type of interaction between defendant and victim status, as measured by status indexes such as racial, economic, and occupational status.

## Third Law of Law

*The level of social dominance orientation among hierarchy-enhancing people of the criminal justice system will be relatively high, whereas the level of social dominance orientation among hierarchy-attenuating people of the criminal justice system will be relatively low.*[11]

Because we have assumed that the security apparatus and criminal justice system are particularly important as hierarchy-enhancing social institutions, there is then reason to expect that such institutions will tend to recruit personnel who are well-suited to their hierarchy-enhancing social roles. Among other things, such personnel should have particularly high levels of SDO. As we will recall, SDO is defined as the degree to which one supports a group-based system of social hierarchy. Social dominance theory would expect that the higher one's SDO, the more one wishes to maintain the integrity of the hierarchical social system, and thus the more likely one is to join hierarchy-enhancing social institutions. Similarly, the extent to which any component of the broad criminal justice system functions in a hierarchy-attenuating fashion, we should expect that these hierarchy-attenuating institutions will also recruit personnel who are well-suited to their social roles. Among other things, this implies that such personnel should have particularly low levels of SDO, compared with other members of the social system. In other words, the social orientations of personnel should tend to match the social functions these personnel serve.

To explore these predictions, our research team assessed levels of social dominance orientation among four different groups: (a) officers in the Los Angeles Police Department (i.e., hierarchy enhancers), (b) members of the Los Angeles County Public Defenders' Office (i.e., hierarchy attenuators), (c) adults called for jury duty in Los Angeles County, and (d) UCLA undergraduates (for specific details of the sampling, see Sidanius, Liu, Pratto, & Shaw, 1994).

We expected that the hierarchy enhancers (e.g., police officers) would have significantly higher levels of social dominance orientation than all other

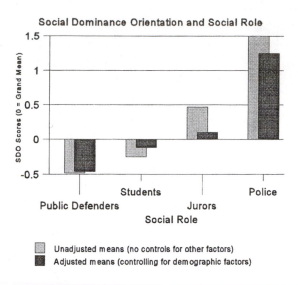

**Figure 6.5.** Social Dominance Orientation as a Function of Social Role
NOTE: The adjusted means are explained in the text.

categories (i.e., jurors, students, and public defenders), and that the hierarchy attenuators (e.g., public defenders) would have significantly lower SDO scores than all other categories. Inspection of the unadjusted means on SDO for each social role supported our expectations regarding both police officers and public defenders (see Figure 6.5).[12] As shown in Figure 6.5, police officers had significantly higher SDO scores than all other groups, and public defenders had significantly lower SDO scores than all other groups. The only pair-wise group difference that was not statistically significant was between public defenders and university students.

Because research has shown SDO to be related to factors such as gender, ethnicity, age, education, and social class (see Sidanius, Pratto, & Bobo, 1994), it is possible that people in these different social roles might have differing levels of SDO simply due to these demographic factors. If, however, the assumptions of SDT are correct, we would expect that the police officers (i.e., hierarchy enhancers) should still have significantly higher SDO scores than the other groups, whereas public defenders should have significantly lower SDO scores than the other groups, even after controlling for these demographic factors. In addition, if the demographic controls are operating properly, we should no longer expect the university students and the jurors to differ in their mean levels of SDO, because age, educational level, and socioeconomic status should be the only factors differentiating university students from people in general (i.e., jurors). After controlling for the five factors (i.e., social class, age, education, gender, and ethnicity), the data showed that the difference in SDO between the jurors and the university students was no longer statistically significant. Even with these controls in place, however, police officers (i.e., hierarchy enhancers) still had significantly higher SDO scores than all other groups, and public defenders (i.e., hierarchy attenuators) had significantly lower SDO scores than all other groups, including the university students (see the adjusted means[13] in Figure 6.5).

Although these data are consistent with our third law of law, they do not identify the processes by which people with given SDO levels and associated attitudes are matched with given social roles. There are at least four different processes by which the personality and ideological characteristics of personnel could become compatible with the social roles these personnel are expected to perform: (a) self-selection of social roles compatible with one's specific personality and ideological characteristics; (b) institutional selection of individuals with particular personality and ideological profiles; (c) institutional socialization, or the process by which the personality-ideological characteristics of personnel are molded by the social roles they perform; and (d) differential attrition, where those with personality-ideological characteristics that do not match their social roles experience higher rates of attrition from these roles than those whose personality-ideological characteristics do match their social roles. Because the matching of personality-ideological characteristics and social roles is so important, there is reason to suspect that all four matching processes will be involved. We will now provide evidence demonstrating some of these processes.[14]

Using two samples of UCLA students, we have recently found evidence supporting the self-selection process. In one sample, we examined the correlation between social dominance orientation (SDO$_6$ Scale) and the perceived attractiveness of four hierarchy-enhancing careers (i.e., criminal prosecutor, police officer, FBI agent, and business executive) and four hierarchy-attenuating careers (i.e., public defender, civil rights lawyer, social worker, and human rights advocate) (see Sidanius, Pratto, Sinclair, & van Laar, 1996). Consistent with expectations, the data showed that the greater one's level of social dominance orientation, the more attractive hierarchy-enhancing careers were perceived to be. Similarly, the greater one's social dominance orientation, the less attractive hierarchy-attenuating careers were perceived to be.

Because some have argued that SDO is simply an index of political conservatism, we decided to make sure that SDO had relationships with perceived hierarchy-attenuating/hierarchy-enhancing career attractiveness over and above any possible effects of either socioeconomic status (SES) or political conservatism. To this end, all three variables were entered into multiple regression analyses to examine the unique effect of each predictor over and above the effect of the other two predictors. In all cases in which SDO showed any significant bivariate relationship with perceived career attractiveness, it maintained a significant relationship with career attractiveness, even when SES and political conservatism were considered. The single exception to this general pattern concerned the perceived attractiveness of being a government prosecutor. This variable, however, failed to be related not only to SDO, but to both SES and political conservatism as well.

Along similar lines, Pratto and her colleagues (Pratto, Stallworth, Sidanius, & Siers, 1997) have shown that even within given occupations (e.g., the police occupation), those attracted to more hierarchy-enhancing social roles were found to have higher SDO levels than those less attracted to such roles.

There is also some evidence consistent with the institutional socialization process. For example, Teahan (1975a) examined the attitudes of 97 white police officers from the time of their entrance into the police academy and over an 18-month period. As police training progressed, white officers became more ethnocentric and hostile toward blacks. In another study, Teahan (1975b) found the same increase in antiblack hostility among white police officers even in a training program ostensibly designed to increase racial understanding.

Not only is there evidence of increasing negative affect toward racial minorities among police officers, but there is also evidence that antiblack attitudes and behaviors are actually rewarded among police officers. For example, in a study of university campus police officers, Leitner and Sedlacek (1976) found that racial prejudice was positively and significantly associated with the officers' performance evaluations by their supervisors, even when a number of other factors were controlled. Similarly, follow-up studies of civilian complaints about police brutality reveal that such brutality complaints rarely make any difference in a police officer's career (see greater detail in the next section). Even more to the point, however, police officers who are accused of brutality are often rewarded by promotions within their departments (Christopher, 1991). Furthermore, evidence from a number of nations indicates that police officers are often rewarded rather than punished for acts of brutality and severity against members of low-status groups (see Chevigny, 1995).

### Fourth Law of Law

*The degree of negative sanctions against the security forces for abuses of power will tend to be exceedingly small, especially in cases of abuse against members of subordinate groups.*

Some empirical evidence for this principle can be found in the Warren Christopher report of 1991. This report was commissioned as a result of the beating of Rodney King by several members of the Los Angeles Police Department and, among other sources, used data taken from the complaint database of the LAPD (Christopher, 1991). The Christopher Commission examined the disposition of all allegations of excessive force or improper tactics leveled against the LAPD by members of the public between January 1986 and December 1990. There were 3,419 such cases, the overwhelming majority of which were not sustained (i.e., 96.8%); only 3% were sustained. Of those complaints found to have merit, only 7.6% of them resulted in the removal of the police officer involved. Putting all of this information together, we see that the probability of having an officer removed from the LAPD for complaints of excessive force or improper tactics is 0.00228, or essentially zero.

In addition, one must also keep in mind that these data, if anything, probably overestimate the degree of police accountability. Not only are members of subordinate groups reluctant to bring formal charges against police officers, but there is also some evidence that the police officers themselves will actively discourage and threaten those attempting to file such complaints (Chevigny, 1995). In other words, and consistent with the observations of former Los Angeles police officer Mark Fuhrman,[15] police officers are, for all intents and purposes, almost completely invulnerable to being fired for acts of brutality against citizens. Even more to the point, although the issue has not been put to rigorous empirical test, there is some evidence that the lack of accountability of the police is not restricted to Los Angeles or even the United States, but is generalizable across several different countries such as Brazil, Mexico, Argentina, and Jamaica (Chevigny, 1995). Other examples can be found in the death squad activities carried out with impunity in South Africa and Central and South America during the 1970s and 1980s (Hedges, 1994; McCuen, 1988; Pauw, 1991).

If this fourth law of law is correct, we would also expect that the probability of a police officer being fired will be even lower in cases where a member of an ethnic minority group brings a charge of brutality against a Euro-American officer.[16] This hypothesis is given greater credibility by the fact that a disproportionate amount of police violence is directed "downward" against members of subordinate social and ethnic groups (see Chevigny, 1995; Lefkowitz, 1975).

### Fifth Law of Law

*The greater the degree of social hierarchy, the greater the use of terror will be.*

Social dominance theory and other group conflict models (see also Scott, 1990) suggest that the consensual endorsement of hierarchy-enhancing ide-ologies (e.g., racism, classism) serves as one of the primary means by which group-based social hierarchies are maintained. Because, however, hierarchy-enhancing ideologies will rarely be perfectly consensual,[17] there will tend to be some residual ideological tension or ideological dissensuality within the social system (for a fuller discussion of the construct of dissensual ideology, see Sidanius, Levin, & Pratto, 1996; Sidanius, Pratto, Martin, & Stallworth, 1991). There is some reason to believe that the more hierarchically structured a system is, the more difficult it will be to keep it in place by the use of ideological consensus alone: The use of terror will also be necessary.

Because SDT and other group dominance theories tend to look at the death penalty as one form of state-sponsored terrorism, we tested this idea by studying the use of the death penalty as a function of the degree of group-based social hierarchy both in the United States and across several different coun-tries (Mitchell & Sidanius, 1995). In the U.S. case, we used the 50 states of the United States as the units of analysis. We examined the number of prisoners executed in each state as a function of nine variables: (a) degree of violent crime in each state, (b) political conservatism of the state, (c) per capita income, (d) population size, (e) population density, (f) educational level of the state, (g) proportion of the state's population that was white, (h) proportion of whites murdered in the state, and (i) degree of social hierarchy within the state.

We expected that even after controlling for other demographic and crimi-nality differences between the states, we should find that those states that were more hierarchically structured had a greater propensity to use capital punish-ment. The results of multiple regression analyses showed that only three of the nine variables had statistically significant and unique effects on a state's use of the death penalty. In order of the magnitude of their effects, these variables were the following: (a) the degree of violent crime within the state, (b) the degree of group-based social hierarchy within the state, and (c) the degree of political conservatism in the state.[18]

The international generalizability of this social hierarchy effect was examined by studying both whether or not and the degree to which different countries used the death penalty. Mitchell and Sidanius (1995) analyzed the 147 countries around the world for which there was sufficient information about the use of capital punishment. They examined the effect of (a) social hierarchy (defined by the degree of economic inequality within the country) on a country's use of the death penalty, while simultaneously controlling for the possible effects of (b) the murder rate within the country, (c) the size of the government, (d) the size of the nation, (e) the nation's educational level, (f) the gross national product, and (g) the population size.

The results of a logistic regression analysis revealed that whether or not a country used capital punishment was dependent on only two of the seven independent variables named previously: (a) the murder rate within the country and, more important, (b) the level of social hierarchy within the country. Not only was the level of social hierarchy an independent contributor to whether or not a nation used the death penalty, but also, consistent with the U.S. data, separate analysis of death penalty frequency showed that the degree of social hierarchy was uniquely related to the degree to which nations used the death penalty as well. There is also some evidence that the overall level of police brutality and terror will be a function of the degree to which societies are hierarchically organized (see Chevigny, 1995, p. 249).

## ■ Criminal Activity and Self-Handicapping Behavior

Although the first five laws of law offer plausible explanations as to why members of low-status groups will be disproportionately arrested, imprisoned, and executed by the criminal justice system, they offer far from a complete picture. SDT also suggests that the relative social position of subordinate groups is not only a function of oppression at the hands of dominant groups, but also a function of the self-destructive and self-handicapping[19] behaviors of people within subordinate groups as well. In other words, social hierarchy is not simply the result of direct and indirect forms of oppression from above, but also the result of cooperation from below (see Sidanius, 1993).

Criminal justice data from both the United States and Great Britain indicate that, on the whole, only about 22% of the racial disparity in the prison population can be attributed to the discriminatory behavior of the criminal justice system or its agents. This implies that approximately 78% of the overrepresentation of minority groups in prisons is a function of higher rates and more serious forms of criminal behavior among these groups.[20] At least in the United States, however, the degree to which the criminal justice system functions in a discriminatory fashion varies radically as a function of the type of criminality involved. Recent U.S. data seem to indicate that for drug offenses, approximately 50% of the racial disparity in imprisonment can be explained by the discriminatory behavior of the criminal justice system (Blumstein, 1993).

Just as discrimination within the criminal justice system against members of subordinate groups appears widespread, so does the observation that members of subordinate groups actually commit a disproportionate number of criminal acts. This latter phenomenon also appears to be quite general, occurring among the Maori of New Zealand (Older, 1984), Aborigines in Australia (Sanson-Fisher, 1978), Native Americans in the United States (Young, 1993), Native Americans in Canada (Moyer, 1992), Native Algerians under the French occupation (Fanon, 1963), Caribbean immigrants in England (Hood & Cordovil, 1992), the Burakumin and Koreans of Japan (Kristof, 1995), foreign immigrants in The Netherlands (Junger & Polder, 1992), the Lapps of Finland (Poikalainen et al., 1992), Arabs of Israel (Sherer, 1990), and African Americans in the United States (Mauer & Huling, 1995).

## ■ Criminality and Social Status—The "Why" Question

The data showing that members of subordinate groups commit crimes at higher rates than members of dominant groups is quite clear and irrefutable. The more difficult question is "Why?" There are two broad approaches to answering this question, the inherency approach and the situational or contingency approach.

### The Inherency Approach

Proponents of the inherency paradigm would attribute the relatively high criminality rates among subordinate groups to certain "inherent" characteristics that are disproportionately found within these groups, including such things as lower impulse control and lower intelligence. One recent example of an inherency explanation that has become increasingly popular in the United States can be found in the book *The Bell Curve* (Herrnstein & Murray, 1994). The authors of this volume would argue that the high overlap between low group status and criminality is due to the relative inability of members of low-status groups to adjust to the increasingly complex demands of postindustrial society. In the "information economy," a successful or even viable lifestyle will increasingly depend on one's intellectual acumen and the ability to learn complex skills. According to supporters of this version of the inherency perspective, these are exactly the kinds of intellectual abilities in which the poor and certain ethnic minorities (e.g., blacks) suffer an inherent disadvantage. The fact that explanations of this type clearly function to reinforce group-based social inequality does not automatically imply that they are incorrect. There is, however, good reason to suspect that explanations of this type are based on a number of faulty interpretations of the empirical evidence, which we will not spend time debating here (see Fraser, 1995).

## The Situational Approach

Rather than regarding high criminality as inherent to individuals from certain races, ethnicities, or social classes, various models within the general situational approach consider the structural, situational, and psychosocial conditions under which subordinates live, and emphasize the effects of these environmental conditions on criminal behavior. Although the inherency and situational approaches differ in many ways, it is instructive to note the one important feature they have in common. Both approaches assume that a major reason for the differential rates of criminality between members of high- and low-status groups is their differential command of the skills and resources necessary for success within the "legal" economy. In the postindustrial age, one of the most important general assets to have, besides access to accumulated financial capital, is access to human capital such as a good education. The major point of contention between the inherency and situational approaches actually hinges on the explanation as to why members of low-status groups are so poorly educated and possess such relatively low human capital. Within the situational approach, there are at least six nonmutually exclusive answers to this question.

The first major answer might be labeled a "resource accessibility" explanation. People in subordinate groups tend to live in areas that are economically depressed, where there are (a) relatively few socially acceptable jobs paying a living wage (*Kids Count in Michigan 1995 Data Book,* 1995, p. 6), (b) substandard educational opportunities (see, e.g., Cobb & Hops, 1973; Love & Bachara, 1975; Senna, Rathus, & Seigel, 1974), and (c) more obstacles to getting business loans and business experience from one's social network. There is some indication that the higher rate of criminality within subordinate communities is, in part, a response to these economic and social realities. For example, a recent study by the RAND Corporation (Reuter, MacCoun, & Murphy, 1990) found that approximately two thirds of the young black males arrested for drug trafficking in Washington, D.C., had been employed at the time of their arrest, mostly in low-paying jobs that provided a median income of $800 a month, which is less than a living wage in Washington, D.C., and most other large U.S. cities. Drug dealing had become a supplementary source of income for these young men, providing a median income of $2,000 a month for daily traders.

The second major explanation within the general situational approach can be labeled the "culture of subordination" model. This model suggests that people within subordinate groups have come to develop cultural values and interaction patterns that make it difficult for them to adequately realize and exploit their human potential. This culture of subordination manifests itself in several forms of self-handicapping behaviors such as high rates of out-of-wedlock births, lower motivation for school achievement, higher rates of drug abuse (e.g., cigarette, cocaine, and alcohol abuse), higher rates of child and spousal abuse, and a greater tendency to use extreme violence in the resolution of disputes (see, e.g., Moynihan, 1967). The model proposes that these self-handicapping behaviors are the result of the self-loathing and inner-directed aggression that result from severe and long-standing oppression and subordination.

A third and closely related explanation within the situational approach could be called the "false consciousness" or role-playing model. This model posits that consensual belief systems within hierarchically organized societies include the notion that subordinates are comparatively and inherently inferior, dangerous, and incompetent. Because these consensual ideas are shared by dominants and subordinates alike, these negative images are incorporated into the self-images and self-definitions of subordinates. Once part of the self-image, these negative images of the self serve as behavioral schemas producing self-fulfilling prophecies. There are some interesting empirical data consistent with this thesis. For example, it has been shown that people would rather seek out negative information about themselves that is consensually held, than positive information about themselves that is not consensually held (see, e.g., Swann & Read, 1981a, 1981b). This line of research would lead one to expect that subordinates will also actually behave so as to confirm consensually held negative stereotypes about themselves, even though these behaviors will lead to suboptimal results. This pattern of behavior is considered self-handicapping.

The fourth model within the general situational family might be titled the "group solidarity model." This perspective argues that among, for example, black children from inner-city neighborhoods, high academic achievement will be interpreted as "trying to act white," an act of in-group disloyalty. John Ogbu (1991, 1994), a major proponent of this approach, suggests that academic achievement will be discouraged not only by peers, but also in more subtle ways by family members. A second component of this general approach is the idea that lack of investment in academic success is also a form of out-group resistance and defiance. This defiance is directed against both teachers and school authorities, who are disproportionately members of the dominant group, and whom the subordinate students regard with a certain degree of suspicion and mistrust.

A fifth explanation concerns the effects of the physical environment on criminal behavior. Recent evidence suggests that exposure to lead may be the single most important cause of criminality, outweighing the effects of any other social or economic factor. As a case in point, 300 boys from Pittsburgh's inner city were tested for lifetime exposure to lead. Those with above-average levels of lead were found to be more aggressive and delinquent, according to teacher, parent, and self-evaluations. Even small doses of lead were associated with the antisocial and delinquent behaviors of youths (e.g., vandalism, arson, theft, and fighting) that precede more violent adult criminality. Moreover, the effects of lead were found to be independent of race, suggesting that the relatively high criminality rates among African American males do not result from a greater predisposition toward crime, as inherency theorists would argue, but rather from the fact that pollutants such as lead tend to accumulate in residential areas populated predominantly by blacks (Needleman, Riess, Tobin, Biesecker, & Greenhouse, 1996). It should be noted, however, that even if this "lead poisoning" hypothesis is ultimately found to be as important as the data now suggest, this fact is still not independent of the dynamics of social hierarchy. Because of their relative lack of power, members of subordinate groups are more likely to be exposed to environmental hazards of all sorts, even when the deleterious effects of these environmental hazards are well-known. Some have referred to this phenomenon as "environmental racism."

Finally, there is reason to suspect that the unusually high rates of imprisonment themselves further contribute to the deterioration of conditions within low-status communities. For example, the 1995 Sentencing Project has pointed out that the extremely high incarceration rate of African American males not only removes "criminals" from the street, but also has a number of damaging, communitywide effects (Mauer & Huling, 1995). Incarceration undermines black males' earning potential because the prison system fails to seriously increase their educational skills and their subsequent ability to earn legal, living wages on release. Their inability to earn livings then makes them less attractive as marriage partners and less able to provide for the children that they father.

Therefore, from a general situational perspective, the initial causes of the relatively high levels of criminality among males in subordinate communities are to be found in the extreme levels of oppression suffered by these communities. Initially brought on by situational factors, it can be argued that criminality subsequently becomes an integral part of the culture and the general conditions of life within subordinate communities. As a result, self-handicapping behaviors become the means by which subordinate groups actually participate in and contribute to their own continued subordination, the continuation of group stereotypes, and the resultant perpetuation of the system of group-based social hierarchy. Although there is some empirical data to suggest that all of the situational explanations mentioned previously contribute to the higher rates of self-handicapping criminality among members of subordinate groups, there is not yet enough empirical evidence to rank-order them by relative importance or plausibility. Only further research will enable us to do this.

How would changes in the levels of institutional discrimination and self-handicapping behavior affect each other and the level of social hierarchy? In answering this question, social dominance theorists would suggest that because individual discrimination, institutional discrimination, institutional terror, and self-handicapping behavior are all interacting and mutually reinforcing components of the same social system, any major change in one of these components will most likely produce changes in other components. Thus, for example, if the average level of self-handicapping behavior among African Americans were to suddenly plummet, and let's say 70% of all African Americans were to suddenly earn admission to elite universities, graduate at or near the top of their classes, and become leading business persons in society, this change would most certainly produce changes in other hierarchical components of the social system. Among other things, this new reality would probably lead to an attenuation of the degree of institutional discrimination and terror directed against African Americans.

From a social dominance perspective, however, there are at least two important points to keep in mind. First, it is exactly because the various hierarchical components are interconnected and codependent that makes major change in any one of them so difficult. A change in one component will necessarily mean a change in many others as well. Second, even if a subordinate group were to effect a substantial positive change in its circumstances, this would by no means imply the end of group-based social inequality and institutional terror, or even its attenuation. Social dominance theory would suggest that as African Americans moved up in the hierarchical structure of U.S. society, they would only begin to adopt derogatory attitudes toward groups below them, and their place on the bottom of this hierarchy would simply be taken by some other social group (e.g., illegal immigrants). We would suggest that this is one of the reasons why efforts at social egalitarianism almost always end in failure (e.g., see the French, Russian, Mexican, and Cambodian revolutions and the U.S. civil rights movement as examples). On the other hand, we are also clearly not suggesting that group-based social hierarchies cannot be attenuated, for there are too many examples of some societies being a great deal more egalitarian than others (e.g., Sweden vs. Saudi Arabia). We have, however, yet to fully understand the precise conditions under which relatively egalitarian societies can be created and maintained.

## ■ Summary and Conclusion

Rather than viewing institutional discrimination within the criminal justice system and self-handicapping behavior as two independent processes, we would argue that they are better seen as interdependent and mutually reinforcing mechanisms. The fact that members of subordinate groups are systematically discriminated against helps create the general social conditions (e.g., poor academic skills) under which higher rates of criminality flourish within subordinate communities. Subsequently, the fact that members of subordinate communities are disproportionately involved in criminal behavior helps to feed the group-based stereotypes of inherent criminality, which, in turn, contribute to continued discrimination within the criminal justice system and other social institutions and the continued relative impoverishment of these communities. The net result of these mutually reinforcing processes is that the overall nature of the group-based social hierarchy is reinforced and stabilized.

At the same time, however, this does not imply that any given subordinate group will always remain subordinant, behave in self-handicapping ways, and suffer from institutional discrimination. There are many examples of given groups changing their relative positions within the social structure, and subsequently ceasing to engage in self-handicapping behaviors and no longer suffering oppression at the hands of the justice system.[21] Although the degree and precise nature of group-based hierarchies are dynamic and forever changing, social dominance theorists argue that what does not appear to change is the existence of group-based social hierarchy itself. It is further suggested that as long as social systems are structured as group-based social hierarchies, there will always be some group that is both terrorized by the justice system and also cooperatively engages in self-handicapping behavior. Although equal justice, regardless of group membership, is a noble and worthy goal for those with democratic values, social dominance theory maintains that there is no strong empirical nor theoretical reason to expect that this goal will ever be achieved as long as human societies remain hierarchically structured.

# Appendix

## *SDO$_6$ Scale*

### ■ Instructions

Below is a series of statements with which you may either agree or disagree. For each statement, please indicate the degree of your agreement-disagreement by *circling* the appropriate number from "1" to "7." Please remember that your first responses are usually the most accurate.

| | Strongly Disagree | | | | | | Strongly Agree |
|---|---|---|---|---|---|---|---|
| 1. Some groups of people are just more worthy than others. | 1 | 2 | 3 | 4 | 5 | 6 | 7 |
| 2. In getting what your group wants, it is sometimes necessary to use force against other groups. | 1 | 2 | 3 | 4 | 5 | 6 | 7 |
| 3. Superior groups should dominate inferior groups. | 1 | 2 | 3 | 4 | 5 | 6 | 7 |
| 4. To get ahead in life, it is sometimes necessary to step on other groups. | 1 | 2 | 3 | 4 | 5 | 6 | 7 |
| 5. If certain groups of people stayed in their place, we would have fewer problems. | 1 | 2 | 3 | 4 | 5 | 6 | 7 |
| 6. It's probably a good thing that certain groups are at the top and other groups are at the bottom. | 1 | 2 | 3 | 4 | 5 | 6 | 7 |
| 7. Inferior groups should stay in their place. | 1 | 2 | 3 | 4 | 5 | 6 | 7 |
| 8. Sometimes other groups must be kept in their place. | 1 | 2 | 3 | 4 | 5 | 6 | 7 |
| 9. It would be good if all groups could be equal. | 1 | 2 | 3 | 4 | 5 | 6 | 7 |
| 10. Group equality should be our ideal. | 1 | 2 | 3 | 4 | 5 | 6 | 7 |
| 11. All groups should be given an equal chance in life. | 1 | 2 | 3 | 4 | 5 | 6 | 7 |
| 12. We should do what we can to equalize conditions for different groups. | 1 | 2 | 3 | 4 | 5 | 6 | 7 |
| 13. Increased social equality. | 1 | 2 | 3 | 4 | 5 | 6 | 7 |
| 14. We would have fewer problems if we treated different groups more equally. | 1 | 2 | 3 | 4 | 5 | 6 | 7 |
| 15. We should strive to make incomes more equal. | 1 | 2 | 3 | 4 | 5 | 6 | 7 |
| 16. No one group should dominate in society. | 1 | 2 | 3 | 4 | 5 | 6 | 7 |

Note to users: Items 9-16 should be reverse coded.

# ■ Notes

1. The "three-strikes" law stipulates that anyone convicted of three felonies is subject to a mandatory prison sentence of 25 years to life.

2. By putting the term "race" in quotation marks, we are implying that the term "race" does not refer to natural categories, but rather to socially constructed categories, the exact meanings and definitions of which will vary across different societies and historical time periods.

3. The high validity and reliability of the $SDO_6$ Scale have been documented by Pratto et al. (1994). It is also important to note that SDO is both conceptually and empirically distinguishable from constructs such as personal dominance, political conservatism, authoritarianism, and racism (see Pratto et al., 1994).

4. Although the laws of law are thought to be applicable cross culturally, a disproportionate amount of the empirical work we will cite is derived from U.S. studies because most of the work in this area is conducted in the United States. These laws of law are not listed in the order of their importance, but rather in the order in which they were incorporated into social dominance theory.

5. The stages during which these differences will manifest themselves include the following: likelihood of arrest (Blumstein, 1982; Bourg & Stock, 1994; Hawkins & Jones, 1989; Hepburn, 1978; Holcomb & Ahr, 1988; Hollinger, 1984; Petersen, Schwirian, & Bleda, 1977; Sarri, 1986; Schellenberg, Wasylenki, Webster, & Goering, 1992; Smith, Visher, & Davisdon, 1984; Thornberry, 1973; Visher, 1983; Weisz, Martin, Walter, & Fernandez, 1991), severity of charges filed (Bradmiller & Walters, 1985; Bourg & Stock, 1994; Sorensen & Wallace, 1995; Stewart, 1985), likelihood of plea bargain offered (Sarri, 1986), likelihood of conviction (Bernard, 1979; Cohen & Peterson, 1981; Kelley, 1976; Lichtenstein, 1982; Lipton, 1983; Mazzella & Feingold, 1994; Poulson, 1990; Wilbanks, 1988), likelihood of probation (Austin, 1985; Petersen & Friday, 1975), severity of sentence imposed (Austin, 1985; Kelley, 1976; Lichtenstein, 1982; Osborne & Rappaport, 1985; Pruitt & Wilson, 1983; Sidanius, 1988; Stewart, 1980, 1985; Sweeney & Haney, 1992; Thornberry, 1973; Towers, McGinley, & Pasewark, 1992), and likelihood of early parole (Dunwoody & Frank, 1994; Myers, 1985).

6. Exactly why racial bias is most likely to occur at earlier rather than later stages of the criminal justice process is not precisely understood as yet. Among other reasons, however, we strongly suspect that the personal values of criminal justice personnel and decision makers contribute to this effect. There is a good deal of evidence indicating that racial prejudice decreases with increasing levels of formal education (see, e.g., Ekehammar, Nelson, & Sidanius, 1987; Sidanius et al., 1991; Wagner & Zick, 1995). Because police officers have lower levels of education than judges, there is some reason to expect that police officers will also exhibit greater levels of racial discrimination than judges, everything else being equal. Racial bias is more likely to occur at the earlier stages of the criminal justice process because police officers are more involved at these stages.

7. On the other hand, there is some evidence of high rates of violence associated with the trafficking of crack cocaine. The U.S. Sentencing Commission also concluded, however, that this violence did not appear to have any inherent connection with the nature of crack per se, but rather with the establishment of a new drug market and the associated competition for market share (see U.S. Sentencing Commission, 1995, pp. 108, 202-203).

8. The National Institute on Drug Abuse annually conducts the National Household Survey on Drug Abuse (NHSDA). The NHSDA is a self-report survey that produces estimates of drug usage among household members aged 12 years and older within the contiguous United States. The 1991 NHSDA found that of those who used powder cocaine, 75% were white and only 25% were black or Latino. On the other hand, of those who used crack cocaine, 52% were white and 48% were either black or Latino. Because the NHSDA is based on self-reported drug usage,

however, we cannot be absolutely sure that different ethnic groups are giving accurate answers to the same degree.

9. Note that there was a slight exception to this general trend in that the conviction rate for Latinos was slightly lower than their actual use rate.

10. These data are for 1992 or 1993, depending on the most recent data available. The data are somewhat limited, however, in that surveys were not administered to the homeless, prisoners, or those residing in residential drug treatment centers. Because of this, very low-income African Americans are probably somewhat underrepresented in these data.

11. Note that this law is a revision of the Third Law of Law as described in Sidanius, 1993.

12. Unadjusted means are average SDO scores, not controlling for the effects of any other factors.

13. Adjusted means are average SDO scores, controlling for the effects of the demographic factors.

14. For an informative discussion of the psychology of police torturers and others engaged in other forms of police brutality, see Crelinsten, 1995.

15. Mark Fuhrman was a key prosecution witness in the O. J. Simpson murder trial.

16. We have tried, unsuccessfully, to get the LAPD to release the data bearing on this point.

17. Typically, the degree to which people in subordinate groups endorse hierarchy-enhancing ideologies is likely to be somewhat smaller than the degree to which people in dominant groups endorse these ideologies.

18. Social hierarchy was operationalized by the use of three indicators: (a) class hierarchy (or the amount of economic inequality within each state), (b) caste hierarchy (the degree of economic inequality between blacks and whites and the degree to which blacks were underrepresented in the state legislature), and (c) membership in the old Confederacy (whether or not the state was part of the states of the old Confederacy). Because it is well known that southern states have a higher rate of execution than other parts of the United States (Mitchell & Sidanius, 1995), one might argue that these results are an artifact of the fact that we included "old Confederacy" as part of our definition of "social hierarchy." We would argue, however, that the South's tendency to put people to death is not an accident, but a result of the fact that this part of the United States has a legacy of being, by far, the most hierarchically structured portion of the nation, as manifested in its practice of chattel slavery. Nonetheless, to demonstrate that these results were not merely an artifact of membership in the southern Confederacy, we reanalyzed the data by removing the old Confederacy factor from our definition of "social hierarchy." The new results showed that the more restrictive index of "social hierarchy" still had a statistically significant and relatively powerful independent effect on the use of capital punishment.

19. We do not use the term *self-handicapping* in the manner used by Jones and his associates (see, e.g., Jones & Berglas, 1978). By the term "self-handicapping," Jones and his associates described the phenomenon where underachievement and other personal failures are attributed to external causes (e.g., alcohol use) rather than to internal causes (e.g., lack of ability). These strategies protect the self-image of those with low self-esteem. We use the term "self-handicapping behavior" to simply describe suboptimal behaviors, regardless of the possible self-esteem protecting function these behaviors might be serving.

20. The data seem to indicate that this discriminatory effect appears to be slightly higher in the United States (24%; see Blumstein, 1993) than in Great Britain (20%; see Hood & Cordovil, 1992).

21. Another clear U.S. example of this is the disproportionate amount of criminal behavior among Irish immigrants to the United States starting in the mid-1850s. As later immigrants to the United States began to occupy the bottom ranks of the white ethnic hierarchy and the relative status of the Irish improved, these later immigrants also became disproportionately involved in criminal behavior (see Lupsha, 1986).

# PART II

## The Response

# 7

# Racism and Self-Esteem

*Jennifer Crocker*
*Diane Quinn*

acial prejudice and discrimination are pervasive features of U.S. society. Several of the chapters in this volume document the sometimes subtle and sometimes blatant nature of racial prejudice. The focus of this chapter is on the effects of racial prejudice on the self-esteem of members of stereotyped or stigmatized groups. We will argue that, contrary to popular and established psychological wisdom, racism does not always take a toll on the self-esteem of its targets. We will consider both situational and personal factors that may protect self-esteem for the targets of racism. Specifically, we will argue that when the situation permits the targets of racism to attribute the negative events they experience to prejudice, rather than to their own shortcomings, their self-esteem will be protected. Furthermore, those individuals whose self-esteem is relatively independent, or noncontingent on approval and regard from others, will have self-esteem that is not harmed by racism.

Prejudice and discrimination have many pernicious effects on stereotyped individuals, of course, and our focus on their effects on self-esteem is not meant to imply that self-esteem is the only, or even the most important consequence of prejudice on it targets. Nonetheless, we believe that the effects of racism on self-esteem are interesting and important for several reasons. First, self-esteem is a central aspect of the subjective experience and quality of life. Self-esteem is powerfully related to variables that influence the affective tone of one's daily experience, with high self-esteem individuals

AUTHORS' NOTE: Preparation of this chapter was supported by National Science Foundation grant BNS to Jennifer Crocker.

reporting, for example, more positive affect (Pelham & Swann, 1989), more life satisfaction (Diener, 1984; Myers & Diener, 1995), less hopelessness (Crocker, Luhtanen, Blaine, & Broadnax, 1994), and fewer depressive symptoms (e.g., Crandall, 1973) than individuals who are low in self-esteem. Indeed, in a review of the literature, Diener (1984) concluded that self-esteem is the strongest predictor of life satisfaction in the United States, outstripping all demographic and objective outcomes, such as age, income, education, physical health, and marital status, and all other psychological variables. Second, effects of racism on self-esteem represent one means by which individuals who are devalued by others may internalize that devaluation, by coming to believe that they are worthless, or less deserving than others. Thus, effects of racism on self-esteem may represent a particularly pernicious consequence of racism because the targets of racism may eventually participate in their own devaluation.

To most people who are not the targets of racial prejudice, it seems obvious that racial prejudice must take a toll on the self-esteem of its targets. How could people endure the knowledge that their social identity is devalued by others, confront negative stereotypes about their group, and face prejudice and discrimination without being low in self-regard? This assumption that racial prejudice leads to low self-esteem is one that is shared by many psychologists, and predicted by several social psychological theories. For example, the "looking glass self" hypothesis (Cooley, 1956; Mead, 1934) argues that people develop a sense of themselves from how they are regarded by other people. Thus, self-worth is dependent on the regard of specific others in one's life and on how other people in general regard one. This theory would suggest that because targets of racial prejudice know that many other people have negative views of them, they will incorporate these negative views into their self-concepts and consequently have lowered self-esteem.

The idea that targets of prejudice have low self-esteem has been taken for granted by many social scientists. For example, Cartwright (1950) argued that "The group to which a person belongs serves as primary determinants of his self-esteem. To a considerable extent, personal feelings of worth depend on the social evaluation of the group with which a person is identified. Self-hatred and feelings of worthlessness tend to arise from membership in underprivileged or outcast groups" (p. 440). Erik Erikson (1956) claimed that "there is ample evidence of inferiority feelings and of morbid self-hate in all minority groups" (p. 155). Gordon Allport (1954) recognized that responses to oppression vary widely, but suggested that a common consequence was low self-esteem: "Group oppression may destroy the integrity of the ego entirely, and reverse its normal pride, and create a groveling self-image" (p. 152).

Surprisingly, however, empirical research contradicts the view that racial prejudice is always internalized in the targets of prejudice as low self-esteem. Crocker and Major (1989) reviewed studies comparing the self-esteem of a wide variety of stigmatized groups and concluded: "In short, this research, conducted over a time span of more than 20 years, leads to the surprising conclusion that prejudice against members of stigmatized or oppressed groups generally does not result in lowered self-esteem for members of those groups. These findings generalize across a variety of stigmatizing conditions, a variety of measures of global self-esteem, and a wide range of subject populations, from adolescents to college students to adults" (p. 611). Research on racial and ethnic minorities, in particular, indicates that being a target of prejudice does not necessarily result in low self-esteem. Many studies have found that African Americans on average have levels of self-esteem that are equal to or higher than that of Americans of European descent (see Hoelter, 1983; Porter & Washington, 1979, for reviews). Similar findings have been reported for Americans of Mexican descent (Jensen, White, & Galliher, 1982). Yet, some ethnic groups do seem to be vulnerable to low self-esteem. Of ethnic minorities in the United States, Asian Americans appear to be most susceptible to low self-esteem, although cultural differences in self-report styles may account for some of this effect (e.g., Crocker et al., 1994).

Thus, despite widespread popular belief and compelling social psychological theory, research suggests that targets of racial prejudice do not inevitably internalize negative views of themselves, and suffer from low self-esteem. The more interesting question, then, is when and how the targets of racial prejudice maintain their self-worth in the face of persistent devaluation. We will consider first how a feature of the situation—attributional ambiguity—can protect self-esteem from racism. We then turn to a characteristic of people—independent self-esteem—that can protect self-esteem from racism.

## ■ Attributional Ambiguity

There are a variety of ways that the self-esteem of the targets of prejudice may be protected (Crocker & Major, 1989; Steele, 1992). For example, individuals who are disadvantaged may protect their self-esteem by comparing themselves only with similarly disadvantaged individuals (Crocker &

Major, 1989; Major, 1987, 1994). Alternatively, the targets of prejudice may devalue the importance of domains in which they fare poorly relative to others (Crocker & Major, 1989; Steele, 1992). In this chapter, we will focus on a third reason the targets of prejudice do not always, or even usually, have low self-esteem: attributional ambiguity.

Underlying the attributional ambiguity notion is the idea that the consequences of being disadvantaged, discriminated against, and the target of prejudice depends on the meaning of those experiences to the individual. One aspect of this meaning concerns one's understanding of the causes of one's disadvantaged status, or negative events in one's life. This idea is consistent with a great deal of research and theory on emotions indicating that emotional reactions to events are influenced by one's interpretations of those events. Negative events, in particular, may have negative consequences for mood and self-esteem if they are explained as due to internal causes, such as one's own shortcomings, but will not have such negative consequences when they are attributed to external causes, such as other people, or circumstances (e.g., Weiner, 1985).

For people who belong to groups that are sometimes the targets of prejudice, the causes of negative outcomes may often be unclear. On one hand, negative outcomes received from others could be due to one's lack of merit, inferior qualifications, poor performance, or other shortcomings. Alternatively, they could be due to prejudice and discrimination based on one's ethnic or racial identity. Uncertainty regarding whether events happen because of prejudice, or because one deserves them, has been called "attributional ambiguity" by Crocker and Major (1989; Major & Crocker, 1993). This uncertainty, or attributional ambiguity, may protect the self-esteem of stigmatized individuals, because it provides an external attribution for negative events. For people who are targets of prejudice and discrimination, knowing that one possible cause of negative outcomes is the prejudice of other people, rather than one's own faults or shortcomings, may protect self-esteem. Thus, differences in self-esteem among stigmatized groups, for example between African Americans and Asian Americans, as well as the differences among individuals who belong to the same group, may be explained in part by the attributions or explanations that they generate for the negative outcomes they experience.

Less obviously, positive outcomes may also be attributionally ambiguous for the stigmatized. Positive outcomes determined by others can reflect one's merit. Indeed, the personal significance of positive outcomes might even be augmented for the stigmatized (Kelley, 1972), because they occurred despite one's devalued social identity. Alternatively, positive outcomes could be discounted if the stigmatized believed they were obtained because of membership in a stigmatized group. Why would the stigmatized have this suspicion? A number of researchers have found that responses toward the stigmatized are sometimes more positive than responses to the nonstigmatized. These exaggerated positive responses may be due to genuine feelings of admiration and respect (Carver, Glass, & Katz, 1977); ambivalence, which amplifies both positive and negative responses (Katz, 1981; Katz, Wackenhut, & Hass, 1986); the wish to avoid the appearance of being prejudiced (Carver et al., 1977); or the desire to demonstrate one's egalitarian and nonprejudiced values (Gaertner & Dovidio, 1986). When positive outcomes could be due to one's stigmatized identity, rather than to one's personal merits, then it is more difficult for the stigmatized individual to "own" or take credit for those outcomes. Thus, although attributional ambiguity regarding the causes of negative events should protect self-esteem, ambiguity about the causes of positive events may be damaging to self-esteem, if the beneficiary of positive outcomes believes that those outcomes reflect favorable treatment toward one's group, rather than a high level of personal deserving.

## ■ Research on Attributional Ambiguity

To test the idea that attributional ambiguity may protect the self-esteem of targets of prejudice, Crocker and her colleagues (Crocker, Voelkl, Testa, & Major, 1991) conducted an experiment in which college students were recruited to participate in a study of friendship development. Participants were told that we were interested in factors that lead to or interfere with the development of friendship. Both African American and European American students were recruited to participate. All participants were told that they would be interacting with a same-sex person who was seated in the next room. Actually, no other person existed, but we convinced our participants that there was another person in the next room who was going to be learning about them and deciding if they could become friends. To this end, participants were asked to describe their likes and dislikes in a paragraph, which was then shown to the "other student." The other student was then supposed to indicate whether or not the two participants could be come friends.

Several aspects of the study were systematically varied. As already noted, participants were either African American or European American college students. Second, the type of reaction each participant received from the hypothetical other student was also varied. Half of the participants were led to believe that the other person really did want to become friends, whereas the remaining participants were led to believe that the other person did not want to become friends. Finally, all subjects were seated in a room with a one-way mirror with attached blinds. The blinds on the mirror were either left up so that the participants believed that the other person could see them, or the blinds were lowered and participants were told that the other could not see them at all. After the participants received feedback indicating that the other person did or did not think they could become friends, their attributions for why they received this outcome and changes in their level of personal self-esteem were measured.

We predicted that when the blinds were up, participants would think that the other person was aware of their race. For the African Americans this would provide one possible explanation for the reaction they received from the other student. When the blinds were down, however, the participants knew that the other person had no knowledge of their race, and, therefore, race could not be an explanation for the outcome. Therefore, we predicted that when the blinds were up, and negative feedback was received, African Americans would attribute the negative feedback to the possible racism of the other student, and their self-esteem would not be hurt. When the blinds were down, however, receiving negative feedback would hurt the African Americans' self-esteem because there was no ambiguity about the cause of the feedback—the other simply did not want to be friends.

We first examined the extent to which our research participants thought the other students' reaction to them was caused by their own race, the other students' racism, and prejudice. These three attributions were highly similar, so we combined them into a composite measure of attributions to prejudice. Table 7.1 presents the results for African American participants. Two patterns emerged in these data: First, when they received a negative reaction, they were more likely to indicate that prejudice and racism was the cause than when they received a positive reaction. This was true regardless of whether the other student knew their race (i.e., regardless whether the blinds were up or down). Second, when the blinds were raised and the other student presumably knew the participant's race, participants were more likely to attribute the reaction to prejudice—regardless of whether the reaction was positive or negative. For European American students, neither of these patterns emerged in attributions to prejudice.

Of particular interest in this study was what happened to the self-esteem of the African American students. Their self-esteem was measured both at the beginning of the experiment and at the end of the experiment, so changes in self-esteem over the course of the study could be assessed. If the attributional

**TABLE 7.1** Attributions to Prejudice as a Function of Race of Subject, Feedback, and Visibility

| | *Race* | | | |
| | *Black* | | *White* | |
| | *Visibility* | | | |
| *Feedback* | *Seen* | *Unseen* | *Seen* | *Unseen* |
|---|---|---|---|---|
| Positive | 5.62 | 3.40 | 4.70 | 4.40 |
| Negative | 9.58 | 7.70 | 5.63 | 4.81 |

SOURCE: Crocker, Voelkl, Testa, and Major (1991). Copyright © 1991 by the American Psychological Association. Reprinted with permission.
NOTE: Means fall on a scale ranging from 3 *not at all due to prejudice* to 15 *very much due to prejudice.*

ambiguity hypothesis is correct, the African American students' self-esteem should not be hurt when negative outcomes can be attributed to prejudice. The results, presented in Table 7.2, indicate that this is exactly what happened. In the blinds-up condition, when African American students believed they could be seen and they received a negative reaction, their self-esteem did not change. In the blinds-down condition, however, when it was unlikely that racial prejudice caused the reaction they received, self-esteem dropped. Again, this pattern was not observed for European American participants. Thus, the possibility that negative outcomes were due to the prejudice of another appeared to protect self-esteem.

When changes in self-esteem following a positive reaction from the other student were examined, an interesting pattern emerged. In the blinds-down condition, when African American subjects received a positive reaction from someone they believed was unaware of their race, their self-esteem increased. But, when they received a positive reaction from the other student whom they believed was aware of their race, self-esteem dropped. It seems that when African American students receive positive outcomes, yet know that the other person is aware of their race, they do not trust the positive reaction. Again, this pattern was not observed among European American students.

The drop in self-esteem in the attributionally ambiguous (blinds up) positive feedback condition is somewhat surprising. According to attribution theory (Abramson, Seligman & Teasdale, 1978; Kelley, 1972; Weiner, 1985), participants might discount the positive feedback in this condition, and if so, the self-esteem boost provided by the positive feedback might be attenuated, or even eliminated. Most attribution research, however, would not suggest that

**TABLE 7.2**  Changes in Self-Esteem as a Function of the Race of the Subject, Valence of Feedback, and Visibility of the Subject

| | Race | | | |
|---|---|---|---|---|
| | Black | | White | |
| | Visibility | | | |
| Feedback | Seen | Unseen | Seen | Unseen |
| Positive | −0.50 | 0.40 | 0.38 | 0.04 |
| Negative | 0.06 | −0.47 | 0.07 | −0.03 |

SOURCE: Crocker, Voelkl, Testa, and Major (1991). Copyright © 1991 by the American Psychological Association. Reprinted with permission.
NOTE: Means are difference scores calculated after standardizing pretest and posttest scores.

positive outcomes whose cause is unclear would actually cause harm to self-esteem. It is possible that ambiguity surrounding a positive outcome on one occasion might also cause one to reconsider the causes of other positive outcomes received in the past. Attributional ambiguity may sometimes trigger suspicions about whether one personally deserved positive outcomes on others occasions, in a sort of "spill-over" of attributions effect, which may be particularly deflating for self-esteem. For example, an African American student who receives a minority fellowship to graduate school may wonder whether he or she would have qualified for other fellowships, as well. This ambiguity may lead the student to question whether positive evaluations from professors received previously were influenced by the student's race. This "spill-over" of attributions might account for the decrement in self-esteem we observed when a positive evaluation was attributionally ambiguous. Similar negative effects of positive outcomes may occur when the stigmatized receive unsolicited, and often unneeded, help from a nonstigmatized individual. Such "assumptive" help implies that the stigmatized individual is inferior, in the context of an apparently well-intentioned behavior. Research demonstrates that unsolicited help received by stigmatized individuals also can have negative consequences for self-esteem (Schneider, Major, Luhtanen, & Crocker, 1996), as well as spoiling one's identity in the eyes of an observer (Gilbert & Silvera, 1996).

In sum, our study suggests that the targets of racial prejudice tend to believe that racial prejudice may have influenced their outcomes, particularly when those outcomes are negative rather than positive, and when others are aware of one's race rather than blind to race. Furthermore, our study supports the idea that attributional ambiguity can protect the self-esteem of targets of prejudice from the self-relevant implications of negative outcomes. It is important to note, however, that attributional ambiguity for negative outcomes may not always be self-protective. Although recognizing the possibility that prejudice caused negative events may be better for self-esteem than the certainty that it did not, a certain attribution to prejudice should be even better for self-esteem. When negative outcomes really are the result of prejudice and discrimination, ambiguity or uncertainty surrounding the true causes of those outcomes may lead to lower self-esteem than if the true cause of the outcome—prejudice—is clear.

This point was demonstrated in a study by Ruggiero and Taylor (1995) in which women received a negative evaluation from a male evaluator. The likelihood that the evaluator was prejudiced against women was experimentally manipulated. Subjects attributed the negative evaluation to prejudice more than to the poor quality of their work only when the a priori likelihood of prejudice was close to 100%. When the likelihood that the evaluator was prejudiced was more ambiguous, the women tended to blame the negative evaluation more on the poor quality of their work than on the evaluator's prejudice. In later research, this pattern of not recognizing the role of prejudice was replicated and shown to have negative effects on performance self-esteem (Ruggiero & Taylor, 1997). Thus, ambiguity about the causes of negative events can also have detrimental effects on self-esteem, when the real cause of one's negative events is prejudice.

Although the Ruggiero and Taylor (1997) results may seem to be inconsistent with our own, we think the apparent inconsistencies can be resolved. Most important, in both studies attributions to prejudice had self-protective consequences for self-esteem (performance self-esteem, in Ruggiero and Taylor's studies). The discrepancy lies more in whether the targets of prejudice tend to perceive prejudice when the causes of their negative outcomes are ambiguous. Subjects in Ruggiero and Taylor's studies tended to attribute negative evaluations to the poor quality of their work more than to discrimination, unless it was nearly certain that prejudice was the cause. Thus, they seemed somewhat more reluctant to make attributions to prejudice than the Crocker et al. (1994) subjects. We suspect that differences in the specific procedures of the studies, and also the societal context of the research may account for this discrepancy. Crocker et al. did not alert their subjects to the prior likelihood that an evaluator was prejudiced. In addition, Ruggiero and Taylor's studies were all conducted in Montreal, Canada, whereas the Crocker et al. studies were conducted in Buffalo, New York. The social meaning of

gender and race, and beliefs about the pervasiveness of prejudice and discrimination, may be quite different for these two social contexts. We suspect that
U.S. college students are much more aware of the pervasiveness of racial and
gender discrimination than the Canadian students in Ruggiero and Taylor's
studies.

Our results also suggest that negative outcomes that result from subtle,
unconscious, or modern forms of prejudice, such as the aversive racism
described in the chapter by Dovidio and Gaertner (Chapter 1, this volume),
are more likely to be ambiguous than are negative outcomes that result from
blatant or "old-fashioned" forms of prejudice (Crocker & Major, 1989).
Because behavior that results from modern racism or aversive racism is not
recognized or labeled as racist by the actor, it may be unclear to the target of
modern or aversive racism whether to attribute such behavior to prejudice. In
contrast, old-fashioned, blatant forms of racism typically involve conscious
and unapologetic rejection or devaluing of others because of their ethnic
identity, and hence can clearly be attributed to prejudice.

Attributional ambiguity may have a variety of additional negative consequences for stigmatized individuals. For example, when the outcomes or
evaluations one receives from others are attributionally ambiguous, it may be
difficult to assess one's abilities and potential (Major & Crocker, 1993).
Should the female graduate student who is told that she does not belong in
graduate school accept that evaluation, and drop out, or should she write it off
as sexism? Should the African American student who receives a "minority
fellowship" feel pride in her accomplishments, or should she be concerned
about whether or not she would have qualified for a standard "nonminority"
fellowship? This added difficulty in assessing one's skills and abilities may
make it difficult to determine appropriate goals, career choices, and strategies.
Ambiguity about the causes of important events might use up cognitive
resources, as the stigmatized person engages in an analysis of why the
outcome was received (e.g., Weary, Marsh, Gleicher, & Edwards, 1993). It
might also undermine motivation, if it weakens the perceived link between
personal efforts and outcomes (Major & Crocker, 1993). Finally, attributional
ambiguity may lead to suspicion and mistrust in relationships.

## ■ Perceived Disadvantage, Discrimination, and Self-Esteem

Our argument that attributing negative outcomes to prejudice and racism
can have the effect of protecting self-esteem led us to hypothesize that the

more individuals believe they are discriminated against, the higher their self-esteem will be. Many social scientists have argued, quite correctly we believe, that racism constitutes a stressor in the lives of African Americans and other ethnic minorities, which can lead to lower levels of physical and psychological well-being (Mays, Coleman, & Jackson, in press; Neighbors, Jackson, Bowman, & Gurin, 1983). Although we share this perspective, our analysis suggests that among individuals who are the targets of prejudice and racism, it is better for psychological well-being if those individuals recognize that prejudice and racism, and not their own faults or failures, explain the negative outcomes they experience.

To examine this hypothesis, we conducted a survey in which we assessed beliefs about disadvantage, discrimination, and psychological well-being in a sample of 96 European American, 91 African American, and 96 Asian American college students at a large, predominantly European American public university (Crocker, Blaine, Luhtanen, & Broadnax, 1995). Included in the survey were measures of (a) perceived personal disadvantage across six domains (quality of education, employment including salaries and wages, recreation, political power and influence, housing, and quality of medical care), and (b) perceived discrimination—the perceived frequency and extent to which the students had personally experienced racial discrimination. These measures were all highly reliable. We also included several measures of psychological well-being, including the Rosenberg Self-Esteem Inventory, which is a highly valid and reliable measure of global, personal self-esteem.

Just over half of the participants in each ethnic group were male. The European American and the African American students were almost all U.S. citizens and native English speakers, but only about half the Asian students were U.S. citizens, and only one quarter of them reported that English was their native language. Interestingly, the Asian students who were U.S. citizens did not differ significantly from those who were not U.S. citizens on any of the analyses reported here. Although their parents were just as educated as the parents of the European American students, both the African American and the Asian students were relatively disadvantaged, as indicated by family income. The European American students reported a median family income between $50,000 and $59,000, whereas the African American and Asian students both reported a median family income between $30,000 and $39,000.

Not surprisingly, African American and Asian students reported more personal disadvantage and discrimination than did European American students (see Table 7.3). Consistent with previous research, there was a marginally significant tendency for African American students to be higher in

**TABLE 7.3**  Perceived Personal Disadvantage and Discrimination and Self-Esteem
Among White, Black, and Asian College Students (standard deviations
in parentheses)

|  | Racial-Ethnic Group | | |
|---|---|---|---|
|  | *Whites* | *Blacks* | *Asians* |
| Disadvantage | 3.05$_a$ | 3.96$_b$ | 3.75$_b$ |
| SD | (1.00) | (1.15) | (1.12) |
| Discrimination | 1.61$_a$ | 4.45$_b$ | 4.45$_b$ |
| SD | (1.11) | (1.37) | (1.29) |
| Self-esteem | 32.58$_a$ | 33.70$_a$ | 29.90$_b$ |
| SD | (4.63) | (4.82) | (4.89) |

NOTE: Means not sharing a common subscript differ at $p < .05$.

self-esteem than European Americans. Asian American students, however,
were lower than both African Americans and European Americans in self-
esteem. Of course, these differences between groups may be due, at least in part,
to cultural differences in self-report biases. Specifically, norms encouraging
modesty in Asian American cultures may make Asian American students less
willing to report about positive aspects of the self than are European American
or African American students (Abe & Zane, 1990; Markus & Kitayama, 1991).

Correlations with other measures, however, suggest that the poor well-
being of Asian American students is not simply due to self-report biases. The
different reactions of these three groups of students to perceived disadvantage
were quite striking (see Table 7.4). Among Asian American students, perceiving that one is personally disadvantaged was strongly and negatively related
to self-esteem, whereas among African American and European American
students perceived disadvantage was unrelated to self-esteem. The correlations also suggested that perceived discrimination was positively related to
self-esteem among African American students, but negatively and nonsigni-
ficantly related to self-esteem among European American and Asian students.

We conducted a more rigorous test of these group differences by comput-
ing regression analyses in which the demographic variables of sex of subject
and family income were controlled. As Table 7.5 shows, perceived disadvantage had negative effects on the self-esteem of Asian students, but not on that
of African American or European American students. Perceived discrimination, on the other hand, had positive effects on the self-esteem of black
students, but not on that of white and Asian students.

**TABLE 7.4** Zero-Order Correlations Between Perceived Personal Disadvantage and Discrimination and Self-Esteem Among Black, White, and Asian College Students

| | Racial-Ethnic Group | | |
| --- | --- | --- | --- |
| | *Whites* | *Blacks* | *Asians* |
| Disadvantage | .02 | −.003 | −.43 |
| | n.s. | n.s. | .001 |
| Discrimination | −.10 | .20 | −.18 |
| | n.s. | .07 | .10 |

These data suggest that perceiving that one is personally disadvantaged is related to lower self-esteem among Asian students, but not among blacks or whites. Perceiving that one is discriminated against, on the other hand, is related to higher self-esteem among black students, but not among Asians or whites. Clearly, the relation between perceiving disadvantage and discrimination and self-esteem differs across disadvantaged groups. In the next section of this chapter, we will consider what makes some people and some groups who are targets of racial prejudice and discrimination vulnerable to low self-esteem, when they perceive that they are discriminated against.

■ **Basing Self-Esteem on Approval and Regard From Others**

For whom does having a devalued social identity translate into, or become internalized as, low personal self-esteem? We will argue that the effects of perceived discrimination on self-esteem depend, in part, on contingencies of worth, or the extent to which targets of prejudice base their self-esteem on the opinions others hold of them.

We have recently become interested in individual and group differences in the extent to which self-esteem is contingent on approval from others. The notion of contingencies of worth, or conditions of self-esteem, has its origins in the theorizing of psychotherapist Carl Rogers (1959). Recently, however, the notion that for some individuals self-worth or self-regard is contingent, whereas for others it is noncontingent, or at least less contingent, has begun to appear in a variety of literatures, including research on depression (Kuiper & Olinger, 1986; Kuiper, Olinger, & MacDonald, 1988; Roberts, Gotlib, &

**TABLE 7.5**  Betas for Effects of Personal Disadvantage and Discrimination on
Self-Esteem Separately for White, Black, and Asian Students,
Controlling for Effects of Sex of Subject and Family Income

|                | Whites | Blacks | Asians |
|----------------|--------|--------|--------|
| Disadvantage   | .00    | .00    | −.40   |
|                | n.s.   | n.s.   | .001   |
| Discrimination | −.10   | .23    | −.01   |
|                | n.s.   | .05    | n.s.   |

Kassel, 1996), intrinsic motivation (Deci & Ryan, 1995), and our own work
on social stigma (Crocker, 1994; Kerr, Crocker & Broadnax, 1995; Crocker,
Quinn, & Wolfe, 1996; Quinn & Crocker, in press).

Sociologists such as Mead and Cooley argued that the self-concept
develops through a process of imagining how we are perceived and evaluated
by others. They called this process the "looking glass self" or "reflected
appraisals," because the self is reflected in or contingent on the reactions that
one receives from other people. As noted earlier, the notion that the self-
concept develops out of reflected appraisals is one theoretical vantage point
that suggests that stigmatized, disadvantaged, or devalued individuals should
have low self-esteem.

At the heart of our argument is the idea that people differ in the degree to
which their self-esteem depends on reflected appraisals. Those individuals
whose self-esteem is contingent on approval or regard from others should be
more vulnerable to low self-esteem if they are a member of a devalued group
than individuals whose self-esteem is not contingent on approval or regard
from others.

To test this notion, we have developed a 10-item measure of the extent to
which individuals base their self-esteem on approval from others, shown in
Table 7.6. This measure has been completed by several hundred college
students and has shown good internal consistency. Scores on this measure are
related to having low self-esteem for college students (Quinn & Crocker, in
press). Of particular concern here, however, is the question of whether basing
self-esteem on approval from others constitutes a vulnerability factor for low
self-esteem among individuals who are stigmatized or devalued.

We have investigated this issue in the context of the stigma associated
with being, or feeling, fat (Quinn & Crocker, in press). Our sample consisted
of 244 female students enrolled in the Introduction to Psychology course at

**TABLE 7.6**  Items on the Basing Self-Esteem on Approval From Others Scale

1. It is important to me to be well thought of by others.
2. I don't care if other people have a negative opinion about me.
3. I can't respect myself if others don't respect me.
4. When other people have a good opinion about me, I have a good opinion about myself.
5. I don't care what other people think of me.
6. Being criticized by others really takes a toll on my self-respect.
7. What others think of me has no effect on what I think of myself.
8. My self-esteem gets a boost when I receive a compliment or praise.
9. What I think about myself is unrelated to how other people view me.
10. My self-esteem depends on the opinions others hold of me.

the University of Michigan. Of the women, 129 indicated that they felt fat, by rating themselves somewhat or very overweight on a measure of perceived weight (described next), and indicating that they were more than 5 pounds overweight. Of the women, 115 classified as normal weight indicated that they did not feel fat by either of these criteria, or indicated that they were overweight by less than 5 pounds. The women completed the Rosenberg Self-Esteem Inventory, and our measure of basing self-esteem on approval from others. We conducted a set of regression analyses in which we predicted self-esteem from self-perceived weight and the extent to which their self-esteem is based on reflected appraisals on the full sample. The analysis indicated that both feeling fat (beta $= -.13$, $p < .05$) and basing self-esteem on reflected appraisals (beta $= -.38$, $p < .0001$) were significant risk factors for low self-esteem among all women. Adding the interaction between self-perceived weight and reflected appraisals increased the variance explained ($p < .055$).

To examine the nature of this interaction, we looked at the relationship between basing self-esteem on reflected appraisals and self-esteem separately for women who felt thin and those who felt fat. Among women who felt thin, basing self-esteem on reflected appraisals was related to being low in self-esteem ($r = -.28$, $p < .01$), but this relationship was even stronger among women who felt fat ($r = -.46$, $p < .01$). Thus, basing self-esteem on reflected appraisals does appear to be a risk factor for low self-esteem for all of the women in our sample, but especially for those women who felt fat.

We suspect that the group differences described earlier in the extent to which perceived disadvantage and discrimination leads to low self-esteem may also be related to differences among groups in the extent to which self-esteem is based on reflected appraisals. At the University of Buffalo, a sample of black, white, and Asian college students completed a shorter version of our measure. Black students were significantly less likely than white or Asian students to agree that their self-esteem depends on the opinions of others. We have also found in a sample of women ranging in age from 18 to 90 from the Buffalo community that black women are much less likely than white women to agree with these items. Most recently, Wolfe and Crocker (1996) collected data on 89 black and 65 white students in an introductory psychology course at the University of Michigan, and found that black students were, once again, significantly less likely than white students to agree that their self-esteem is based on approval from others.

Are African Americans less likely to base their self-esteem on approval from all others, or do they specifically not base their self-esteem on the approval from whites? It is possible that the "others" that black students have in mind when they complete our scale are whites, and the race differences we observe on this measure reflect a tendency—perhaps true of all groups—not to base self-esteem on the approval of out-group members. We addressed this question in our University of Michigan sample by creating another version of the measure in which the questions specifically asked about others "of your racial group." If black students base their self-esteem on what other blacks think of them, but not on what whites think of them, then we should find that the race differences in scores on this measure go away when same-race others are specified, and we should find that blacks score lower on the measure when race is not specified than when same-race others are specified.

We did, indeed, find that the race differences in basing self-esteem on approval from others went away when same-race others were specified. As these means in Table 7.7 show, however, the scores of black students did not change from one version of the scale to the other. It was white students who indicated that they were less likely to base their self-esteem on approval from others when same-race others were specified. We are not sure why white students' scores changed when same-race others were specified in the items. We suspect that white students change their responses because the same-race other version of the measure does not make sense to them. Alternatively, white students may have thought that when race was explicitly mentioned, their racial attitudes were being assessed. Hence, they may have changed their responses to avoid appearing prejudiced. Regardless, it is clear is that black students were not scoring lower than whites just because the "other" they had in mind in the original version of the scale was whites.

In sum, both individual and group differences in the effects of perceived discrimination on self-esteem may depend on which of those individuals and

**TABLE 7.7**  Scores on the Basing Self-Esteem on Approval From Others Scale for Blacks and Whites, When the Race of Other Others is Unspecified (general other) or Specified as Same Race

|  | *Whites* | *Blacks* |
|---|---|---|
| General other | 4.37 | 3.75 |
| Same-race other | 3.42 | 3.67 |

groups have self-esteem that is contingent on approval from others. For individuals and groups who base their self-esteem on approval from others, self-esteem may indeed be lower if they perceive that they are targets of discrimination.

Why do some people base their self-esteem on approval and regard from others, while others do not (or do so less)? The answer to this question is likely to be complex, involving an interaction of cultural, situational, and personality factors. For example, early childhood experiences may create a predisposition to have specific conditions of self-esteem (Bowlby, 1988; Crocker & Wolfe, 1997; Rogers, 1959). Cultural influences on the self-concept may account, at least in part, for the differences we observed between Asian and African American college students. Markus and Kitayama (1991) have suggested that individuals from Western cultures tend to have self-concepts that are relatively independent, stressing the self as a bounded, autonomous individual. In these cultures, self-esteem tends to be based on one's ability to express the self, and validate one's internal attributes. In Asian cultures, the self-concept is more interdependent, and the self is construed in the context of one's relationships with others. In these cultures, self-esteem is based on one's ability to adjust, restrain the self, and maintain harmony with the social context. We suspect that whereas in the highly individualistic cultures such as the United States, self-esteem is related to being independent and self-sufficient, in collectivist cultures it may be more strongly related to gaining approval from others.

The meaning given to one's disadvantaged position in society may also affect the basis of self-esteem. Some individuals and groups may view their disadvantaged status as a relatively permanent consequence of the hierarchies of groups in a society, whereas others may view their disadvantaged status as a more temporary state. For example, those who voluntarily immigrate to the United States to improve their economic circumstances may view the United States as a meritocracy and a land of opportunity. These individuals may consider the system in which they are disadvantaged to be legitimate, and consequently tend to base their self-esteem on how they are doing, and how they are regarded in that system (Ogbu, 1986). Other groups, such as African Americans, who came to the United States involuntarily may be more aware of the long history of discrimination against their group and see their disadvantaged status as more stable. As noted, African Americans tend to regard the system in which they are disadvantaged as illegitimate, and may consequently disengage their self-esteem from approval and regard from others. This may be a highly adaptive strategy. In a system in which the opinions others hold of one's group are influenced by centuries of oppression and prejudice, why should one base one's self-esteem on approval and regard of others?

## ■ Conclusions

A great deal of social psychological theorizing has suggested that the experience of being devalued, or being the target of prejudice, must inevitably take a toll on self-esteem. Yet numerous studies have indicated that the targets of prejudice do not always internalize the devaluation they experience, and often they have high self-esteem. Our research has identified two factors—one situational and one personal—that may help explain why being a target of prejudice does not necessarily result in low self-esteem. First, targets of prejudice are often aware of the possibility that the rejection or negative outcomes they experience result from other people's prejudice, rather than their own shortcomings. This external attribution, we have shown, can protect self-esteem in the face of rejection.

We hasten to add, however, that although attributional ambiguity may protect self-esteem, it can also have a number of costs. Attributional ambiguity for positive events makes it more difficult for individuals to take credit for their success. Thus, minority graduate students admitted under special programs may exist under a cloud of suspicion—sometimes even in their own minds—that they would not have been admitted without the special program. Beyond self-esteem, however, attributional ambiguity may have other deleterious effects on students. Attempts to resolve the ambiguity regarding the role prejudice plays in one's experiences may demand cognitive resources, detracting from the amount of attention that is devoted to other information in one's environment. The black student, for example, who wonders if a remark a faculty member has just made has racist overtones may lose her ability to concentrate on the content of the lecture. This demand on cognitive resources may ultimately undermine academic performance.

In addition, attributional ambiguity can make it difficult for students to assess accurately their ability and potential, and therefore make life decisions more difficult. Consider, for example, the student of color who is complimented by her professor on her class performance. The student may wonder whether she is really doing a good job, or whether the professor is just eager to be encouraging to students of color, or even simply trying not to appear prejudiced. This student may find it difficult to evaluate whether she has the potential to succeed in more difficult courses. Thus, although attributional ambiguity can sometimes protect self-esteem, it places a heavy burden on students of color.

Yet our survey study of perceived discrimination and self-esteem among black, white, and Asian college students clearly indicates that awareness of discrimination does not always protect self-esteem. This has led us to consider personal factors—individual differences—that lead some people to internalize the prejudice they experience more than others do. Specifically, we hypothesized that the notion of "reflected appraisals" describes the basis of self-esteem for some individuals more than others. People who have self-esteem that is relatively noncontingent, or independent of approval and regard from others have self-esteem that is less vulnerable to prejudice.

Clearly, blanket statements that prejudice leads to low self-esteem, or prejudice does not lead to low self-esteem, are likely to be overly simple. Prejudice leads to low self-esteem in its targets in some circumstances more than others, and for some individuals more than others. Our research suggests that the consequences of prejudice on self-esteem depend on the meanings that disadvantage has for stigmatized individuals—both the meaning of specific negative events the individual experiences, and the meaning of the disadvantaged status of one's social group.

# To Identify or Not to Identify

*Preserving, Ignoring, and Sometimes
Destroying Racial (Social) Identity*

*Audrey J. Murrell*

The negative impact of prejudice and racism on members of minority groups has been well documented. Clearly, prejudice, stereotyping, and discrimination act as a social detour for many ethnic minorities, rerouting them away from success and toward a path obstructed by the roadblocks of economic despair and social disenfranchisement. It has been difficult for any single psychological theory or social psychological concept to adequately describe the impact of racism on historically disadvantaged groups. Some research has attempted to quantify the loss of key resources from our economy because of the exclusion of talent and skill caused by racial discrimination (e.g., Fernandez, 1985; Greenhaus, Parasuraman, & Wormley, 1990). Others have drawn connections between racism and the prevalence of negative social conditions, with the message being the shared negative impact of racism on our society (Duckitt, 1992b). Our competitiveness as a society into the next century depends on the elimination of the social and economic barriers created by racial prejudice and discrimination (Alderfer, Alderfer, Tucker, & Tucker, 1980; Fernandez, 1985; Ilgen & Youtz, 1986).

How members of disadvantaged groups deal with and react to racism is a critical yet understudied area that clearly warrants more attention from social psychological research. Examining adaption to prejudice can tell us an important story about how disadvantaged individuals cope with and respond to severely adverse conditions. Although the extant literature on the negative impact of prejudice on disadvantaged groups is sparse, several theories currently provide a good starting point for understanding how individuals respond to the negative effects of racism. The purpose of this chapter is to review two major theoretical models that focus on understanding the impact of racism on the nature of intergroup relations and the strength of intragroup identification. In addition to this review, my focus will be to explore the similarities and differences between these two sets of theories about racial and social group identity and to offer some suggestions on future issues that should be addressed by social psychology.


## ■ Racism and Its Impact

A variety of previous research in social psychology has examined the impact of prejudice and racism on members of minority and other disadvantaged groups. One central theme within this body of work has been that the negative impact of racial prejudice and stereotypes exerts a strong and detrimental effect on the targets of these actions and attitudes (Taylor, 1980; Weber, 1961). More recently, discussions on the impact of racism on minority group members have expanded to include a focus on how the targets of prejudice are affected by acts of discrimination and negative attitudes. The basic idea is that responses by the victims of racial discrimination and prejudice may take many different forms. One response may be accepting or preserving these negative views and conditions. This response is characterized by traditional social psychological concepts such as stigma (Crocker & Major, 1989), marginality (Frable, 1993), and negative self-concept among minority group members (Banks & Grambs, 1972; Houston, 1984). In addition to accepting the ill effects of racism, another response could be rejection. Social protest and black nationalism (Murrell & Brown, in press; Taylor, Underwood, Thomas, & Zhang, 1990; Terrell & Taylor, 1980; Terrell, Taylor, & Terrell, 1980) focus on how disadvantaged groups reject or ignore the dominant identity and actively attempt to change the social forces that adversely affect them.

A third response among targets of racial prejudice and discrimination has received considerably less attention by traditional social psychological theories. Classic theories of adaption to prejudice focus on the individual's decision (either conscious or unconscious) to accept the domination identity or to reject it. Models of Nigrescense (or "becoming black") describe reactions to prejudice in which new identity formations emerge. Here, reactions to prejudice may take the form of changing or destroying traditional views of racial and cultural identity in favor of new, often multiracial and multicultural racial identities. Clearly, any of these outcomes are likely responses to racism by the targets of prejudice. Jones (1997) writes the following:

> One's racial and ethnic identity is shaped in part by one's adaptions to the predicaments of prejudice. This adaption may be conscious—as in choosing a particular style of dress, one's cohorts of friends, one's attitudes toward schooling, career values, and so forth. Or it may be reflected in the more or less automatic cumulative experiences of, say, being a person of color in the United States. (p. 288)

Thus, reactions of disadvantaged group members to prejudice and discrimination can take many different forms. Although notions of negative racial group identity among minority group members have somewhat dominated traditional social psychological discourse on racial relations, several models try to represent the variety of ways in which these individuals attempt to understand and reconcile their individual view of themselves with society's view of their racial group members. In general, these models of racial identity do not assume that the impact of prejudice and discrimination is universally negative; rather, these models often begin with the idea that identity represents an individual's struggle to understand, adapt, and perhaps change what society has defined as the meaning of group (or racial) identity.

## ■ Models of Racial Identity

One such model of racial group identity is based on a variety of research conducted primarily at the University of Pittsburgh. This work, stimulated by early research by Milliones (1973, 1980), involves a number of empirical and theoretical pieces by Taylor and his colleagues (Taylor, 1990; Taylor & Grundy, in press; Taylor, Henderson, & Jackson, 1991; Taylor & Jackson, 1990a, 1990b; Taylor & Jackson, in press; Taylor, Jackson, & Quick, 1982; Taylor & Rogers, 1993). According to this work, racial identity can be characterized by what is labeled as "identity prototypes." The preconsciousness prototype describes racial identity as identification with mainstream values such as capitalism, democracy, fairness, and a free market economy. Individuals within this prototype have an antipathy toward their culture of origin and tend to identify with white majority values. There is a high degree of internalization of negative racial stereotypes within this group. Thus, individuals falling within this prototype will endorse conceptions of blacks as mentally defective, physically gifted, emotional, and highly sexual.

The emergence prototype is described as a "painful awakening often triggered by a critical event" (Taylor, 1990, p. 46). Individuals within this group are consumed with notions of identity validation, and a great deal of energy is devoted to challenging the values held by those in the preconscious prototype. Because of this type of challenging and reevaluation of one's identity, individuals in the confrontation-internalization prototypes are often seen as highly "militant." One could, however, also characterize individuals of this type as having a high degree of racial group pride that takes the form of seeing one's own racial group as superior and the majority group as oppressive and evil.

The last two prototypes focus on a less polarized view of intragroup identity. Individuals within the integration prototype experience an openness to working with members from different racial and cultural groups. The central concern for individuals within this prototype, however, remains the advancement of their own in-group community. In contrast, although individuals within the double consciousness prototype have a similar willingness to interact with individuals from diverse racial groups, the central concern for these individuals is the advancement of human and social equality. According to Taylor and his colleagues, the negative effects of internalized racism prevalent within the preconsciousness prototype are least evident among these individuals.

Research based on Taylor's model has shown that when racial group identity is defined as preencounter, individuals are at greater risk of social maladjustment compared with any other group (Denton, 1985; Taylor, 1980, in press; Terrell et al., 1980). These individuals tend to express more aggression and express less warmth and acceptance of other blacks. Barrett (1974) demonstrated, using a laboratory manipulation of attribution, that blacks with preencounter attitudes were less able to identity with the situation of the black protagonist. Those with preencounter attitudes tend to report less marital satisfaction (Taylor, 1990, Taylor & Zhang, 1990) and tend to report more sexual partners than other blacks (Taylor & Franklin, in press). Consistently, individuals with preencounter attitudes show lower self-esteem and ego identity compared with other blacks (Denton, 1985), and tend to doubt their ability to lead and are more emotionally constricted than other blacks (Brown, 1976). A relationship between racial identity and self-esteem indicates that individuals characterized as preencounter in their racial group identity report by far the lowest levels of self-esteem across the four stages. Client-therapist relationships, drug and alcohol consumption, likelihood to experience depression, low marital satisfaction, and low ego maturity have all been demonstrated to occur among individuals whose racial group identity can be characterized as preencounter. In addition, achievements in educational and work environments are lower for those with preencounter identities.

The Pittsburgh model of racial identity is quite similar to other models whose aim is to explain the different forms that identification with one's racial group may take. Cross (1991) describes "stages" of black identity in his model known as Nigrescense. In this model, five stages of racial group identity that are similar to the prototypes of the Pittsburgh model are proposed by Cross: preencounter, encounter, immersion-emersion, and internalization. The initial stage of racial identity development begins with the negative impact of racial group membership. Thus, preencounter is defined by antiblack attitudes causing the person to think, act, and behave in ways that devalue his or her own racial group identity. Similar to other models of racial identity, a critical event or "encounter" causes the individual to question social definitions of their group identity. This encounter experience causes the person to search for different meanings of their racial group membership.

The next three stages in the model developed by Cross outline different forms of racial group identity than ones defined in exclusively negative terms. Immersion-emersion is a stage described as identity in "transition." Here, people are focused on trying to develop a different understanding of their race, or search for what it means to be "black." Thus, an almost total immersion in one's own racial group identity is the defining feature of the immersion-emersion stage. Racial group pride is very high during this stage and, often, negative other-group attitudes are present during this stage.

Although it is unclear what events or experiences cause a person to emerge from the immersion-emersion stage, the next stage according to Cross is internalization. Here, conflicts about racial identity are resolved and negative other-group attitudes are replaced by an overall concern for humanity. An interesting feature of Cross's stage of internalization that is distinct from other models of racial identity is the notion of ego-defenses and personal efficacy orientation that develops during this internalization stage. According to Cross, individuals within this stage recognize that racism is a part of the fabric of this society and actively engage in the development of coping strategies to help buffer against the negative impact of prejudice and discrimination. At the same time, these individuals develop a personal efficacy orientation that deflects negative outcomes and prejudicial acts from the self-concept. Thus, this efficacy orientation protects against negative events that are seen as racially motivated from returning the individual to earlier stages of negative racial identity and self-denigration. This notion is quite similar to the concept of attributional ambiguity that is discussed in Chapter 7 of this volume.

The final stage of racial identity described by Cross is that of internalization-commitment. In this stage, some sense of attachment and commitment to racial and social equality is formed. The ideas described by Cross in the internalization-commitment stage and by Taylor in the double consciousness prototype are related to notions of multiculturalism (Berry, 1984; LaFromboise, Coleman, & Gerton, 1993) in which individuals are able to maintain distinct identities that represent their own culture or racial group identity along with other culture or racial identities (e.g., the dominant cultural identity). For many, this type of multiple identities perspective best describes an accurate, adaptive, and healthy way to structure group identity within a diverse and global society.

Another model of racial identity that has received considerable attention is proposed by Helms (1990). Based somewhat on the work of Cross, the model by Janet Helms and her colleagues focuses on statuses rather than stages (i.e., Cross ) or prototypes (i.e., Taylor). The need to focus on statuses rather than stages is to avoid some of the assumptions of developmental models in which stages occur in a linear sequence of events or periods. The statuses proposed by Helms, however, are quite similar in their content to the other two models of racial group identity. Helms proposed five statuses: conformity, dissonance, immersion-emersion, internalization, and integrative awareness. Three of the five statuses have similar labels to the stages outlined by Cross and the definitions within these statuses are also similar to Cross's model. The fifth status, integrative awareness, has a slightly different label yet describes a similar complex, multigroup identity forming in this period.

The dissonance status as described by Helms, however, differs from both the encounter stage and from the emergence prototype. Recall that Taylor describes a "trigger event" that causes the person to challenge the values and definitions of their own racial group as deficient and defective. Cross describes the encounter stage in a similar fashion as an "eye-opening" period in which the individual challenges but is also confused about the meaning of race in this society. Helms, in her notion of dissonance, characterizes a period in which the individual is ambivalent or confused about the meaning of race. She describes this period as one in which there is a loss of clarity and the individual feels marginalized within the society. In this sense, the dissonance status appears to be more similar (yet somewhat less extreme) to the initial status of conformity. The Helms model also differs from that of Taylor and Cross in that she has developed a widely used measure of racial identity that assesses individual identity across a 50-item set that represent each of her five statuses of racial group identity (Helms, 1990; Parham & Helms, 1985a, 1985b; Yanico, Swanson, & Tokar, 1994).

Clearly, these three prominent models of racial identity each attempt to understand the ways in which members of oppressed groups recognize, understand, and internalize concepts of their racial group identity. The advantages of these models are that they represent a range of different responses to racial prejudice and discrimination. Instead of assuming the impact of racial prejudice to be negative, these models explore the idea that individuals can be active participants in the reconstruction of their own racial group identity. These "disadvantaged" individuals can accept the negative images presented to them or they can ignore these images in favor of more positive ones, or they can cognitively destroy these images in favor of more integrative and inclusive ones. The recognition that racial identity can take on many different forms can have important implications for research on intergroup and race relations. Notions of adaption and coping can provide useful tools to help develop these more positive responses among individuals who are stigmatized by negative racial conditions. In addition, issues such as self-concept, achievement, mental and physical health, interpersonal relationships, and intergroup interactions should be quite different depending on an individual's prototype, stage, or status. Incorporating these notions into existing concepts within social psychology should stimulate a number of interesting questions for future social psychological research.

Although models of racial group identity present a number of interesting questions that promise to expand our understanding of the impact of racial prejudice, there are some limitations to the models developed to date. A major concern is that the notions of racial identity have been developed almost exclusively from the perspective of one racial group: African Americans. There has been some attempt to expand this understanding and focus on ethnic identity rather than racial identity (Phinney, 1990a, 1990b). The challenge here is to test whether models of racial identity based on the experiences of African Americans can be used to understand the racial and ethnic identity of other disadvantaged groups (e.g., Hispanic Americans and some groups of Asian Americans). Ideas such as the role of the family and religious orientation are important issues within the Hispanic and Latino cultures that are not clearly represented in current models of racial group identity. Similarly, notions of self-control, patience, and moderation are associated with some Asian cultures yet are currently absent from the models of racial identity discussed here. These limited examples suggest that although models of racial identity help advance our understanding of the impact of prejudice and racism on members of oppressed groups, we are still in need of models that represent the complexity of racial as well as ethnic group identity.

## ■ Social Identity Theory

Although models of racial group identity have explored the consequences of racial group membership primarily from the perspective of specific racial groups (e.g., African Americans), principles of social identity theory (Tajfel, 1978; Tajfel & Turner, 1979) have been adapted by a variety of research and applied to the notion of racial and ethnic group membership. The notion of one's social identity provides an interesting perspective to add to models of racial group membership because this perspective begins with the idea that individuals are motivated to maintain a positive view of their social or group membership. Thus, applying social identity theory to the issue of racial and ethnic group membership makes the notions of self-denigration and racial stigmatization seem antithetical; that is, maintaining a negative rather than a positive sense of social identity is an exceptional rather than a normative state.

According to social identity theory (Tajfel & Turner, 1985), a person's identity is formed and shaped by a number of experiences both direct and indirect. These experiences include successes, failures, challenges, critical events, and personal relationships, just to name a few. Part of the identity that is created and maintained through these experiences is an identity associated with what Tajfel (1978) called "social categories" and "human groups." In understanding and explaining interactions and relations between groups, the notion of identity is central. A natural consequence of these social categories is that one distinguishes between those within the group that contains the self, or one's in-group, and all others labeled as the out-group. The meaning and significance of these social categories depends on the nature of social reality, that is, the specific dynamics within the social context. As the social context changes, one would expect, so does the meaning and significance of these social groups. Thus, the categorization of people is done in reference to the self within a particular social context. When social categories of people are formed, it has direct implications for how the self is perceived, evaluated, and categorized. Our understanding of social categories of people has direct implications for how we see ourselves in relation to others.

Clearly then, if one sees oneself in positive terms relative to others, then social identity will be positive. If a person belongs to a group that is negatively viewed by others, it becomes difficult (yet not impossible) to maintain a positive social identity. The central assumption of social identity theory, however, is that individuals are motivated to maintain a positive rather than a negative view of the self. Thus, attention and energy are channeled toward establishing and maintaining this positive identity. Success or failure of these efforts depends on a variety of both individual and social factors (Wills, 1981).

Interestingly, social identity theory outlines any number of ways individuals may engage in what are called "self-enhancing" processes (see Crocker & Major, 1989; Chapter 7, this volume) to protect or restore a positive sense of social identity. If an individual is a member of a group that is viewed negatively by others, he or she may reject these negative attributes of group membership in favor of a more positive image. Clearly, the rejection of a negatively defined group membership is similar to what is described in the emergence prototype of Taylor, the encounter stage by Cross, and the dissonance status described by Helms. For example, rather than rejecting negative notions that members of minority groups are too fatalistic and superstitious, minority members may view themselves positively as more religious and spiritual than majority group members. The behavior labeled as in-group favoritism or bias according to Tajfel is consistent with notions of racial pride as defined by models of racial group identity (Taylor, Cross, and Helms).

Another strategy for enhancing positive social identity is to redefine the context for intergroup definitions and interactions. Social creativity strategies involve the development of new forms of intergroup comparisons that will create positive, rather than negative, in-group identity. For example, intergroup comparisons may occur on new dimensions. Thus, members of minority groups may draw attention to dimensions that are more likely to lead to positive outcomes for minority group members, or emphasize those unique characteristics of one's ethnicity. Within this redefinition, minority members may also reassess the value that is placed on these different dimensions. For example, a movement away from focusing on individual achievement versus collective (e.g., familial, community, racial group) achievement is one such attempt to attach new values to attributes that define previously group membership.

Another example of a social creativity strategy is to change the nature or target of intergroup comparisons. Thus, low-status or stigmatized groups may examine their own status in reference to other minority or low-status groups rather than the majority or high-status group. This type of lateral comparison is one approach that may ensure a more positive outcome of these comparisons and, thus, enhance perceived individual social status. The idea here is "our group may not be the best, but we are better than them."

In addition to social creativity, people can use social competition strategies to enhance the overall position of their social group. These strategies involve more direct competition between minority and majority groups on dimensions that are directly relevant to defining group membership. Social identity theory predicts social competition when the comparisons between social groups are perceived to be insecure or the existing social status hierarchy is called into question. This category of strategies involves activism, political action, civil rights activity, and other behaviors that directly challenge and attempt to change the overall social status structure that defines intergroup boundaries.

Although there is no evidence that examines the overall effectiveness of social creativity versus social competition strategies, the outcomes, according to their use, are expected to be somewhat different. The outcome of social competition strategies is to alter the status quo of how group boundaries are defined. The use of social creativity strategies may alter the cognitive and affective framework for the individual, but the social status within larger society remains unchanged. Social competition, if successful, has the potential to change not only individual social identity but social order and status as well. The impact, however, of unsuccessful attempts at social competition can be withdrawal on the part of minority group members, isolation and exclusion by majority members, and in extreme cases, backlash and retaliation by majority group members.

Interestingly, social identity theory does not devote a great deal of attention to the notion of acceptance of negative in-group status. A distinction is made, however, between groups that an individual may choose to belong to (ascribed) versus those without a choice of membership (assigned). When negative characteristics of group membership exist, individuals can choose to exit the group. As Tajfel (1978) discusses, however, this is more easily accomplished when group membership is ascribed rather than assigned. Although Tajfel focuses on a number of cognitive mechanisms for the enhancement of in-group status (especially when exit from the group is not possible), notions of marginality are the closest to the first categories of racial group identity described by the three models.

Clearly then, there are a number of similarities between models of racial group identity and Tajfel's notion of social identity. How the various concepts within racial identity models correspond to the range of strategies for the enhancement of social identity is described in Table 8.1. This table is an attempt to integrate the description of racial group identity that has been devised and researched within the realm of Nigrescense models and the principles outlined by social identity theory that explain intergroup relations and behavior. Although each of the models discussed here has several strengths and limitations, using an inclusive approach that incorporates notions of in-group rejection as well as in-group enhancement is the best approach to take in future explorations of racial or social identity among disadvantaged groups.

## ■ Conclusions

A great deal of social psychological research on race and intergroup relations has focused on the impact of discrimination, marginality, and stereotyping of minority group members. Historically, this research has examined the impact of racism and discrimination by focusing on the self-concept of minority group members with a particular emphasis on the concept of self-esteem. Several earlier studies sought to explain what was perceived to be the most extreme consequence of prolonged discrimination, self-own group rejection, and majority group identification (e.g., Clark & Clark, 1939). Since the mid-1960s until the present, a paradox within these research findings has emerged. It appears that positive rather than negative self-concept has been found among minority group members that takes the form of high self-esteem among these individuals across a wide range of empirical measures (Banks, 1981; Banks & Grambs, 1972). Many have argued that to explain this apparent inconsistency and to better our understanding of the nature of race relations from the perspective of minority group members, we must focus not on the issues of self-concept or self-esteem exclusively; rather, we must focus our attention and research efforts toward a better understanding of racial group identity or what others have labeled black consciousness (Banks, 1981).

As Cross (1971, 1991) explains, some identities for individuals are very important to their self-concept. These are known as core identities. The notion of a core identity describes how a person sees him- or herself and how central some dimensions of this definition are to this view of the self. In a sense, core identities are focal points that have a significant impact on behavior, attitudes, and social interactions. Some aspects of these group identities are more important that others. Thus, we should not assume that the impact of racial

**TABLE 8.1**  Black Identity Prototypes and Strategies to Improve Social Identity

| Taylor Model of Racial Identity (prototypes) | Cross Model of Racial Identity (stages) | Helms Model of Racial Identity (statuses) | Social Identity Theory (self-enhancement strategies) |
|---|---|---|---|
| Preconsciousness | Preencounter | Conformity | Social mobility or acceptance |
| Emergence | Encounter | Dissonance | In-group favoritism-bias |
| Confrontation-internalization | Immersion-emersion | Immersion-emersion | Social competition |
| Integration | Internalization | Internalization | Social creativity |
| Double consciousness | Internalization-commitment | Integrative awareness | Social integration |

discrimination and prejudice is universal or the same for all minority group members. According to the models of racial group identity developed by Taylor, Helms, and Cross, we must take into account the extent to which negative definitions of racial identity are acknowledged and accepted by the individual. In addition, Cross adds that we must also understand whether racial group identity represents a core identity for the individual.

As discussed within this chapter, models of racial group identity are quite similar to how the concept of social identity was defined by Tajfel (1978) as "the individual's knowledge that he or she belongs to certain social groups together with some emotional and value significance to his or her of the group membership" (p. 61). These self-images, according to Tajfel, will vary in their richness, complexity, content, and so forth. Individuals are motivated to maintain positive social identity. Therefore, the outcomes of intergroup comparisons will vary depending on whether the individuals involved have a positive or a negative social (racial) identity. Previous research has focused primarily on the type of resolution to being a member of a disadvantaged group that can be characterized as psychological exit; that is, decreasing identification with the low-status group and identifying strongly with the out-group. The argument here is that principles of social identity theory can explain the range of options that may be available to individuals who are members of disadvantaged groups in which group status is assigned. Similarly, models of racial group identity also help to explain the range of outcomes that individuals can select to adapt to a disadvantaged social status.

The result of merging these two perspectives within this discussion is to explore the implications for intergroup behavior and to determine the areas in need of enhanced understanding and research.

In reviewing the research and theory on black identity and intergroup relations, I can offer several conclusions. First and foremost is the idea that black racial identity is not unidimensional. As social identity theory outlines, individuals maintain multiple identities that are either more or less salient depending on the specific context (Tajfel & Turner, 1979). Similarly, Cross (1991) argues that blacks have had and continue to have a reference group orientation that is multifaceted. Therefore, the finding that some blacks have positive self-images rather than negative self-images should not be surprising. If aspects of collective self-esteem contribute to overall feelings of personal worth, then variability in how racial group identity is defined and maintained should produce a range of outcomes in overall level of personal identity.

A second conclusion that is important to note here is also echoed in the work by Cross (1991). As his and other models of black identity state, reference group orientation (or social identity) does not necessarily predict personal identity. The principles of social creativity and competition illustrate a range of alternatives that will strongly mediate the impact of socially defined group membership on social (racial) identity. A rich area of future research would be to explore the variety of consequences of these strategies for improving social identity among blacks and other minority group members on the nature of intergroup relations and outcomes.

One area of concern in the study of racial group identity is that models of Nigrescense have almost exclusively focused on racial group identity among African Americans. Little theory or research has focused on these issues among members of other racial and ethnic groups. Recent attention in the areas of multiculturalism (e.g., Andreasen, 1990; Berry, 1984; LaFromboise et al., 1993) offers some new insights into this area; however, much work has yet to be done.

What is clear from the integration of racial identity models and social identity theory is that the potential response by minority group members to racism and discrimination can take many forms. A socially defined negative racial group identity can be preserved in the form of internalized racism and negative self-esteem. This negative social definition can be ignored, however, and take the form of in-group or racial pride. In still some other cases, this negative status can be destroyed and replaced by a new social (racial) identity. It is critical that social psychological research move beyond merely seeing racial identity as either positive or negative. Such a view underrepresents the importance and complexity of the concept of racial (social) identification. The implication for developing a better understanding of the response to racism among members of disadvantaged groups is the development of strategies for adapting to the effects of racism and prejudice and the enhancement of healthy and productive race relations in the future.

# 9

# A Threat in the Air

## How Stereotypes Shape Intellectual Identity and Performance

### Claude M. Steele

From an observer's standpoint, the situations of a boy and a girl in a math classroom or of a Black student and a White student in any classroom are essentially the same. The teacher is the same; the textbooks are the same; and in better classrooms, these students are treated the same. Is it possible, then, that they could still experience the classroom differently, so differently in fact as to significantly affect their performance and achievement there? This is the central question of this article, and in seeking an answer, it has both a practical and a theoretical focus. The practical focus is on the perhaps obvious need to better understand the processes that can hamper a group's school performance and on what can be done to improve that performance. The theoretical focus is on how societal stereotypes about groups can influence the intellectual functioning and identity development of individual group members. To show the generality of these processes and their relevance to important outcomes, this theory is applied to two groups: African Americans, who must contend with negative stereotypes about their abilities in many scholastic domains, and women, who must do so primarily in math and the physical sciences. In trying to understand the schooling outcomes of these two groups, the theory has a

AUTHOR'S NOTE: The research reported in this article was supported by National Institutes of Health Grant MH5 1977, Russell Sage Foundation Grant 879.304, and Spencer Foundation and James S. McDonnell Foundation postdoctoral fellowships. Completion of the research was aided by the Center for Advanced Study in the Behavioral Sciences.

distinct perspective, that of viewing people, in Sartre's (1946/1965) words, as "first of all beings in a situation" such that if one wants to understand them, one "must inquire first into the situation surrounding [them]" (p. 60).

The theory begins with an assumption: that to sustain school success one must be identified with school achievement in the sense of its being a part of one's self-definition, a personal identity to which one is self-evaluatively accountable. This accountability—that good self-feelings depend in some part on good achievement—translates into sustained achievement motivation. For such an identification to form, this reasoning continues, one must perceive good prospects in the domain, that is, that one has the interests, skills, resources, and opportunities to prosper there, as well as that one belongs there, in the sense of being accepted and valued in the domain. If this relationship to schooling does not form or gets broken, achievement may suffer. Thus, in trying to understand what imperils achievement among women and African Americans, this logic points to a basic question: What in the experience of these groups might frustrate their identification with all or certain aspects of school achievement?

One must surely turn first to social structure: limits on educational access that have been imposed on these groups by socioeconomic disadvantage, segregating social practices, and restrictive cultural orientations, limits of both historical and ongoing effect. By diminishing one's educational prospects, these limitations (e.g., inadequate resources, few role models, preparational disadvantages) should make it more difficult to identify with academic domains. To continue in math, for example, a woman might have to buck the low expectations of teachers, family, and societal gender roles in which math is seen as unfeminine as well as anticipate spending her entire professional life in a male-dominated world. These realities, imposed on her by societal structure, could so reduce her sense of good prospects in math as to make identifying with it difficult.

But this article focuses on a further barrier, one that has its effect on the already identified, those members of these groups who, having survived structural obstacles, have achieved identification with the domain (of the present groups, school-identified African Americans and math-identified women). It is the social-psychological threat that arises when one is in a situation or doing something for which a negative stereotype about one's group applies. This predicament threatens one with being negatively stereotyped, with being judged or treated stereotypically, or with the prospect of conforming to the stereotype. Called *stereotype threat,* it is a situational threat—a threat in the air—that, in general form, can affect the members of any group about whom a negative stereotype exists (e.g., skateboarders, older adults, White men, gang members). Where bad stereotypes about these groups apply, members of these groups can fear being reduced to that stereotype. And for those who identify with the domain to which the stereotype is relevant, this predicament can be self-threatening.

Negative stereotypes about women and African Americans bear on important academic abilities. Thus, for members of these groups who are identified with domains in which these stereotypes apply, the threat of these stereotypes can be sharply felt and, in several ways, hampers their achievement.

First, if the threat is experienced in the midst of a domain performance—classroom presentation or test-taking, for example—the emotional reaction it causes could directly interfere with performance. My colleagues and I (Spencer, Steele, & Quinn, 1997; C. M. Steele & Aronson, 1995) have tested this possibility with women taking standardized math tests and African Americans taking standardized verbal tests. Second, when this threat becomes chronic in a situation, as for the woman who spends considerable time in a competitive, male-oriented math environment, it can pressure *disidentification,* a reconceptualization of the self and of one's values so as to remove the domain as a self-identity, as a basis of self-evaluation. Disidentification offers the retreat of not caring about the domain in relation to the self. But as it protects in this way, it can undermine sustained motivation in the domain, an adaptation that can be costly when the domain is as important as schooling.

Stereotype threat is especially frustrating because, at each level of schooling, it affects the vanguard of these groups, those with the skills and self-confidence to have identified with the domain. Ironically, their susceptibility to this threat derives not from internal doubts about their ability (e.g., their internalization of the stereotype) but from their identification with the domain and the resulting concern they have about being stereotyped in it. (This argument has the hopeful implication that to improve the domain performance of these students, one should focus on the feasible task of lifting this situational threat rather than on altering their internal psychology.) Yet, as schooling progresses and the obstacles of structure and stereotype threat take their cumulative toll, more of this vanguard will likely be pressured into the ranks of the unidentified. These students, by not caring about the domain vis-à-vis the self, are likely to underperform in it regardless of whether they are stereotype threatened there. Thus, although the identified among these groups are likely to underperform only under stereotype threat, the unidentified (casualties of sociocultural disadvantage or prior internalization of stereotype threat) are likely to underperform and not persist in the domain even when stereotype threat has been removed.

In these ways, then, the present analysis sees social structure and stereotypes as shaping the academic identities and performance outcomes of large segments of society. But first, for the two groups under consideration, what are these outcomes?

As is much discussed, these outcomes are in a crisis state for African Americans. Although Black students begin school with standardized test scores that are not too far behind those of their White counterparts, almost immediately a gap begins to appear (e.g., Alexander & Entwistle, 1988; Burton & Jones, 1982; Coleman et al., 1966) that, by the sixth grade in most school districts, is two full grade levels (Gerard, 1983). There have been encouraging increases in the number of African Americans completing high school or its equivalence in recent years: 77% for Black students versus 83% for White students (American Council on Education, 1995-1996). And there have been modest advances in the number of African American high school graduates enrolling in college, although these have not been as substantial as in other groups (American Council on Education, 1995-1996). Perhaps most discouraging has been the high dropout rate for African American college students: Those who do not finish college within six years is 62%, compared with a national dropout rate of 41% (American Council on Education, 1995-1996). And there is evidence of lower grade performance among those who do graduate of, on average, two thirds of a letter grade lower than those of other graduating students (Nettles, 1988). On predominantly White campuses, Black students are also underrepresented in math and the natural sciences. Although historically Black colleges and universities now enroll only 17% of the nation's Black college students they produce 42% of all Black BS degrees in natural science (Culotta & Gibbons, 1992). At the graduate level, although Black women have recently shown modest gains in PhDs received, the number awarded to Black men has declined over the past decade more than for any other subgroup in society (American Council on Education, 1995-1996).

Women clearly thrive in many areas of schooling. But in math, engineering, and the physical sciences, they often endure lesser outcomes than men. In a meta-analysis involving over 3 million participants, Hyde, Fennema, and Lamon (1990), for example, found that through elementary and middle school, there are virtually no differences between boys and girls in performance on standardized math tests but that a trend toward men doing better steadily increases from high school ($SD = .29$) through college ($SD = .41$) and into adulthood ($SD = .59$). And, as their college careers begin, women leave these fields at a rate two and a half times that of men (Hewitt & Seymour, 1991). Although White women constitute 43% of the U.S. population, they earn only 22% of the BS degrees and 13% of the PhDs and occupy only 10% of the jobs in physical science, math, and engineering, where they earn only 75% of the salary paid to men (Hewitt & Seymour, 1991).

These inequities have compelled explanations ranging from the sociocultural to the genetic. In the case of African Americans, for example, past and ongoing socioeconomic disadvantage, cultural orientations (e.g., Ogbu, 1986), and genetic differences (e.g., Herrnstein & Murray, 1994; Jensen, 1969) have all been proposed as factors that, through singular and accumulated effect, could undermine their performance. In the case of women's performance in math and the physical sciences, there are parallel arguments: structural and cultural gender role constraints that shunt women away from these areas; culturally rooted expectations (e.g., Eccles, 1987; Eccles-Parsons et al., 1983); and, again, genetic limitations (Benbow & Stanley, 1980, 1983). But, like crumbs along the forest floor, several findings lead away from these analyses as fully sufficient.

For one thing, minority student achievement gaps persist even in the middle and upper socioeconomic classes. Using data from the Coleman report (Coleman et al., 1966) and a more recent College Board study of Scholastic Assessment Test (SAT) scores, Miller (1995, 1996) found that the gaps in academic performance (grades as well as standardized test scores) between Whites and non-Asian minorities (e.g., African Americans, Hispanics, and Native Americans) were as large, or larger, in the upper and middle classes (as measured by parental education and occupation) than in the lower classes. Group differences in socioeconomic status (SES), then, cannot fully explain group differences in academic performance.

Another point is that these differences are not even fully explained by group differences in skills. This is shown in the well-known *overprediction* or *underperformance* phenomenon of the test bias literature. Overprediction occurs when, at each level of performance on a test of preparation for some level of schooling (e.g, the SAT), students from one group wind up achieving less—getting lower college grades, for example—than other students with the same beginning scores. In this sense, the test scores of the low-performing group overpredict how well they will actually achieve, or, stated another way, the low-performing group underperforms in relation to the test's prediction.

But the point here is that because the students at each test-score level have comparable initial skills, the lower eventual performance of one group must be due to something other than skill deficits they brought with them.

In the case of African Americans, overprediction across the academic spectrum has been so reliably observed as to be almost a lawful phenomenon in American society (e.g., Jensen, 1980; Vars & Bowen, 1997). Perhaps the most extensive single demonstration of it comes from a recent Educational Testing Service study (Ramist, Lewis, & McCamley-Jenkins, 1994) that examined the predictiveness of the SAT on 38 representative college and university campuses. As is typically the case, the study found that the predictive validity to the SAT—its correlation with subsequent grades—was as good for African American, Hispanic, and Native American students as for White and Asian students. But for the three non-Asian minority groups, there was sizable overprediction (underperformance) in virtually all academic areas. That is, at each level of preparation as measured by the SAT, something further depressed the grades of these groups once they arrived on campus.

As important, the same study found evidence of SAT overprediction for female students (i.e., women performing less well than men at comparable SAT levels) in technical and physical science courses such as engineering, economics, and computer science but not in nontechnical areas such as English. It is interesting though that women in this study were not overpredicted in math per se, a seeming exception to this pattern. The overprediction of women's college math performance has generally been unreliable, with some studies showing it (e.g., Benbow & Arjmand, 1990; Levin & Wyckoff, 1988; Lovely, 1987; Ware, Steckler, & Leserman, 1985) and others not (e.g., Adelman, 1991; DeBoer, 1984; Ware & Dill, 1986). However, a recent study (Strenta, Elliott, Adair, Scott, & Matier, 1993) involving over 5,000 students at four prestigious northeastern colleges identified a pattern of effects that suggests why these different results occur: Underperformance reliably occurred among women who were talented in math and science and who, perhaps for that reason, took courses in these areas that were intended for majors, whereas it did not occur among women with less math and science preparation who took courses in these areas intended for nonmajors. Thus, women may be reliably overpredicted in math and the physical sciences, just as Black students are more generally, but only when the curriculum is more advanced and only among women who are more identified with the domain. Among this vanguard, though, something other than skill deficits depresses their performance. What are these further processes?

### ■ Social and Stereotype Structure as Obstacles to Achievement Identification

The proposed answer is that at least one of these processes is a set of social psychological phenomena that obstructs these groups' identification with domains of schooling.[1] I turn first to school identification.

### ■ Academic Identification

As noted, this analysis assumes that sustained school achievement depends, most centrally, on identifying with school, that is, forming a relationship between oneself and the domains of schooling such that one's self-regard significantly depends on achievement in those domains. Extrinsic rewards such as better career outcomes, personal security, parental exhortation, and so on, can also motivate school achievement. But it is presumed that sustaining motivation through the ebb and flow of these other rewards requires school identification. How, then, is this identification formed?

Not a great deal is known about the process. But several models (e.g., Schlenker & Weigold, 1989; C. M. Steele, 1988; Tesser, 1988) share an implicit reasoning, the first assumption of which is that people need positive self-regard, a self-perception of "adaptive and moral adequacy" (C. M. Steele, 1988, p. 289). Then, the argument goes, identification with a given domain of life depends, in large part, on the self-evaluative prospects it offers. James (1890/1950) described the development of the self as a process of picking from the many, often incompatible, possible selves, those "on which to stake one's salvation" (p. 310). This choice and the assessment of prospects that goes into it are, of course, multifaceted: Are the rewards of the domain attractive or important? Is an adequate opportunity structure available? Do I have the requisite skills, talents, and interests? Have others like me succeeded in the domain? Will I be seen as belonging in the domain? Will I be prejudiced against in the domain? Can I envision wanting what this domain has to offer? and so on. Some of these assessments undergird a sense of efficacy in the domain (e.g., Bandura, 1977, 1986). Others have to do with the rewards, importance, and attractiveness of the domain itself. And still others have to do with the feasibility and receptiveness of the domain. The point here is that students tacitly assess their prospects in school and its subdomains, and, roughly speaking, their identifications follow these assessments: increasing when they are favorable and decreasing when they are unfavorable. As for the two groups under consideration, then, this analysis suggests that something systematically downgrades their assessments of, and thus their identification with, critical domains of schooling.

## ■ Threats to Academic Identification

*Structural and cultural threats.* Both groups have endured and continue to endure sociocultural influences that could have such effects. Among the most replicable facts in the schooling literature is that SES is strongly related to school success and cognitive performance (e.g., Coleman et al., 1966; Miller, 1996). And because African Americans have long been disproportionately represented in lower socioeconomic classes, this factor surely contributes to their achievement patterns in school, both through the material limitations associated with lower SES (poor schools, lack of resources for school persistence, etc.) and through the ability of these limitations, by downgrading school-related prospects, to undermine identification with school. And beyond socioeconomic structure, there are cultural patterns within these groups or in the relation between these groups and the larger society that may also frustrate their identification with school or some part of it, for example, Ogbu's (1986) notion of a lower-class Black culture that is "oppositional" to school achievement or traditional feminine gender roles that eschew math-related fields (e.g., Eccles-Parsons et al., 1983; Linn, 1994).

*Stereotype threat.* Beyond these threats, waiting for those in these groups who have identified with school is yet another threat to their identification, more subtle perhaps but nonetheless profound: that of stereotype threat. I define it as follows: the event of a negative stereotype about a group to which one belongs becoming self-relevant, usually as a plausible interpretation for something one is doing, for an experience one is having, or for a situation one is in, that has relevance to one's self-definition. It happens when one is in the *field* of the stereotype, what Cross (1991) called a "spotlight anxiety" (p. 195), such that one can be judged or treated in terms of a racial stereotype. Many analysts have referred to this predicament and the pressure it causes (e.g., Allport, 1954; Carter, 1991; Cose, 1993; Goffman, 1963; Howard & Hammond, 1985; Jones et al., 1984; Sartre, 1946/1965; C. M. Steele, 1975; C. M. Steele & Aronson, 1995; S. Steele, 1990). The present definition stresses that for a negative stereotype to be threatening, it must be self-relevant. Then, the situational contingency it establishes—the possibility of conforming to the stereotype or of being treated and judged in terms of it—becomes self-threatening. It means that one could be limited or diminished in a domain that is self-definitional. For students from groups in which abilities are negatively stereotyped in all or some school domains and yet who remain identified with those domains, this threat may be keenly felt, felt enough, I argue, to become a further barrier to their identification with the domain.

There is, however, a more standard explanation of how negative stereotypes affect their targets. Beginning with Freud (as cited in Brill, 1938) in psychology and Cooley (1956) and Mead (1934) in sociology, treatises on the experience of oppression have depicted a fairly standard sequence of events: Through long exposure to negative stereotypes about their group, members of prejudiced-against groups often internalize the stereotypes, and the resulting sense of inadequacy becomes part of their personality (e.g., Allport, 1954; Bettelheim, 1943; Clark, 1965; Erikson, 1956; Fanon, 1952/1967; Grier & Coobs, 1968; Kardiner & Ovesy, 1951; Lewin, 1941).

In recent years, the tone of this argument has constructively lightened, replacing the notion of a broad self-hatred with the idea of an inferiority anxiety or low expectations and suggesting how situational factors contribute to this experience. S. Steele's (1990) essays on *racial vulnerability* (i.e., a vulnerability of both Blacks and Whites that stems, in part, from the situational pressures of reputations about their groups) offered an example. This work depicts the workings of this anxiety among African Americans in an interconnected set of ideas: *integration shock* that, like Goffman (1963), points to settings that integrate Blacks and Whites as particularly anxiety arousing; *objective correlatives* or race-related situational cues that can trigger this anxiety; and the inherent sense of risk, stemming from an internalized *inferiority anxiety* and from a *myth of inferiority* pervading integrated settings, of being judged inferior or of confirming one's own feared inferiority. Howard and Hammond (1985) earlier made this argument specifically in relation to the school achievement of Black students. They argued that once "rumors of inferiority" (stereotypes; p. 18) about Black students' abilities pervade the environment—through, for example, national debates over the genetic basis of racial differences in IQ—they can intimidate Black students; become internalized by them; and, in turn, lead to a low sense of self-efficacy, demotivation, and underperformance in school. Analogous arguments have been applied to women interested in math-related areas (cf. Eccles-Parsons et al., 1983).

These models recognize the situational influence of negative stereotypes (e.g., Allport, 1954; Howard & Hammond, 1985; S. Steele, 1990) but most often describe it as a process in which the stereotype, or more precisely the possibility of being stereotyped, triggers an internalized inferiority doubt or low expectancy. And because this anxiety is born of a socialization presumed to influence all members of the stereotyped group, virtually all members of the group are presumed to have this anxiety, to one degree or another.

Stereotype threat, in contrast, refers to the strictly situational threat of negative stereotypes, the threat that does not depend on cuing an internalized anxiety or expectancy. It is cued by the mere recognition that a negative group stereotype could apply to oneself in a given situation. How threatening this recognition becomes depends on the person's identification with the stereotype-relevant domain. For the domain identified, the situational relevance of the stereotype is threatening because it threatens diminishment in a domain that is self-definitional. For the less domain identified, this recognition is less threatening or not threatening at all, because it threatens something that is less self-definitional.

Stereotype threat, then, as a situational pressure "in the air" so to speak, affects only a subportion of the stereotyped group and, in the area of schooling, probably affects confident students more than unconfident ones. Recall that to be identified with schooling in general, or math in particular, one must have confidence in one's domain-related abilities, enough to perceive good prospects in the domain. This means that stereotype threat should have its greatest effect on the better, more confident students in stereotyped groups, those who have not internalized the group stereotype to the point of doubting their own ability and have thus remained identified with the domain—those who are in the academic vanguard of their group.[2]

Several general features of stereotype threat follow:

1. Stereotype threat is a general threat not tied to the psychology of particular stigmatized groups. It affects the members of any group about whom there exists some generally known negative stereotype (e.g., a grandfather who fears that any faltering of memory will confirm or expose him to stereotypes about the aged). Stereotype threat can be thought of as a subtype of the threat posed by negative reputations in general.

2. That which turns stereotype threat on and off, the controlling "mechanism" so to speak, is a particular concurrence: whether a negative stereotype about one's group becomes relevant to interpreting oneself or one's

behavior in an identified-with setting. When such a setting integrates stereotyped and nonstereotyped people, it may make the stereotype, as a dimension
of difference, more salient and thus more strongly felt (e.g., Frable, Blackstone, & Sherbaum, 1990; Goffman, 1963; Kleck & Strenta, 1980; Sartre,
1946/1965; S. Steele, 1990). But such integration is neither necessary nor
sufficient for this threat to occur. It can occur even when the person is alone,
as for a woman taking an important math test alone in a cubicle but under the
threat of confirming a stereotyped limitation of ability. And, in integrated
settings, it need not occur. Reducing the interpretive relevance of a stereotype
in the setting, say in a classroom or on a standardized test, may reduce this
threat and its detrimental effects even when the setting is integrated.[3]

3. This mechanism also explains the variabilities of stereotype threat: the
fact that the type and degree of this threat vary from group to group and, for
any group, across settings. For example, the type and degree of stereotype
threat experienced by White men, Black people, and people who are overweight differ considerably, bearing on sensitivity and fairness in the first
group, on school performance in the second, and on self-control in the third.
Moreover, for any of these groups, this threat will vary across settings (e.g.,
Goffman, 1963; S. Steele, 1990). For example, women may reduce their
stereotype threat substantially by moving across the hall from math to English
class. The explanation of this model is straightforward: Different groups
experience different forms and degrees of stereotype threat because the
stereotypes about them differ in content, in scope, and in the situations to
which they apply.

4. To experience stereotype threat, one need not believe the stereotype
nor even be worried that it is true of oneself. The well-known African
American social psychologist James M. Jones (1997) wrote,

> When I go to the ATM machine and a woman is making a transaction, I think
> about whether she will fear I may rob her. Since I have no such intention, how
> do I put her at ease? Maybe I can't . . . and maybe she has no such expectation.
> But it goes through my mind. (p. 262)

Jones felt stereotype threat in this situation even though he did not believe that
the stereotype characterized him. Of course, this made it no less a life-shaping
force. One's daily life can be filled with recurrent situations in which this
threat pressures adaptive responses.

5. The effort to overcome stereotype threat by disproving the stereotype—for example, by outperforming it in the case of academic work—can

be daunting. Because these stereotypes are widely disseminated throughout society, a personal exemption from them earned in one setting does not generalize to a new setting where either one's reputation is not known or where it has to be renegotiated against a new challenge. Thus, even when the stereotype can be disproven, the need to do so can seem Sisyphean, everlastingly recurrent. And in some critical situations, it may not be disprovable. The stereotypes considered in this work allege group-based limitations of ability that are often reinforced by the structural reality of increasingly small group representations at more advanced levels of the schooling domain. Thus, for group members working at these advanced levels, no amount of success up to that point can disprove the stereotype's relevance to their next, more advanced performance. For the advanced female math student who has been brilliant up to that point, any frustration she has at the frontier of her skills could confirm the gender-based limitation alleged in the stereotype, making this frontier, because she is so invested in it, a more threatening place than it is for the nonstereotyped. Thus, the work of dispelling stereotype threat through performance probably increases with the difficulty of work in the domain, and whatever exemption is gained has to be rewon at the next new proving ground.

### ■ Empirical Support for a Theory of Stereotype Threat and Disidentification

In testing these ideas, my and my colleagues' research has had two foci: The first is on intellectual performance in the domain in which negative group stereotypes apply. Here, the analysis has two testable implications. One is that for domain-identified students, stereotype threat may interfere with their domain-related intellectual performance. Analysts have long argued that behaving in a situation in which one is at risk of confirming a negative stereotype about one's group, or of being seen or treated stereotypically, causes emotional distress and pressure (e.g., Cross, 1991; Fanon, 1952/1967; Goffman, 1963; Howard & Hammond, 1985; Sartre, 1946/1965; C. M. Steele & Aronson, 1995; S. Steele, 1990). The argument here is that for those who identify with the domain enough to experience this threat, the pressure it causes may undermine their domain performance. Disruptive pressures such as evaluation apprehension, test anxiety, choking, and token status have long been shown to disrupt performance through a variety of mediating mechanisms: interfering anxiety, reticence to respond, distracting thoughts, self-consciousness, and so on (Baumeister & Showers, 1984; Geen, 1991; Lord & Saenz, 1985; Sarason, 1980; Wine, 1971). The assumption of this model is that stereotype threat is another such interfering pressure. The other testable implication is that reducing this threat in the performance setting, by reducing its interfering pressure, should improve the performance of otherwise stereotype-threatened students.

The second research focus is the model's implication that stereotype threat, and the anticipation of having to contend with it unceasingly in school or some domain of schooling, should deter members of these groups from identifying with these domains, and, for group members already identified, it should pressure their disidentification.[4]

### ■ Stereotype Threat and Intellectual Performance

Steven Spencer, Diane Quinn, and I (Spencer et al., 1997) first tested the effect of stereotype threat on intellectual performance by testing its effect on the standardized math test performance of women who were strong in math.

*The stereotype threat of women performing math.* At base, of course, the stereotype threat that women experience in math-performance settings derives from a negative stereotype about their math ability that is disseminated throughout society. But whether this threat impaired their performance, we reasoned, would depend on two things. First, the performance would have to be construed so that any faltering would imply the limitation of ability alleged in the stereotype. This means that the performance would have to be difficult enough so that faltering at it would imply having reached an ability limit but not so difficult as to be nondiagnostic of ability. And second, as has been much emphasized, the women in question would have to be identified with math, so that faltering and its stereotype-confirming implication would threaten something they care about, their belongingness and acceptance in a domain they identify with. Of course, men too (at least those of equal skill and identification with math) could be threatened in this situation; faltering would reflect on their ability too. But their faltering would not carry the extra threat of confirming a stereotyped limitation in math ability or of causing them to be seen that way. Thus, the threat that women experience, through the interfering pressure it causes, should worsen their performance in comparison to equally qualified men. Interestingly, though, these otherwise confident women should perform equally as well as equally qualified men when this situational threat is lessened.

To explore these questions, Spencer, Quinn, and I (Spencer et al., 1997) designed a basic research paradigm: We recruited female and male students, mostly college sophomores, who were both good at math and strongly identified with it in the sense of seeing themselves as strong math students and seeing math as important to their self-definition. We then gave them a very difficult math test one at a time. The items were taken from the advanced math General Records Examination (GRE) and we assumed would frustrate the skills of these students without totally exceeding them. As expected, and presumably reflecting the impairing effects of stereotype threat, women significantly underperformed in relation to equally qualified men on this difficult math test. But more important, in another condition of this experiment in which the test was an advanced literature test rather than a math test and in which participants had been selected and matched for their strong literature skills and identification, women performed just as well as equally qualified men. This happened, we reasoned, because women are not stereotype threatened in this area.

A second experiment replicated women's underperformance on the difficult math test and showed that it did not happen when the test was easier, that is when the items, taken from the regular quantitative section of the GRE, were more within the skills of these strong math students. The lack of performance frustration on this easier test, presumably, reduced women's stereotype threat by making the stereotype less relevant as an interpretation of their performance.

*Stereotype threat versus genes.* So went our interpretation. But an alternative was possible: The biological limits of women's math ability do not emerge until the material tested is difficult. It is this very pattern of evidence that Benbow and Stanley (1980, 1983) used to suggest a genetic limitation in women's math ability. Thus, the first two experiments reproduced the gender effects on math performance reported in the literature: that women underperform primarily in math and mainly when the material is difficult. But they fall short of establishing our interpretation.

To do this, we would need to give women and men a difficult math test (one capable of producing women's underperformance) but then experimentally vary stereotype threat, that is, vary how much women were at risk of confirming the stereotype while taking the test. A third experiment did this by varying how the test (the same difficult one used in the earlier experiments) was represented. Participants were told either that the test generally showed gender differences, implying that the stereotype of women's limitations in math was relevant to interpreting their own frustration, or that it showed no gender differences, implying that the gender stereotype was not relevant to their performance and thus could not be confirmed by it on this particular test. The no-gender-differences representation did not challenge the validity of the stereotype; it simply eliminated the risk that the stereotype could be fulfilled on this test. In the gender-differences condition, we expected women (still stereotype threatened) to underperform in relation to equally qualified men, but in the no-gender-differences condition, we expected women (with stereotype threat reduced) to perform equal to such men. The genetic interpretation, of course, predicts that women will underperform on this difficult test regardless of how it is represented.

In dramatic support of our reasoning, women performed worse than men when they were told that the test produced gender differences, which replicated women's underperformance observed in the earlier experiments, but they performed equal to men when the test was represented as insensitive to gender differences, even though, of course, the same difficult "ability" test was used in both conditions (see Figure 9.1). Genetic limitation did not cap the performance of women in these experiments. A fourth experiment showed that reducing stereotype threat (through the no-gender-differences treatment) raised women's performance to that of equally qualified men, even when participants' specific performance expectancies were set low, that is, when participants were led to expect poor test performance. Also, a fifth experiment (that again replicated the treatment effects of the third experiment) found that participants' posttreatment anxiety, not their expectancies or efficacy, predicted their performance. Thus, the disruptive effect of stereotype threat was mediated more by the self-evaluative anxiety it caused than by its lowering of performance expectations or self-efficacy.

*Internal or situational threat.* These findings make an important theoretical and practical point: The gender-differences conditions (including those in which the possibility of gender differences was left to inference rather than stated directly) did not impair women's performance by triggering doubts they had about their math ability. For one thing, these women had no special doubts of this sort; they were selected for being very good at math and for reporting high confidence in their ability. Nor was this doubt a factor in their test performance. Recall that the math test was represented as an ability test in all conditions of these experiments. This means that in the no-gender-differences conditions, women were still at risk of showing their own math ability to be weak—the same risk that men had in these conditions. Under this risk (when

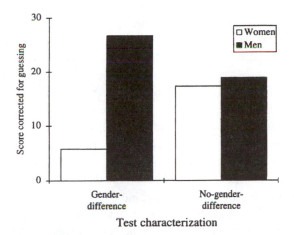

**Figure 9.1.** Mean Performance on a Difficult Math Test as a Function of Gender and Test Characterization

their own math ability was on the line), they performed just as well as men. Whatever performance-impairing anxiety they had, it was no greater than that of equally qualified men. Thus, the gender-differences conditions (the normal condition under which people take these tests) could not have impaired their performance by triggering some greater internalized anxiety that women have about their own math ability—an anxiety acquired, for example, through prior socialization. Rather, this condition had its effect through situational pressure. It set up an interpretive frame such that any performance frustration signaled the possible gender-based ability limitation alleged in the stereotype. For these women, this signal challenged their belongingness in a domain they cared about and, as a possibly newly met limit to their ability, could not be disproven by their prior achievements, thus its interfering threat.

*The stereotype threat of African Americans on standardized tests.* Joshua Aronson and I (C. M. Steele & Aronson, 1995) examined these processes among African American students. In these studies, Black and White Stanford University students took a test composed of the most difficult items on the verbal GRE exam. Because the participants were students admitted to a highly selective university, we assumed that they were identified with the verbal skills represented on standardized tests. The first study varied whether or not the stereotype about Black persons' intellectual ability was relevant to their performance by varying whether the test was presented as *ability-diagnostic,* that is, as a test of intellectual ability, or as *ability-nondiagnostic,* that is, as a laboratory problem-solving task unrelated to ability and thus to the stereotype about ability. Analysis of covariance was used to remove the influence of participants' initial skills, measured by their verbal SAT scores, on their test performance. This done, the results showed strong evidence of stereotype threat: Black participants greatly underperformed White participants in the diagnostic condition but equaled them in the nondiagnostic condition (see Figure 9.2). A second experiment produced the same pattern of results with an even more slight manipulation of stereotype threat: whether or not participants recorded their race on a demographic questionnaire just before taking the test (described as nondiagnostic in all conditions). Salience of the racial stereotype alone was enough to depress the performance of identified Black students (see Figure 9.3).

*The cognitive mediation of stereotype threat.* Stereotype threat, then, can impair the standardized test performance of domain-identified students; this effect generalizes to several ability-stereotyped groups, and its mediation seems to involve anxiety more than expectancies. But do these manipulations cause a specific state of stereotype threat, that is, a sensed threat specifically about being stereotyped or fitting the stereotype? To address this question, Aronson and I (C. M. Steele & Aronson, 1995) tested two things: whether manipulating stereotype threat actually activates the racial stereotype in the thinking and information processing of stereotype-threatened test takers and whether it produces in them a specific motivation to avoid being seen stereotypically. Again, Black and White participants were run in either an ability-diagnostic or ability-nondiagnostic condition, except that just after the condition instructions and completion of the sample test items (so that participants could see how difficult the items were) and just before participants expected to take the test, they completed measures of stereotype activation and avoidance. The stereotypeactivation measure asked them to complete 80 word fragments, 10 of which we knew from pretesting could be completed with, among other words, words symbolic of African American stereotypes (e.g., _ _ce [race], la_ _ [lazy], or _ _ or [poor]) and 5 of which could be completed with, among other words, words signifying self-doubts (e.g., lo_ _ _ [loser], du_ _ [dumb], or sha_ _ _ [shame]). The measure of participants' motivation to avoid being seen stereotypically simply asked them how much they preferred various types of music, activities, sports, and personality

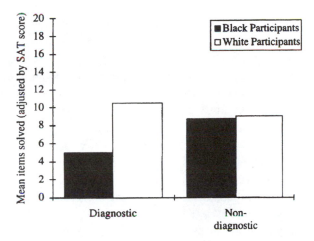

**Figure 9.2.** Mean Performance on a Difficult Verbal Test as a Function of Race and Test Characterization

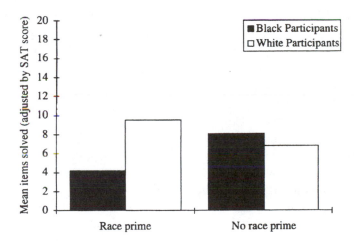

**Figure 9.3.** Mean Performance on a Difficult Verbal Test as a Function of Whether Race Was Primed

traits, some of which a pretest sample had rated as stereotypic of African Americans.[5]

If expecting to take a difficult ability-diagnostic test is enough to activate the racial stereotype in the thinking of Black participants and to motivate them to avoid being stereotyped, then these participants, more than those in the other conditions, should show more stereotype and self-doubt word completions and fewer preferences for things that are African American. This is precisely what happened. Black participants in the diagnostic condition completed more word fragments with stereotype- and self-doubt-related words and had fewer preferences for things related to African American experience (e.g., jazz, basketball, hip-hop) than Black participants in the nondiagnostic condition or White participants in either condition, all of whom were essentially the same (see Figure 9.4). Also, as a last item before participants expected to begin the test, they were given the option of recording their race, a measure we thought might further tap into an apprehension about being viewed stereotypically. Interestingly, then, all of the Black participants in the nondiagnostic condition and all of the White participants in both conditions listed their race, whereas only 25% of the Black participants in the diagnostic condition did so.

*Self-rejection or self-presentation?* A troubling implication of the earlier mentioned internalization models (e.g., Allport, 1954; Bettelheim, 1943; Clark, 1965; Erikson, 1956; Fanon, 1952/1967; Grier & Coobs, 1968; Kardiner & Ovesy, 1951) is that negative stereotypes about one's group eventually become internalized and cause rejection of one's own group, even of oneself—*self-hating* preferences. The famous finding of Clark and Clark (1939) that Black children preferred White dolls over Black dolls has been interpreted this way. The preferences of Black participants in the diagnostic condition fit this pattern; with negative stereotypes about their group cognitively activated, they valued things that were African American less than any other group. But the full set of results suggests a different interpretation. In those conditions in which Black participants did not have to worry about tripping a stereotypic perception of themselves, they valued things that were African American more strongly than did other participants. Thus, rather than reflecting self- or own-group rejection, their devaluing of things that were African American in the diagnostic condition was apparently a strategic self-presentation aimed at cracking the stereotypic lens through which they could be seen. So it could be, then, in the general case, rather than reflecting real self-concepts, behavior that appears group rejecting or self-rejecting may reflect situation-bound, self-presentational strategies.

Stereotype activation measure

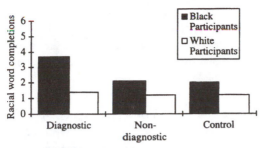

Self-doubt activation measure

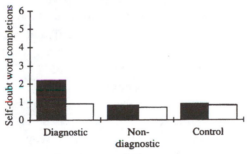

Stereotype avoidance measure

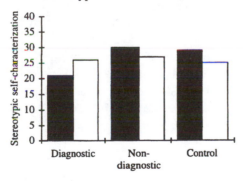

**Figure 9.4.** Indicators of Stereotype Threat

*Stereotype threat and domain identification.* Not being identified with a domain, our (C. M. Steele & Aronson, 1995) theory reasons, means that one's experience of stereotype threat in the domain is less self-threatening. Although we have yet to complete a satisfactory test of this prediction, partially completed experiments and pretests show that stereotype threat has very little, if any, effect on participants not identified with the domain of relevance. Most typically, these participants give up and underperform on the difficult test regardless of whether they are under stereotype threat. Although not yet constituting a complete test of this implication of the theory, these data do emphasize that the above results generalize only to domain-identified students.

*Stereotype threat and the interpretation of group differences in standardized test performance.* Inherent to the science of quantifying human intelligence is the unsavory possibility of ranking societal groups as to their aggregated intelligence. It is from this corner of psychology that the greatest controversy has arisen, a controversy that has lasted throughout this century and that is less about the fact of these group differences than about their interpretation (cf. Herrnstein & Murray, 1994; Kamin, 1974). To the set of possible causes for these group differences, our (C. M. Steele & Aronson, 1995) findings add a new one: the differential impact of stereotype threat on groups in the testing situation itself. Thus, stereotype threat may be a possible source of bias in standardized tests, a bias that arises not from item content but from group differences in the threat that societal stereotypes attach to test performance. Of course, not every member of an ability-stereotyped group is going to be affected by stereotype threat every time they take a test. As our research has shown, the experience of success as one takes the test can dispel the relevance of the stereotype. Nonetheless, among the most identified test takers in the stereotype-threatened group—those in its academic vanguard who have the greatest confidence and skills—this threat can substantially depress performance on more difficult parts of the exam. And this depression could contribute significantly to the group's underperformance in comparison with nonstereotype-threatened groups.[6]

### ■ Reaction of Disidentification

Stereotype threat is assumed to have an abiding effect on school achievement—an effect beyond its impairment of immediate performance—by preventing or breaking a person's identification with school, in particular, those domains of schooling in which the stereotype applies. This reasoning has several implications for which empirical evidence can be brought to bear: the resilience of self-esteem to stigmatization; the relationship between stigmatized status and school achievement; and, among ability-stigmatized people, the relationship between their school performance and self-esteem.

*Self-esteem's resilience to stigmatization.* In a recent review, Crocker and Major (1989) were able to make a strong case for the lack of something that common sense suggests should exist: a negative effect of stigmatization on self-esteem. Following the logic of the internalization models described above and viewing stigmatization as, among other things, an assault to self-esteem, one might expect that people who are stigmatized would have lower self-esteem than people who are not. Yet, as Crocker and Major reported, when the self-esteem of stigmatized groups (e.g., Blacks, Chicanos, the facially disfigured, obese people, etc.) is actually measured, one finds that their self-esteem is as high as that of the nonstigmatized.

Crocker and Major (1989) offered the intriguing argument that stigma itself offers esteem-protective strategies. For example, the stigmatized can blame their failures on the prejudice of out-group members, they can limit their self-evaluative social comparisons to the ingroup of other stigmatized people, and they can devalue the domains in which they feel devalued. Other models have also described esteem-saving adaptations to stigma. For example, models that assume internalization of stereotype-related anxieties often posit compensatory personality traits (e.g., grandiosity) that protect self-esteem but leave one poorly adapted to the mainstream (e.g., Allport, 1954; Clark, 1965; Grier & Coobs, 1968; Kardiner & Ovesy, 1951; S. Steele, 1990). In the present reasoning, stigmatization stems from stereotype threat in specific domains. Thus, it adds to the list of stigma adaptations the possibility of simple domain disidentification, the rescuing of self-esteem by rendering as self-evaluatively irrelevant the domain in which the stereotype applies. Herein may lie a significant source of the self-esteem resilience shown in stigmatized groups. This idea also implies that once domain disidentification is achieved, the pressure for adaptations of attribution and personality may be reduced.

*A universal connection between stigmatization and poor school achievement.* If disidentification with school, and the resulting underachievement, can be a reaction to ability-stigmatizing stereotypes in society, then it might be expected that ability stigmatization would be associated with poor school performance wherever it occurs in the world. Finding such a relationship would not definitively prove the present theory; the direction of causality could be quarreled with, as could the mediation of such a relationship. Still, it would be suggestive, and, in that respect, Ogbu (1986) reported an interesting fact: Among the caste-like minorities in industrial and nonindustrial nations throughout the world (e.g., the Maoris of New Zealand, the Baraku of Japan, the Harijans of India, the Oriental Jews of Israel, and the West Indians of Great Britain), there exists the same 15-point IQ gap between them and the nonstigmatized members of their society as exists between Black and White Americans. These groups also suffer poorer school performance, higher dropout rates, and related behavior problems. Moreover, these gaps appear even when the stigmatized and nonstigmatized are of the same race, as in the case of the Baraku and other Japanese. What these groups share that is capable of explaining their deficits is a caste-like status that, through stereotypes in their societies, stigmatizes their intellectual abilities—sowing the seeds, I suggest, of their school disidentification.

*The dissociation of self-esteem and school achievement.* If the poor school achievement of ability-stigmatized groups is mediated by disidentification, then it might be expected that among the ability stigmatized, there would be a disassociation between school outcomes and overall self-esteem. Several kinds of evidence suggest this process among African Americans. First, there is the persistent finding that although Black students underperform in relation to White students on school outcomes from grades to standardized tests (e.g., Demo & Parker, 1987; Simmons, Brown, Bush, & Blyth, 1978; C. M. Steele, 1992), their global self-esteem is as high or higher than that of White students (e.g., Porter & Washington, 1979; Rosenberg, 1979; Wylie, 1979). For both of these facts to be true, some portion of Black students must have acquired an imperviousness to poor school performance.

Several further studies suggest that this imperviousness is rooted in disidentification. In a study of desegregated schools in Champaign, Illinois, Hare and Costenell (1985) measured students' school achievement; overall self-esteem; and self-esteem in the specific domains of home life, school, and peer-group relations. Like others, they found that although Black students performed less well than White students, they still had comparable levels of overall self-esteem. Their domain-specific measures suggested why: Although Black students were lower than White students in school and home-life self-esteem, Blacks slightly exceeded Whites in peer-group self-esteem. Here then, perhaps, was the source of their overall self-regard: disidentification with domains in which their evaluative prospects were poor (in this case, school and home life) and identification with domains in which their prospects were better (i.e., their peers).

A recent study suggests that this may be a not uncommon phenomenon. Analyzing data available from the National Educational Longitudinal Survey (National Center for Educational Statistics, 1992; a nationally representative longitudinal survey begun in 1988), Osborne (1994) found that from the 8th through 10th grades, Black students had lower achievement and somewhat higher self-esteem than White students, which replicated the general pattern of findings described above. But more than this, he found evidence of increasing Black students' disidentification over this period: The correlation between their school achievement and self-esteem for this period decreased significantly more for Black than for White students. Also, using a scale measure of school disidentification, Major, Spencer, Schmader, Wolfe, and Crocker (in press) found that Black students were more disidentified than White students in several college samples and that for disidentified students of both races, negative feedback about an intellectual task had less effect on their self-esteem than it did for identified students. Major et al. further showed that when racial stereotypes were primed, neither negative nor positive feedback affected Black students' self-esteem, whereas the self-esteem of White students followed the direction of the feedback. Ability stigmatization of the sort experienced by African Americans, then, can be associated with a protective "disconnect" between performance and self-regard, a disconnect of the sort that is consistent with disidentification theory.

Can stereotype threat directly cause this disconnect? To test this question, Kirsten Stoutemeyer and I varied the strength of stereotype threat that female test takers (Stanford students) were under by varying whether societal differences between women and men in math performance were attributed to small but stable differences in innate ability (suggesting an inherent, gender-based limit in math ability) or to social causes such as sex-role prescriptions and discrimination (suggesting no inherent, gender-based limit in math ability). We then measured their identification with math and math-related careers, either before or after they took a difficult math test. Regardless of when identification was measured, women under stronger stereotype threat disidentified with math and math-related careers more than women under weaker stereotype threat. Although domain identification has several determinants, these findings suggest that stereotype threat is an important one of them.

## ■ "Wise" Schooling: Practice and Policy

As a different diagnosis, the present analysis comes to a different prescription: The schooling of stereotype-threatened groups may be improved through situational changes (analogous to those manipulated in our experiments) that reduce the stereotype threat these students might otherwise be under. As noted, psychological diagnoses have more typically ascribed the problems of these students to internal processes ranging from genes to internalized stereotypes. On the face of it, at least, internal states are more difficult to modify than situational factors. Thus, the hope of the present analysis, encouraged by our research, is that these problems might be more tractable through the situational design of schooling, in particular, design that secures these students in the belief that they will not be held under the suspicion of negative stereotypes about their group. Schooling that does this, I have called *wise,* a term borrowed from Erving Goffman (1963), who borrowed it from gay men and lesbians of the 1950s. They used it to designate heterosexuals who understood their full humanity despite the stigma attached to their sexual orientation: family and friends, usually, who knew the person beneath the stigma. So it must be, I argue, for the effective schooling of stereotype-threatened groups.

Although "wisdom" may be necessary for the effective schooling of such students, it may not always be sufficient. The chief distinction made in this analysis (between those of these groups who are identified with the relevant school domain and those who are not) raises a caution. As noted, stereotype threat is not keenly felt by those who identify little with the stereotype-threatening domain. Thus, although reducing this threat in the domain may be necessary to encourage their identification, it may not be sufficient to build an identification that is not there. For this to occur, more far-reaching strategies that develop the building blocks of domain identification may be required: better skills, greater domain self-efficacy, feelings of social and cultural comfort in the domain, a lack of social pressure to disidentify, and so on.

But for the identified of these groups, who are quite numerous on college campuses, the news may be better than is typically appreciated. For these students, feasible changes in the conditions of schooling that make threatening stereotypes less applicable to their behavior (i.e., wisdom) may be enough. They are already identified with the relevant domain, they have skills and confidence in the domain, and they have survived other barriers to identification. Their remaining problem is stereotype threat. Reducing that problem, then, may be enough to bring their performance on par with that of nonstereo-typed persons in the domain.

This distinction raises an important and often overlooked issue in the design of schooling for stereotype-threatened students, that of *triage,* the issue of rendering onto the right students the right intervention. Mistakes can easily be made. For example, applying a strategy to school-identified students (on the basis of their membership in a stereotype-threatened group) that assumes weak identification, poor skills, and little confidence could backfire. It could increase stereotype threat and underperformance by signaling that their abilities are held under suspicion because of their group membership. But the opposite mistake could be made by applying a strategy that assumes strong identification, skills, and confidence to those who are actually unidentified with the relevant domain. Merely reducing stereotype threat may not accomplish much when the more primary need of these students is to gain the interests, resources, skills, confidences, and values that are needed to identify with the domain.

Some wise strategies, then, may work for both identified and unidentified students from these groups, but others may have to be appropriately targeted to be effective. I offer some examples of both types.

For both domain-identified and domain-unidentified students:

1. *Optimistic teacher-student relationships.* The prevailing stereotypes make it plausible for ability-stigmatized students to worry that people in their schooling environment will doubt their abilities. Thus, one wise strategy, seemingly suitable for all students, is to discredit this assumption through the authority of potential-affirming adult relationships. The Comer (1988) Schools Project has used this strategy with great success at the elementary school level, and Johnides, von Hippel, Lerner, and Nagda (1992) have used it in designing a mentoring program for incoming minority and other students at the University of Michigan. In analogous laboratory experiments, Geoffrey Cohen, Lee Ross, and I (Cohen, Steele, & Ross, 1997) found that critical feedback to African American students was strongly motivating when it was coupled with optimism about their potential.

2. *Challenge over remediation.* Giving challenging work to students conveys respect for their potential and thus shows them that they are not regarded through the lens of an ability-demeaning stereotype. Urie Treisman (1985) used this strategy explicitly in designing his successful group-study workshops in math for college-aged women and minorities. Taking students where they are skillwise, all students can be given challenging work at a challenging, not overwhelming, pace, especially in the context of supportive adult-student relationships. In contrast, remedial work reinforces in these students the possibility that they are being viewed stereotypically. And this, by increasing stereotype threat in the domain, can undermine their performance.

3. *Stressing the expandability of intelligence.* The threat of negative-ability stereotypes is that one could confirm or be seen as having a fixed

limitation inherent to one's group. To the extent that schooling can stress what Carol Dweck (1986) called the *incremental* nature of human intelligence—its expandability in response to experience and training—it should help to deflect this meanest implication of the stereotype. Aronson (1996) recently found, for example, that having African American college students repeatedly advocate the expandability of intelligence to their elementary school tutees significantly improved their own grades.

For domain-identified students:

1. *Affirming domain belongingness.* Negative-ability stereotypes raise the threat that one does not belong in the domain. They cast doubt on the extent of one's abilities, on how well one will be accepted, on one's social compatibility with the domain, and so on. Thus, for students whose primary barrier to school identification is stereotype threat, direct affirmation of their belongingness in the domain may be effective. But it is important to base this affirmation on the students' intellectual potential. Affirming social belonging alone, for those under the threat of an ability stereotype, could be taken as begging the question.

2. *Valuing multiple perspectives.* This refers to strategies that explicitly value a variety of approaches to both academic substance and the larger academic culture in which that substance is considered. Making such a value public tells stereotype-threatened students that this is an environment in which the stereotype is less likely to be used.

3. *Role models.* People from the stereotype-threatened group who have been successful in the domain carry the message that stereotype threat is not an insurmountable barrier there.

For domain-unidentified students:

1. *Nonjudgmental responsiveness.* Research by Lepper, Woolverton, Mumme, and Gurtner (1993) has identified a distinct strategy that expert tutors use with especially poor students: little direct praise, Socratic direction of students' work, and minimal attention to right and wrong answers. For students weakly identified with the domain, who are threatened by a poor reputation and who probably hold internalized doubts about their ability, this Socratic strategy has the wisdom of securing a safe teacher-student relationship in which there is little cost of failure and the gradual building of domain efficacy from small gains.

2. *Building self-efficacy.* Based on Bandura's (1977, 1986) theory of self-efficacy, this strategy attempts to build the student's sense of competence and self-efficacy in the schooling domain. Howard and Hammond (1985) have developed a powerful implementation of this strategy for African American and other minority students, especially in inner-city public schools.

## ■ Existence Proof: A Wise Schooling Intervention

Providing a definitive test of wise schooling theory will require, of course, an extensive research program. But as a first step, something might be learned from what Urie Treisman (1985) called an existence proof, in this case, a demonstration that an intervention derived from the theory could stop or reverse a tenacious negative trajectory in the school performance of stereo-type-threatened students. Such an intervention would of necessity confound things: different wise practices as well as other practices and structures, peculiar to that setting, that could also affect academic outcomes. It could not stand as a test of the psychological theory per se. But if a particular architecture of wise strategies succeeded, it would encourage their applicability to the real-world schooling of these students.

With this rationale, my colleagues and I (Steven Spencer, Richard Nisbett, Mary Hummel, David Schoem, Kent Harber, Ken Carter) implemented a freshman-year program at the University of Michigan aimed at the under-achievement and low retention rates of African American students. Each year, the program included approximately 250 freshmen in the ethnic proportions of the larger campus but with an oversampling of approximately 20% Black students and 20% non-Black minority students (i.e., Asian, Hispanic, and Native American students as a single group). Program students were randomly selected from the students admitted to Michigan and then recruited by phone to participate. All program participants lived together in the wing of a large, 1,200-student dormitory throughout their freshman year.

In this context, we implemented several wise strategies. The program was presented as a transition program aimed at helping students maximize the advantages of university life. We also recruited students honorifically; they were told that, as Michigan admittees, they had survived a very competitive selection process and that our program was designed to help them maximize their strong potential. These practices represented the program as nonreme-diational and represented the university as having acknowledged their intellectual potential and as having high expectations for them—all things that signal the irrelevance of negative group stereotypes. Once the students were in the program, these expectations were reinforced by their being offered a "challenge" workshop, modeled on those developed by Treisman (1985) for calculus, in either freshman calculus, chemistry, physics, or writing. These were taken on a voluntary basis in the dormitory. Students also participated in small weekly discussion groups, centered on brief readings, that allowed discussion of adjustment-relevant social and even personal issues. This activity has the wisdom of letting students know that they, or other members of their group, are not the only ones with concerns about adjusting to university life—an insight that can deflect the relevance of negative group stereotypes. These formal program components lasted for the first 10 weeks of the school year, and, as voluntary activities, approximately half of the students regularly participated in either one or both of them.

The first-semester grades averaged over the first two years of this ongoing project give a reliable picture of the program's initial impact. To show the size of the program's effect on students at different levels of preparation, Figure 9.5 graphs first-semester grades, using regression lines, for the different student groups as a function of standardized test scores on entry into the university (they are presented as standard deviation units in this figure to provide a common scale for students who took either the SAT or American College Test exam). The first thing to notice is the two essentially parallel lines for White and Black students outside of any program at Michigan. They replicate the standard overprediction—underperformance of Black students alluded to earlier, and it is against this pattern that the effects of the program can be evaluated. Looking first at the line for White students in our program, there is a modest tendency for these students to do better than the White control students (i.e., those outside the program), but given our accumulation of $n$ throughout these first two years, this difference is not significant. It is the results for Black students in our program (but who were not also in the campus minority program) that are most promising. Their line is considerably above that for Black control students (i.e., Black students outside any program) and, even with the modest sample size ($n = 27$), is significantly higher than this control line in the top one third of the standardized test distribution, $t = 2.72$, $p < .05$. It is important that this group of Black students showed almost no underperformance; in the top two thirds of the test distribution, they had essentially the same grades as White students. We also know from follow-up data that their higher grade performance continued at least through their sophomore year and that as long as four years later, only one of them had dropped out.

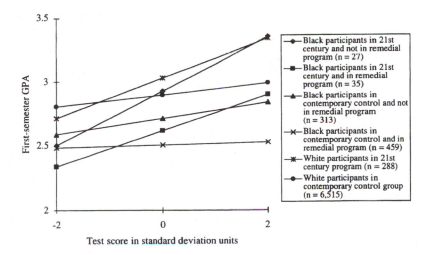

**Figure 9.5.** First-Semester Grade Point Average (GPA) as a Function of Program and Race Controlling for High School GPA

Theoretically just as important is the bottom line in Figure 9.5, depicting the results for Black students in a large minority remediation program. Despite getting considerable attention, they performed worse than the other groups at nearly every level of preparation. The difference between Black students in the minority program and Black students not in any program becomes significant at 1.76 standard deviations below the mean for test performance and is significant from that point on, $p < .05$. Also, by the beginning of their junior year, 25% of these students had failed to register, and among those who entered with test scores in the top one third of the test distribution, this figure was 40%. Some selection factor possibly contributed to this. Despite our having controlled for test scores and high school grade point averages in these analyses, some portion of these students may have been assigned to this program because they evidenced other risk factors. Still, these results suggest that the good intentions of the minority-remediation framework for schooling African American students can backfire by, in our terms, institutionalizing the racial stereotype by which they are already threatened.

Although these findings are preliminary and we do not know that they were mediated as our theory claims, they are a step toward an existence proof; they show that wise practices can reduce Black students' underachievement in a real-school context and, as important, that unwise practices seem to worsen it.

# ■ Conclusion

In social psychology, we know that as observers looking at a person or group, we tend to stress internal, dispositional causes of their behavior, whereas when we take the perspective of the actor, now facing the circumstances they face, we stress more situational causes (e.g., Jones & Nisbett, 1972; Ross, 1977). If there is a system to the present research, it is that of taking the actor's perspective in trying to understand the intellectual performance of African American and female students. It is this perspective that brings to light the broadly encompassing condition of having these groups' identification with domains of schooling threatened by societal stereotypes. This is a threat that in the short run can depress their intellectual performance and, over the long run, undermine the identity itself, a predicament of serious consequence. But it is a predicament—something in the interaction between a group's social identity and its social psychological context, rather than something essential to the group itself. Predicaments can be treated, intervened on, and it is in this respect that I hope the perspective taken in this analysis and the early evidence offer encouragement.

# ■ Notes

1. Other factors may also contribute. For example, there are persistent reports of women and minorities being treated differently in the classroom and in other aspects of schooling (e.g., Hewitt & Seymour, 1991). This treatment includes both the "chilly-climate" sins of omission—the failure to call on them in class or to recognize and encourage their talents, and so on—and, in the case of low-income minorities, sins of commission—disproportionate expulsion from school, assignment to special education classes, and administration or corporal punishment ("National Coalition of Advocates for Students Report," 1988).

2. The point is not that negative stereotypes are never internalized as low self-expectancies and self-doubts. It is that in such internalization, disidentification is the more primary adaptation. That is, once the stereotype-relevant domain (e.g., math) is dropped as a self-definition, the negative stereotype (e.g., that women are limited in math) can be accepted as more self-descriptive (i.e., internalized) without it much affecting one's self-regard (as for the woman who, not caring about math, says she is lousy at it). But this internalization is probably resisted (e.g., Crocker & Major, 1989) until disidentification makes it less self-threatening. Once this has happened, the person is likely to avoid the domain because of both disinterest and low confidence regardless of whether stereotype threat is present.

3. As a process of social devaluation, stereotype threat is both a subform of stigmatization and something more general. It is that form of stigmatization that is mediated by collectively held, devaluing group stereotypes. This means that it does not include stigmatization that derives from nonstereotyped features such as a facial disfigurement or, for example, what Goffman (1963) called abominations of the body. Stereotype threat is a situational predicament. And, in this sense,

it is also more general than stigmatization. It is a threat that can befall anyone about whom a negative reputation or group stereotype exists.

4. Moreover, a protective avoidance of identification can become a group norm. In reaction to a shared sense of threat in school, for example, it can become a shared reaction that is transmitted to group members as the normative relation to school. Both research (e.g., Ogbu, 1986; Solomon, 1992) and the media have documented this reaction in minority students from inner-city high schools to Harvard University's campus. Thus, disidentification can be sustained by normative pressure from the in-group as well as by stereotype threat in the setting.

5. Participants did not actually take the test in this experiment, as completing these measures would likely have activated the stereotype in all conditions.

6. Those who are less domain identified in the stereotype-threatened group may also underperform on standardized tests. Because they care less about the domain it represents, they may be undermotivated or they may withdraw effort in the face of frustration. And for all of the reasons I have discussed, the greater portion of the stereotype-threatened group may be academically unidentified. This fact too, then, may contribute to the group's overall weaker performance on these tests in comparison with nonstereotype-threatened groups.

# 10

# The Rocky Road to
# Positive Intergroup Relations

*Patricia G. Devine*
*Kristin A. Vasquez*

**D**eveloping an understanding of the origins and nature of *intergroup tension*—tension between members of different groups—has been on the research agenda of social scientists seemingly forever. And they are not the only ones interested in this endeavor. Legislators, politicians, and regular old folks face similar challenges as they try to decide legal policy and how to negotiate everyday circumstances in which they encounter and interact with people different from themselves. The difference might be race, ethnicity, sexual orientation, religion, age, nationality . . . the list could go on and on. Social scientists have often argued that intergroup tension arises from feelings of negativity between group members. We don't deny this to be one source of intergroup tension. We believe, however, that there are a variety of sources of intergroup tension, and that our overall efforts to promote positive intergroup relations would be served well by expanding the way we think about intergroup tension. Not to give too much away early in the chapter, but we argue, somewhat counterintuitively, that intergroup tension can arise out of positive motivations—that is, efforts to be nonprejudiced and to get along well with members of other groups. To set the stage for our analysis, consider the following true story that happened to one of us not too long ago.

## ■ Why Is This So Hard?

Once upon a time, a student was charged with the task of bringing refreshments to a meeting. Naturally, as a student, she did not cook, so she

234

decided to order a pizza. Then she remembered that among those to be fed at the meeting would be the Princess.

The Princess was a kind and friendly person, and a real-life princess. She was the daughter of a Sultan in Mindanao, in the southern Philippines. She had spoken often, in her brief acquaintance with the student, about her pride in her heritage and the value she placed on her Muslim culture and values. Unfortunately, in all their conversations, the issue of pizza—or other dietary practices—had never come up.

The student felt trapped. Should she order pizza for everyone? Would the Princess be able to eat it? Would assuming the Princess couldn't eat it be a sign of prejudice? Or was it a sign of prejudice not to know if there were particular Muslim dietary restrictions? If there were, would the Princess keep them? Would making a special case of the Princess, or not making a special case, be the worse error? And most of all, if the student spent the better part of every day thinking about issues of prejudice and discrimination, why weren't any of these answers more apparent?

The unhappy student puzzled over the pizza. She asked friends and family members if the Princess could eat pizza, but no one knew the answer. Finally, her professor clarified the issue, saying, "Why don't you call and ask her?"

The student was dumbfounded. It had never once entered her mind to ask the Princess. She had been convinced that, if she were a nonprejudiced person as she wished to be, she should have automatically known the answer.

The call to the Princess was not easy to make. The student thought hard, trying to find a way around it. What could she say? "Excuse me, but do you happen to eat pizza?" "I was just wondering if there are any rules for Muslims against pizza eating?" She felt acutely embarrassed and self-conscious, and that was before she even picked up the phone.

She called. The Princess answered. The student was grateful to be on the phone so she didn't have to look the Princess in the eye as she asked, but even so, she noticed she was shuffling her feet as she spoke. "Uh," she stuttered, "I'm bringing the food tonight, and, well, I, um, is pizza . . . OK? Do you eat pizza?"

"Oh, sure," the Princess replied.

The student had an answer to the pizza problem. But somehow, she didn't feel that much better. "Did I sound like a moron?" she asked herself. "Does the Princess think I'm an insensitive clod?"

The next time the student met the Princess, she was filled with apprehension. But the Princess was as kind and gracious as ever, and continued to tell the student fascinating stories about her homeland. The student was relieved, to say the least. The situation did not have to turn out as well as it did, she knew. But this time, the risk paid off for everyone.

You may never have to buy dinner for a Muslim princess. But every day, there is the chance for you to come into contact with members of groups with whom you are unfamiliar or have had little personal experience. When it happens to you, what do you do? How do you know what to say? How will the other person respond? Should you explicitly acknowledge your differ- ences or should you act like there are no differences at all? Are you ever afraid that you will be seen as prejudiced, even though you don't mean to be? These questions are at the heart of the dilemma that many people face as they try to get along in a diverse social world.

## ◼ Old Problems and New Challenges

As the United States becomes an increasingly multicultural society, contact between members of different groups—intergroup contact—is both important and inevitable. If we, individually and as a society, are going to be successful and do well in the future, we are going to have to learn to be comfortable within a multicultural environment. It is vital that the feelings of uncertainty and confusion that can complicate relations between people from different groups be explored. Such feelings might easily lead people tȯ retreat to their own groups, where the risk of being misunderstood or labeled as "prejudiced" is lessened, but that withdrawal would be unfortunate on both personal and societal levels.

Before we consider the nature of the dilemmas that can arise in intergroup settings, let us take a minute to reflect on how we got to this point in relations between groups. There has been a dramatic change in the social and political climate in the United States with regard to race relations and issues of culture. In the wake of the civil rights movement, attitudes of white Americans about racial matters have changed (e.g., Schuman, Steeth, & Bobo, 1985). At some levels, the changes have been dramatic, and the effects, positive. No longer are there separate restrooms, water fountains, or lunch counters for blacks and whites. In addition, recent survey studies indicate that most people no longer subscribe as strongly to the negative views that were once commonplace in the United States. White Americans are, overall, more positive toward inte- gration, their racial attitudes are more favorable, and fewer white people indicate that they would not vote for a well-qualified black presidential candidate. In short, overt, explicit, obvious kinds of prejudice have clearly decreased in frequency.

So, then, what's the problem? These changes should bode well for improving intergroup relations. And, in fact, they do. The remaining problems are two. First, although the majority of white Americans have renounced overtly racist beliefs (e.g., Dovidio & Gaertner, 1986b; Gaertner & Dovidio, 1986; Katz, Wackenhut, & Hass, 1986; McConahay, 1986; Schuman et al., 1985), there still remain people who hold extremely negative, hostile views toward members of other groups. We do not deny that some such people exist, nor that their prejudiced attitudes pose a real problem on both theoretical and practical levels.

For the purposes of this chapter, however, we will focus instead on the greater number of majority group members who hold relatively nonprejudiced attitudes. As we look at this group, a second problem becomes evident: Although we are cautiously optimistic, it is important to recognize that with the positive changes come new challenges in how to think about intergroup relations both for majority group members (historically the perpetrators of prejudice) and for minority group members (historically the targets of prejudice). Our specific interest focuses on how these challenges are played out in the context of interpersonal interactions between majority and minority group members. Ironically, the challenges faced by both groups are tied directly to the facts that (a) overt prejudice is no longer socially acceptable and (b) there are no good guidelines for "how to do the intergroup thing well." The question of interest is how we make sense of majority group members' efforts to respond in nonprejudiced ways. The fact that there is a perceived societal pressure to respond without prejudice can, paradoxically, create difficulties for both majority and minority group members. Let's take a closer look.

## ■ Challenges for Majority Group Members

Ask yourself (as did the student in the story) what it means to be nonprejudiced. Then ask yourself what you can do to show another person that you are nonprejudiced. You may be able to think of some concrete actions you can perform, but more likely you will find yourself with a list of "should nots." For example, you may tell yourself that you should not stare. You should not ask questions based on the stereotype of the group. You may even tell yourself to "be yourself" or "act natural." The question then becomes how to act "natural" while your head is full of prohibitions, you're feeling a little nervous anyway, and you'd like to make a good impression—not be labeled as prejudiced.

In other words, with positive changes in attitudes among many majority group members, there also come some new challenges for people who are trying to figure out how to behave the "right" way when interacting with members of other groups. Some of these challenges are rooted in the fact that for individuals who do not hold prejudiced attitudes, there are not good explicit norms or guidelines about how to behave in intergroup interactions. There are many rules about what not to do and what not to say (e.g., don't make ethnic or racial slurs), but few guidelines about what actions are appropriate. We believe that the lack of clear guidelines, combined with a fear of appearing prejudiced in these settings, creates difficulties for people who are trying to behave in nonprejudiced ways.

What is the result of these difficulties? The frustration that can result from the lack of guidance in these intergroup settings can be heard in the comments of students who say "I tried, but it didn't work. I feel damned if I do and damned if I don't. If I acknowledge race I am being racist; if I hide from it or say I don't notice race, other people say I am insensitive. How do I do this right? What are the guidelines?" The risk we are most concerned about is that in the face of these difficulties, some people will declare intergroup contact too difficult, or not worth the bother, and withdraw from intergroup interactions. This withdrawal would functionally take care of the tension associated with intergroup interactions, but it seems a less than desirable solution.

## ■ Challenges for Minority Group Members

A decrease in overt prejudice also changes the situation for minority group members. Minority group members are, in general, in touch with the ideas that there are explicit norms in our society against the overt expression of prejudice (see Crocker & Major, 1989; Duke & Morin, 1992; Feagin, 1989). As a result, some may become mistrusting of the majority group members who respond in positive ways or profess to be nonprejudiced. Are these responses reflections of true changes in attitudes, or do they reflect efforts to hide their truly-felt prejudices and to respond in socially desirable ways? How can one tell? Indeed, for many, there is a cloud of suspicion and mistrust casting a shadow on prospects for positive intergroup relations. These suspicions are echoed in the comments of minority group members, such as, "It's the 'is it or isn't it' [prejudice] debate that can churn inside a black person confronted with poor service in a restaurant, a social slight, or an inconsiderate act by a white . . . it's the second guessing we do" (Duke & Morin, 1992, p. A24). This feeling of uncertainty about the motives or intentions underlying the behavior of majority group members is referred to as attributional ambiguity in the social psychology literature (Chapter 5, this volume; Crocker & Major, 1989; Crocker, Voelkl, Testa, & Major, 1991; Major & Crocker, 1993). In short, uncertainty about how to make sense of majority group members' behavior, however sensible it may be when considered in historical context, is likely to contribute to tension in intergroup settings.

## ■ What Happens When Uncertainties Collide?

Our thinking about these issues is organized around two central themes. The first is that contact between members of different groups often results in specific types of interpersonal dilemmas that have to be managed by both parties if the interaction is to succeed. The second theme is that because so much of social behavior is ambiguous, there is the potential for miscommunication between majority group and minority group members that arises out of the kind of expectations, goals, and concerns that each brings to the intergroup situation. Such miscommunication can easily result in the escalation of tension. Ironically, although there are many possible sources of tension in a intergroup encounter, such tension is often given the most pejorative interpretation: prejudice. Once the tension is explained as prejudice, a positive outcome to the interaction is unlikely. These potential pitfalls are the reason we call the road to positive intergroup relations a rocky one.

Social interaction, especially between members of different groups, is very complex. It often becomes very confusing and difficult for people on either side of an interaction to figure out how to manage the situation. As a result, tension can even arise between *interactants* (people in the interaction) who have good intentions, who want the interaction to go well. In other words, we believe that one does not have to be prejudiced to have the interaction to go poorly. We looked to the existing literature on intergroup relations for advice on how to think about, and hopefully improve, intergroup relations. Unfortunately, we found little guidance; in our opinion the existing literature left us ill-equipped to address these kinds of issues. Our most recent work has focused on exploring the nature of tension experienced in intergroup interactions and on understanding why people find such interactions so difficult to manage. Our goal is to understand the practical challenges associated with the *interpersonal dynamics*—the constantly changing "give and take" between the people in the interaction—of intergroup contact. We will outline a framework for addressing such challenges that may help us to understand why intergroup encounters can be difficult and fraught with tension. To set the stage for this work and to provide adequate context, we briefly review what we consider to be major limitations of past theorizing on intergroup relations.


### ■ Limitations of Past Research

The literature on intergroup relations offers a peculiar perspective on how individuals, both majority and minority group members, manage specific interpersonal encounters with members of other groups. The issue of key interest is how two people from different groups affect each other in an interaction. Traditionally, however, most research has examined majority group and minority group members in isolation. Such a strategy is, by definition, limited in its ability to address the dynamic aspects of negotiating intergroup encounters. Moreover, there has been no attempt to integrate the findings from these separate literatures to consider how dynamic interactions unfold over time. Let's look at these limitations in more detail to see why they pose a challenge for understanding how majority and minority group members deal with the practical challenges involved in negotiating intergroup interactions.


### ■ Limitation 1: There Are Two People Here, But We Look at Them One at a Time

Somewhat symptomatic of the limitations of existing theory is that the previous work has examined majority group members (e.g., whites and heterosexuals) and minority group members (e.g., blacks and homosexuals) separately. Such a position neglects some practical challenges of intergroup contact in contemporary society. As a result, the literature has had very little to offer to help us understand the nature of the interpersonal dynamics of intergroup contact. For example, the central focus of the "majority group literature" has been on the nature of the attitudes and stereotypes majority group members hold with regard to minority group members (e.g., Allport, 1954; Cook, 1985; Devine, Monteith, Zuwerink, & Elliot; 1991; Dovidio & Gaertner, 1986b; McConahay, 1986; Stephan, 1987). The concern has been prejudice: its origins, and efforts to eliminate it. The literature on minority group members has often emphasized the self-esteem and adjustment consequences of being a member of a stigmatized group (e.g., Crocker & Major, 1989; Jones et al., 1984; Seligman & Welch, 1991).

When thinking about what goes on between people in intergroup interactions, these literatures offer only an analysis of prospective interactants. Although these literatures have taught us a great deal, they offer an incomplete picture. We have not yet examined carefully and fully the nature of interpersonal dynamics that emerge between majority and minority group members when they are brought together in a specific interpersonal situation. In other words, we do not know what happens once the interaction begins.

To effectively address the problem of intergroup tension, the study of intergroup relations must be broadened to include analyses of how individuals think about the interactions, about themselves and their partners during these interactions, and about the outcomes of the interactions. We have to take seriously the practical considerations involved in negotiating the fluid, interpersonal aspects of intergroup contact. If we do not, we will not be in a very good position to try to develop effective interventions that ultimately might facilitate positive, harmonious intergroup relations.

## ■ Limitation 2: And Then We Ignore One of Them

Social psychologists have generally thought about the issue of intergroup tension and prejudice as a majority group problem. According to this logic, the key obstacle to positive intergroup relations was that majority group members had negative attitudes toward minority group members. At the heart of the strategies that have been developed to try to reduce intergroup hostilities was the assumption that majority group members' negative attitudes (prejudice) needed to be changed. The assumption was that if the attitudes changed, the stage would be set for smooth, positive, and harmonious intergroup relations. Indeed, some researchers have argued that in the study of race relations, for example, that the minority views are "conspicuous by their absence" (Seligman & Welch, 1991, p. 1). Although we agree that it is clearly necessary to address majority group members' negative attitudes, we believe that attitude change by itself is unlikely to be sufficient to solve the problem. Any effective analysis of the interpersonal intergroup situation needs to take into consideration the perspective of both majority and minority group members. In addition, it must take into consideration the nature of the reciprocal dynamics (how things change in the situation as each person's actions affect the other person) that emerge when people engage in interaction situations.

*Can majority attitudes really be changed?* There are a lot of strategies that have been tried to change attitudes of majority group members—for example, propaganda techniques, education, therapy, and insight training. Perhaps the most important and well-investigated strategy for trying to reduce intergroup tension derives from the contact hypothesis (Allport, 1954; Amir, 1969; Cook, 1984; 1985; Stephan, 1985). The contact hypothesis delineates the conditions that should promote positive attitudes among majority group members. Based on the research of a number of insightful investigators, we find that there are a number of situations that, if achieved, would contribute to positive attitudes, or encourage attitude change among majority group members (see Stephan, 1987, for a review). Some of these conditions include the following:

■ Contact should be between people of equal status.
■ Interactions should be cooperative rather than competitive.
■ Contact should have institutional support.
■ Outcomes of the contact should be positive.
■ Contact should occur between similarly competent others.
■ Contact should be with a nonstereotypic other.

There are, however, a number of shortcomings to the contact hypothesis that limit its power as a solution to the problem of intergroup tension. First, these conditions are extremely difficult to achieve in an intergroup situation. For example, think about the typical classroom situation. The classroom is an important setting for thinking about intergroup contact because, historically, it has been an arena where there was great hope that contact could produce positive intergroup attitudes. But, if you remember back to being in elementary school, you will recall that it is a very competitive environment; students compete for grades and the teacher's attention. As another example, consider the employment setting, where affirmative action policies are enacted to encourage contact among groups. Not only is that environment very often competitive, but it is also hierarchical, violating the equal status condition of the contact hypothesis. A second problem with the contact hypothesis is that there are also interdependencies among the different conditions. That is, cooperation may facilitate development of positive attitudes, but only when it is combined with a successful outcome. When cooperative endeavors end in failure, there is often escalation of conflict, which may take the form of blaming of the minority group member. Indeed, the most succinct and accurate summary of research on the contact hypothesis is that contact sometimes produces positive attitudes among majority members (Stephan, 1987). Clearly we have a difficult situation here—conditions assumed to be necessary to promote positive intergroup relations are difficult, if not impossible, to achieve in most real-world settings.

*If majority attitudes change, will it be enough?* Considered from the vantage point of the history of race relations, thinking about the problem of intergroup prejudice as a majority problem makes a lot of sense; after all, majority group members have typically been the ones in positions of power. Such an emphasis also grew naturally out of the kind of sociopolitical climate in which social scientists were trying to solve the U.S. race problem. But even if all majority group members could be induced to hold positive attitudes through cooperative contact, the analysis of the problem offered by the contact hypothesis is too global and incomplete for an understanding of the nature of the complex interpersonal dynamics associated with intergroup contact. Not only does it focus solely on the majority group member, but it assumes that if attitudes are positive, tension will disappear. Remember the student in the story at the beginning of this chapter? She held very positive attitudes toward the Princess, and toward members of the Princess's cultural group in general. She was highly motivated to do well in the interaction and not to offend the Princess. We would not consider the student to be prejudiced against the Princess. And yet, the interaction between them still held the potential for miscommunication, and possibly, the student feared, the escalation of tension. This story, then, demonstrates that establishing positive attitudes is not sufficient to ensure smooth encounters. There are other obstacles that make the road to intergroup relations a bit rough, even when intentions are good.

## ■ A Classic Look at Dynamic Interactions

Part of the reason so much emphasis has focused on attitude change as the ultimate goal of contact is that very few studies have examined what goes on in actual interactions between majority and minority group members. The few that have are very similar in design and in their conclusions. If we examine these studies carefully, we can see not only the overemphasis on majority group members, but also important assumptions about the attitudes that majority group members hold. The premise of these studies, consistent with prevailing themes in the literature, is that majority group members' negative attitudes toward minority group members will lead majority group members to treat minority group members less favorably than majority group members. That is, the prejudice of the majority group members will lead them to discriminate against minority group members. One particularly well-designed study serves as an example for our purposes.

This research was done by Word, Zanna, and Cooper in 1974 to study the nature of dynamic interactions between majority and minority group members—in this case, blacks and whites. In the first of two experiments, the researchers created an interview context for the interaction. White experimental participants were assigned to the role of interviewer, and black and white students were identified as applicants who were to be interviewed by the white interviewer. The important thing to know about the applicants was that they were actually *confederates* (helpers of the experimenter). They knew everything that was going on and they had a preprogrammed prescribed role in the interview situation.

The researchers were particularly interested in how the majority group members would handle themselves and conduct themselves in this interaction. The outcomes they were most interested in included a variety of nonverbal behaviors including things like eye gaze (how much time the interviewer spent looking at the applicant), awkward speech patterns (e.g., saying "um" or "er" a lot) or hesitations, the length of the interview, and interpersonal distance (how close the interviewer sat to the applicant).

What were the findings? Very much as they expected, Word et al. (1974) found that the black and white applicants were treated differently in this interaction situation. The black applicants were met with less eye contact, greater interpersonal distance, more speech errors, and shorter interviews. Clearly, the black applicants were discriminated against, in the sense that they were treated differently than the white applicants.

The conclusion from this study, and those like it in the social psychology literature, is that majority group members' discriminatory behavior (their avoidant nonverbal behavior) was a manifestation of their hidden prejudice. Other possible interpretations of that behavior were not offered in the report of the experiment, nor are they interpretations that had been considered by very many social psychologists at that time. Can you think of any alternative reasons why the white interviewers might have shown awkward or avoidant nonverbal behaviors in the Word et al. (1974) study? Keep in mind that Word et al. assumed that all majority members were basically prejudiced toward minority group members, yet they did not take any type of individual difference measure of prejudice. That is, they did not ask the participants any questions about their attitudes toward African Americans. They assumed, as did many social psychologists (e.g., Crosby, Bromley, & Saxe, 1980) that self-report measures of attitudes are untrustworthy and thus preferred to look at behaviors that are not easy to control (e.g., nonverbal behaviors). We believe, however, that it is simplistic to categorize all majority group members as prejudiced on the basis of their nonverbal behaviors alone. Moreover, we believe that individual differences in self-reported levels of prejudice are important and should be taken into consideration as we try to understand contemporary race relations and relations between minority and majority group members more generally. Specifically, we believe that individual differences in prejudice have implications for the nature of tension experienced in intergroup situations.

### ■ Individual Differences in Prejudice: Personal Standards for How to Treat Minority Group Members

To illustrate these important differences in levels of prejudice, we will review some of our own research in this area (Devine, 1989; Devine & Monteith, 1993; Devine et al., 1991; Monteith, 1993; Monteith, Devine, & Zuwerink, 1993, Zuwerink, Devine, Monteith, & Cook, 1996). The first question we asked is whether people have different standards about how they should treat members of minority groups (Devine, 1989). We found that although people of high and low levels of prejudice toward blacks, as measured by a self-report scale, had equal knowledge of the cultural stereotype of blacks, only people who reported being low in prejudice made a conscious and deliberate attempt to keep those negative stereotypes from influencing their behavior.

Because people of differing prejudice levels appeared to have different personal standards about how to behave toward minority group members, we then investigated the nature and consequences of those standards (Devine et al., 1991). The way we did this was rather straightforward: We described a situation in which they imagined themselves encountering a member of another group in a variety of settings. We then asked them two questions: How they thought they should react in such a setting, and how they thought they would react. For example, we told them to imagine that they were sitting on a bus and a black person sat down next to them. Then we asked them if they should feel uncomfortable, and if they would feel uncomfortable.

Note that we believe people are able to reflect accurately on their own standards, and are willing to report honestly about their standards. If this were not the case, what would we expect to see? Most college students are probably aware that it is not considered "politically correct" to make overtly prejudiced statements. If all of the participants in our studies were answering according to such "PC" guidelines, we would expect everyone to answer like this: "No, it shouldn't bother me at all if a black person sat down next to me on a bus, and no, it wouldn't bother me at all." In other words, the "should" scores and "would" scores would all be at the low extreme, and the *discrepancy* (the difference between their "should" score and their "would" score) would be zero. If we saw that most participants were answering our questionnaires in that way, then we would wonder what was happening. Either all of them were really completely nonprejudiced, or those who were higher in prejudice were manipulating their responses, either to fool themselves (because they didn't want to admit to prejudice) or to fool us (so we didn't make negative judgments about them).

The results we obtained, however, were rather different—strikingly so if you believe that people are unwilling or unable to answer honestly about their views on prejudice. A large majority of participants reported positive discrepancies—according to themselves, what they would do is more prejudiced than what they should do. Moreover, higher total "should" scores (i.e., personal standards allowing more prejudiced responses) were associated with higher levels of prejudice. Higher total "would" scores were also associated with higher levels of prejudice. These findings are consistent regardless of whether we ask respondents about their standards about thoughts, feelings, or behavior toward minority groups (Monteith et al., 1993); see Table 10.1.

Thus, when we compared people who report being low versus high in prejudice on self-report attitude measures, we found that they have different standards for how they should treat members of a minority group. Low-prejudice people's personal standards required that they respond in nonprejudiced or nonbiased ways. The personal standards of high-prejudice people permitted higher levels of prejudice, as would be expected given their attitudes.

We also found that, overall, low-prejudice people's personal standards were more internalized than were the standards of their high-prejudice counterparts (Devine et al., 1991; Monteith et al., 1993). That is, compared to high-prejudice people, low-prejudice people told us that it was more important for them to live up to their personal standards, that they were more committed to living up to their personal standards, and that they saw living up to their personal standards as a central part of their self-concepts. Low-prejudice

**TABLE 10.1**  Predicted Values for Total Should and Total Would Ratings as a
Function of Prejudice Level and Response Type

|  | Feeling Response | | Thought Response | | Behavior Response | |
|---|---|---|---|---|---|---|
| Rating | LP | HP | LP | HP | LP | HP |
| Total should | 1.53 | 3.61 | 1.82 | 3.93 | 1.16 | 2.24 |
| Total would | 2.43 | 5.04 | 3.31 | 5.37 | 1.37 | 2.93 |

SOURCE: Monteith, Devine, and Zuwerink (1993). Copyright © 1993 by the American Psychological
Association. Reprinted with permission.
NOTE: LP = low prejudice; HP = high prejudice. Responses for "should" and "would" scores range from 1 to
7, where higher numbers indicate more prejudiced responses. For each dependent measure, comparisons between
low- and high-prejudice participants within each domain were performed. The effect for prejudice was
significant in every case ($p < 0.05$).

people also feel more obligated to respond consistently with their personal
standards; see Table 10.2. High-prejudice people have personal standards
that are less internalized and carry less obligation to conform to those standards.

Another very important finding is that when low-prejudice people vio-
late their personal standards (i.e., when they slip up, often unintentionally,
and respond with more prejudice than they personally believe is acceptable), a number of important psychological consequences follow (see Devine
& Monteith, 1993). In the face of failures to live up to their standards,
low-prejudice people feel guilty and self-critical. As shown in Figure 10.1,
low-prejudice people with large discrepancies—that is, people who say that
what they "would" do is more prejudiced than what they "should" do—experience high levels of negative feelings directed toward themselves; they feel
guilty, regretful, ashamed, disappointed with themselves, and self-critical.
In contrast, high-prejudice people do not report high levels of such feelings, whether they were faced with large or small discrepancies. In other
words, a high-prejudice person may do something even more prejudiced than
his or her personal standards deem appropriate, but he or she still doesn't feel
very guilty about it (Devine et al., 1991). In fact, if he or she feels anything,
it is likely to be anger toward the minority group member (Monteith et al.,
1993).

The guilt associated with discrepancies for people of lower prejudice
levels can be a motivating condition for people to try to figure out how to avoid
prejudice in the future; it drives them to try to figure out what went wrong and

**TABLE 10.2**  Internalization of Personal Standards and Obligation as a Function of
Prejudice Level

|  | Prejudice Level | | |
|---|---|---|---|
|  | Low | Moderate | High |
| Internalization of personal standard | 6.29$_a$ | 5.50$_b$ | 4.99$_b$ |
| Obligation to conform to personal standard | 5.44$_a$ | 5.17$_{ab}$ | 4.26$_b$ |

NOTE: Responses range from 1 to 7, where higher numbers indicate higher levels of the construct. Means with
different subscripts differ significantly from each other ($p < .05$).
SOURCE: Devine, Monteith, Zuwerink, and Elliot (1991).

how they can respond consistently with their standards in the future so as to
avoid such failures (Monteith, 1993). We can conclude, then, that low-
prejudice people and high-prejudice people have very different standards for
how to treat minority group members, and that these standards have implications for the possibility of further prejudice reduction.

The differences between the self-reports of high- and low-prejudiced
people in our studies are theoretically important because they demonstrate
that some people are willing to state that they are relatively prejudiced, and
others tell us that although they would like to be nonprejudiced, they sometimes fail to live up to those standards. For researchers who believe that the
nonprejudiced responses of white participants are merely symptomatic of
the fact that overt prejudice has been driven underground (e.g., Kinder &
Sears, 1981, McConahay, 1986), the responses of these participants are
difficult to explain. Although there may be some respondents whose ambivalence about racial issues contains unacknowledged negative feelings toward
minority groups (Gaertner & Dovidio, 1986), many of our respondents are
very much aware of the times when their own thoughts, feelings, and behaviors are more prejudiced than they would like. That is, not only are our
participants aware of their own standards, but unlike "aversive racists," our
participants are also consciously aware that they sometimes fail to live up to
those standards. We do not claim that our results are incompatible with the
theory of aversive racism; indeed, both perspectives are important to a complete understanding of the phenomenon of prejudice. We do argue, however,
that because a significant number of individuals are aware of their violations
of their own standards, they are in a much better position to work to continue
to reduce their biases than are aversive racists, who are unaware of their
prejudice.

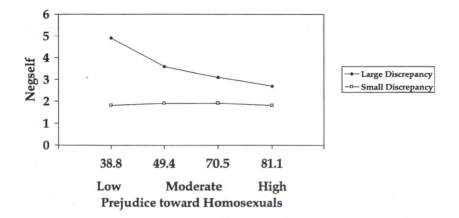

**Figure 10.1.** Predicted Values of Negative Feelings Toward the Self for High- and Low-Discrepancy Subjects as a Function of Prejudice
SOURCE: Devine, Monteith, Zuwerink, and Elliot (1991). Copyright © 1991 by the American Psychological Association. Reprinted with permission.

Our past work has taken into consideration the differences in people's standards and motivations to respond without prejudice toward members of other groups. But what implications does this work hold for real intergroup encounters? Indeed, an important limitation of this work is that it deals only with majority group members' thoughts and feelings, and only in imagined encounters with minority group members. We have focused on the nature of the conflict within a person (i.e., guilt) associated with trying to reduce prejudice. To address this shortcoming in our own work, the goal of our more recent research is to extend our analysis into the interpersonal intergroup arena. That is, until recently we had not explored how these individual differences in personal standards affect what happens between people in an intergroup interaction. We believe that the differences we see in people's attitudes and standards affect how they think about the interactions, how they think about themselves in the interactions, and how they behave during the interactions.

## ■ Prejudice Reduction as a Process

Instead of thinking of prejudice reduction as an all-or-nothing event, in which a person is either prejudiced or not, we think of it as a gradual process.

In a way, becoming a low-prejudiced person is like breaking a bad habit, the habit of prejudiced responses. The first thing a person must do when breaking any habit is to make a commitment. Then the person must develop the skills necessary to change the unwanted behavior.

In our work, we have conceived of prejudice reduction as just such a process, involving number of interrelated stages (see Figure 10.2). The first thing that people have to do, if they are going to overcome prejudiced tendencies, is to establish nonprejudiced attitudes and standards. The second thing that they have to do is internalize those standards. Those two steps together will establish the motivation to respond without prejudice. As our previous work suggests, however, attitude change is not sufficient to overcome prejudice. Once motivated, people have to develop the ability to respond consistently with those nonprejudiced standards. During the prejudice reduction process, low-prejudice people are confronted with rather formidable challenges from within, as they battle their spontaneous negative responses, and from interpersonal settings in which their standards are truly "put on the line."

We find that many white students interacting with blacks, and many heterosexual students interacting with homosexuals, have said that they are really concerned about doing and saying the wrong thing. They want the interactions to go well; they want to do the right thing. These people have accomplished Steps 1 and 2 of the prejudice reduction process. Where they seem to get tripped up is at Step 3: learning to behave in a nonprejudiced way. They have the motivation, but are uncertain about how to translate their nonprejudiced standards into behaviors that are consistent with those standards. Have you ever had this kind of experience? Your experience may be much like that of the bemused student from our story. She was committed to behaving in a nonprejudiced, sensitive way, but she had no idea how to do so. Indeed, it appears that her motivation to convey her positive attitudes to the Princess led her to "overthink" the situation, and to miss the most direct resolution to her dilemma—simply asking the Princess if she ate pizza.

## ■ Individual Differences in Prejudice and Anticipated Responses in Intergroup Settings

To understand how low- and high-prejudice individuals think about intergroup situations, we ask them what their thoughts are with regard to impending interactions with members of different groups (Devine, Evett, &

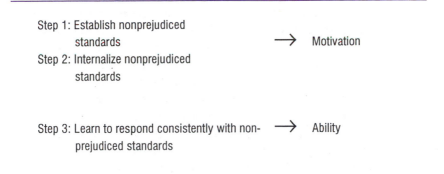

Step 1: Establish nonprejudiced
    standards                               ⟶    Motivation
Step 2: Internalize nonprejudiced
    standards

Step 3: Learn to respond consistently with non-  ⟶   Ability
    prejudiced standards

**Figure 10.2.** The Prejudice Reduction Process

Vasquez-Suson, 1996; Evett & Devine, 1996). The analysis for high-prejudice people is fairly straightforward and it follows from the kind of overt prejudice that you might expect from people who are high in prejudice. They report to us that they expect to feel hatred and antipathy toward the minority group member, that they would feel hostile in these kinds of interactions, and that they would like to get out of the situation as fast as possible. Think back to the Word et al. (1974) study for just a moment and the key outcome measures that they examined. We might expect that the decreased eye contact, the increase in the speech errors, the increased personal distance that they found might follow, for these high-prejudice people, directly from those negative attitudes.

But what about low-prejudice people? We found that low-prejudice people fall into two different categories. These two different categories of low-prejudice people are equally motivated to respond without prejudice; being nonprejudiced is a very important goal for them. We have found, however, that their anticipated reactions to members of minority groups are determined jointly by motivation and their self-perceived ability to respond consistently with their standards. Attitude change is not enough, having motivation is not enough; we must consider the issue of ability.

Let's think, first, about the individuals whose motivation is high and their self-perceived ability is high. Under these circumstances they report that they will not experience any interpersonal difficulty. They expect to have smooth and positive interactions with members of minority groups, and they expect the interaction to go well. They also say that they would act "normally," and that there would be nothing particularly unusual for them about the intergroup exchange. These people are motivated and they believe that they have the requisite skills to translate that motivation into reality.

What about the individuals whose motivation is high, but their self-perceived ability is low? First, how does one have low self-perceived ability? One of the things is that people could have what is called *low self-presentational efficacy expectancy* (Leary & Atherton, 1986), a fancy term that means that people doubt their ability to accurately convey their nonprejudiced identity. In short, they are not convinced that they can present themselves in the way that they would like to. These are the people who colloquially say that they don't want to say something wrong or dumb. "I don't want to be insensitive. I don't want to offend the other person." When people have low self-presentational efficacy expectancy they don't expect the interaction to go particularly well.

To complicate matters, it is also possible to have what called *low self-presentational outcome expectancy* (Leary & Atherton, 1986). In this situation, people might think they have the requisite skills to convey the impression they want to convey, but they are not sure that the interaction partner is going to trust their responses. In other words, they are not sure that their behavior will be received by the other person as sincere or as truly representing their nonprejudiced views. As with self-presentational efficacy expectancy, when people come to an interaction with low self-presentational outcome expectancy, they do not expect the interaction to go well.

When motivation is high and self-perceived ability is low, the stage is set for a variety of interpersonal difficulties. For low-prejudice people who are uncertain about their ability to convey an nonprejudiced image or to have their behavior interpreted accurately, their motivation to respond without prejudice may actually interfere with their efforts to convey their nonprejudiced intentions. In a very real sense, their good intentions go awry. That is, it has been shown that when people have a specific interpersonal goal (e.g., to present a nonprejudiced identity) and either self-presentational efficacy or outcome expectancies are low, people will experience heightened self-awareness, discomfort, and anxiety in the interaction (Leary & Atherton, 1986; Schlenker & Leary, 1982). What does this mean in an intergroup context?

To illustrate, consider the interpersonal consequences of being high in self-focus or self-awareness (Schlenker & Leary, 1982). One of the things that people who are high in self-awareness do is to monitor their behavior and to compare their behavior to their standards. Low-prejudice people know what their standards are; they want to present a nonprejudiced identity in this circumstance. They begin to wonder how well they are doing. To assess how well they are doing they start to monitor their nonverbal behaviors (Am I standing too close? Am I staring?), aspects of interaction styles to which we normally don't give a second thought, let alone monitor carefully. To complicate matters, these types of behaviors are hard to control (DePaulo, 1992; Polanyi, 1962). The more people start to monitor the nonverbal aspects of behavior, the more distracted they become and the more likely they are to disrupt the typically smooth and coordinated aspects of social behavior, until their behavior is neither smooth nor particularly coordinated. The bottom line is that their efforts, coupled with the anxiety that arises out of their uncertainties about the success of their efforts, result in interaction styles that are awkward and strained.

Of central importance for our current analysis is that *social anxiety,* the feeling of anxiety that arises in a social situation (real or imagined) when a person believes that he or she is being evaluated by others (Schlenker & Leary, 1982), is associated with a specific set of nonverbal behaviors including decreased eye contact, increased interpersonal distance, and increased speech errors (see Figure 10.3). This list should look familiar to you. These are exactly the same outcomes that have been taken as evidence of majority group members' antipathy or prejudice toward minority group members (as in the Word et al., 1974, study reviewed earlier). These awkward and disaffiliative nonverbal behaviors can originate from very different psychological experiences; when considered alone they are inherently ambiguous. They may be signs of antipathy and hatred in high-prejudice people, but may be related to social anxiety and self-focus among well-intentioned, low-prejudice people. The key point is that the same outcomes, these avoidant nonverbal behaviors, can occur for different psychological reasons. Given that the behaviors are ambiguous and therefore open to alternative interpretations, the stage is set for miscommunication between majority and minority group members.

When we first started thinking about these issues, we thought that they could provide us with some reason to be optimistic about the future of intergroup relations. So we set out to examine the nature of people's expectations in encounters with members of other groups. We asked white, heterosexual participants to imagine themselves interacting for the first time with a black person or a homosexual person. They answered questions about their motivation to appear nonprejudiced, self-efficacy expectancy (whether they thought they could behave in a nonprejudiced way), outcome expectancy (whether they thought the other person would accept them as nonprejudiced), self-awareness, social anxiety, and antipathy. The results are presented in Table 10.3. Very low-prejudice respondents were highly motivated to respond

| Nonverbal signs of social anxiety | Nonverbal signs of antipathy or prejudice |
|---|---|
| • Decreased eye contact | • Decreased eye contact |
| • Increased interpersonal distance | • Increased interpersonal distance |
| • Shorter interactions | • Shorter interactions |

**Figure 10.3.** Ambiguous Nonverbal Behavior

without prejudice, and they expected to be able to do so and to be accepted by the minority group member; they also expected to experience very little social anxiety. Participants that we label "moderately low-prejudice" are just as motivated to behave in a nonprejudiced way as are the very low-prejudice participants, but they are not as confident that they can act in an appropriate manner, nor that they will be believed by the minority group member. In other words, their self-efficacy and outcome expectancies are lower. These moderately low-prejudice subjects also expected to experience more self-awareness and anxiety in this social interaction. Finally, it is of interest to note that none of our low-prejudice subjects reported anticipating feelings of antipathy or hostility, which was clearly expected by our respondents who were high in prejudice.

In summary, although high-prejudice people anticipate a negative interaction with minority group members, there is some good news in these data. Some low-prejudice people think they are pretty good at intergroup encounters; they tell us that they have smooth and positive intergroup relations. In addition, there are some other low-prejudice people who have good intentions, but are uncertain about how to behave to convey those good intentions.

We have to be careful here, however. So far we've been focusing on majority group members almost exclusively. We don't want to fall into the trap of thinking about the problem of intergroup tension as a majority group problem alone; it would be a mistake to focus only on the good intentions of majority group members. We must consider the perspective of minority group members: How will they interpret the awkward interaction styles of some majority group members? Keep in mind that intentions cannot be seen directly and are most often inferred from behavior. Indeed, the good intentions of the majority group member are useful only if they can be conveyed by the majority group member and accurately interpreted by the minority group member. Well, what interpretation should minority group members make if what they

**TABLE 10.3** Mean Scores on Six Indexes as a Function of Prejudice Level

| | Prejudice Level | | | |
|---|---|---|---|---|
| | *Very Low* | *Moderately Low* | *Moderate* | *High* |
| Motivation | 5.47$_a$ | 5.43$_a$ | 4.45$_b$ | 2.32$_c$ |
| Self-efficacy expectancy | 5.23$_a$ | 4.71$_b$ | 4.53$_{bc}$ | 4.11$_c$ |
| Outcome expectancy | 4.44$_a$ | 4.14$_b$ | 3.66$_c$ | 3.58$_c$ |
| Self-awareness | 3.93$_a$ | 4.68$_b$ | 4.64$_b$ | 4.22$_b$ |
| Anxiety | 2.69$_a$ | 3.97$_b$ | 4.80$_c$ | 5.54$_d$ |
| Antipathy and suspicion | 1.51$_a$ | 2.10$_b$ | 2.82$_c$ | 4.07$_d$ |

SOURCE: Devine, Evett, and Vasquez-Suson (1996).
NOTE: For each index, possible scores range from 1 to 7 with higher scores representing higher levels of the construct. These scores are responses to an imagined interaction with a homosexual student. Similar results were obtained for an imagined interaction with a black student. For each row, means not sharing a subscript differ at $p < .01$.

see is awkward, nervous, and disaffiliative behaviors? As we argued above, it is crucial that we consider the perspectives of both the majority and minority group members as we think about these issues.

## ■ The Minority Perspective Revisited

The historical social psychological research on the minority group perspective has focused on the long-term adjustment and esteem consequences of being members of a stigmatized group (see Chapter 7, this volume). In this work, minority group members are often seen as rather passive targets of prejudice. The conception, however, of minority group members as simply passive recipients of majority group prejudice has been challenged in recent theorizing (e.g., Crocker & Major, 1989; Jones et al., 1984; Major & Crocker, 1993). For example, Jones et al. (1984) noted that the stigmatized person is neither "interpersonally powerless nor bereft of belief or expectations of his own." One type of belief or expectation that minority group members, in general, may bring to the intergroup situation is a suspicion or mistrust of majority group members' intentions.

If these are the expectations that are brought to an intergroup situation, how are the minority group members going to deal with negative or positive responses from majority group members? In a series of very clever experiments, Crocker, Major, and their colleagues (Chapter 7, this volume; Crocker et al., 1991; Crocker & Major, 1989; Major & Crocker, 1993) have shown that minority group members accept both negative and positive feedback when their minority status is unknown to majority group evaluators. When their minority status is known, however, both negative and positive feedback are viewed as manifestations of prejudice. The negative feedback is seen as a direct reflection of negative attitudes. Positive feedback is interpreted as the majority group members' efforts to appear nonprejudiced to others (i.e., to behave in socially acceptable ways).

Anticipating negative reactions from majority group members is likely to be a source of tension in intergroup settings. Consider the following quotation from an interview with an African American concerning the cumulative effect of racial discrimination: "I think that it causes you to have to look at things from two perspectives. You have to decide whether things that are done are slights that are made because you are black or are because the person is just rude, or unconcerned, or uncaring. So, it's the kind of situation where you're always kind of looking to see with a second eye or second antenna just what's going on" (Feagin, 1989, p. 115). Crocker, Major, and colleagues (e.g., Crocker & Major, 1989; Crocker et al., 1991; Major & Crocker, 1993) have argued that minority group members live in a chronic state of attributional ambiguity with regard to the causes of majority group members' behavior toward them. Many minority group members face this type of attributional ambiguity, and it is likely to lead to a fair amount of stress and uncertainty among minority group members about how to handle intergroup encounters with majority group members.

Minority group members must decide if their suspicions are valid, and if so, whether they should act in accordance with their suspicions. Moreover, they must weigh the consequences to themselves and others if they are wrong . . . or if they are right. We do not suggest that these uncertainties are not understandable; they are quite understandable in the context of the history of prejudice and discrimination in this country. Interpersonal interactions have important real-world consequences, and if they go poorly, the minority group member may face serious disadvantages. For instance, in the Word et al. study (1974) we reviewed earlier, black applicants were discriminated against (treated differently than whites) in a simulated job hiring situation. It is important to ask the question of whether the way people are treated affects their performance in such interpersonal settings. Word et al.'s second study suggests that the answer to this question is yes, and dramatically emphasizes the importance of the goal of developing strategies to reduce discriminatory treatment.

In their second study, Word et al. had white participants in the role of job applicants interact with confederate interviewers who were trained to behave as the participant interviewers had in the first study. Thus, the interviewers displayed little eye contact, greater interpersonal distance, and awkward speech patterns (i.e., they exhibited the behaviors that black participants had been subjected to in Study 1) for half the interviews, and in the other half of the interviews did not exhibit these disaffiliative behaviors (i.e., they exhibited the behavior that white participants had been subjected to in Study 1). Word et al. were interested in how well the applicants, all white, performed in the interview. Judges who knew nothing about the study watched the interview and rated each applicant's performance. The findings indicated that white applicants who were confronted with the discriminatory, disaffiliative behavior performed less well in the interview and were evaluated more negatively. In a very real sense, poor performance was drawn out of the applicants based on how they were treated by the interviewer.

The important point here is that discriminatory treatment, whether intended to be discriminatory or not, has tangible effects on the target. If the same processes were in effect in a real job interview, and a qualified black candidate therefore was not hired because of an impression that the interviewer elicited, it would be irresponsible of us to minimize the impact of the situation just because the white interviewer "meant well." Nonetheless, although we must keep in mind the impact that discrimination has on minority group members regardless of its source, we believe it is extremely important to differentiate between sources of intergroup tension. Interactions that go awry because of miscommunication are, theoretically, easier to improve than those that fail because of hostility. The route to remedy depends on the nature of underlying problem.

The uncertainties faced by minority group members, although understandable, could increase the potential for miscommunication between majority and minority group members as they come to the intergroup situation. These uncertainties may lead a minority group member to interpret the anxious behaviors of well-intentioned majority group members as manifestations of hostility and prejudice; to the extent that such an interpretation is made, it could create complications for the ensuing interaction.

We have been working to get individual difference measures on the trust that minority group members experience in interactions with majority group members. We do not believe that all minority group members are suspicious of majority group members; in fact, we find that there is a fair amount of variability in the amount of suspicion that people have with regard to majority

group members. We have found among homosexuals, for example, that trust
is related to the quality of experience they have had with heterosexuals and to
how comfortable they are with their sexual orientation (Conley, Devine, Evett,
& Veniegas, 1996). Those who are trusting generally have positive expectations regarding the interaction and their interaction partner. They expect the
interaction to go well. Those who are generally suspicious, in contrast, have
much more negative expectations regarding the quality and outcome of their
interactions with heterosexuals. We believe that these expectations are equally
important to determining the outcome of intergroup interactions as are the
expectations reported by majority group members.

At this point, we can conclude that both majority and minority group
members bring expectations about how the intergroup contact is going to
occur, what the other interactant is going to do, and how they themselves are
going to function in the intergroup situation. We want to be clear that our
analysis is not meant to place blame at the hands of either majority or minority
group members. Our purpose has been to develop an understanding of the
practical challenges confronted by members of both groups as they approach
the interpersonal aspects of intergroup contact. What is needed at this point
is a way to think about what happens when these people, who clearly have
expectations, come together in a dynamic interaction situation.

## ■ A Dynamic Model of Intergroup Interactions

Studying the reciprocal dynamics of interactions is extremely difficult.
To set the stage for how we might consider the dynamic aspects of intergroup
contact, consider a general model of the reciprocal dynamics of interactions
(Darley & Fazio, 1980). Any interaction will have at least two people. Darley
and Fazio refer to one as the perceiver and the other as the target; they outlined
a five-step model to explain what goes on between perceiver and target in
dynamic interactions. Figure 10.4 displays the model. As we go through the
model, try to imagine all that really goes on in an interaction: the ways in
which perceivers and targets make judgments about each other, and how they
influence each other during the interaction. First, a perceiver develops an
expectation about a target. Second, the perceiver behaves toward the target in
accordance with the expectation. Third, the target has to interpret the behavior
of the perceiver. Fourth, based on that interpretation, the target responds to
the perceiver's actions. Fifth, the perceiver then interprets the target's action,
updates his or her expectation, and then reenters the interaction sequence at

Step 1: Perceiver develops expectation about target

Step 2: Perceiver behaves consistently with expectation about target

Step 3: Target interprets perceiver's behavior

Step 4: Target responds to perceiver's behavior

Step 5: Perceiver interprets target's response, updates expectation about target, returns to Step 2

**Figure 10.4.** Darley & Fazio's Model of Dynamic Interactions
SOURCE: Darley and Fazio (1980).

Step 2, where the perceiver then has to behave toward the target based on the updated expectation.

There are a couple of points that we need to keep in mind whenever we talk about an interaction. First, as you probably noted, each of the interaction participants is both a perceiver and a target. Think about what that means and imagine trying to keep track of what happens during even a brief interaction—both members of the interaction bring expectations to the interaction, interpret the other's behavior in light of those expectations, update their expectations as the interaction unfolds, and behave in accordance with their expectations. Dynamic interactions are extraordinarily complex. A second complication is that neither party in the interaction is necessarily explicit about his or her goals, intentions, or concerns. Therefore, each interactant must make assumptions about the other's goals or intentions. Very often the important part of what is happening to people's expectations occurs silently in the heads of the respective interaction partners. As a result, the stage is set for various levels of interpersonal difficulties and misunderstanding between the interaction partners.

Whether miscommunication and tension result from an intergroup situation depends largely on the extent to which the goals or expectations of the interaction partners match. Consider a few of the myriad possibilities. First, think about a high-prejudice majority group member interacting with a suspicious minority group member. What is the majority group member thinking? "I'm not going to like this. I'd like to terminate the interview as quickly as possible." The minority group member may set in motion attributional processes to protect self-esteem and may be just as happy to get out of the interaction. Here the goals may match, and the interaction may go smoothly, if not positively. So there will be tension, but the tension will not necessarily escalate. What about the situation in which a low-prejudice majority group member, who has the requisite skills to behave consistently with his or her nonprejudiced identity, interacts with a trusting minority group member? Again, we have a match. Miscommunication is unlikely and tension is unlikely. Under these circumstances we can anticipate a positive and smooth exchange between interactants.

Consider now a situation in which a well-intentioned, highly motivated, but unskilled low-prejudice person interacts with a suspicious minority group member. The low-prejudice person, who feels anxious about the encounter, may be perceived as hostile due to the awkward, nervous kinds of behaviors he or she exhibits. The target, in this case the minority group member, may interpret those behaviors as consistent with his or her expectations that the majority group member is prejudiced, and based on that interpretation, this individual may respond in a cool, aloof fashion, or with hostility of his or her own. Now what's the well-intentioned, low-prejudice person to think? He or she now has to interpret the minority group member's behavior. He or she may say "I tried, but I've been rebuffed," and may not make further efforts to try to have a positive intergroup interaction. Ultimately, there may be the escalation of hostility or tension, rather than the alleviation of tension, even under circumstances where the majority group member had the best of intentions.

Why is that problematic? Pettigrew (Chapter 11, this volume) suggested that when intergroup interactions are awkward, strained, or uncomfortable for some reason, people seek patterns of avoidance. We see this on college campuses with increasing frequency. Indeed, the kind of escalation of tension we have outlined could lead to withdrawal and decreased interest in future contact. Because intergroup interactions are often difficult to negotiate, many majority and minority group members may decide to retreat from intergroup contact situations, rather than putting themselves at risk for the difficult or negative interaction. This kind of separatism, even when voluntary, seems an unsatisfactory solution to the problem of intergroup tension.

## ■ Conclusions

We are encouraged that many low-prejudice people have the motivation to respond without prejudice in intergroup interactions. Our enthusiasm and optimism about the impact of low-prejudice people's good intentions on intergroup relations, however, must be somewhat tempered. That is, in a very real sense, people's good intentions are useful only if they are accurately interpreted by the target of those intentions. Intentions cannot be seen and must be inferred from behavior. This could be a problem if, for example, minority group members rely on the types of nonverbal behaviors that do not distinguish between social anxiety and hostility. To the extent that we do not make intentions explicit, there exists the potential for miscommunication between interactants that could lead to the escalation, rather than the alleviation, of tension.

The practical aspects of intergroup interactions are difficult. It is not obvious how to produce more smooth and positive intergroup interactions. There is a great deal of potential for miscommunication that arises out the expectations and concerns that both majority and minority group members bring to the interaction. If the miscommunication produces a negative interaction, then real, negative consequences will result for one or both parties. At that point, the quality of intentions of the interactants becomes moot. Despite these difficulties, however, we are optimistic that intergroup tension can be reduced, but to create those circumstances we have to understand that majority and minority group members are interdependent.

If we take seriously the kinds of practical challenges that each interactant identifies—the kinds of things they say are difficult about intergroup interaction situations—then we will be at a good point of departure for developing effective interventions for reducing intergroup tension and improving the interpersonal communication between majority and minority group members. Members of different groups must be willing to trust each other. They must be willing to talk to each other. And they must be willing to admit when they don't know what to do.

We began this chapter with a story about a very specific intergroup encounter. As you read it, you may have asked why we chose to relate that incident to you. What does it have to do with you? Well, although the specifics of the story may not be relevant to your life, the theme may be. It seems that many of us might be making our encounters with members of other groups more difficult than they need to be. The student assumed that, because she wanted to be nonprejudiced, she was supposed to know the answer to the "Pizza Question," although objectively there is no reason that a woman reared in the American Midwest should be aware of the dietary practices of Muslims in the southern Philippines. More generally, in our concern about not wanting to appear insensitive (or worse, *prejudiced*), we manage to disrupt not only our behavior in the interaction, but our ability to identify relatively obvious solutions to our dilemmas (such as "why don't you call and ask?"). What if we gave up the pretense that we "should know what to do"? What if we admitted ignorance when it exists and confessed our desire to learn and understand? True, much will still depend on our interaction partner. But this approach may be a better starting point for alleviating tension than trying to fake it through the interaction and worrying the whole time about what we're doing wrong. Almost certainly, it is preferable to withdrawing from intergroup contact altogether because the challenges are too daunting.

Perhaps the single most important problem facing us over time is that we are afraid to communicate. So many people are afraid to say "I don't know how to do it." They tell their friends about the difficulties they encounter, but they don't tell minority group members. Many minority group members are reluctant to try to educate majority group members. These are issues that we have to put on the table and try to work through as interaction partners if we are ultimately going to solve the problem of intergroup tension. Then we can learn, together, to navigate this rocky road.

# 11

# Prejudice and Discrimination
# on the College Campus

*Thomas F. Pettigrew*

**P**rejudice is all too human. So, too, is intergroup discrimination. Unfortunately, as students, administrators, and the general public are well aware, basic features of human beings and society make both phenomena prevalent. This reality does not mean, however, that prejudice and discrimination are so inevitable that we cannot effectively combat and limit them on the college campus.

Over the past six decades, social psychology has focused attention on these topics. The discipline's work is most popularly known through the best-selling volume *The Nature of Prejudice.* Written by Gordon Allport (1958), it summarizes what was known on the subject 40 years ago and shaped the direction of later work.

Found in both psychology and sociology departments, social psychologists look at prejudice and discrimination from three perspectives. Allport emphasized the individual level—why some people are prone to prejudice against out-groups and others are not. He also noted the importance of the immediate intergroup situation for shaping the expression of prejudice and discrimination. But what shapes these situations? The third perspective is the macrolevel—social institutions and the larger society.

This chapter analyzes intergroup prejudice and discrimination at all three levels of analysis. First, it describes the two phenomena. In summarizing social psychology's findings, it shows that the interconnections between

AUTHOR'S NOTE: Reprinted with permission of the *Higher Education Extension Service Review.*

prejudice and discrimination are more complex than popularly appreciated. Second, it indicates how critical the intergroup situation is to prejudice and discrimination. Third, it reviews four social psychological processes that underlie normative change, and finally, it relates these processes to ways that a college can move from mere desegregation to genuine integration. Because expressions of prejudice and the process of discrimination reflect the norms for intergroup interaction in a specific situation and established by the governing institution, the key goal of administrative policy in this realm must be to set firm institutional norms of intergroup acceptance (not merely tolerance).

## ■ Defining and Relating Prejudice and Discrimination

### ■ Prejudice

Definitions of prejudice abound. Prejudice, one aphorism asserts, is being down on something you are not up on. Prejudice, goes another, is a vagrant opinion without visible means of support. Like "intelligence" and other concepts adapted from popular parlance, the scientific definition of prejudice is at once both broader and narrower than its common meanings. In popular language, it can refer to bias, partiality, or a predilection—in the law, to harm and injury.

For intergroup relations, it is useful to think of prejudice as having two essential components—one negative and emotional, the other irrational and cognitive. Prejudice consists of opinions against an out-group without an adequate basis. When combating prejudice, it is important to keep both components in mind.

For the emotional side of prejudice, social science limits itself to negative feelings toward the out-group. In popular speech, loyal group members can have positive prejudice toward their in-group—"love prejudice" in Spinoza's words. The scientific definition does not include this phenomenon. Hatred is a major, but not the only, emotion of prejudice; feelings such as envy, resentment, and irritation are also common.

For the irrational side of prejudice, the problem of deciding what constitutes "an adequate basis" is usually not at issue. We can detect blatant prejudice by its gross overgeneralizations—stereotypes applied to most members of the out-group. If the "facts" justify our dislike of Nazis, it is not prejudice. Applying this dislike to all Germans, regardless of their relationship with Nazis, is prejudice.

Thus, prejudice consists of negative attitudes against certain out-groups and their members that are irrationally based. It is an antipathy toward out-groups accompanied by a faulty generalization. It can be felt or expressed. It is directed toward an entire out-group, and toward individuals as members of the out-group.

In recent years, a more subtle form of prejudice has developed in Europe as well as in North America (Kovel, 1970; Pettigrew, 1989; Pettigrew & Meertens, 1995; Sears, 1988; Chapter 4, this volume). This newer form rejects gross stereotypes and blatant discrimination. Its opposition to racial reform takes ostensibly nonprejudicial forms. Thus, a person favors racial desegregation of public schools, but opposes the "busing" of children that is necessary to achieve the desegregation. The subtly prejudiced try not to be openly unfair to minorities, but they avoid them and their issues. They typically deceive not just others but themselves as well; they "unconsciously pass . . . judgments on themselves and bring . . . in a unanimous verdict of Not Guilty" (Ryan, 1971, p. 28). The acting out of subtle prejudice is especially prevalent on campuses today. The "innocent jokes" and other cues that symbolize for minorities that they are unappreciated are typically what students of color mean when they report intergroup tension and racial harassment. Yet their very subtlety makes these forms hard to document; minority students who claim such harassment often appear to whites as "too sensitive." Such forms are also difficult for administrators to define. Most campus approaches cover only blatant discrimination that is easily documented.

## ■ Discrimination

Prejudice, then, is internal to an individual. By contrast, discrimination is overt; it directly affects out-group members by limiting their opportunities. Individual acts of unfairness toward out-group members represent a low-level form of discrimination, not the major concern. Focusing on the institutional and societal levels of analysis, discrimination is most usefully viewed as a social system of intergroup relations (Pettigrew & Taylor, 1992).

Group discrimination takes so many forms that it is best defined by its results. Discrimination against a minority group occurs when the group's life chances and life choices are limited in comparison to those of the majority group. There are two forms of the phenomenon—direct and indirect (Pettigrew, 1985; Pettigrew & Taylor, 1992).

Direct discrimination occurs at points where the group inequality is generated, often intentionally. Here decisions are directly based on race, gender, or ethnicity. This form predominated before the civil rights movement.

After the 1960s, it became easier to attack in legislation and the courts. So a more subtle, indirect form of group discrimination has emerged.

Indirect discrimination is the perpetuation or magnification of the original injury. It occurs when the inequitable results of direct discrimination form the basis for later decisions (past-in-present discrimination) or decisions in linked institutions (side-effect discrimination; Feagin & Feagin, 1986). Thus, discrimination is indirect when seemingly neutral criteria serve as proxies for race or gender in determining social outcomes. As such, like newer forms of prejudice, indirect discrimination is more subtle and ostensibly fair.

Anyone in higher education knows these discrimination forms. A few decades ago, many colleges and professional schools applied strict ceiling limits to the admission of particular religious and racial groups. A few may covertly continue these limits. Such a practice illustrates direct discrimination.

Indirect forms of discrimination are still common on many campuses. They especially apply to the many minority groups that are poorer on average than the majority and typically live in segregated areas. Here, decisions with a social class component will disproportionately affect them. For example, colleges that raise tuition without fully compensating for the increase in their scholarship funds particularly hurt these students. Sharply raising admissions requirements to include course prerequisites rarely provided by barrio and ghetto schools also strikes hardest at minority students. Indeed, it provides a clear example of past-in-present discrimination.

## ■ The Relationship

Systems of indirect discrimination can operate without prejudiced institutional leaders; or, for that matter, without even their awareness of the existence of discrimination. Thus, the relationship between prejudice and discrimination is not as simple as many think. Thoroughly unprejudiced white southerners and white South Africans in prior decades had to participate daily in racial discrimination. They lived in societies that enforced intense forms of discrimination. In reverse, highly prejudiced people do not engage in discrimination when they find themselves in situations where such behavior is not tolerated.

So it is diverting and often unjust to accuse those who manage institutions that indirectly discriminate of prejudice (or worse). Their personal characteristics are not the issue, and the charge naturally makes the managers defensive. It obscures the real problem of altering the symptoms of indirect discrimination.

The fact that these systems often perform positive functions for the institution makes the problem of combating indirect discrimination more difficult. It is not enough to end the discriminatory practice, when the practice itself is deeply embedded in institutional arrangements that serve the campus well. The difficult task is to alter appointments, admissions, and other systems so that, for example, they no longer exclude whole groups of Americans, while they retain their positive benefits for the institution.

Consider Harvard University's tenure system. During the 1930s, Harvard President James Conant tried to improve his faculty with a rigorous new appointment system. One component of the new system sought an objective measure of scholarship—publications in books and journals. The system worked well; Harvard's faculty grew in eminence under the selection system, so it served a vital function for the university. Yet it also served to exclude African Americans. Undoubtedly, such exclusion was far from Conant's mind when he designed the system. Nonetheless, a generation later Harvard had only four black Americans in a faculty of about 750.

Here we see how unintentional indirect discrimination works. Segregation concentrated promising black scholars onto the faculties of the 122 historically black institutions of higher learning. They published little, because they lacked the time, research facilities, and publishing connections. They typically taught four or five courses a semester, compared to Harvard instructors' two. Is there any wonder why those at Harvard could publish more than black scholars?

Note the cumulative manner in which past-in-present indirect discrimination operates. Prior discrimination had concentrated black scholars on black campuses. Further discrimination limited the resources of these campuses. In turn, these limited resources made it impossible for the faculty at these colleges to publish as frequently as the faculty of better-funded institutions. Using publications as a key criterion, Harvard and other predominantly white universities then did not hire promising black scholars. Such cumulative cycles are difficult to break, and they continue unless informed intervention is made.

## ■ The Critical Importance of Situational Norms

One of the strongest findings from social psychological research is the power of situational norms to shape intergroup interaction. Such norms constitute widely shared expectations about how the groups should and will interact. When most members of all groups share similar expectations and behave toward each other in similar ways, intergroup norms are strong, stable, and controlling. Intergroup norms, then, are widely accepted and legitimated standards for intergroup interaction (Pettigrew, 1991).

The most convincing evidence for the importance of norms in intergroup interaction is provided by an array of research studies conducted in the 1940s and 1950s (Allport, 1958; Pettigrew, 1961). These studies used field observation of interactions between black and white Americans in a variety of situations. They asked the following: (a) What happens when racial norms are strong, consistent, and sanctioned with rewards and punishments? (b) What happens when racial norms are strong but in conflict across different institutions? (c) What happens when norms are changing? And (d) what happens when there are no operating norms at all?

## ■ Strong, Consistent, Sanctioned Norms

Strong racial norms, whether racist or egalitarian in character, have led to consistent behavior by most black and white Americans. Sanctions maintained this massive conformity of two generations ago. In the then-segregated South, harsh punishments were swift for both blacks and whites who broke the "white supremacy" norms. Research also showed this phenomenon worked in reverse. When sanctioned, egalitarian racial norms developed in some institutions, most blacks and whites managed to conform to these norms, too.

## ■ Strong but Conflicting Norms

Such egalitarian racial norms in U.S. society were rare 40 years ago, however. When they did exist in particular institutions, they clashed with those of surrounding institutions. How, then, did the same black and white Americans behave when faced with egalitarian norms in one sector of their lives and racist norms in other sectors?

The results of field studies on this question provide further evidence for the importance of situational norms. Most people proved fully capable of immediate behavioral change as they moved from one set of institutional norms to another. Thus, in a coal-mining area, most black and white miners followed a pattern of racial integration below the ground and racial segregation above the ground (Minard, 1952). Social psychology abounds with similar examples (e.g., Biesanz & Smith, 1951; Killian, 1949).

The most striking instance came from a Chicago suburb where there was a large steel mill. Inside the mill, black and white workers were fully integrated in a multiracial labor union. Wages, jobs, promotions, and elected positions within the union were distributed equally between the racial groups. Yet, these workers went home to racially segregated residential areas. Indeed, most of the same white workers who believed strongly in an interracial union belonged to a neighborhood organization that kept black citizens from living in the area (Reitzes, 1953).

What looks to outside observers as inconsistent, illogical behavior does not appear that way to most people in these situations. In each of the situations, most people followed a consistent, "psychological" rule: They simply conformed to the prevailing racial norms. Normative demands made on them were inconsistent, not their norm-following behavior. Such widespread conformity to intergroup norms does not imply that generalized, prejudiced attitudes are never invoked. Some of the white coal-miners were either egalitarian or racist both below and above the ground. A small minority of the white steel workers either accepted or rejected blacks in both their work and housing situations (Reitzes, 1953). These were the people whose racial attitudes were so salient that they defied the racial norms in one or the other of the conflicting normative situations. The key point is that most people followed the norms of whatever institution they were in, even when they conflicted with those in another institution of their daily lives.

## ■ Changing Norms

The power of intergroup norms is also revealed when the norms undergo rapid change. Firmly established norms are necessary for smooth social interaction. Shared expectations guide the behavioral flow and allow people to interpret their contact in similar ways. In short, norms shape social interaction and provide it with a common meaning.

So, when norms are shifting, smooth interaction becomes difficult. The old norms have not completely disappeared, yet new norms have not won full acceptance. Intergroup interactions become awkward, even tense. Each side does not quite know how to act, or what to expect from the other. Often members of the more powerful group yearn for the "good old days," when traditional norms were firmly in place and unequal interaction was unproblematic. Intergroup interaction can be so uncomfortable during such transitions that patterns of avoidance develop. Avoiding contact with the out-group reduces the tension.

As many readers are aware, such avoidance has become a widespread pattern on college campuses. Although the civil rights movement began the process of eroding traditional racist norms, egalitarian norms of interracial interaction have been slow to emerge. Both black and white Americans really believe old patterns of imperious, dominant behavior by whites and obsequious, subservient behavior by blacks are "wrong"—that is, counternormative—yet both races must learn new patterns of equality. The awkwardness and discomfort, not to mention resistance, that results from this major normative shift has led to widespread patterns of interracial avoidance by both groups on campuses today.

A related social psychological process also deters the development of a new normative structure. Blatant racism, a reflection of the older norms, is now disparaged in North America and Western Europe. Yet many whites comply with the new egalitarian norms without internalizing them. Most majority group members publicly reflect in their intergroup behavior what they understand to be the new expectations, but many have not accepted these new norms as "right." This disparity between compliance with and internalization of the new norms has led to the development of the subtle forms of prejudice described earlier.

■ Absence of Norms

When no norms for intergroup interaction exist, their absence reveals the strong need for them. Kohn and Williams (1956) showed this vividly in rural New York State where few black citizens lived. The bars in the area had never developed racial norms for service. Teams of black and white graduate students tested this service in these all-white bars. When the black tester entered, confusion was the typical response. Without norms to guide them, waitresses did not know whether to serve the new customer or not. Often the slightest cue from other staff members or customers, even a facial gesture, decided the issue. If the bartender and customers paid no attention, waitresses usually served the black customer without incident. But if there were any negative attention, they often refused to serve the black student—even though this violated the state's antidiscrimination law.

In short, the pointed reactions to strong racial norms, to conflicting or changing norms, and to the absence of norms highlight the significance of norms. From these and other research findings, four basic principles for changing racial norms emerge.

## ■ Four Social Psychological Processes Underlying Normative Change

Before discussing campus policy, it is reassuring to know that, difficult as effective policies are to establish, there are processes that favor their acceptance. Once firm institutional initiatives toward change in intergroup norm processes begin, four interrelated processes can generate acceptance for the new policies far more rapidly than conventional wisdom allows.

(1) *The perception of the inevitability of the institutional changes is critical.* Popular support for the changes is not necessary. The perception of their inevitability and permanence is sufficient. If such perceptions are not created, however, hope that strong, even violent, protest can "turn back the clock" strengthens resistance. This possibility is a particular danger when conflicting intergroup policies have come and gone frequently in the past.

(2) *Behavioral change typically leads to attitude change.* Conventional wisdom holds that attitude change must precede behavioral change. Yet hundreds of social psychology studies have shown the efficacy of precisely the opposite causal sequence: Behavior change is often the precursor of attitude changes. Institutional alterations that require new intergroup behavior become powerful attitude change mechanisms in themselves.

So, it might be asked, why have the new intergroup norms not been internalized more than they have? It is probably because intergroup behavioral change has not been as extensive as many think. The great majority of white college students, for example, have lived in virtually all-white neighborhoods and attended virtually all-white schools. Their failure to internalize equalitarian norms reflects our society's failures over the past several decades to adopt and apply the integrationist vision of the civil rights movement.

(3) *Intergroup contact under optimal conditions can reduce conflict and prejudice.* Allport (1958) listed four optimal conditions for beneficial intergroup contact: equal status treatment in the situation; common goals; intergroup cooperation toward the common goals, or "interdependence" (Sherif, 1966); and authority support for the intergroup contact. When these conditions do not hold, intergroup contact can lead to increased intergroup hostility, distrust, and conflict. Although the contact hypothesis has its limitations (Pettigrew, 1986), research supports the hypothesis in intergroup situations throughout the world.

(4) *Dispelling intergroup fears can reduce both prejudice and discrimination even without intergroup contact.* Intergroup contact is not essential for positive change. Just having your worst fears and expectations about the

out-group convincingly shown to be unjustified has positive effects. Dispelling fears is especially important in tense situations, where extreme fears make doing so easier. The challenge in such situations is in overcoming the resistance to perceiving and accepting the disconfirming evidence. Yet this process, like the others, is a two-edged sword: Its converse—the confirmation of intergroup fears—leads to further entrenchment of intergroup prejudice and conflict.

The focus on changing intergroup norms is more useful than concern about what is loosely termed "campus climate." Intergroup climates emerge from normative structures established by an institution's leaders. This view provides a foundation for remedial policies to alleviate current intergroup problems on campus.

## ■ Moving From Desegregation to Integration

It helps to make a distinction between desegregation and integration. Mere desegregation involves only a mixture of groups no longer formally separated. It does not refer to the quality of the intergroup interaction. Desegregated campus life can range from positive intergroup contact to a living hell of intergroup strife. Desegregation, then, is a prerequisite for an integrated institution; it is not the ultimate goal.

Genuine integration refers to positive intergroup interaction that meets Allport's (1958) conditions for prejudice-reducing contact. It does not refer to an institution that simply allows minorities to enter, while maintaining its past arrangements designed for an exclusively white student body. Nor is it a synonym for assimilation. Integration goes beyond present-day U.S. society by providing the conditions for removing the racial and ethnic threats and stereotypes that divide Americans.

To be sure, integration by this definition is a tall order. Cynics say such institutions do not exist in the United States today. In response, two considerations are important. First, the desegregation-integration distinction forms a continuum, not an absolute dichotomy. True integration is the goal toward which higher learning must strive—not simply numbers or legal requirements.

Second, colleges are, of course, part of U.S. society, and they are burdened by the nation's legacy of racial and intergroup conflict. Big-city universities cannot escape the effects of race conflicts and minority despair that surround them. All colleges must work with the products of the nation's still largely segregated elementary and secondary schools. Campuses, therefore, mirror society's intergroup tensions. Yet, we aspire in other realms for the campus to reflect the ideal; it should be no different in the intergroup realm.

Intergroup policies affect three areas: student recruitment and selection, intergroup staffing, and campus life for students. Before each is discussed, several caveats are in order. This discussion cannot be exhaustive; it is intended to supplement previous discussions (see especially Ascher, 1990). Moreover, there are no magical cures for intergroup problems. They have been years in the making; their solutions will be neither painless nor immediate. The points raised here derive from the normative perspective just described, hardened by three decades of the author's consulting in varied educational settings. Each must be customized to fit a particular campus situation.

## ■ Student Recruitment and Selection

Here, four issues require discussion. The first is obvious: the need for substantial, nontoken percentages of minority groups. How to implement this goal is not so obvious, however. There is little discussion on college campuses, much less action concerning the remaining points. Second, the correlation between minority status and social class should be kept as low as possible. Third, roughly balanced ratios of females to males within each major group improves campus social life. Finally, campus life, as well as elementary and secondary schools, would benefit if higher education treated prior interracial experience as an asset in selecting majority students.

*Critical mass.* The requirement of a critical mass of minority students on campus is now generally accepted. Beyond that, however, there is considerable confusion over what this is and the difficulty in reaching the goal. Social psychology speaks to both issues.

Critical mass, borrowed from physics, refers to the absolute number as well as percentage of a group's representation on a campus. No fixed percentage fits all situations. The often-mentioned figure of 20% derives from research on elementary and secondary schools that involved only two groups—black and white students. Some observers use the 20% figure as if it referred not to one group but to the total minority representation. But this use ethnocentrically assumes all minorities are essentially alike. Filipino Americans and Cherokee Americans culturally share more with the majority group than they do with each other. Within the large, artificial ethnic categories used in the United States today—Hispanic and Asian Americans—there is at least as much variation as there is among European Americans.

The key point about critical mass concerns a group's representation throughout the entire social structure of the campus. It is unlikely for various groups to scatter randomly throughout the structure—from the basketball team and student government to Phi Beta Kappa and the dormitories. Still, if critical proportions are achieved and there are no "steering" processes, we should consistently find mixed groups working, playing, and living together. Moreover, these mixed groups need to avoid solo roles where a student is the only member from their group—the only female in an otherwise all-male group, the only black in an otherwise all-white group. Research shows the special difficulties inherent in such conspicuous, "on stage" positions (Kanter, 1977; Pettigrew & Martin, 1987; Taylor, Fiske, Etcoff, & Ruderman, 1978).

Admittedly, this perspective on critical mass adds to the difficulties of recruiting a varied student body. There are so many U.S. minorities that it is impossible to have a critical mass on campus of each group represented. The *Harvard Encyclopedia of American Ethnic Groups* lists 122 separate ethnicities—from Acadians to Zoroastrians (Thernstrom, Orlov, & Handlin, 1980). Nonetheless, this perspective pinpoints where efforts are most needed to achieve such a goal for the major groups on campus.

*Social class and minority-majority status.* Several decades ago, one university decided to direct its minority recruitment efforts toward only attracting students from lower-status families. This university later experienced unusually serious intergroup strife. As in high schools, complications arise when an institution has a high correlation between social class and minority-majority status. In U.S. society, race is salient and class almost denied. So class differences are typically interpreted as racial differences. (Interestingly, Latin America has the reverse myopia.) Compounding class and racial differences lessens the probability of common interests. So any recruitment and admissions policies should strive to outline a substantial social class mix within racial and ethnic groups.

*Male-female ratios.* Sexual tensions of the larger society spill over to the campus. So, much of the tension within and across groups on campus revolves around dating. These tensions are lessened if the admissions policies of coeducational institutions also achieve a rough balance of males and females within each major group.

*Prior interracial experience as an asset.* After talks on integrated education at the precollege level, upper-status white parents frequently ask me a blunt question: "What's in it for my child?" Unfortunately, answers that stress justice and national unity generally fall on deaf ears. Some answers are not politic: "Your child will not grow up to be a bigot like you!" But one answer draws rapt attention: "It will help your child get into Harvard." I knew that the then-Dean of Admissions granted, among other considerations, special attention to students with prior interracial experience. He did it to further a harmonious campus community, but the practice also serves to motivate white parents to have their children attend interracial schools. By making such an admissions policy public, higher education can support positive reform in elementary and secondary schools.

Although private colleges and universities in great demand can more easily implement this policy, most can make use of it. The policy should, however, be limited to majority applicants for two reasons. First, most minority students have had considerable interracial exposure before coming to campus. This is not the case for majority students. A Stanford report shows that about 90% of its minority students had prior extensive contact with whites (Camarillo, 1989). But only a fourth of Stanford's white students had previous contact with African, Mexican, or Asian Americans. Second, minorities typically lack the same degree of school choice. To penalize them for having attended segregated schools would compound the original injury.

## ◼ Intergroup Staffing

The value of a diverse faculty and staff is obvious. Yet, discussion centers on the need for minority staff to provide role models and counseling for minority students. Such a point has merit, of course, but is far too limited. Minority staff members are also important for majority students. And rarely mentioned are two additional reasons for intergroup staffing—intellectual breadth and "muddling through together."

Diversity enriches academic departments intellectually by broadening their perspectives. This seldom-mentioned fact is especially meaningful in the humanities and social sciences. In my field of social psychology, women and minorities have brought fresh new ideas and interests to bear. This contribution means that affirmative action in faculty is not a paternalistic process to "help" women and minorities: It is a process that strengthens the intellectual mission of higher education.

Diverse staffing also contributes to the development of integration on the campus. College campuses need all the insight they can get in this difficult task. Social science can provide research and ideas, but few Americans have experience with truly integrated institutions. Campuses need minority staff members for their unique perspectives in this muddling through together process.

Colleges have employed a variety of programs to achieve diverse staffing. One effective method involves set-aside positions that departments can compete for if they nominate qualified faculty who would add to departmental diversity. The campus monitors quality in the same manner as other appointments. This arrangement fits snugly under the emphasis on diversity in the Supreme Court's *Bakke* ruling. Thus, white males can lend diversity to some nursing school faculties.

The University of California at Santa Cruz used this program to attract 29 top-level minority and female appointments beyond those hired regularly. Of these appointments, 24 remain on the campus. Unfortunately, the administration terminated the program as part of funding cut-backs. Lectures on the subject by prominent speakers replaced it. This was a serious blow to the campus's intergroup norms, for words can never replace effective actions.

Affirmative action efforts also can be deterred by a confusion between legally required goals and the diverse staffing needs of the campus. Explicit goals are necessary to monitor the progress of any program. The problem arises when rigid availability ratios limit the goals. Diversity in some sectors of a university often takes an effort to attract women and minorities in particular specialties who are in short national supply. Federal goals, based on availability, will not require the effort; yet successful integration of the campus may depend on it. Hence, although campuses must meet federal goals, they must go beyond them as befits their special situation.

## ■ Campus Life for Students

There is much current discussion of "multiculturalism" and "pluralism." When commentators use these terms in the context of a thoroughly open, integrated campus that reflects its diverse community, this discussion is consistent with the normative perspective offered here. That is not, however, always the case.

Often these concepts, pluralism in particular, are twisted into arguments for segregation on the campus. A women's center on one public university campus informally excludes males from many of its events; other campuses restrict some dormitories to one ethnicity; many campuses look the other way when social organizations that receive campus support openly discriminate by race, ethnicity, religion, and gender. These actions constitute violations of Title VI of the 1964 Civil Rights Act. The principal point goes beyond their illegality, however; such public breaches of a professed open institution undercut efforts to establish solid norms of intergroup acceptance. They loudly advertise that the campus is not truly serious about its publicly announced intergroup policies.

When demands for such discriminatory practices come from majority students, they are usually explained as part of the "good old traditions" of the institution. The contention is that student life on campus should continue as it was when minorities (and often women) were not members of the student body. Conservative alumni often join the fray. They threaten to halt their contributions if the campus does not remain as it was when they were students. Such controversies test an administrator's resolve. New norms take root at such critical times. After Williams College withstood the storm and admitted women, it developed one of the most effective coeducational programs of any previously unisex campus.

When demands for such discriminatory practices come from minority students, they usually signal the failure of the campus to achieve an effectively open, multicultural environment. Such demands are a retreat from the long-term aim of African, Asian, and Hispanic Americans to be included on equal terms in the larger society. It is a minority proclamation that they would rather segregate then continue as the campus operates. As such, it is a call to action for a campus, but not the separatist actions called for by the students. Some administrations, regretfully, grant minority demands for separate facilities with a haste never before shown minority concerns. Although such actions may buy peace in the short run, later problems at these sites reveal their long-term costs.

The alternative strategy for an administration is to listen to the minority students' reasons for wanting separation, rather than to their proposed action. Their reasons represent a list of past efforts that have failed—at least in minority perceptions. Often, the minority protesters accurately point out how the college allows a separatist majority social life. So they wonder why the campus should not allow them to emulate it. Firm denial of separatist structures in student life has to be the policy for all groups.

So how can an institution achieve both integrated structures and cultural fairness? Some believe the two are antithetical. The normative perspective maintains they can enhance each other—once the campus establishes a solid normative structure of intergroup acceptance and nondiscrimination. Three tests are critical: (a) Is there open access to all campus opportunities in fact as well as theory? (b) Are the structures that shape student life on campus reinforcing cross-group bonds? (c) Is there optimal cultural fairness?

*Open access in practice.* Equal access to libraries and other physical facilities is rarely at issue. Differential access is a problem for what many students care most about—the college's social resources. Do the cheerleading club, student government, and athletic teams reflect the diverse student body? Precise proportions are not needed; mixed representation is the goal.

Most institutions claim open access in theory. But what about in practice? A periodic check of group participation in all student organizations and activities provides a useful gauge of progress on the desegregation-integration continuum. Can all students interested in regional studies participate freely in the college's cultural clubs—Chinese, Hispanic, and so on? Do they? There is a problem when only one group participates in an activity that receives college support and recognition.

This test may exclude religious and other off-campus organizations that receive no support or recognition from the college. Rarely, however, does this exempt fraternities and sororities. Directly or indirectly, these social groups are still typically considered integral parts of the campus. As such, many (not all) of these organizations remain bastions of intergroup segregation and discrimination.

*Reinforcing cross-group bonds.* A related way to view campus activities is to evaluate whether they serve to divide or bring together students from across the spectrum of racial and ethnic groups. Athletic teams offer the optimal example of an activity that can develop a sense of "we-ness" as members of the college community. Social scientists often test Allport's (1958) contact hypothesis with athletic teams, because they frequently meet the conditions for optimal intergroup contact.

Other activities also can reinforce students' shared identity as members of the academic community. College administrators should encourage coaches, faculty advisers, and student leaders to seek members of underrepresented groups in their activities. Such encouragement is enhanced when the college's support is partly contingent on success in this effort.

*Optimal cultural fairness.* Cultural fairness is not a simple issue. Educational institutions find themselves in a dilemma. On one hand, they wish to recognize the many cultures from which their students come. On the other hand, U.S. society expects colleges to prepare their students for a labor market that is neither culturally fair nor multicultural, and students expect good jobs on graduation. Critics on both sides fail to appreciate the tension that results from attempts to reconcile these positions.

There is no easy resolution to this dilemma. The normative approach can only suggest several operating guidelines. Simply celebrating Cinco de Mayo and Martin Luther King Jr.'s birthday is not enough. Students readily recognize halfhearted attempts at multicultural events for what they are—halfhearted. Larger institutions can implement focused programs of regional and cultural studies. Such programs help to meet the need when the programs boast an intergroup faculty and attract students from all groups. All too often, however, such programs have faculties and attract students comprised only of the ethnicity involved. Research shows that this situation isolates the program, its teachers, and its majors from the larger campus community.

All campuses can strive to integrate the role of minority cultures in the general curriculum—not just in history but throughout the humanities and social sciences. Critics of multiculturalism often see this as somehow diluting the "true" subject matter. By true, they apparently mean the traditional course content that ignored the great achievement of the United States as a highly diverse "nation of immigrants." Modern scholarship is increasingly multicultural. Broadening the curriculum does not encourage faculty members to teach ideological distortions or some "politically correct" dogma; avoidance of past scholarly inadequacies is sufficient.

# 12

# The Essential Power of Racism

---

## *Commentary and Conclusion?*

*James M. Jones*

It is rare for a social psychologist to write a book about racism (see Dovidio & Gaertner, 1986a; Jones, 1972, 1997 for exceptions). Generally, social psychologists have been concerned with prejudice based on race, and its enabling psychological mechanisms of stereotyping and social categorization (Allport, 1954). Race prejudice is a characteristic of individuals (their thoughts, feelings, and behaviors) and, hence, properly falls under the purview of social psychology, which typically analyzes social psychological phenomena at the level of the individual. This volume on racism is something of a departure from the traditional ways of analyzing racial bias. Does this focus on racism suggest a different approach to racial bias? Does it suggest a different level of analysis of the causes and consequences of racial bias? Or is it just a different label for a traditional approach?

In our contemporary popular culture, egregious examples of racial bias or insensitivity are almost never labeled as "prejudice." A joke about the sexual preferences and appetites of blacks cost Earl Butz his job as agriculture secretary because he told a "racist" joke. It would seem awkward, if not a little silly, to say he told a "prejudiced" joke. In a more contemporary vein, the professional golfer Fuzzy Zoeller ("Fanfare," 1997) got in trouble when he cavalierly dismissed young multiracial Tiger Woods's romp through the 1997 Masters Golf Tournament by 12 shots, setting the lowest-scoring record of all time, with the following observation:

> That little boy is tearing up this course. The way he's playing, here's what you do. You pat him on the back and say, just don't serve fried chicken at the

dinner, okay? [He snapped his fingers and turned as he walked away and said]
Or collard greens or whatever they serve.

Zoeller's implication that black people could be lumped together entitatively as *they are* (cf. Campbell, 1958) and actitatively by what *they do* (eat collard greens; cf. Abelson, 1994) goes to the core of the race notion *essence*.[1] Prejudice does not make such essential claims, and thus, is usually not implicated when racial insensitivity of some magnitude occurs. Is it just a semantic distinction made prominent by the linguistic divergence between science and popular culture? Or is it important to understand that prejudice and racism are different dynamics of human behavior whose consequences diverge in meaningful ways? Given the title of this volume, and the history of social psychological research on race, we may wonder if this is meant to suggest something new, and, if so, what? Is the problem of racism different from the problem of prejudice? Is the response required different? These questions are not simply rhetorical, but raise important conceptual distinctions in need of analysis.

This volume does not, in general, tackle the distinction between prejudice and racism. In his analysis of racism and U.S. politics, Sears (Chapter 4) defines racism "narrowly as a categorical hostility or antagonism toward African Americans because of their race." That this definition does not differ from what we might call race prejudice is noted with the caveat, "I do not intend any important distinction between 'racism' and 'prejudice.' " Operario and Fiske (Chapter 2), however, make an explicit and meaningful distinction—race prejudice is converted to racism through race-based power.

Although this volume does not seek to distinguish racism from prejudice, I believe the two notions differ in meaningful ways. In the first edition of *Prejudice and Racism* (Jones, 1972), I argued that racism could and should be distinguished from prejudice because racism involved two specific properties that were not required of prejudice: (a) It rested on a belief in the biological inferiority of a racial group, relative to one's own group, and (b) it implied a power differential in favor of one's own group. Prejudice requires neither of these properties. Why do these differences between prejudice and racism matter?

On the first property, the belief in the biological distinctions between races invokes a view of "essential" differences between groups, which suggests that the differences are "fundamental" and "immutable." Medin (1989) demonstrates the power of this essentializing tendency with respect to general perceptions; and, Hirschfeld (1996) applies this analysis to race. Thus, the tendency to categorize people into groups is abetted by the idea that the groups are distinguishable in defining and unchangeable ways. The strategies for reducing the negative effects of social categorization, then, must work against the prevailing human tendency to keep groups and their members distinctive.

The second property, racial difference in meaningful power, is influential because it suggests that being in control allows one to endorse options that serve their self-interests and often, but not always, dis-serve the interests of racial out-groups. Thus, groups are not only possessed of certain attributes (intelligence, beauty, work ethic, and other entative characteristics), but they enjoy active control over others by determining their life outcomes (they evaluate, select, punish, reward, among other actative behaviors). When the power to act in race-based, self-serving ways is taken for granted, the disadvantage of racial out-groups is either unseen, or explained away by the moral obligation to maintain the natural status quo, based on self-contained individualism (cf. Sampson, 1977). Perhaps more important, the subtle influence of power means that those who enjoy it, directly or indirectly, may be unaware of all the ways they are privileged by it.

Prejudice is defined in many different ways, but, in general, they all suggest that it is the attitudes, beliefs, or behaviors of people that define its essence. That is, prejudice is an individual-level phenomenon and is attached to individuals. Individuals are prejudiced and the problems that arise can be defined with respect to specific encounters among people. Bigots, right-wing authoritarians, and highly prejudiced people can be defined by their answers to particular questions, or the pattern of judgment they make about novel stimuli, or their beliefs about others. Prejudiced people can have a cumulative impact on the quality of life and the availability of opportunities for their targets.

In 1965, President Lyndon Johnson suggested that achieving civil rights via the Civil Rights Act of 1964 and the Voting Rights Act of 1965 only established equality in theory, not in fact. It was therefore necessary to continue to ensure that those who had faced historical discrimination would be able to achieve equality as a result, not just a theory. The result of this belief was the establishment of the Equal Employment Opportunity Commission and the enactment of the remedial policies now known as affirmative action. By this reckoning, the problem of racial bias was institutional, and the remedy, therefore, was also institutional.

The significant point of departure between prejudice and racism is that racism exists not only at the level of the individual, but at the higher levels of institutions and culture (cf. Jones, 1997). Operario and Fiske implicate the

power differential as the element that transforms individual-level race prejudice to individual-level racism. Although individuals make institutions work,
and culture is the cumulative experiences of individuals over time, both
institutions and culture have a life of their own. To resolve the questions about
the distinction between prejudice and racism up front, it is clear that prejudice
functions to create immediate and direct discrimination based on race. That
discrimination is all the more meaningful when it co-occurs with a societal
structure that aligns choice and chances with racial group membership. When
this alignment privileges one race over another, and does so over centuries
and with an accompaniment of theories, rationales, and beliefs, this recurring
dynamic transcends simple race prejudice. Thus, the cumulative effects of race
prejudice over time combine with the cultural rationales and beliefs about
racial essences to enable the institutional implementation of racism. Race
prejudice operates in a bottom-up way; cultural racism operates in a top-down
way; and their joint effect is institutional racism. The problems of racism
developed in the chapters of this volume address this dynamic in different
ways and from different perspectives.

## ■ The Problem(s) of Racism

The problems of race are that (a) race provides a visible and easily used
basis for categorizing people into groups; (b) our race-relations history is one
of conflict, negative evaluation, dislike, and fear; (c) although the negativity
of race relations has been rejected in our contemporary society, people may
still harbor vestiges of those hostile feelings; (d) those hostile feelings influence people to behave in negative ways (unfair stereotypical biases); (e)
distrust, ignorance, and uncertainty make interracial communication difficult,
and these differences often lead people to behave unwittingly in ways that
exaggerate the differences; (f) racism has consequences, often, but not always,
negative for its targets; (g) the fact that whites have been persistently in a
powerful relationship relative to the targets of racism, has perpetuated their
privilege at the same time that racial targets have been disadvantaged. Each
of these problems is implicated in one way or another by the chapters of this
volume. The following brief summaries illustrate how the present volume
illuminates our understanding of these problems of racism.

*Race provides a visible and easily used basis for categorizing people into
groups.* Banks and Eberhardt (Chapter 3) provide a detailed and cogent

summary of the fact that people tend to place others into social categories, and to assign essential properties to those social categories that make the people placed in them similar to each other, and different from those outside the category. Because race is such an "essentializing" social category, it offers a natural human tendency toward what we might call *racialism* (cf. Appiah, 1990; Jones, 1997)—the tendency to ascribe essential, but not readily visible or confirmable, properties to people categorized into racial groups. These racial difference are not simply descriptions of ways in which social categories differ, but come to define moral and intellectual qualities by which evaluation of merit is made. Thus a "meritocracy," in a racialized society, is a formalization of racism. Rules for maintaining a racialized meritocracy include unwritten psychological rules by which racial stereotypes persist and are unresponsive to disconfirming evidence. The fact that race rests on biological assumptions of its essential nature, in spite of the fact that it remains unsupported by scientific evidence, does not deter its use in our society. In fact, Banks and Eberhardt offer a "legal" construction of race argument which suggests that it is not flawed scientific notions of race at fault, but that "legal norms and decision making have created race" (p. 60).

Race, then, is socially constructed and inserted into our legal system in such a way as to embed it squarely in the functional institutions of our society. In this way, we may see legal decisions as the agents of racialization. That is, historically, legal decisions have supported the notion of racial categories and defined the essential properties that maintain their mutual exclusivity. By contrast, in contemporary times, legal decisions are moving to deracialize our society. Ironically, the blurring of racial boundaries, to the point of legally obliterating them, is seen by many as a "new racism." By ignoring race, we have eliminated the legal capacity to remedy egregious discrimination in its name. The formal taking of race into account (e.g., *Plessy v. Ferguson,* 1896) is replaced by the *Hopwood v. Texas* (1996) ruling that race tells us nothing of a person and to assume so is to "stereotype him." The judgment of U.S. Supreme Court Justice Brennan in *Regents of the University of California v. Bakke,* in 1978, that "to get beyond racism you must first take account of race," is impugned by *Hopwood,* which concludes that we may not take race into account for any reasons. This leaves us in a peculiar position in which the "blatant" factors of "old-fashioned" racism are replaced with a modern form of objectivity that leaves open the door for "subtle" bias by race. We are thus susceptible to the historical influences of race and its subtle psychological intrusions. Most of this volume tells us the increasingly subtle story of racism in our contemporary minds and hearts, institutions, and culture at large.

*Racism is a subtle expression of the confusion and ambivalence of its psychological history.* Racism is no longer a matter of hatred, disgust, and hostility, but is increasingly seen as an expression of ambivalence, ambiguity, and a matter of some subtlety. We have progressed beyond the overt expression of racial animosity and contempt, at least to some degree and by some accounts. Dovidio and Gaertner (Chapter 1) argue that the problem is no longer simply overt hostility, but the expression of discomfort that accompanies being with someone not "like you." The discomfort escalates to fear when the other is not only different, but also the target of oppression by members of your group. The soliloquy might go like this, "Maybe they don't like me, or maybe they are out to get me, or maybe, they are just not as good as us. I want to be fair, I'm a decent person, but . . . " Devine and Vasquez (Chapter 10) argue that proof of one's decency is most easily accomplished when the rules for decency are clear. For example, when low-prejudice whites were put in a jury simulation and required to reevaluate a case that carried a death penalty, jurors were less likely to give the death penalty to a black defendant when the jury was all white (possibly implying racial prejudice). But, when there was a black juror who supported the death penalty, these low-prejudice white jurors were as likely as high-prejudice whites to support the death penalty for black defendants. When it is not so clear how to express one's decency, what comes out is discriminatory racial bias. This biased behavior is not "intentional," but it occurs nevertheless. Subtle racism is in many ways more insidious than overt racism. Why? Because the perpetrator is unaware of his or her motivations or of the racial bias. Because he or she "feels" fair minded, protestations of bias fall on deaf and well-defended ears.

This subtlety of discrimination is not limited to the United States, where blacks are the least well liked, as Jackson, Brown, and Kirby (Chapter 5) show. In Europe, there is a general tendency for each European country to have its disfavored group. The Dutch and the Germans hate the Turks, the French hate the North Africans, and the British hate both the South Asians and the West Indians. If racism can be defined as negative policy positions toward out-groups (Chapter 5, this volume), then modern and traditional racism, economic threat, and negative feelings for out-group members account for it. This accounting is the same whether in the United States or Western Europe. Although the groups may differ across countries, the pattern is the same. In each case, countries reject the overt or traditional expressions of racism, but, in each case, the subtle expression explains a lot of the negative racial antipathy. A "subtle racist," by the Pettigrew (Chapter 11, this volume) findings, would hold negative public policy views regarding negative out-groups only when there is a rational basis for it. "Export immigrants only when they commit a crime or do not have their papers in order." Subtle or aversive racists have not changed their negative views, only raised the bar for "acceptable" reasons for their negativity.

The cup is half empty, it seems. Blatant racists are racist by any standard. The subtle racists are only waiting for an excuse to be so. That they do not see themselves as racists only makes the problem more elusive and insidious. Sears sees the racial world through unforgiving lenses. There has been real progress in race relations in Sears's view; racial supremacy has waned and egalitarianism is a real U.S. norm. Yet racial polarization persists, and the racial gap is widening. For example, Sears points out that 79% of whites believe blacks are better off than they were 10 years ago, but only 48% of blacks believe that. Even more dramatic, 80% of blacks, compared to 39% of whites, felt that blacks did not receive fair treatment in the courts and in the criminal justice system. Perhaps this explains the racial divergence in reactions to the O. J. Simpson criminal trial verdict. Although there is progress, racial divergence in public opinion notwithstanding, far worse is the continuing evidence of white racial antagonism.

Sears offers compelling data that answers the question of whether white antagonism contributes to whites' opposition to policies thought to have a positive benefit to African Americans and to African American political candidates. In a democracy based on political freedoms as the basis for personal freedoms, racialization that sustains a white-dominated status quo augurs badly for racial progress. The problem, stated in different ways in different chapters, is simple—racial progress, although definite and real, is well short of the ideal color-blind and raceless guarantee of individual freedoms. It seems that opportunities are denied and opposition mounted in the name of race at the same time that we proclaim society to be raceless and colorless. The subtlety of racism is its most sinister characteristic.

Distrust, ignorance, and uncertainty exaggerate interracial relations and harm all parties. Devine and Vasquez point out a sinister and subtle problem of racism, a desire to "do the right thing." By their account, there are substantial numbers of white Americans who reject racial bias as unacceptable personal behavior, and who strive in all sincerity to behave in a fair and unbiased way. Such people have self-conceptions as fair-minded people, and feel upset if evidence is obtained to the contrary. As with Gaertner and Dovidio's aversive racist, however, the absence of the norms for "right doing" leave them vulnerable to "wrong doing." Failing to have the "efficacy" to behave in an egalitarian fashion, or, perhaps worse, believing that one will not be perceived as one intends, is a source of fear, anxiety, and threat to the self. In a circular sort of self-fulfilling prophecy, well-intentioned behavior violates out-group expectations and out-group members whose negative reaction rejects the actor's intended fairness. The target is uncertain how to take the actor's behavior. The actor is uncertain how to "communicate" his or her good intentions. What remains is another failed communication that confirms all the worst fears in the situation. So, by this account, racism is not just a matter of poor intentions, it can be a result of good intentions. In this regard, it resembles the aversive racism of Gaertner and Dovidio. But how is one to know, and how does one fix it? We'll return to this later.

*Racism has consequences, often negative, for its targets.* So much of our analysis of racism has focused on the so-called "perpetrators" of racism. I have called this the redemption approach (Jones, 1997), because this remedy to racism is the conversion of racists to nonracists. The only question is how to do it. In our scientific history, we have paid relatively little attention to the targets of racism. Crocker and Quinn (Chapter 7) show us why this is a problem. It seems logical that being the target of stigmatizing perceptions and unfair, biased, and discriminatory treatment may take its toll. For every complex problem there is a simple answer and it is usually wrong. The prevailing "wisdom" was that being a target of such animosity and hostility over so many years had to have a negative impact on psychological well-being. Kardiner and Ovesy (1951) went so far as to claim that

> the Negro, in contrast to the white, is a more unhappy person; he has a harder environment to live in, and the internal stress is greater. . . . There is not one personality trait of the Negro the source of which cannot be traced to his difficult living conditions. There are no exceptions to this rule. The final result is a wretched internal life. (p. 81)

Crocker and Quinn, however, counted the teeth in the horse's mouth and discovered that diminished self-esteem of African Americans is not an empirical fact. They have described this work elsewhere, but in the present volume they offer the general premise that externalizing explanatory attribution for negative feedback is ego protective. They further suggest that when self-esteem is not contingent on others for its maintenance, it is less vulnerable to prejudice and other stigmatizing behaviors. So, empirical evidence suggests that to a greater extent the self-esteem of blacks is less contingent on external feedback, and, in general, "noncontingent" self-esteem is less vulnerable to prejudice. This view demands that we recognize the contextual nature of self-relevant perceptions and judgments. Like standards of social comparison, we have choices. We can choose to whom we compare, and we can choose what feedback we internalize. Negative judgments from someone outside our group provide the immediate possibility that the feedback is biased. If the group has well-known tendencies for negative and perhaps irrational or nonobjective judgments, then it is easy to discount the evaluation. So, for Crocker and Quinn, racism does not have the impact it might be expected to have.

Murrell (Chapter 8) offers another perspective on the targets of racism. She suggests that although there are a variety of options for a member of a stigmatized group to derive positive esteem from their group identification (social mobility, social creativity, and social competition), racial identity may be one of the most compelling. Racial identity allows one to gain control over the meaning of the racial group, and to define it in such a way that in spite of its generally negative social evaluation in society at large, from their perspective it has positive value and the capability of conferring positive social identity. The interesting and difficult problem exposed by this racial approach to social identity is that the more successful racial identity is as an antidote to racism, the more distance it is likely to put between the person and other groups. Thus, successful coping may, at worst, exaggerate intergroup conflict (cf. Jones & Morris, 1993), and, at best, make intergroup communication harder.

Steele (Chapter 9) offers an at once devastating and hopeful analysis of the effects of racial bias on its targets. Tennessee Williams's "Big Daddy" smelled mendacity. For Steele, African Americans can feel "stereotype threat" in the air of academic situations. A stereotype threat occurs in any situation in which there is a negative stereotype about one's group. The threat arises when one considers the possibility, perhaps probability, that one will be judged or treated in accordance with the negative stereotype, or, perhaps even worse, will conform to the stereotype. Thus, stereotype threat is a burden to those who fall under its influence. It is bad enough that Steele's research shows that stereotype threat contributes to the dramatic decline in performance by people who are otherwise quite capable. It is even worse that reactions to stereotype threat can include heightened racial vigilance, self-doubt, and retreat from one's racial identification. It is interesting that Murrell's analysis of racial identity seems to be precluded by Steele's stereotype threat reactivity. It seems that heightened racial identity, according to Steele's data, may contribute to a lowering of academic performance. It is possible that those African Americans with high racial identity may be less susceptible to stereotype threat. It could be that those students who have demonstrated this effect may be in the moderate to low range of racial identification. The important aspect of the stereotype threat notion, though, and the basis for the "hopefulness," is that the threat is in the air, it is not in the genes. If the situational cues are changed, as Steele shows in his research, the threat goes away and the performance reaches its true level. Cleaning the air is do-able and we will return to this a bit later when we consider the response to racism.

*Whites have been persistently in a powerful relation relative to the targets of racism.* The racial dominance of whites in the United States goes without saying. But, the sociological fact of this dominance has, according to Operario and Fiske, psychological consequences. The structure of an interpersonal power relation is one in which the less powerful person's outcomes are dependent on the more powerful one. This outcome dependency has not only consequences for the dependent one (cf. Thibault & Kelley, 1959), but also for the persons in power. Powerful people need not and do not pay attention to those less powerful. When they do, they use stereotypes and categorical thinking to explain things to their satisfaction, and to justify or rationalize their power privilege. As Banks and Eberhardt suggest, stereotypes create race. Here, stereotypes create the racialized explanation for superiority that is at the heart of racism. Moreover, and here it gets really sinister, people who identify with others in power are susceptible to that same distorted cognition. Thus, in-group identification along racial lines can create a condition by which distorted stereotypic thinking can reinforce, indeed invent, a rationale by which members of subordinate racial groups are deserving of their fate. The history of racism suggests strongly that excesses of racial bias, as well as gender bias, have been planted squarely in the belief in natural law. That the social order is "natural" is close to saying it is "inevitable." Thus, the power stricture reinvents itself perpetually by the cognitive processes delineated at length throughout this volume.

Racism entails a belief in superiority based on race. Making such beliefs natural instantiates racism as an unchallenged status quo. In this racial scenario, white privilege, white entitlement, white superiority is a given. Selective transport of some nonwhites across the racial osmotic membrane is possible and validates even more the naturalness of white dominance.[2] The inevitability of white dominance is given a further boost and theoretical rationale by Sidanius, Levin, and Pratto (Chapter 6). They advance the notion that all societies in recorded time have been group-based social hierarchies, defined largely by gender, age, and social class. In addition, differences defined by race or ethnicity have been common bases of social hierarchies. Thus, racism is an instance of social-group hierarchical processes. The story they tell is not very hopeful.

They take their story to the criminal justice system where ample evidence supports the notion that criminal incarceration is disproportionately high for African Americans in the United States. For example, across the United States, 32% of all 20- to 29-year-old males are involved with the criminal justice system. In California, that number increases to 40%. The rate of imprisonment in California under the "three strikes and you're out" law is 17 times greater for African Americans than for European Americans. Sidanius et al. offer two explanations for this disproportionate involvement: institutional discrimination and self-handicapping criminality. Racism, if you will, explains part of this bias and criminal behavior explains the rest. Although the precise basis for this claim is not presented, the authors suggest that only 22% of the racial disparity in prison populations is explained by institutional discrimination. This leaves 78% of the disparity to be explained by the criminal behavior of these groups. Why? Sidanius et al. suggest several situational explanations, including the following: (a) African Americans live disproportionately in depressed economic areas, (b) they are subjected to a "culture of subordination" (behavioral patterns that undermine their human potential), and (c) false consciousness (acceptance of the notion that they are subordinate because they are inferior). There are other explanations but what we are left with is a theoretical explanation, social dominance theory (SDT), which suggests a line from *West Side Story* (Bernstein, 1959)—"I'm depraved on account of I'm deprived." The problem is that racial disparities exist not only in the criminal justice system, but also in society at large and have for centuries. The SDT explanation for racial disparities is "that's what socially hierarchical societies do." The future is bleak because by the SDT account (Chapter 6, this volume), "there is no strong empirical nor theoretical reason to expect that this goal [equal justice] will ever be achieved as long as human societies remain hierarchically structured." The last to leave, turn out the lights! SDT describes the facts, then predicts them. What is important about SDT is that it provides a coherent story for how these facts come to be, and how they are interwoven with other aspects of the system and the psyche. Operario and Fiske provide psychological models that both follow from social hierarchy and can be shown to perpetuate it. By SDT analysis, it seems, the victim has committed the crime.

Perhaps college campuses are inherently less morbid, but Pettigrew (Chapter 11) offers a more upbeat story. For Pettigrew, discrimination amounts to what Operario and Fiske call power—"discrimination against a minority group occurs when the group's life chances and life choices are limited in comparison to those of the majority group." In other words, a social hierarchy tends to perpetuate its dominance! The problem of discrimination is both direct and indirect. The direct forms are familiar to us. The indirect forms are less familiar, but are implicated in a far greater way in our contemporary society. Two of these indirect forms are "past-in-present" discrimination by which past direct discrimination influences the unequal life chances and choices in the present. Racial bias in hiring, access to bank loans, and real estate red-lining continue to adversely affect the educational and economic choices and possibilities for the children of those who experienced this direct discrimination. A second form, "side-effect" discrimination explains that when discrimination occurs in one domain, say education, then others such as health, housing, economics are affected. Social policy is often articulated on a direct discrimination basis (we need a victim and we need intention to determine when discrimination occurs), but this analysis suggests the problem is far more subtle and complex. Taken together, the chapters of this volume paint a fairly bleak picture. Good intentions are not good enough. There are lots of bad-intentioned people as well. Reactions of racial targets can exacerbate race relations, or worse, undermine their own viability and racial standing. Although progress has been made in race relations, there is ample evidence that antagonism and polarization persists. Whether in the United States or Europe, the story is pretty much the same. Considering it all, racial disparities may just be inevitable and "natural." So what is our response to this story?

### ■ The Response(s) to Racism

As the several chapters of this volume clearly show, racism is a complex, insistent, and insidious set of problems in the United States and Europe. The problems run the gamut from subtle inconsistencies of feelings and beliefs eventuating in ambiguous or ambivalent behavior, to canonical cultural tendencies toward social hierarchies and group dominance. The history of racial relations enters the picture, but in vague and often transparent ways. Doing right and doing wrong are not dichotomous choices linked separately to good and bad, but a duality that is often inseparable. For example, treating people without regard to color, historically thought to be a good thing, can now be shown to be difficult, if not impossible, to do. Insisting on this color-blind possibility may well shrink rather than expand opportunities. Eldridge Cleaver, one of the leaders of the Black Panther party in the 1960s, reduced the struggle for justice to a simple litmus test: "You are either part of the problem or part of the solution." One of the problems of racism is that it is not totally clear whether an action, approach, or policy serves to solve the problem or becomes an additional problem.

The response to racism is necessarily as complex and multifaceted as the problems themselves. In my recent book on racism (Jones, 1997), I devoted one out of 18 chapters to reducing racial bias. The discussion was largely extrapolations of studies showing ways to reduce intergroup conflict, and the conditions under which interaction among diverse peoples can lead to closer, less conflicted relations. Social psychology prides itself on the cause-effect clarity of experimental research. We have done a great deal of such research on many aspects of prejudice and racism. But we are still left without a simple cause-effect statement of what the responses to racism should be. The present chapters offer several approaches.

Dovidio and Gaertner suggest we need to make people aware of subtle racism and how it works. Devine and Vasquez believe that miscommunication fuels prejudice and better communication will lessen it. President Clinton's 1997 national conversation on race is certainly one approach that is consistent with this prescription. Powerful people perpetuate racism in part because of what their power inclines them to do. Operario and Fiske advise that removing those power hierarchies linked consistently to race is the way to invalidate, and thus eliminate, those racist consequences of power. Sidanius et al. also implicate social hierarchies, but seem rather sanguine about the chances of actually doing that. Sears, too, seems to despair. The problems of racism in the United States have evolved over a very long time and "society at large has played a large role in creating the problem" (Chapter 4, this volume). Thus, society at large has a large role to play in its amelioration. Sears's hope lies in the Declaration of Independence, that we are all equal, and possessed of inalienable rights to life, liberty, and the pursuit of happiness. This ideal is a moral commitment that ensures we must and will continue to struggle to bring it closer to reality. Perhaps this is, indeed, our most profound goad to action.

Pettigrew continues to make the most eloquent and effective argument for the benefit of contact across racial and other divides. Diversity in our society means integration of the ultimate kind for Pettigrew. The effective response to racism, for Pettigrew, promotes normative change in our society. New social norms would replace racial animosity and discrimination with adherence to equality and cross-race friendships. This is a tall order, but its likelihood is increased if we convince ourselves that institutional change toward diversity is inevitable; that behavioral change leads to attitude change; that contact among diverse groups will reduce conflict; and that reducing fears people have about other groups will reduce prejudice and discrimination. These are caveats and guides that can be useful in assessing the likely success of specific actions. Embracing these principles and implementing them is clearly more than half of the battle.

The responses are defined by Steele, Crocker and Quinn, and Murrell. Disidentification, noncontingent self-esteem, and racial identity unfold as processes by which one maintains positive and meaningful self-regard in the face of prejudice and racism. There are positive outcomes in these approaches. Self-esteem is maintained even if racial stigma persists. Academic performance can be enhanced by simply removing the threat of negative expectancies. But we must also be careful that these strategies do not leave the culprits of prejudice and racism unchanged, or exacerbate relations across racial divides.

And, finally, perhaps the biggest problem of all is that we have a problem, racism, which has no essential basis in race. Banks and Eberhardt show convincingly that race is socially constructed, in part, by the decisions that are handed down in our courts, not by the biological scientists who define human essence. The meaning of race is confused, conflicted, and inconsistent. Race means nothing and everything at the same time. The courts say we have to take it into account to remove its worst effects, and, at the same time, say we must never take it into account because that moves us away from the ideal of individual inalienable rights. It is difficult to get a good hold on race because it changes continually as a result of the legal, political, and scientific efforts to define it. The problem, in part, is the concept of race itself.

The response that makes sense is to keep responding! Approaching the multiple problems of racism allows us to conceive a variety of possible responses. Some may be more important than others, but as Sears proposes, the moral commitment to freedom and equality propels us forward. I am reminded of Isaac Asimov's *Foundation Series* in which mathematical calculations had secured a precise knowledge of the future. But the certainty of that future was dependent on the natural processes of human society. Informing them of the certain future rendered it uncertain. So, we must struggle to do the right thing, trying to figure out what the right thing is, and daring to fail.

This book is testament to that struggle. It will take its place within the arsenal of efforts to realize the dream of a fair, just, and free society for all.

## ■ Notes

1. Entitativity refers to the fact that people can be grouped together as a single entity by virtue of the fact that they are assumed to have similar features, to be seen in close proximity to each other, and to have common purpose and common fate (Campbell, 1958). Actitativity is the property of a group that reflects its ability to act and, hence, to affect others (Abelson, 1994). It is characterized by mass action, common purpose. . . . Zoeller downplayed his remarks because "he didn't mean anything by them." They clearly implied, however, that blacks could be stereotyped by what they were like and what they did. This plays into the social categorization on which so much of our prejudicial and racist actions rest.

2. This view, labeled the "exception that proves the rule," has been called "enlightened racism," (Jhally & Lewis, 1992), and proposes that those occurrences of racial success strengthen the notion that all those in the group who do not succeed are personally flawed. Is it the personal inadequacy, not the systematic discrimination, that explains the racial group disparities?

# References

Aboud, F. (1988). *Children and prejudice.* New York: Basil Blackwell.

Abe, J. S., & Zane, N. W. S. (1990). Psychological maladjustment among Asian and white American college students: Controlling for confounds. *Journal of Consulting and Clinical Psychology, 37,* 437-444.

Abelson, R. P. (1994, June). *In-group perceptions of activity by the collective other.* Invited address presented at the Presidential Symposium, American Psychological Society, Washington, DC.

Abramowitz, A. I. (1994). Issue evolution reconsidered: Racial attitudes and partisanship in the U.S. electorate. *American Journal of Political Science, 38*(1), 1-24.

Abramson, L. Y., Seligman, M. E. P., & Teasdale, J. (1978). Learned helplessness in humans: Critique and reformulation. *Journal of Abnormal Psychology, 87,* 49-74.

Adelman, C. (1991). *Women at thirty-something: Paradoxes of attainment.* Washington, DC: U.S. Department of Education, Office of Research and Development.

Adorno, T. W., Frenkel-Brunswik, E., Levinson, D. J., & Sanford, R. N. (1950). *The authoritarian personality.* New York: Harper.

Alba, R. D. (1990). *Ethnic identity: The transformation of white America.* New Haven, CT: Yale University Press.

Alderfer, C. P., Alderfer, C. J., Tucker, L., & Tucker, R. (1980). Diagnosing race relations in management. *Journal of Applied Behavioral Science, 27,* 135-166.

Alexander, K. L., & Entwistle, D. R. (1988). Achievement in the first two years of school: Patterns and processes. *Monographs of the Society for Research in Child Development, 53*(2).

Allport, G. W. (1958). *The nature of prejudice.* Garden City, NY: Doubleday.

Allport, G. W. (1979). *The nature of prejudice* (2nd ed.). Reading, MA: Addison-Wesley.

Alpern, D. (1995). Why women are divided on affirmative action. *Working Women, 20*(18).

Altemeyer, B. (1988). *Enemies of freedom: Understanding right-wing authoritarianism.* San Francisco: Jossey-Bass.

American Council on Education. (1995-1996). *Minorities in higher education.* Washington, DC: Office of Minority Concerns.

295

*American National Election Survey Studies 1948-1994.* (1995). Ann Arbor, MI: Interuniversity Consortium for Political and Social Research.

Amir, Y. (1969). Contact hypothesis of ethnic relations. *Psychological Bulletin, 71,* 319-343.

Anastasio, P. A., Bachman, B. A., Gaertner, S. L., & Dovidio, J. F. (1997). Categorization, recategorization, and common in-group identity. In R. Spears, P. J., Oakes, N. Ellemers, & S. A. Haslam (Eds.), *The social psychology of stereotyping and group life* (pp. 236-256). Oxford, UK: Basil Blackwell.

Anderson, J. (1996, April 29/May 6). Black and blue. *New Yorker,* 62-64.

Anderson, N. B., McNeily, M. D., Armstead, C., Clark, R., & Pieper, C. (1993). Assessment of cardiovascular reactivity: A methodological overview. *Ethnicity & Disease, 3*(1), 29-37.

Andreasen, A. R. (1990). Cultural interpretation: A critical research issue for the 1990s. In M. E. Goldberg, G. Gorn, & R. Pollay (Eds.), *Advances in consumer research* (Vol. 17, pp. 847-849). Provo, UT: Association for Consumer Research.

Appiah, K. A. (1990). Racisms. In D. T. Goldberg (Ed.), *Anatomy of racism* (pp. 3-17). Minneapolis: University of Minnesota Press.

Arkin, S. D. (1980). Discrimination and arbitrariness in capital punishment: An analysis of post-Furman murder cases in Dade County, Florida, 1973-1976. *Stanford Law Review, 33,* 75-101.

Aronson, J. (1996). *Advocating the malleability of intelligence as an intervention to increase college grade performance.* Unpublished manuscript, University of Texas.

Ascher, C. (1990). Recent initiatives to institutionalize pluralism on predominantly white campuses. *Higher Education Extension Service Review, 2*(1), 1-10.

Ashmore, R. D., & Del Boca, F. K. (1981). Conceptual approaches to stereotypes and stereotyping. In D. L. Hamilton (Ed.), *Cognitive processes in stereotyping and intergroup behavior* (pp. 1-35). Hillsdale, NJ: Lawrence Erlbaum.

Austin, T. L. (1985). Does where you live determine what you get? A case study of misdemeanant sentencing. *Journal of Criminal Law and Criminology, 76,* 490-511.

Baldus, D. C., Pulaski, C. A., & Woodsworth, G. (1983). Comparative review of death sentences: An empirical study of the Georgia experience. *Journal of Criminal Law and Criminology, 74,* 661-753.

Baldus, D. C., Woodsworth, G., & Pulaski, C. A. (1985). Monitoring and evaluating contemporary death sentencing systems: Lessons from Georgia. *U.C. Davis Law Review, 18,* 1375-1407.

Baldus, D., Woodsworth, G., & Pulaski, C. (1990). *Equal justice and the death penalty: A legal and empirical analysis.* Boston: Northeastern University Press.

Banaji, M. R., & Greenwald, A. G. (1994). Implicit stereotyping and prejudice. In M. P. Zanna & J. M. Olson (Eds.), *The psychology of prejudice: The Ontario Symposium* (Vol. 7, pp. 55-76). Hillsdale, NJ: Lawrence Erlbaum.

Bandura, A. (1977). Self-efficacy: Toward a unifying theory of behavior change. *Psychological Review, 84,* 191-215.

Bandura, A. (1986). *Social foundations of action: A social-cognitive theory.* Englewood Cliffs, NJ: Prentice Hall.

Banks, J. (1981). *Multiethnic education: Theory and practice.* Boston: Allyn & Bacon.

Banks, J., & Grambs, J. (1972). *Black self-concept.* New York: McGraw-Hill.

Banton, M. (1986). Pluralistic ignorance as a factor in racial attitudes. *New Community, 8*(1), 18-25.

Bargh, J. A. (1996). Automaticity in social psychology. In E. T. Higgins & A. W. Kruglanski (Eds.), *Social psychology: Handbook of basic principles* (pp. 169-183). New York: Guilford.

Barrett, R. K. (1974). *A study of attribution of responsibility as a function of internal-external locus of control and interracial person perception.* Unpublished doctoral dissertation, University of Pittsburgh, Pittsburgh, PA.

Baumeister, R. F., & Showers, C. J. (1984). A review of paradoxical performance effects: Choking under pressure in sports and mental tests. *European Journal of Social Psychology, 16,* 361-383.

Baumeister, R. F., & Leary, M. R. (1995). The need to belong: Desire for interpersonal attachments as a fundamental human motivation. *Psychological Bulletin, 117,* 497-529.

Beaman, A. L., Barnes, P. J., Klentz, B., & McQuork, B. (1978). Increasing helping rates through information dissemination: Teaching pays. *Personality and Social Psychology Bulletin, 3,* 406-411.

Beijers, W. M. E. H., Hille, H., & de Leng, A. W. (1994). *Selectiviteit nader bekeken: Een onderzoek naar de OM-afdoeing van strafzaken teken verdachten behorende tot etnische minderheisgroepen.* Amsterdam: Vrije Universiteit.

Benbow, C. P., & Arjmand, O. (1990). Predictions of high academic achievement in mathematics and science by mathematically talented students: A longitudinal study. *Journal of Educational Psychology, 82,* 430-441.

Benbow, C. P., & Stanley, J. C. (1980). Sex differences in mathematical ability: Fact or artifact? *Science, 210,* 1262-1264.

Benbow, C. P., & Stanley, J. C. (1983). Sex differences in mathematical reasoning ability: More facts. *Science, 222,* 1029-1031.

Benedict, R. (1959). *Race: Science and politics.* New York: Viking.

Bennett, C. E. (1992). The black population of the United States: March 1991. *Current population reports* (Series P-20, No. 464). Washington, DC: U.S. Bureau of the Census.

Bernard, J. L. (1979). Interaction between the race of the defendant and that of jurors in determining verdicts. *Law and Psychology Review, 5*(Fall), 103-111.

Bernstein, L. (1959). *West side story.* New York: G. Schirmer.

Berry, J. W. (1984). Cultural relations in plural societies: Alternatives to segregation and their sociopyschological implications. In N. Miller & M. B. Brewer (Eds.), *Groups in contact* (pp. 11-27). San Diego, CA: Academic Press.

Bettelheim, B. (1943). Individual and mass behavior in extreme situations. *Journal of Abnormal and Social Psychology, 38,* 417-452.

Biesanz, J., & Smith, L. M. (1951). Race relations of Panama and the Canal Zone. *American Sociological Review, 57*(1), 7-14.

Blair, I., & Banaji, M. R. (1996). Automatic and controlled processes in gender stereotyping. *Journal of Personality and Social Psychology, 70,* 1142-1163.

Blauner, R. (1968). Internal colonialism and ghetto revolt. *Social Problems, 16,* 395-408.

Blumer, H. (1958). Race prejudice as a sense of group position. *Pacific Sociological Review, 1*(1), 3-7.

Blumstein, A. (1982). On the racial disproportionality of U.S. prison populations. *Journal of Criminal Law and Criminology, 73,* 1259-1281.

Blumstein, A. (1993). Racial disproportionality of U.S. prison populations revisited. *University of Colorado Law Review, 64*(3), 743-759.

Bobo, L. (1983). Whites' opposition to busing: Symbolic racism or realistic group conflict? *Journal of Personality and Social Psychology, 45,* 1196-1210.

Bobo, L. (1987). Group conflict, prejudice, and the paradox of contemporary racial attitudes. In P. A. Katz & D. A. Taylor (Eds.), *Eliminating racism: Means and controversies* (pp. 85-114). New York: Plenum.

Bobo, L. (1988). Attitudes toward the black political movement: Trends, meaning, and effects on racial policy preferences. *Social Psychology Quarterly, 51,* 287-302.

Bobo, L., & Hutchings, V. L. (1996). Perceptions of racial group competition: Extending Blumer's theory of group position to a multiracial social context. *American Sociological Review, 51,* 950-962.

Bobo, L., Johnson, J. H., Oliver, M. L., Sidanius, J., & Zubrinsky, C. (1992). *Public opinion before and after a spring of discontent: A preliminary report on the 1992 Los Angeles County Survey.* Los Angeles: UCLA Center for the Study of Urban Poverty.

Bobo, L., & Kluegel, J. R. (1991, May). *Modern American prejudice: Stereotypes, social distance, and perceptions of discrimination toward blacks, Hispanics, and Asians.* Paper presented at the annual meeting of the American Sociological Association, Cincinnati, OH.

Bobo, L., & Kluegel, J. R. (1993). Opposition to race targeting: Self-interest, stratification ideology, or racial attitudes? *American Sociological Review, 58,* 443-464.

Bobo, L., Kluegel, J. R., & Smith, R. A. (1997). Laissez faire racism: The crystallization of a "kinder, gentler" antiblack ideology. In S. A. Tuch & J. K. Martin (Eds.), *Racial attitudes in the 1990s: Continuity and change* (pp. 15-44). Westport, CT: Praeger.

Bobo, L., Zubrinsky, C. L., Johnson, J. H., Jr., & Oliver, M. L. (1994). Public opinion before and after a spring of discontent. In M. Baldassare (Ed.), *The Los Angeles riots: Lessons for the urban future* (pp. 103-134). Boulder, CO: Westview.

Bonger, W. W. (1916). *Criminality and economic opportunity.* Boston: Little, Brown.

Bosma, J. J. (1985). *Allochtonen en strafoemeing.* Groningen: Uitgave Criminologisch Instituut Groningen.

Bourg, S., & Stock, H. V. (1994). A review of domestic violence arrest statistics in a police department using a pro-arrest policy: Are pro-arrest policies enough? *Journal of Family Violence, 9,* 177-189.

Bowers, W. J., & Pierce, G. L. (1980). Arbitrariness and discrimination under post-Furman capital statutes. *Crime and Delinquency, 26,* 563-635.

Bowlby, J. (1988). *A secure base: Parent-child attachment and healthy human development.* New York: Basic Books.

Bowser, B. P. (Ed.). (1995). *Racism and antiracism in world perspecive.* Thousand Oaks, CA: Sage.

Braddock, J. H., & McPartland, J. M. (1987). How minorities continue to be excluded from equal opportunities: Research on labor market and institutional barriers. *Journal of Social Issues, 43*(1), 5-39.

Bradmiller, L. L., & Walters, W. S. (1985). Seriousness of sexual assault charges: Influencing factors. *Criminal Justice and Behavior, 12,* 463-484.

Brewer, M. B. (1979). In-group bias in the minimal intergroup situation: A cognitive-motivational analysis. *Psychological Bulletin, 86,* 307-324.

Brewer, M. B. (1988). A dual process model of impression formation. In R. Wyer & T. Srull (Eds.), *Advances in social cognition* (Vol. 1, pp. 1-36). Hillsdale, NJ: Lawrence Erlbaum.

Brewer, M. B., & Brown, R. J. (1998). Intergroup relations. In D. T. Gilbert, S. T. Fiske, & G. Lindzey (Eds.), *The handbook of social psychology* (4th ed.). New York: McGraw-Hill.

Brill, A. A. (Ed.). (1938). *The basic writings of Sigmund Freud.* New York: Random House.

Brislin, R. W. (1990). *Applied cross-cultural psychology.* Newbury Park, CA: Sage.

Brown, A. (1976). *Personality correlates of the Developmental Inventory of Black Consciousness.* Unpublished master's thesis, University of Pittsburgh, Pittsburgh, PA.

Brown, K. T., Torres, M., & Jackson, J. S. (1996). *Structure of racial attitudes in Western European nations.* Unpublished manuscript, University of Michigan, Ann Arbor.

Brown, T., Crocker, J., Jackson, J. S., Lightborn, T., & Torres, M. (1996). *What drives the bus: Modeling the causal linkages among prejudice, affect, and beliefs toward ethnic and racial out-groups in Western Europe.* Unpublished manuscript, University of Michigan, Ann Arbor.

Brown v. Memphis & C. R. Co., 4F.37 (C.C.W.D. Tenn. 1880).

Burton, N. W., & Jones, L. V. (1982). Recent trends in achievement levels of Black and White youth. *Educational Researcher, 11,* 10-17.

Camarillo, A. M. (1989). *Building a multiracial, multicultural university community* (Final Report of the University Committee on Minority Issues). Stanford, CA: Stanford University.

Campbell, D. T. (1958). Common fate, similarity, and other indices of the status of aggregates as social entities. *Behavioral Science, 3*(1), 14-25.

Carmines, E. G., & Merriman, W. R., Jr. (1993). The changing American dilemma: Liberal values and racial policies. In P. M. Sniderman, P. E. Tetlock, & E. G. Carmines (Eds.), *Prejudice, politics, and the American dilemma* (pp. 237-255). Stanford, CA: Stanford University Press.

Carmines, E. G., & Stimson, J. A. (1989). *Issue evolution: Race and the transformation of American politics.* Princeton, NJ: Princeton University Press.

Carter, S. (1991). *Reflections of an affirmative action baby.* New York: Basic Books.

Cartwright, D. (1950). Emotional dimensions of group life. In M. L. Raymert (Ed.), *Feelings and emotions* (pp. 439-447). New York: McGraw-Hill.

Carver, C. S., Glass, D. C., & Katz, I. (1977). Favorable evaluations of blacks and the disabled: Positive prejudice, unconscious denial, or social desirability? *Journal of Applied Social Psychology, 8,* 97-106.

Cavalli-Sforza, L. L., & Feldman, M. W. (1973). Cultural versus biological inheritance: Phenotypic transmission from parents to children. *American Journal of Human Genetics, 25,* 618-637.

Chevigny, P. (1995). *Edge of the knife: Police violence in the Americas.* New York: New Press.

Chicago & Northwestern Railway Company v. Anna Williams, 55 Ill. 185 (1870).

Christopher, W. (1991). *Report of the independent commission on the Los Angeles Police Department.* Los Angeles: Independent Commission on the Los Angeles Police Department.

Citrin, J., Green, D. P., & Sears, D. O. (1990). Whites' reactions to black candidates: When does race matter? *Public Opinion Quarterly, 54*(1), 74-96.

Citrin, J., Sears, D. O., Muste, C., & Wong, C. (1996). *Multiculturalism versus liberalism in mass opinion: Normative consensus or group conflict?* Unpublished manuscript, University of California, Berkeley.

Clark, K. B. (1965). *Dark ghetto: Dilemmas of social power.* New York: Harper & Row.

Clark, K. B., & Clark, M. K. (1939). The development of consciousness of self and the emergence of racial identification of Negro school children. *Journal of Social Psychology, 10,* 591-599.

Clayton, S. D., & Tangri, S. S. (1989). The justice of affirmative action. In F. A. Blanchard & F. J. Crosby (Eds.), *Affirmative action in perspective* (pp. 177-192). New York: Springer-Verlag.

Cobb, J. A., & Hops, H. (1973). Effects of academic survival skill training on low-achieving first graders. *Journal of Educational Research, 67*(3), 108-113.

Cohen, D. L., & Peterson, J. L. (1981). Bias in the courtroom: Race and sex effects of attorneys on juror verdicts. *Social Behavior and Personality, 9*(1), 81-87.

Cohen, G., Steele, C. M., & Ross, L. (1997). *Giving feedback across the racial divide: Overcoming the effects of stereotypes.* Unpublished manuscript, Stanford University.

Cohen, S., Kessler, R. C., & Gordon, L. U. (1995). *Measuring stress: A guide or health and social scientists.* New York: Oxford University Press.

Coleman, J. S., Campbell, E. Q., Hobson, C. J., McPartland, J., Mood, A. M., Weinfield, E. D., & York, R. L. (1966). *Equality of educational opportunity.* Washington, DC: U.S. Government Printing Office.

Comer, J. (1988, November). Educating poor minority children. *Scientific American, 259,* 42.

Conley, T. D., Devine, P. G., Evett, S. R., & Veniegas, R. C. (1996, May). *Minority group expectations in interpersonal intergroup interactions.* Paper presented at the annual meeting of the Midwestern Psychological Association, Chicago.

Converse, P. E., Clausen, A. R., & Miller, W. E. (1965). Electoral myth and reality: The 1964 election. *American Political Science Review, 59,* 321-336.

Converse, P. E., & Markus, G. B. (1979). Plus ça change . . . : The new CPS election study panel. *American Political Science Review, 73*(March), 32-49.

Cook, S. W. (1984). Cooperative contact in multiethnic contexts. In N. Miller & M. B. Brewer (Eds.) *Groups in contact: The psychology of desegregation* (pp. 155-185). New York: Academic Press.

Cook, S. W. (1985). Experimenting on social issues: The case of school desegregation. *American Psychologist, 40,* 452-460.

Cooley, C. H. (1956). *Human nature and the social order.* New York: Free Press.

Copeland, J. T. (1994). Prophecies of power: Motivational implications of social power for behavioral confirmation. *Journal of Personality and Social Psychology, 67,* 264-277.

Cose, E. (1993). *The rage of a privileged class.* New York: Harper Collins.

Cox, O. C. (1948). *Caste, class, and race.* New York: Monthly Review Press.

Crandall, R. (1973). The measurement of self-esteem and related constructs. In J. Robinson & P. R. Shaver (Eds.), *Measures of social psychological attitudes.* Ann Arbor, MI: Institute for Social Research.

Crelinsten, R. D. (1995). In their own words: The world of the torturer. In R. D. Crelinsten & A. P. Schmid (Eds.), *The politics of pain: Torturers and their masters* (pp. 35- 64). Boulder, CO: Westview.

Crocker, J. (1994, October). *Who cares what you think? Reflected and deflected appraisals.* Paper presented at the annual meeting of the Society for Experimental Social Psychology, Incline Village, NV.

Crocker, J., Luhtanen, R., Blaine, B., & Broadnax, S. (1994). Collective self-esteem and psychological well-being among white, black, and Asian college students. *Personality and Social Psychology Bulletin, 20,* 502-513.

Crocker, J., Blaine, B., Luhtanen, R., & Broadnax, S. (1995). *Perceived disadvantage, discrimination, and psychological well-being among black, white, and Asian college students.* Unpublished manuscript, University of Michigan, Ann Arbor.

Crocker, J., & Major, B. (1989). Social stigma and self-esteem: The self-protective properties of stigma. *Psychological Review, 96,* 608-630.

Crocker, J., Quinn, D. M., & Wolfe, C. T. (1996, May). *Feeling fat: Affective consequences of the stigma of overweight.* Paper presented at the annual meeting of the Society for the Psychological Study of Social Issues, Ann Arbor, MI.

Crocker, J., Thompson, L. L., McGraw, K. M., & Ingerman, C. (1987). Downward comparison, prejudice, and evaluations of others: Effects of self esteem and threat. *Journal of Personality and Social Psychology, 52,* 907-916.

Crocker, J., Voelkl, K., Testa, M., & Major, B. (1991). Social stigma: The affective consequences of attributional ambiguity. *Journal of Personality and Social Psychology, 60,* 218-228.

Crocker, J., & Wolfe, C. T. (1997). *Contingencies of self-esteem: An integrative perspective.* Unpublished manuscript, University of Michigan, Ann Arbor.

Crosby, F., Bromley, S., & Saxe, L. (1980). Recent unobtrusive studies of black and white discrimination and prejudice: A literature review. *Psychological Bulletin, 35,* 546-563.

Crosby, F. J. (1994). Understanding affirmative action. *Basic and Applied Social Psychology, 15,* 13-42.

Cross, W. E. (1971). The Negro-to-black conversion experience: Toward a psychology of black liberation. *Black World, 20*(9), 13-37.

Cross, W. E. (1991). *Shades of black: Diversity in African American identity.* Philadelphia, PA: Temple University Press.

Culotta, E., & Gibbons, A. (Eds.). (1992, November 13). Minorities in science [Special section]. *Science, 258,* 1176-1232.

Cummings, S. (1980). White ethnics, racial prejudice, and labor market segmentation. *American Journal of Sociology, 85,* 938-950.

Darley, J. M., & Fazio, R. H. (1980). Expectancy confirmation processes arising in the social interaction sequence. *American Psychologist, 35,* 867-881.

Darley, J. M., & Latané, B. (1968). Bystander intervention in emergencies: Diffusion of responsibility. *Journal of Personality and Social Psychology, 8,* 377-383.

Davis, F. G. (1991). *Who is black? One nation's definition.* Philadelphia, PA: Temple University Press.

Davis, J. A., & Smith, T. W. (1994). *General social surveys, 1972-1994: Cumulative codebook.* Chicago: National Opinion Research Center.

DeBoer, G. (1984). A study of gender effects in science and mathematics course-taking behavior among students who graduated from college in the late 1970's. *Journal of Research in Science Teaching, 21,* 95-103.

Deci, E. L., & Ryan, R. M. (1995). Human autonomy: The basis for true self-esteem. In M. H. Kernis (Ed.), *Efficacy, agency, and self-esteem* (pp. 31-49). New York: Plenum.

Demo, D. H., & Parker, K. D. (1987). Academic achievement and self-esteem among Black and White college students. *Journal of Social Psychology, 4,* 345-355.

Denton, S. E. (1985). *A methodological refinement and validational analysis of the Developmental Inventory of Black Consciousness (DIB-C).* Unpublished doctoral dissertation, University of Pittsburgh, Pittsburgh, PA.

DePaulo, B. M. (1992). Nonverbal behavior and self-presentation. *Psychological Bulletin, 111,* 203-243.

Dépret, E. F., & Fiske, S. T. (1993). Social cognition and power: Some cognitive consequences of social structure as a source of control deprivation. In G. Weary, F. Gleicher, & K. Marsh (Eds.), *Control motivation and social cognition* (pp. 176-202). New York: Springer-Verlag.

Dépret, E. F., & Fiske, S. T. (1996). *Perceiving the powerful: Intriguing individuals versus threatening groups.* Unpublished manuscript, University of Massachusetts at Amherst.

Derry v. Lowry, 6 Phil Rep. 30 (1865).

Devine, P. G. (1989). Stereotypes and prejudice: Their automatic and controlled components. *Journal of Personality and Social Psychology, 56*(1), 5-18.

Devine, P. G., & Elliot, A. J. (1995). Are racial stereotypes really fading? The Princeton trilogy revisited. *Personality and Social Psychology Bulletin, 21,* 1139-1150.

Devine, P. G., Evett, S. R., & Vasquez-Suson, K. A. (1996). Exploring the interpersonal dynamics of intergroup contact. In R. M. Sorrentino & E. T. Higgins (Eds.), *Handbook of motivation and cognition: The interpersonal context* (Vol. 3, pp. 423-464). New York: Guilford.

Devine, P. G., & Monteith, M. J. (1993). The role of discrepancy-associated affect in prejudice reduction. In D. M. Mackie & D. L. Hamilton (Eds.), *Affect, cognition, and stereotyping: Interactive processes in intergroup perception* (pp. 317-344). Orlando, FL: Academic Press.

Devine, P. G., Monteith, M. J., Zuwerink, J. R., & Elliot, A. J. (1991). Prejudice with and without compunction. *Journal of Personality and Social Psychology, 60,* 817-830.

De Vos, G. A. (1992). *Social cohesion and alienation: Minorities in the United States and Japan.* Boulder, CO: Westview.

Diener, E. (1984). Subjective well-being. *Psychological Bulletin, 95,* 542-575.

Divale, W., & Harris, M. (1976). Population, warfare, and the male supremacist complex. *American Anthropologist, 78,* 521-538.

Dollard, J., Doob, L., Miller, N. E., Mowrer, O., & Sears, R. (1939). *Frustration and aggression.* New Haven, CT: Yale University Press.

Dovidio, J. F. (1995, August). *Stereotypes, prejudice, and discrimination: Automatic and controlled processes.* Paper presented at the annual meeting of the American Psychological Society, New York.

Dovidio, J. F., Brigham, J. C., Johnson, B. T., & Gaertner, S. L. (1996). Stereotyping, prejudice, and discrimination: Another look. In N. Macrae, C. Stangor, & M. Hewstone (Eds.), *Foundations of stereotypes and stereotyping* (pp. 276-319). New York: Guilford.

Dovidio, J. F., Evans, N., & Tyler, R. B. (1986). Racial stereotypes: The contents of their cognitive representations. *Journal of Experimental Social Psychology, 22,* 22-37.

Dovidio, J. F., & Fazio, R. H. (1992). New technologies for the direct and indirect assessment of attitudes. In J. Tanur (Ed.), *Questions about survey questions: Meaning, memory, attitudes, and social interaction* (pp. 204-237). New York: Russell Sage.

Dovidio, J. F., & Gaertner, S. L. (1981). The effects of race, status, and ability on helping behavior. *Social Psychology Quarterly, 44,* 192-203.

Dovidio, J. F., & Gaertner, S. L. (Eds.). (1986a). *Prejudice, discrimination, and racism.* New York: Academic Press.

Dovidio, J. F., & Gaertner, S. L. (1986b). Prejudice, discrimination, and racism: Historical trends and contemporary approaches. In J. F. Dovidio & S. L. Gaertner (Eds.), *Prejudice, discrimination, and racism* (pp. 1-34). Orlando, FL: Academic Press.

Dovidio, J. F., & Gaertner, S. L. (1991). Changes in the nature and expression of racial prejudice. In H. Knopke, J. Norrell, & R. Rogers (Eds.), *Opening doors: An appraisal of race relations in contemporary America* (pp. 201-241). Tuscaloosa: University of Alabama Press.

Dovidio, J. F., Mann, J. A., & Gaertner, S. L. (1989). Resistance to affirmative action: The implication of aversive racism. In F. A. Blanchard & F. J. Crosby (Eds.), *Affirmative action in perspective* (pp. 83-102). New York: Springer-Verlag.

Dovidio, J. F., & Mullen, B. (1992). *Race, physical handicap, and response amplification.* Unpublished manuscript, Colgate University, Hamilton, NY.

Dovidio, J. F., Smith, J. K., Donnella, A. G., & Gaertner, S. L. (1997). Racial attitudes and the death penalty. *Journal of Applied Social Psychology, 27,* 1468-1487.

Duckitt, J. (1992a). *The social psychology of prejudice.* New York: Prager.

Duckitt, J. (1992b). Psychology and prejudice: A historical analysis and integrative framework. *American Psychologist, 47,* 1182-1193.

Duke, L., & Morin, R. (1992, March 8). Focusing on race: Candid dialogue, elusive answers. *Washington Post,* pp. A1, A24, A25.

Duleep, H. O., & Sanders, S. (1992). Discrimination at the top: American-born Asian and white men. *Industrial Relations, 31,* 416-432.

Dunwoody, P. T., & Frank, M. L. (1994). Effects of ethnicity on prison sentencing. *Psychological Reports, 74,* 200.

Dutton, D. G., & Lake, R. A. (1973). Threat of own prejudice and reverse discrimination in interracial situations. *Journal of Personality and Social Psychology, 28,* 94-100.

Dutton, D. G., & Lennox, V. L. (1974). Effect of prior "token" compliance on subsequent interracial behavior. *Journal of Personality and Social Psychology, 29,* 65-71.

Dweck, C. (1986). Motivational processes affecting learning. *American Psychologist, 41,* 1040-1048.

Eberhardt, J. L., & Fiske, S. T. (1996). Motivating individuals to change: What is a target to do? In C. N. Macrae, C. Stangor, & M. Hewstone (Eds.), *Stereotypes and stereotyping* (pp. 369-415). New York: Guilford.

Eberhardt, J. L., & Randall, J. L. (1997). The essential notion of race. *Psychological Science, 8,* 198-203.

Eccles, J. S. (1987). Gender roles and women's achievement-related decisions. *Psychology of Women Quarterly, 11,* 135-172.

Eccles-Parsons, J. S., Adler, T. E., Futterman, R., Goff, S. B., Kaczala, C. M., Meece, J. L., & Midgley, C. (1983). Expectations, values, and academic behaviors. In J. T. Spence (Ed.), *Achievement and achievement motivation* (pp. 75-146). New York: Freeman.

Edsall, T. B., & Edsall, M. D. (1991). When the official subjet is presidential politics, taxes, welfare, crime, rights, or values . . . the real subject is race. *Atlantic Monthly, May,* 53-86.

Edsall, T. B., & Edsall, M. D. (1992). *Chain reaction: The impact of race, rights, and taxes on American politics.* New York: Norton.

Ekehammar, B., Nelson, I., & Sidanius, J. (1987). Education and ideology: Basic aspects of education related to adolescents' sociopolitical attitudes. *Political Psychology, 8,* 395-410.

Erber, R., & Fiske, S. T. (1984). Outcome dependency and attention to inconsistent information. *Journal of Personality and Social Psychology, 47,* 709-726.

Ericson, R. (1982). *Reproducing order: A study of police patrol work.* Toronto: University of Toronto Press.

Erikson, E. (1956). The problem of ego-identity. *Journal of the American Psychoanalytic Association, 4,* 56-121.

Evett, S. R., & Devine, P. G. (1996). [Minority group members' expectancies in intergroup interactions]. Unpublished raw data.

Fanfare. (1997, April 22). *Washington Post,* p. E2.

Fanon, F. (1963). *The wretched of the earth.* New York: Grove.

Fanon, F. (1967). *Black skins, white masks.* New York: Grove Press. (Original work published 1952)

Faranda, J., & Gaertner, S. L. (1979, March). *The effects of inadmissible evidence introduced by the prosecution and the defense, and the defendant's race on the verdicts by high and low authoritarians.* Paper presented at the annual meeting of the Eastern Psychological Association, New York.

Farley, R. (1984). *Blacks and whites: Narrowing the gap?* Cambridge, MA: Harvard University Press.

Fazio, R. H., Jackson, J. R., Dunton, B. C., & Williams, C. J. (1995). Variability in automatic activation as an unobtrusive measure of racial attitudes: A bona fide pipeline? *Journal of Personality and Social Psychology, 69,* 1013-1027.

Feagin, J. R. (1989). The continuing significance of race: Antiblack discrimination in public places. *American Sociological Review, 56*(1), 101-116.

Feagin, J. R., & Feagin, C. B. (1986). *Discrimination American style: Institutional racism and sexism.* Malabar, FL: Krieger.

Federal Glass Ceiling Commission. (1995). *Good for business: Making full use of the nation's human capital.* Washington, DC: Government Printing Office.

Fernandez, J. P. (1985). *Black managers in white corporations.* New York: John Wiley.

Fields, B. J. (1990). Slavery, race, and ideology in the United States of America. *New Left Review, 181,* 95-118.

Fields, J. M., & Schuman, H. (1976). Public beliefs about the beliefs of the public. *Public Opinion Quarterly, 40,* 427-448.

Fineman, H. (1995, April 3). Race and rage. *Newsweek, 125,* 22-34.

Firebaugh, G., & Davis, K. E. (1988). Trends in antiblack prejudice, 1972-1984: Region and cohort effects. *American Journal of Sociology, 94,* 251-272.

Fiske, S. T. (1982). Schema-triggered affect: Applications to social perception. In M. S. Clark & S. T. Fiske (Eds.), *Affect and cognition: The 17th annual Carnegie Symposium on cognition* (pp. 55-78). Hillsdale, NJ: Lawrence Erlbaum.

Fiske, S. T. (1993). Controlling other people: The impact of power on stereotyping. *American Psychologist, 48,* 621-628.

Fiske, S. T. (1998). Stereotyping, prejudice, and discrimination. In D. T. Gilbert, S. T. Fiske, & G. Lindzey (Eds.), *The handbook of social psychology* (4th ed.). New York: McGraw-Hill.

Fiske, S. T., & Neuberg, S. L. (1990). A continuum model of impression formation, from category-based to individuating processes: Influence of information and motivation on attention and interpretation. In M. P. Zanna (Ed.), *Advances in experimental social psychology* (Vol. 23, pp. 1-74). New York: Academic Press.

Fiske, S. T., & Ruscher, J. B. (1993). Negative interdependence and prejudice: Whence the affect? In D. M. Mackie & D. L. Hamilton (Eds.), *Affect, cognition, and stereotyping: Interactive processes in group perception* (pp. 239-268). San Diego, CA: Academic Press.

Fiske, S. T., & Taylor, S. (1991). *Social cognition.* New York: McGraw-Hill.

Forbes, I., & Mead, G. (1992). *Measure for measure: A comparative analysis of measures to combat discrimination in the member countries of the European Community.* London: Department of Employment.

Frable, D. E. S. (1993). Dimensions of marginality: Distinctions among those who are different. *Personality and Social Psychology Bulletin, 19,* 370-380.

Frable, D., Blackstone, T., & Sherbaum, C. (1990). Marginal and mindful: Deviants in social interaction. *Journal of Personality and Social Behavior, 59,* 140-149.

Fraser, S. (1995). *The bell curve wars: Race, intelligence, and the future of America.* New York: Basic Books.

Fyfe, J. J. (1982). Blind justice: Police shootings in Memphis. *Journal of Criminal Law and Criminology, 73,* 707-722.

Gaertner, S. L., & Dovidio, J. F. (1977). The subtlety of white racism, arousal, and helping behavior. *Journal of Personality and Social Psychology, 35,* 691-707.

Gaertner, S. L., & Dovidio, J. F. (1986). The aversive form of racism. In J. F. Dovidio & S. L. Gaertner (Eds.), *Prejudice, discrimination, and racism* (pp. 61-89). Orlando, FL: Academic Press.

Gaertner, S. L., Dovidio, J. F., Anastasio, P. A., Bachman, B. A., & Rust, M. C. (1993). The common in-group identity model: Recategorization and the reduction of intergroup bias. In W. Stroebe & M. Hewstone (Eds.), *European review of social psychology* (Vol. 4, pp. 1-26). New York: John Wiley.

Gaertner, S. L., Dovidio, J. F., Banker, B., Rust, M., Nier, J., Mottola, G., & Ward, C. (1997). Does racism necessarily mean antiblackness? Aversive racism and pro-whiteness. In M. Fine, L. Powell, L. Weis, & M. Wong (Eds.), *Off white* (pp. 167-178). London: Routledge.

Gaertner, S. L., & McLaughlin, J. P. (1983). Racial stereotypes: Associations and ascriptions of positive and negative characteristics. *Social Psychology Quarterly, 46,* 23-30.

Gaertner, S. L., Rust, M. C., Dovidio, J. F., Bachman, B. A., & Anastasio, P. A. (1994). The contact hypothesis: The role of a common in-group identity on reducing intergroup bias. *Small Group Research, 25,* 224-249.

Garcia, L. T., Erskine, N., Hawn, K., & Casmay, S. R. (1981). The effect of affirmative action on attributions about minority group members. *Journal of Personality, 49,* 427-437.

Geen, R. G. (1991). Social motivation. *Annual Review of Psychology, 42,* 377-399.

Gelman, D. (1988, March 7). Black and white in America. *Newsweek, 111,* 24-43.

General Accounting Office. (1990). *Death penalty sentencing: Research indicates patterns of racial disparities* (GAO/GGD-90-57). Washington, DC: Author.

General Accounting Office. (1995). *Military equal opportunity: Certain trends in racial and gender data may warrant further analysis* (GAO/NSIAD Report No. 96-17). Washington, DC: Author.

Gerard, H. (1983). School desegregation: The social science role. *American Psychologist, 38,* 869-878.

Gilbert, D. T., & Silvera, D. S. (1996). Overhelping. *Journal of Personality and Social Psychology, 70,* 678-690.

Gilens, M. (1995). Racial attitudes and opposition to welfare. *Journal of Politics, 57,* 994-1014.

Giles, M. W., & Evans, A. S. (1985). External threat, perceived threat, and group identity. *Social Science Quarterly, 66*(1), 51-66.

Gleick, P. (1993). Water and conflict: Fresh water resources and international security. *International Security, 18*(1), 79-112.

Goddard, R. W. (1986). Postemployment: The changing current in discrimination charges. *Personnel Journal, 65*(October), 34-40.

Goffman, E. (1963). *Stigma: Notes on the management of spoiled identity.* New York: Touchstone.

Goodwin, S. A., & Fiske, S. T. (1996). *Impression formation in asymmetrical power relationships: Does power corrupt absolutely?* Unpublished manuscript, University of Massachusetts at Amherst.

Gossett, T. F. (1963). *Race, the history of an idea in America.* Dallas, TX: Southern Methodist University Press.

Gramsci, A. (1971). *Selections from the prison notebooks.* London: Wishart.

Greenhaus, J. H., Parasuraman, S., & Wormley, W. M. (1990). Effects of race on organizational experiences, job performance evaluations, and career outcomes. *Academy of Management Journal, 33*(1), 64-86.

Grier, W. H., & Coobs, R M. (1968). *Black rage.* New York: Basic Books.

Gross, S. R., & Mauro, R. (1989). *Death and discrimination: Racial disparities in capital sentencing.* Boston: Northwestern University Press.

Grube, J. W., Mayton, D. M., II, & Ball-Rokeach, S. J. (1994). *Journal of Social Issues, 50*(4), 153-173.

Hacker, A. (1995). *Two nations: Black and white, separate, hostile, unequal.* New York: Ballantine.

Hamilton, D. L., & Trolier, T. K. (1986). Stereotypes and stereotyping: An overview of the cognitive approach. In J. F. Dovidio & S. L. Gaertner (Eds.), *Prejudice, discrimination, and racism* (pp. 127-163). Orlando, FL: Academic Press.

Hardt, R. H. (1968). Delinquency and social class: Bad kids or good cops. In I. Deutscher & E. J. Thompson (Eds.), *Among the people: Encounters with the poor* (pp. 132-145). New York: Basic Books.

Hare, B. R., & Costenell, L. A. (1985). No place to run, no place to hide: Comparative status and future prospects of Black boys. In M. B. Spencer, G. K. Brookins, & W. Allen (Eds.), *Beginnings: The social and affective development of Black children* (pp. 201-214). Hillsdale, NJ: Erlbaum.

Hawkins, D. F., & Jones, N. E. (1989). Black adolescents and the criminal justice system. In R. L. Jones (Ed.), *Black adolescents* (pp. 403-425). Berkeley, CA: Cobb & Henry.

Hedges, C. (1994, January 24). Dozens of Islamic rebel suspects slain by Algerian death squads. *New York Times,* p. A4.

Helms, J. E. (1990). The measurement of black racial identity attitudes. In J. E. Helms (Ed.), *Black and white racial identity: Theory, research, and practice* (pp. 83-104). Westport, CT: Greenwood.

Hepburn, J. R. (1978). Race and the decision to arrest: An analysis of warrants issued. *Journal of Research in Crime and Delinquency, 15*(1), 54-73.

Herrnstein, R., & Murray, C. (1994). *The bell curve.* New York: Free Press.

Heussenstamm, F. K. (1971). Bumper stickers and cops. *Transaction, 8,* 32-33.

Hewitt, N. M., & Seymour, E. (1991). *Factors contributing to high attrition rates among science and engineering undergraduate majors.* Unpublished report to the Alfred P. Sloan Foundation.

Hilton, J. L., & Darley, J. M. (1985). Constructing other persons: A limit on the effect. *Journal of Experimental Social Psychology, 21*(1), 1-18.

Hilton, J. L., & Von Hippel, W. (1996). Stereotypes. In J. T. Spence, J. M. Darley, & D. J. Foss (Eds.), *Annual review of psychology* (Vol. 47, pp. 237-271). Palo Alto, CA: Annual Reviews.

Hirschfeld, L. A. (1996). *Race in the making: Cognition, culture, and child's construction of human kinds.* Cambridge: MIT Press.

Hitt, M. A., & Keats, B. W. (1984). Empirical identification of the criteria for effective affirmative action programs. *Journal of Applied Behavioral Science, 20,* 203-222.

Hochschild, J. L. (1995). *Facing up to the American dream: Race, class, and the soul of the nation.* Princeton, NJ: Princeton University Press.

Hoelter, J. W. (1983). Factorial invariance and self-esteem: Reassessing race and sex differences. *Social Forces, 61,* 834-846.

Hoffman, C., & Hurst, N. (1990). Gender stereotypes: Perceptions or rationalization? *Journal of Personality and Social Psychology, 58,* 197-208.

Hogg, M. A., & Abrams, D. A. (1988). *Social identifications: A social psychology of intergroup relations and group processes.* London: Routledge.

Holcomb, W. R., & Ahr, P. R. (1988). Arrest rates among young adult psychiatric patients treated in inpatient and outpatient settings. *Hospital and Community Psychiatry, 39*(10), 52-57.

Hollinger, R. C. (1984). Race, occupational status, and pro-active police arrest for drinking and driving. *Journal of Criminal Justice, 12,* 173-183.

Holmes, S., & Inglehart, M. (1994, July). *The contents of prejudice: A cross-cultural analysis.* Paper presented at the annual meeting of the International Society of Political Psychology, Santiago de Compostela, Spain.

Homer-Dixon, T. (1991). On the threshold: Environmental changes as causes of acute conflict. *International Security, 16*(2), 76-116.

Homer-Dixon, T. (1994). Environmental scarcities and violent conflict. *International Security, 19*(1), 5-40.

Hood, R., & Cordovil, G. (1992). *Race and sentencing: A study in the Crown Court.* Oxford, UK: Clarendon.

Hood, R., & Sparks, R. (1970). *Key issues in criminology.* London: Weidenfeld & Nicholson.

Hopwood v. Texas, 5th Cir. Ct. App., U.S. (1996).

Hosokawa, B. (1969). *Nisei: The quiet Americans.* New York: William Morrow.

Houck v. Southern Pacific Railway, 38 F. 226 (1888).

Houston, L. N. (1984). Black consciousness and self-esteem. *Journal of Black Psychology, 11*(1), 1-7.

Howard, J., & Hammond, R. (1985, September 9). Rumors of inferiority. *New Republic, 72,* 18-23.

Hudson, N. (1995, December 4). Study: Races differ in promotion rates. *Navy Times,* p. 8.

Hyde, J. S., Fennema, E., & Lamon, S. J. (1990). Gender differences in mathematics performance: A meta-analysis. *Psychological Bulletin, 107,* 139-155.

Ignatiev, N. (1995). *How the Irish became white.* New York: Routledge.

Ilgen, D. R., & Youtz, M. A. (1986). Factors affecting the evaluation and development of minorities in organizations. In K. Rowland & G. Ferris (Eds.), *Research in personnel and human resource management: A research annual* (pgs. 307-337). Greenwich, CT: JAI.

Inglehart, M. R., & Yeakley, A. (1993, February). Differences in content—Similarities in reactions: A cross-cultural analysis of responses to out-groups. In C. W. Leach (Chair), *Racism and xenophobia across nations and cultures.* Symposium conducted at the meeting of the Society for Cross-Cultural Research, Washington, DC.

Insko, C. A., Nacoste, R. P., & Moe, J. L. (1983). Belief congruence and racial discrimination: Review of the evidence and critical evaluation. *European Journal of Social Psychology, 13,* 153-174.

Iyengar, S., & Kinder, D. R. (1987). *News that matters: Television and American opinion.* Chicago: University of Chicago Press.

Jackman, M. R., & Muha, M. J. (1984). Education and intergroup attitudes: Moral enlightenment, superficial democratic commitment, or ideological refinements. *American Sociological Review, 49,* 751-769.

Jackson, J. S., Brown, T. B., Williams, D. R., Torres, M., Sellers, S. L., & Brown, K. B. (1996). Racism and the physical and mental health status of African Americans: A 13-year national panel study. *Ethnicity & Disease, 6*(1/2), 132-147.

Jackson, J. S., & Inglehart, M. R. (1995). Reverberation theory: Stress and racism in hierarchically structured communities. In S. E. Hobfoll & M. deVries (Eds.), *Stress and communities: Moving beyond the individual* (pp. 353-373). Norwell, MA: Kluwer.

Jackson, J. S., Kirby, D., Barnes, L., & Shepard, L. (1993). Racisme institutionnel et ignorance pluraliste: Une comparison transnationale. In M. Wievorka (Ed.), *Racisme et modernite* (pp. 246-264). Paris: Editions La Decouverte.

Jackson, J. S., Lemaine, G., Ben Brika, J., & Kirby, D. (1993). *Individual out-group rejection: Western European and United States comparisions.* Unpublished manuscript, University of Michigan, Ann Arbor.

Jackson, J. S., & Tull, S. (1996). *Changes in public opinion toward ethnic immigrants in Western Europe.* Manuscript submitted for publication.

Jacobson, C. K. (1985). Resistance to affirmative action: Self-interest or racism? *Journal of Conflict Resolution, 29,* 306-329.

James, W. (1950). *The principles of psychology* (Vol. 1). New York: Dover. (Original work published 1890)

Jane Doe v. State of Louisiana, through the Department of Health and Human Resources, Office of Vital Statistics and Registrar of Vital Statistics, 479 So.2d 369 (1985).

Jaynes, G. D., & Williams, R. M., Jr. (1989). *A common destiny: Blacks and American society.* Washington, DC: National Academy Press.

Jensen, A. R. (1969). How much can we boost IQ and scholastic achievement? *Harvard Educational Review, 39,* 1-123.

Jensen, A. R. (1980). *Bias in mental testing.* New York: Free Press.

Jensen, G. F., White, C. S., & Galliher, J. M. (1982). Ethnic status and adolescent self-evaluations: An extension of research on minority self-esteem. *Social Problems, 30,* 226-239.

Jessor, T. (1988). *Personal interest, group conflict, and symbolic group affect: Explanations for whites' opposition to racial equality.* Unpublished doctoral dissertation, University of California, Los Angeles.

Jhally, S., & Lewis, J. (1992). *Enlightened racism: The Cosby show, audiences, and the myth of the American dream.* Boulder, CO: Westview.

Johnides, J., von Hippel, W., Lerner, J. S., & Nagda, B. (1992, August) *Evaluation of minority retention programs: The undergraduate research opportunities program at the University of Michigan.* Paper presented at the 100th Annual Convention of the American Psychological Association, Washington, DC.

Johnson, J. D., Whitestone, E., Jackson, L. E., & Gatto, L. (1995). Justice is still not color-blind: Differential racial effects of exposure to inadmissible evidence. *Personality and Social Psychology Bulletin, 21,* 893-898.

Johnson, L. C., & Macrae, C. N. (1994). Changing social stereotypes: The case of the information seeker. *European Journal of Social Psychology, 24,* 581-592.

Johnson, S. L. (1985). Black innocence and the white jury. *Michigan Law Review, 83* 1611-1708.

Jones, E. E., & Berglas, S. (1978). Control of attributions about the self through self-handicapping strategies: The appeal of alcohol and the role of underachievement. *Personality and Social Psychology Bulletin, 4,* 200-206.

Jones, E. E., Farina, A., Hastorf, A. H., Markus, H., Miller, D. T., & Scott, R. A. (1984). *Social stigma: The psychology of marked relationships.* New York: W. H. Freeman.

Jones, E. E., & Nisbett, R. E. (1972). The actor and the observer: Divergent perceptions of the causes of behavior. In E. E. Jones, D. E. Kanouse, H. H. Kelley, R. E. Nisbett, S. Valins, & B. Weiner (Eds.), *Attribution: Perceiving the causes of behavior* (pp. 79-94). Morristown, NJ: General Learning Press.

Jones, J. M. (1972). *Prejudice and racism.* Reading, MA: Addison-Wesley.

Jones, J. M. (1997). *Prejudice and racism* (2nd ed.). New York: McGraw-Hill.

Jones, J. M., & Morris, K. T. (1993) Individual versus group identification as a factor in intergroup racial conflict. In S. Worchel & J. Simpson (Eds.), *Conflict between people and peoples* (pp. 170-189). Chicago: Nelson-Hall.

Jost, J. T., & Banaji, M. R. (1994). The role of stereotyping in system justification and the production of false consciousness. *British Journal of Social Psychology, 33*(1), 1-27.

Junger, M., & Polder, W. (1992). Some explanations of crime among four ethnic groups in The Netherlands. *Journal of Quantitative Criminology, 8*(1), 51-78.

Kamin, L. (1974). *The science and politics of I.Q.* Hillsdale, NJ: Erlbaum.

Kanter, R. M. (1977). Some effects of proportions on group life: Skewed sex ratios and responses to token women. *American Journal of Sociology, 82,* 965-991.

Kardiner, A., & Ovesy, L. (1951). *The mark of oppression.* New York: Norton

Katz, I. (1981). *Stigma: A social-psychological perspective.* Hillsdale, NJ: Lawrence Erlbaum.

Katz, I. (1991). Gordon Allport's *The nature of prejudice. Political Psychology, 12*(1), 125-157.

Katz, I., & Hass, R. G. (1988). Racial ambivalence and value conflict: Correlational and priming studies of dual cognitive structures. *Journal of Personality and Social Psychology, 55,* 893-905.

Katz, I., Wackenhut, J., & Hass, R. G. (1986). Racial ambivalence, value duality, and behavior. In J. F. Dovidio & S. L. Gaertner (Eds.), *Prejudice, discrimination, and racism* (pp. 35-60). Orlando, FL: Academic Press.

Keil, T. J., & Vito, G. F. (1989). Race, homicide severity, and application of the death penalty: A consideration of the Barnett Scale. *Criminology, 27,* 511-531.

Kelley, H. H. (1972). Causal schemata and the attribution process. In E. E. Jones, D. E. Kanouse, H. H. Kelley, R. E. Nisbett, S. Valins, & B. Weiner (Eds.), *Attribution: Perceiving the causes of behavior* (pp. 151-176). Morrison, NJ: General Learning Press.

Kelley, H. E. (1976). A comparison of defense strategy and race as influences in differential sentencing. *Criminology, 14,* 241-249.

Kerr, K., Crocker, J., & Broadnax, S. (1995, August). *Feeling fat and feeling depressed: The stigma of overweight in black and white women.* Paper presented at the annual meeting of the American Psychological Association, New York.

*Kids count in Michigan 1995 data book: County profiles of child and family well-being.* (1995). Lansing, MI: Annie E. Casey Foundation.

Killian, L. W. (1949). *Southern white laborers on Chicago's West Side.* Unpublished doctoral dissertation, University of Chicago.

Kinder, D. R. (1986). The continuing American dilemma: White resistance to racial change 40 years after Myrdal. *Journal of Social Issues, 42,* 151-172.

Kinder, D. R., & Sanders, L. M. (1986). *Revitalizing the measurement of white Americans' attitude: A report to the NES 1985 Pilot Study Committee and NES Board.* Unpublished manuscript, University of Michigan, Ann Arbor.

Kinder, D. R., & Sears, D. (1981). Symbolic racism versus racial threats to "the good life." *Journal of Personality and Social Psychology, 40,* 414-431.

Kirschenman, J., & Neckerman, K. M. (1991). "We'd love to hire them, but . . .": The meaning of race for employers. In C. Jencks & P. E. Peterson (Eds.), *The urban underclass* (pp. 203-232). Washington, DC: Brookings.

Kleck, R. E., & Strenta, A. (1980). Perceptions of the impact of negatively valued physical characteristics on social interactions. *Journal of Personality and Socid Psychology, 39,* 861-873.

Kleppner, P. (1985). *Chicago divided: The making of a black mayor.* DeKalb: Northern Illinois University Press.

Kline, B. B., & Dovidio, J. F. (1982, April). *Effects of race, sex, and qualifications on predictions of a college applicant's performance.* Paper presented at the annual meeting of the Eastern Psychological Association, Baltimore, MD.

Kluegel, J. R. (1990). Trends in whites' explanations of the black-white gap in socioeconomic status, 1977-1989. *American Sociological Review, 55,* 512-525.

Kluegel, J. R., & Smith, E. R. (1986). *Beliefs about inequality: American's views of what is and what ought to be.* New York: Aldine de Gruyter.

Kohn, M. L. (1987). Cross-national research as an analytic strategy: American Sociological Association 1987 presidential address. *American Sociological Review, 52,* 713-731.

Kohn, M. L., & Williams, R. (1956). Situational patterning in intergroup relations. *American Sociological Review, 21,* 164-174.

Kovel, J. (1970). *White racism: A psychohistory.* New York: Pantheon.

Kraiger, K., & Ford, J. K. (1985). A meta-analysis of ratee effects in performance ratings. *Journal of Applied Psychology, 70,* 56-65.

Kramer, R. M., & Brewer, M. B. (1984). Effects of group identity on resource use in a simulated commons dilemma. *Journal of Personality and Social Psychology, 46,* 1044-1057.

Krause, N. (1994). Stressors in salient social roles and well-being in later life. *Journal of Gerontology, 49,* 137-148.

Kravitz, D. A. (1995). Attitudes toward affirmative action plans directed at blacks: Effects of plan and individual differences. *Journal of Applied Social Psychology, 25,* 2192-2220.

Krieger, L. H. (1995). The content of our categories: A cognitive bias approach to discrimination and equal employment opportunity. *Stanford Law Review, 47,* 1161-1248.

Kristof, N. D. (1995, November 30). Japanese outcasts better off than in past but still outcast. *New York Times,* p. A1.

Kuiper, N. A., & Olinger, L. J. (1986). Dysfunctional attitudes and a self-worth contingency model of depression. In P. C. Kendall (Ed.), *Advances in cognitive-behavioral research and therapy* (pp. 115-142). Orlando, FL: Academic Press.

Kuiper, N. A., Olinger, L. J., & MacDonald, M. R. (1988). Vulnerability and episodic cognitions in a self-worth contingency model of depression. In L. B. Alloy (Ed.), *Cognitive processes in depression* (pp. 289-309). New York: Guilford.

Kuzenski, J. C., Bullock, C. S., III, & Gaddie, R. K. (Eds.). (1995). *David Duke and the politics of race in the South.* Nashville, TN: Vanderbilt University Press.

LaFree, G. D. (1989). *Rape and criminal justice: The social construction of sexual assault.* Belmont, CA: Wadsworth.

LaFromboise, T., Coleman, H. L. K., & Gerton, J. (1993). Psychological impact of biculturalism: Evidence and theory. *Psychological Bulletin, 114,* 395-412.

Leach, C. (1995). *Ethnic prejudices as attitudes: An eco-phenomenological view.* Unpublished doctoral dissertation, University of Michigan, Ann Arbor.

Leach, C. W., Kirby, D. C., & Jackson, J. S. (1995). *Prejudice and pluralistic ignorance in Western Europe.* Unpublished manuscript, University of Michigan, Ann Arbor.

Leary, M. R., & Atherton, S. C. (1986). Self-efficacy, social anxiety, and inhibition in interpersonal encounters. *Journal of Social and Clinical Psychology, 4,* 256-267.

Lefkowitz, J. (1975). Psychological attributes of policemen: A review of research and opinion. *Journal of Social Issues, 31*(1), 3-26.

Leippe, M. R., & Eisenstadt, D. (1994). Generalization of dissonance reduction: Decreasing prejudice through induced compliance. *Journal of Personality and Social Psychology, 67,* 395-413.

Leitner, D. W., & Sedlacek, W. E. (1976). Characteristics of successful campus police officers. *Journal of College Student Personnel, 17,* 304-308.

Lenski, G. (1984). *Power and privilege: A theory of social stratification.* Chapel Hill: University of North Carolina Press.

Lepper, M. R., Woolverton, M., Mumme, D. L., & Gurtner, J.-L. (1993). Motivational techniques of expert human tutors: Lessons for the design of computer-based tutors. In S. P. Lajoie & S. J. Derry (Eds.), *Computers as cognitive tools* (pp. 75-104). Hillsdale, NJ: Erlbaum.

Levin, J., & Wyckoff, J. (1988). Effective advising: Identifying students most likely to persist and succeed in engineering. *Engineering Education, 78,* 178-182.

Levine, R. A., & Campbell, D. T. (1972). *Ethnocentrism: Theories of conflict, ethnic attitudes, and group behavior.* New York: John Wiley.

Lewin, K. (1941). *Resolving social conflict.* New York: Harper & Row.

Lewontin, R. C., Rose, S., & Kamin, L. J. (1984). *Not in our genes: Biology, ideology, and human nature.* New York: Pantheon.

Lichtenstein, K. R. (1982). Extra-legal variables affecting sentencing decisions. *Psychological Reports, 50,* 611-619.

Linn, M.C. (1994). The tyranny of the mean: Gender and expectations. *Notices of the American Mathematical Society, 41,* 766-769.

Lippmann, W. (1922). *Public opinion.* New York: Harcourt Brace.

Lipton, J. P. (1983). Racism in the jury box: The Hispanic defendant. *Hispanic Journal of Behavioral Sciences, 5,* 275-290.

Loewen, J. W. (1971). *The Mississippi Chinese: Between black and white.* Cambridge, MA: Harvard University Press.

Lopreato, J. (1984). *Human nature and biocultural evolution.* Boston: Allen & Unwin.

Lord, C. G., & Saenz, D. S. (1985). Memory deficits and memory surfeits: Differential cognitive consequences of tokenism for tokens and observers. *Journal of Personality and Social Psychology, 49,* 918-926.

Louis Spotorno v. August Fourichon, 40 La. Ann. 423 (1888).

Love, W., & Bachara, G. (1975). Delinquents with learning disabilities. In *Youth reporter* (pp. 5-7). Washington, DC: Department of Health, Education, and Welfare.

Lovely, R. (1987, February). *Selection of undergraduate majors by high ability students: Sex difference and attrition of science majors.* Paper presented at the annual meeting of the Association for the Study of Higher Education, San Diego, CA.

Lupsha, P. A. (1986). Organized crime in the United States. In R. Kelly (Ed.), *Organized crime: A global perspective* (pp. 32-57). Totowa, NJ: Rowman & Littlefield.

Lynch, J. P., & Sabol, W. J. (1994, November). *The use of coercive social control and changes in the race and class composition of U.S. prison populations.* Paper presented at the American Society of Criminology, Miami, FL.

Maas, C., & Stuyling de Lange, J. (1989). Selectivitet in de rechsgang van buitenlandse verdachten behorende tot ethnische groepen. *Tidschrift voor Criminologie, 1,* 1-13.

Mackie, D. M., Hamilton, D. L., Susskind, J., & Rosselli, F. (1996). Social psychological foundations of stereotype formation. In C. N. Macrae, C. Stangor, & M. Hewstone (Eds.), *Stereotypes & Stereotyping* (pp. 41-78). New York: Guilford.

Macrae, C. N., Bodenhausen, G. V., Milne, A. B., & Jetten, J. (1994). Out of mind but back in sight: Stereotypes on the rebound. *Journal of Personality and Social Psychology, 67,* 808-817.

Macrae, C. N., Milne, A. B., & Bodenhausen, G. V. (1994). Stereotypes as energy saving devices: A peek inside the cognitive toolbox. *Journal of Personality and Social Psychology, 66*(1), 37-47.

Macrae, C. M., Stangor, C., & Hewstone, M. (Eds.). (1996). *Stereotypes and stereotyping.* New York: Guilford.

Mair, G. (1986). Ethnic minorities, probation, and the magistrates' courts: A pilot study. *British Journal of Criminology, 26,* 147-155.

Major, B. (1987). Gender, justice, and the psychology of entitlement. In P. Shaver & C. Hendrick (Eds.)., *Review of personality and social psychology* (Vol. 7, pp. 124-148). Newbury Park, CA: Sage.

Major, B. (1994). From social inequality to personal entitlement: The role of social comparisons, legitimacy appraisals, and group membership. In M. P. Zanna (Ed.), *Advances in experimental social psychology* (Vol. 26, pp. 293-348). San Diego, CA: Academic Press.

Major, B., & Crocker, J. (1993). Social stigma: The consequences of attributional ambiguity. In D. M. Mackie & D. L. Hamilton (Eds.), *Affect, cognition, and stereotyping* (pp. 345-370). San Diego, CA: Academic Press.

Major, B., & Crocker, J. (1993). Social stigma: The affective consequences of attributional ambiguity. In D. M. Mackie & D. L. Hamilton (Eds.), *Affect, cognition, and stereotyping: Interactive processes in intergroup perception* (pp. 345-370). San Diego, CA: Academic Press.

Major, B., Spencer, S., Schmader, T., Wolfe, C., & Crocker, J. (in press). Coping with negative stereotypes about intellectual performance: The role of psychological disengagement. *Personality and Social Psychology Bulletin.*

Marger, M. N. (1994). *Race and ethnic relations: American and global perspectives.* Belmont, CA: Wadsworth.

Marino, K. E. (1980). A preliminary investigation into behavioral dimensions of affirmative action compliance. *Journal of Applied Psychology, 65,* 346-350.

Markus, H. R., & Kitayama, S. (1991). Culture and the self: Implications for cognition, emotion, and motivation. *Psychological Review, 98,* 224-253.

Martell, R. F., Lane, D. M., & Emrich, C. (1996). Male-female differences: A computer simulation. *American Psychologist, 51,* 157-158.

Marx, K. (1972). *The Marx-Engels reader.* New York: Norton.

Massey, D. S., & Denton, N. A. (1993). *American apartheid: Segregation and the making of the underclass.* Cambridge, MA: Harvard University Press.

Mauer, M., & Huling, T. (1995, October). *Young black Americans and the criminal justice system: Five years later.* (Available from The Sentencing Project, 918 F. St. NW, Suite 901, Washington, DC 20004)

Mays, V. M., Coleman, L. M., & Jackson, J. S. (in press). Perceived race-based discrimination, employment status, and job stress in a national sample of black women: Implications for health outcomes. *Journal of Occupational Health.*

Mazzella, R., & Feingold, A. (1994). The effects of physical attractiveness, race, socioeconomic status, and gender of defendants and victims on judgments of mock jurors: A meta-analysis. *Journal of Applied Social Psychology, 24,* 1315-1344.

McClain, J. D. (1995, April 30). Blacks still lag in pay and job opportunities. *Syracuse Herald American,* p. A11.

McConahay, J. B. (1982). Self-interest versus racial attitudes as correlates of antibusing attitudes in Louisville: Is it the buses or the blacks? *Journal of Politics, 44,* 692-720.

McConahay, J. B. (1986). Modern racism, ambivalence, and the modern racism scale. In J. F. Dovidio & S. L. Gaertner (Eds.), *Prejudice, discrimination, and racism* (pp. 91-125). Orlando, FL: Academic Press.

McConahay, J. B., & Hough, J. C., Jr. (1976). Symbolic racism. *Journal of Social Issues, 32*(2), 23-45.

McCuen, G. E. (1988). *Political murder in Central America: Death squads and U.S. policies.* Hudson, WI: G. E. McCuen.

McGuinn v. Forbes, 37 F. 639 (1889).

Mead, G. H. (1934). *Mind, self, and society.* Chicago: University of Chicago Press.

Medin, D. L. (1989). Concepts and conceptual structure. *American Psychologist, 44,* 1469-1481.

Mendelberg, T. (1997). Executing Hortons: Racial crime in the 1988 presidential campaign. *Public Opinion Quarterly, 61*(1), 134-157.

Meyers, B. (1984). Minority group: An ideological formulation. *Social Problems, 32*(1), 1-15.

Michels, R. (1991). *Political parties: A sociological study of the oligarchical tendencies of modern democracy.* New York: Free Press.

Miller, D. T., & McFarland, D. (1987). Pluralistic ignorance: When similarity is interpreted as dissimilarity. *Journal of Personality and Social Psychology, 53*(2), 298-305.

Miller, L. S. (1995). *An American imperative: Accelerating minority educational advancement.* New Haven, CT: Yale University Press.

Miller, L. S. (1996, March). *Promoting high academic achievement among non-Asian minorities.* Paper presented at the Princeton University Conference on Higher Education, Princeton, NJ.

Milliones, J. (1973). Construction of a black consciousness measure: Psychotherapeutic implications. *Psychotherapy, 17,* 175-182.

Milliones, J. (1980). *Construction of a black consciousness measure: Psychotherapeutic implications.* Unpublished doctoral dissertation, University of Pittsburgh, Pittsburgh, PA.

Milner, D. (1981). Racial prejudice. In J. C. Turner & H. Giles (Eds.), *Intergroup behavior* (pp. 102-143). London: Blackwell.

Minard, R. D. (1952). Race relations in the Pocahontas coal field. *Journal of Social Issues, 8*(1), 29-44.

Mitchell, M., & Sidanius, J. (1995). Social hierarchy and the death penalty: A social dominance perspective. *Political Psychology, 16,* 591-619.

Monteith, M. (1993). Self-regulation of prejudiced responses: Implications for progress in prejudice-reduction efforts. *Journal of Personality and Social Psychology, 65,* 469-485.

Monteith, M. J., Devine, P. G., & Zuwerink, J. R. (1993). Self-directed versus other-directed affect as a consequence of prejudice-related discrepancies. *Journal of Personality and Social Psychology, 64,* 198-210.

Morganthau, T. (1996, June 24). Fires in the night. *Newsweek, 127,* 28-38.

Mosca, G. (1939). *The ruling class: Elements of political science.* New York: McGraw-Hill.

Moyer, S. (1992). Race, gender, and homicide: Comparisons between aboriginals and other Canadians. *Canadian Journal of Criminology, July/October,* 387-402.

Moynihan, D. P. (1967). The Negro family: The case for national action. In L. Rainwater & W. L. Rainwater (Eds.), *The Moynihan report and the politics of controversy* (pp. 47-132). Cambridge: MIT Press.

Mullen, B., Brown, R., & Smith, C. (1992). In-group bias as a function of salience, relevance, and status: An integration. *European Journal of Social Psychology, 22*(2), 103-122.

Mullen, B., & Hu, L. (1989). Perceptions of in-group and out-group variability: A meta-analytic integration. *Basic and Applied Social Psychology, 10,* 233-252.

Murrell, A. (in press). African American women, careers, and family. In N. J. Burgess, E. Brown, & S. Turner (Eds.), *African American women: An ecological perspective.* Ann Arbor, MI: Garland.

Murrell, A. J., & Brown, A. (in press). Racial identity prototypes and black national ideologies. *Journal of Black Psychology.*

Murrell, A. J., Dietz-Uhler, B. L., Dovidio, J. F., Gaertner, S. L., & Drout, C. (1994). Aversive racism and resistance to affirmative action: Perceptions of justice are not necessarily color-blind. *Basic and Applied Social Psychology, 15,* 71-86.

Myers, D. G., & Diener, E. (1995). Who is happy? *Psychological Science, 6,* 10-19.

Myers, S. L. (1985). Statistical tests of discrimination in punishment. *Journal of Quantitative Criminology, 1,* 191-218.

Nacoste, R. W. (1994). If empowerment is the goal: Affirmative action and social interaction. *Basic and Applied Social Psychology, 15,* 87-112.

National Center for Educational Statistics. (1992). *National Educational Longitudinal Study of 1988: First follow-up. Student component data file user's manual.* Washington, DC: U.S. Department of Education, Office of Educational Research and Improvement.

National Coalition of Advocates for Students Report. (1988, December 12). *The Ann Arbor News,* pp. A1, A4.

Needleman, H. L., Riess, J. A., Tobin, M. J., Biesecker, G. E., & Greenhouse, J. B. (1996). Bone lead levels and delinquent behavior. *Journal of the American Medical Association, 275,* 363-369.

Nei, M., & Roychoudhury, A. K. (1983). Genetic relationship and evolution of human races. *Evolutionary Biology, 14,* 1-59.

Neighbors, H. W., Jackson, J. S., Bowman, P. J., & Gurin, G. (1983). Stress, coping, and black mental health: Preliminary findings from a national study. *Prevention in Human Services, 2*(3), 5-29.

Nettles, M. T. (1988). *Toward undergraduate student equality in American higher education.* New York: Greenwood.

Neuberg, S. L. (1989). The goal of forming accurate impressions during social interactions: Attenuating the impact of negative expectancies. *Journal of Personality and Social Psychology, 56,* 374-386.

Neuberg, S. L., & Fiske, S. T. (1987). Motivational influences on impression formation: Outcome dependency, accuracy-driven attention, and individuating processes. *Journal of Personality and Social Psychology, 53,* 431-444.

Nickerson, S., Mayo, C., & Smith, A. (1986). Racism in the courtroom. In J. F. Dovidio & S. L. Gaertner (Eds.), *Prejudice, discrimination, and racism* (pp. 255-278). Orlando, FL: Academic Press.

Nielsen, F. (1985). Toward a theory of ethnic solidarity in modern societies. *American Sociological Review, 50*(2), 133-149.

O'Gorman, H. (1986). The discovery of pluralistic ignorance: An ironic lesson. *Journal of the History of the Behavioral Sciences, 22,* 333-347.

Ogbu, J. (1986). The consequences of the American caste system. In U. Neisser (Ed.), *The school achievement of minority children: New perspectives.* Hillsdale, NJ: Lawrence Erlbaum.

Ogbu, J. U. (1991). Minority coping responses and school experience. *Journal of Psychohistory, 18,* 433-456.

Ogbu, J. U. (1994). From cultural differences in cultural frame of reference. In P. M. Greenfield & R. R. Cocking (Eds.), *Cross-cultural roots of minority child development* (pp. 365-391). Hillsdale, NJ: Lawrence Erlbaum.

Older, J. (1984). Reducing racial imbalance in New Zealand universities and professions. *Australian and New Zealand Journal of Sociology, 20,* 243-256.

Oliver, M. L., & Shapiro, T. M. (1995). *Black wealth-white wealth: A new perspective on racial inequality.* New York: Routledge.

Omi, M., & Winant, H. (1986). *Racial formation in the United States: From the 1960s to the 1980s.* New York: Routledge.

Operario, D., & Fiske, S. T. (1997, October). *Power, interpersonal dominance, and control: Bias and hierarchy maintenance in social interaction.* Paper presented at the annual meeting of the Society for Experimental Social Psychology, Toronto, Canada.

Opotow, S. (1990). Moral exclusion and injustice: An introduction. *Journal of Social Issues, 46*(1), 1-20.

Osborne, J. (1994). Academics, self-esteem, and race: A look at the underlying assumption of the disidentification hypothesis. *Personality and Social Psychology Bulletin, 21,* 449-455.

Osborne, Y. H., & Rappaport, N. B. (1985). Sentencing severity with mock jurors: Predictive validity of three variable categories. *Behavioral Sciences and the Law, 3,* 467-473.

Ostrom, T. M., & Sedikides, C. (1992). Out-group homogeneity effects in natural and minimal groups. *Psychological Bulletin, 112,* 536-552.

Painton, P. (1991, May 27). Quota quagmire. *Time,* 20-22.

Palmore v. Sidoti, 466 U.S. 429 (1984).

Pareto, V. (1979). *The rise and fall of the elites.* New York: Arno.

Parham, T. A., & Helms, J. E. (1985a). Attitudes of racial identity and self-esteem of black students: An exploratory investigation. *Journal of College Student Personnel, 26*(2), 143-147.

Parham, T. A., & Helms, J. E. (1985b). Relation of racial identity attitudes to self-actualization and affective states of black students. *Journal of Counseling Psychology, 32,* 431-440.

Parson, T. (1962). The law and social control. In W. M. Evan (Ed.), *Law and sociology: Exploratory essays* (pp. 56-72). New York: Free Press.

Paternoster, R. (1983). Race of victim and location of crime: The decision to seek the death penalty in South Carolina. *Journal of Criminal Law and Criminology, 74,* 754-785.

Paternoster, R. (1984). Prosecutorial discretion in requesting the death penalty: A case of victim-based racial discrimination. *Law and Society Review, 18,* 437-478.

Pauw, J. (1991). *In the heart of the whore: The story of apartheid's death squads.* Halfway House, South Book Publications.

Pelham, B. W., & Swann, W. B., Jr. (1989). From self-conceptions to self-worth: On the sources and structure of global self-esteem. *Journal of Personality and Social Psychology, 57,* 672-680.

Penner, L. A. (1971). Interpersonal attraction to a black person as a function of value importance. *Personality, 2,* 175-187.

Perdue, C. W., Dovidio, J. F., Gurtman, M. B., & Tyler, R. B. (1990). "Us" and "them": Social categorization and the process of intergroup bias. *Journal of Personality and Social Psychology, 59,* 475-486.

Petersen, D. M., & Friday, P. C. (1975). Early release from incarceration: Race as a factor in the use of "shock probation." *Journal of Criminal Law and Criminology, 66*(1), 79-87.

Petersen, D. M., Schwirian, K. P., & Bleda, S. E. (1977). The drug arrest: Empirical observations on the age, sex, and race of drug law offenders in a Midwestern city. *Drug Forum, 6,* 371-386.

Petrocik, J. R. (1987). Realignment: New party coalitions and the nationalization of the South. *Journal of Politics, 49,* 347-375.

Pettigrew, T. F. (1961). Social psychology and desegregation research. *American Psychologist, 16*(3), 105-112.

Pettigrew, T. F. (1983). Group identity and social comparisons. In C. Fried (Ed.), *Minorities and identity* (pp. 1-60). Berlin: Springer-Verlag.

Pettigrew, T. F. (1985). New black-white patterns: How best to conceptualize them? *Annual Review of Sociology, 11,* 329-346.

Pettigrew, T. F. (1986). The contact hypothesis revisited. In M. Hewstone & R. Brown (Eds.), *Contact and conflict in intergroup encounters* (pp. 169-195). Oxford, UK: Basil Blackwell.

Pettigrew, T. F. (1989). The nature of modern racism in the United States. *Revue Internationale de Psychologie Sociale, 2,* 291-303.

Pettigrew, T. F. (1991). Normative theory in intergroup relations: Explaining both harmony and conflict. *Psychology and Developing Societies, 3*(1), 3-16.

Pettigrew, T. F. (1994, October). *Education and policy.* Paper presented at the University of Massachusetts Conference on Racism, Amherst, MA.

Pettigrew, T. F., Jackson, J. S., Ben Brika, J., Lemaine, G., Meertens, R. W., Wagner, U., & Zick, A. (in press). Out-group prejudice in Western Europe. *European Review of Social Psychology.*

Pettigrew, T. F., & Martin, J. (1987). Shaping the organizational context for black American inclusion. *Journal of Social Issues, 43*(1), 41-78.

Pettigrew, T. F., & Meertens, R. W. (1995). Subtle and blatant prejudice in Western Europe. *European Journal of Social Psychology, 25*(1), 57-76.

Pettigrew, T. F., & Taylor, M. (1992). Discrimination. In E. F. Borgatta & M. L. Borgatta (Eds.), *The encyclopedia of sociology* (Vol. 1, pp. 498-503). New York: Macmillan.

Phinney, J. S. (1990a). Ethnic identity in college students from four ethnic groups. *Journal of Adolescence, 13,* 171-183.

Phinney, J. S. (1990b). Ethnic identity in adolescents and adults: Review of the research. *Psychological Bulletin, 108,* 499-514.

Piliavin, J. A., Dovidio, J. F., Gaertner, S. L., & Clark, R. D., III. (1981). *Emergency intervention.* New York: Academic Press.

Pincus, F. L., & Ehrlich, H. W. (Eds.) (1994). *Race and ethnic conflict.* Boulder, CO: Westview.

Plessy v. Ferguson, 163 U.S. 537 (1896).

Poikalainen, K., Nayha, S., & Hassi, J. (1992). Alcohol consumption among male reindeer herders of Lappish and Finnish origin. *Social Science and Medicine, 35,* 735-738.

Polanyi, M. (1962). *Personal knowledge.* Chicago: University of Chicago Press.

Porter, J. R., & Washington, R. E. (1979). Black identity and self-esteem: A review of the studies of Black self-concept, 1968-1978. *Annual Review of Sociology, 5,* 53-74.

Porter, J. R., & Washington, R. E. (1993). Minority identity and self-esteem. In J. Blake & J. Hagen (Eds.), *Annual review of sociology,* (Vol. 19, pp. 136-61). Palo Alto, CA: Annual Reviews.

Poulson, R. L. (1990). Mock juror attribution of criminal responsibility: Effects of race and the "guilty but mentally ill" (GBMI) verdict option. *Journal of Applied Social Psychology, 20,* 1596-1611.

Pratto, F. (1996). Sexual politics: The gender gap in the bedroom, the cupboard, and the cabinet. In D. M. Buss & N. Malamuth (Eds.), *Sex, power, and conflict: Evolutionary and feminist perspectives* (pp. 179-230). New York: Oxford University Press.

Pratto, F., Sidanius, J., Stallworth, L. M., & Malle, B. F. (1994). Social dominance orientation: A personality variable predicting social and political attitudes. *Journal of Personality and Social Psychology, 67,* 741-763.

Pratto, F., Stallworth, L., Sidanius, J., & Siers, B. (1997). The gender gap in occupational role attainment: A social dominance approach. *Journal of Personality and Social Psychology, 72,* 37-53..

Pruitt, C. R., & Wilson, J. Q. (1983). A longitudinal study of the effect of race on sentencing. *Law and Society Review, 17,* 613-635.

Putnam, R. D. (1995). Tuning in, tuning out: The strange disappearance of social capital in America. *Political Science and Politics, 28,* 664-683.

Quinn, D. M., & Crocker, J. (in press). Vulnerability to the affective consequences of the stigma of overweight. In J. Swim & C. Stangor (Eds.), *Prejudice: The target's perspective*. San Diego, CA: Academic Press.

Quinney, R. (1977). *Class, state, and crime*. New York: David McKay.

Rabier, J. R., Riffault, H., & Inglehart, R. (1986). *Euro-barometer 23: The European currency unit and working conditions*. Ann Arbor, MI: Interuniversity Consortium for Political and Social Research.

Radelet, M. L. (1981). Racial characteristics and the imposition of the death penalty. *American Sociological Review, 46*, 918-927.

Ramist, L., Lewis, C., & McCamley-Jenkins, L. (1994). *Student group differences in predicting college grades: Sex, language, and ethnic groups* (College Board Report No. 93-1, ETS No. 94.27). New York: College Entrance Examination Board.

R. C. Chaires et al. v. City of Atlanta, 164 Ga. 755/139 S.E. 559.

Regents of the University of California v. Bakke, 438 U.S. 265 (1978).

Reitzes, D. C. (1953). The role of organizational structures: Union versus neighborhood in a tension situation. *Journal of Social Issues, 9*(3), 37-44.

*Report of the National Advisory Commission on Civil Disorders*. (1968). New York: Bantam.

Reuter, P., MacCoun, R., & Murphy, P. (1990). *Money from crime: A study of the economics of drug dealing in Washington, D.C.* Santa Monica, CA: RAND.

Rex, J., & Mason, D. (1986). *Theories of race and ethnic relations*. New York: Cambridge University Press.

Roberts, J. E., Gotlib, I., & Kassel, J. D. (1996). Adult attachment security and symptoms of depression: The mediating role of dysfunctional attitudes and low self-esteem. *Journal of Personality and Social Psychology, 70*, 310-320.

Roediger, D. R. (1991). *The wages of whiteness: Race and the making of the American working class*. New York: Verso.

Rogers, C. R. (1959). A theory of therapy, personality, and interpersonal relationships, as developed in the client-centered framework. In S. Koch (Ed.), *Psychology: A study of a science* (Vol. 3, pp. 184-256). New York: McGraw-Hill.

Rokeach, M. (1973). *The nature of human values*. New York: Free Press.

Rokeach, M. (1979). *Understanding human values: Individual and Societal*. New York: Free Press.

Rosch, E. (1975). Cognitive representations of semantic categories. *Journal of Experimental Psychology: General, 104*, 192-233.

Rosenberg, M. (1979). *Conceiving self*. New York: Basic Books.

Ross, L. (1977). The intuitive psychologist and his shortcomings: Distortions in the attribution process. In L. Berkowitz (Ed.), *Advances in experimental social psychology* (Vol. 10, pp. 337-384). New York: Academic Press.

Rothbart, M., & Taylor, M. (1992). Category labels and social reality: Do we view social categories as natural kinds. In G. Semin & K. Fieder (Eds.), *Language and social cognition* (pp. 11-36). Newbury Park, CA: Sage.

Ruggiero, K. M., & Taylor, D. M. (1995). Coping with discrimination: How disadvantaged group members perceive the discrimination that confronts them. *Journal of Personality and Social Psychology, 68*, 826-838.

Ruggiero, K. M., & Taylor, D. M. (1997). Why minority group members perceive or do not perceive the discrimination that confronts them: The role of self-esteem and perceived control. *Journal of Personality and Social Psychology, 72*, 373-389.

Ruscher, J. B., & Fiske, S. T. (1990). Interpersonal competition can cause individuating impression formation. *Journal of Personality and Social Psychology, 58*, 832-842.

Ryan, W. (1971). *Blaming the victim*. New York: Vintage.

Sachdev, I., & Bourhis, R. Y. (1985). Social categorization and power differentials in group relations. *European Journal of Social Psychology, 15,* 415-434.

Sachdev, I., & Bourhis, R. Y. (1991). Power and status differentials in minority and majority group relations. *European Journal of Social Psychology, 21*(1), 1-24.

Saint Francis College v. Al-Khazraji, 481 U.S. 604 (1987).

Sampson, E. E. (1977). Individualism and the American ideal. *Journal of Personality and Social Psychology, 35,* 767-782.

Sanson-Fisher, R. (1978). Aborigines in crime statistics: An interaction between poverty and detection. *Australian and New Zealand Journal of Criminality, 11,* 71-80.

Sarason, I. G. (1980). Introduction to the study of test anxiety. In I. G. Sarason (Ed.), *Test anxiety: Theory, research, and applications* (pp. 57-78). Hillsdale, NJ: Erlbaum.

Sarri, R. C. (1986). Gender and race differences in criminal justice processing. *Women's Studies International Forum, 9*(1), 89-99.

Sartre, J. R (1965). *Anti-Semite and Jew.* New York: Schocken Books. (Original work published 1946)

Sassen, S. (1994). America's immigration "problem." In F. L. Pincus & H. W. Ehrlich (Eds.), *Race and ethnic conflict* (pp. 176-185). Boulder, CO: Westview.

Scheidt, W. (1924). The concept of race in anthropology and the divisions into human races from Linnaeus to Deniker. In E. W. Count (Ed.), *This is race* (pp. 354-391). New York: Henry Schuman.

Schellenberg, E. G., Wasylenki, D., Webster, C. D., & Goering, P. (1992). A review of arrests among psychiatric patients. *International Journal of Law and Psychiatry, 15,* 251-264.

Schermerhorn, R. A. (1970). *Comparative ethnic relations: A framework for theory and research.* New York: Random House.

Schiraldi, V., Kuyper, S., & Hewitt, S. (1996). *Young African Africans and the criminal justice system in California.* San Francisco: Center on Juvenile and Criminal Justice.

Schlenker, B. R., & Leary, M. R. (1982). Social anxiety and self-presentation: A conceptualization and model. *Psychological Bulletin, 92,* 641-669.

Schlenker, B. R., & Weigold, M. E (1989). Goals and the self-identification process: Constructing desired identities. In L. A. Pervin (Ed.), *Goals concepts in personality and social psychology* (pp. 243-290). Hillsdale, NJ: Erlbaum.

Schneider, M. E., Major, B., Luhtanen, R., & Crocker, J. (1996). When help hurts: Social stigma and the costs of assumptive help. *Personality and Social Psychology Bulletin, 22,* 201-209.

Schuman, H., Steeth, C., & Bobo, L. (1985). *Racial attitudes in America: Trends and interpretations.* Cambridge, MA: Harvard University Press.

Scott, J. C. (1990). *Domination and the arts of resistance.* New Haven, CT: Yale University Press.

Sears, D. O. (1983). The persistence of early political predispositions: The roles of attitude object and life stage. In L. Wheeler & P. Shaver (Eds.), *Review of personality and social psychology* (Vol. 4, pp. 79-116). Beverly Hills, CA: Sage.

Sears, D. O. (1988). Symbolic racism. In P. A. Katz & D. A. Taylor (Eds.), *Eliminating racism: Profiles in controversy* (pp. 53-84). New York: Plenum.

Sears, D. O., & Allen, H. M., Jr. (1984). The trajectory of local desegregation controversies and whites' opposition to busing. In N. Miller & M. B. Brewer (Eds.), *Groups in contact: The psychology of desegregation* (pp. 123-151). New York: Academic Press.

Sears, D. O., & Citrin, J. (1985). *Tax revolt: Something for nothing in California* (Enlarged ed.). Cambridge, MA: Harvard University Press.

Sears, D. O., Citrin, J., & Kosterman, R. (1987). Jesse Jackson and the Southern white electorate in 1984. In L. W. Moreland, R. P. Steed, & T. A. Baker (Eds.), *Blacks in Southern politics* (pp. 209-225). New York: Praeger.

318                                                                  CONFRONTING RACISM

Sears, D. O., Citrin, J., & van Laar, C. (1995, September). *Black exceptionalism in a multicultural society.* Paper presented at the joint meeting of the Society for Experimental Psychology and the European Association of Experimental Social Psychology, Washington, D.C.
Sears, D. O., Citrin, J., Cheleden, S. V., & van Laar, C. (1998). Cultural diversity and multicultural politics: Is ethnic balkanization psychologically inevitable? In D. Prentice and D. Miller (Eds.), *Cultural Divides.* New York: Russell Sage Foundation.
Sears, D. O., & Funk, C. L. (1991). The role of self-interest in social and political attitudes. In M. Zanna (Ed.), *Advances in experimental social psychology, Vol. 24* (pp. 1-91). Orlando, FL: Academic Press.
Sears, D. O., Hensler, C. P., & Speer, L. K. (1979). Whites' opposition to "busing": Self-interest or symbolic politics? *American Political Science Review, 73,* 369-384.
Sears, D. O., & Huddy, L. (1992). The symbolic politics of opposition to bilingual education. In J. Simpson & S. Worchel (Eds.), *Conflict between people and peoples* (pp. 145-169). Chicago: Nelson-Hall.
Sears, D. O., & Jessor, T. (1996). Whites' racial policy attitudes: The role of white racism. *Social Science Quarterly, 77*(4), 751-759.
Sears, D. O., & Kinder, D. R. (1971). Racial tensions and voting in Los Angeles. In W. Z. Hirsch (Ed.), *Los Angeles: Viability and prospects for metropolitan leadership* (pp. 51-88). New York: Praeger.
Sears, D. O., & Kinder, D. R. (1985). Whites' opposition to busing: On conceptualizing and operationalizing group conflict. *Journal of Personality and Social Psychology, 48,* 1141-1147.
Sears, D. O., Lau, R. R., Tyler, T. R., & Allen, H. M., Jr. (1980). Self-interest versus symbolic politics in policy attitudes and presidential voting. *American Political Science Review, 74,* 670-684.
Sears, D. O., van Laar, C., Carrillo, M., & Kosterman, R. (1996). Is it really racism? The origins of white Americans' opposition to race-targeted policies. *Public Opinion Quarterly, 61*(1), 16-53.
Seligman, L., & Welch, S. (1991). *Black Americans' views of racial inequality: The dream deferred.* New York: Cambridge University Press.
Sellin, T. (1938). *Culture, conflict, and crime.* New York: Social Science Research Council.
Senna, J., Rathus, S. A., & Seigel, L. (1974). Delinquent behavior and academic investment among suburban youth. *Adolescence, 36,* 481-491.
Shaare Tefila Congregation v. Cobb, 481 U.S. 615 (1987).
Shaw v. Reno, 509 U.S. 113 (1993).
Sherer, M. (1990). Criminal activity among Jewish and Arab youth in Israel. *International Journal of Intercultural Relations, 14,* 529-548.
Sherif, M. (1966). *In common predicament.* Boston: Houghton Mifflin.
Sherif, M., & Sherif, C. W. (1953). *Groups in harmony and tension.* New York: Harper.
Sidanius, J. (1988). Race and sentence severity: The case of American justice. *Journal of Black Studies, 18,* 273-281.
Sidanius, J. (1993). The psychology of group conflict and the dynamics of oppression: A social dominance perspective. In S. Iyengar & W. McGuire (Eds.), *Explorations in political psychology* (pp. 183-219). Durham, NC: Duke University Press.
Sidanius, J., Levin, S., & Pratto, F. (1996). Consensual social dominance orientation and its correlates within the hierarchical structure of American society. *International Journal of Intercultural Relations, 20,* 385-408.
Sidanius, J., Liu, J., Pratto, F., & Shaw, J. (1994). Social dominance orientation, hierarchy-attenuators, and hierarchy-enhancers: Social dominance theory and the criminal justice system. *Journal of Applied Social Psychology, 24,* 338-366.

Sidanius, J., Pratto, F., & Bobo, L. (1994). Social dominance orientation and the political psychology of gender: A case of invariance? *Journal of Personality and Social Psychology, 67*(6), 1-13.

Sidanius, J., Pratto, F., & Bobo, L. (1996). Racism, conservatism, affirmative action, and intellectual sophistication: A matter of principled conservatism or group dominance? *Journal of Personality and Social Psychology, 70*(3), 1-15.

Sidanius, J., Pratto, F., Martin, M., & Stallworth, L. (1991). Consensual racism and career track: Some implications of social dominance theory. *Political Psychology, 12,* 691-721.

Sidanius, J., Pratto, F., Sinclair, S., & van Laar, C. (1996). Mother Teresa meets Genghis Khan: The dialectics of hierarchy-enhancing and hierarchy-attenuating career choices. *Social Justice Research, 9*(2), 145-170.

Siegel, R. (1996). "The rule of love": Wife beating as prerogative and privacy. *Yale Law Journal, 105,* 2117.

Simmons, R. G., Brown, L., Bush, D. M., & Blyth, D. A. (1978). Self-esteem and achievement of Black and White adolescents. *Social Problems, 26,* 86-96.

Skogan, W. (1990). The police and public in England and Wales: A British crime survey report. *Home Office Research Study, 117,* 26-37.

Small, S. (1994). *Racialized barriers: The black experience in the United States and England in the 1980s.* London: Rutledge.

Smedley, A. (1993). *Race in North America: Origin of a worldview.* Boulder, CO: Westview.

Smith, C. A., & Ellsworth, P. C. (1985). Patterns of cognitive appraisal in emotion. *Journal of Personality and Social Psychology, 48,* 813-838.

Smith, D. A., Visher, C. A., & Davisdon, L. A. (1984). Equity and discretionary justice: The influence of race on police arrest decisions. *Journal of Criminal Law and Criminology, 75,* 234-249.

Smith, D. J., & Gray, J. (1985). *Police and people in London* (Policy Studies Institute Report). Aldershot, Hants, UK: Policy Studies Institute.

Smith, T. W. (1984). The polls: Gender and attitudes toward violence. *Public Opinion Quarterly, 48,* 384-396.

Sniderman, P. M., & Hagen, M. G. (1985). *Race and inequality: A study in American values.* Chatham, NJ: Chatham House.

Sniderman, P. M., & Piazza, T. (1993). *The scar of race.* Cambridge, MA: Harvard University Press.

Sniderman, P. M., & Tetlock, P. E. (1986). Symbolic racism: Problems of motive attribution in political debate. *Journal of Social Issues, 42,* 173-188.

Snyder, M. (1992). Motivational foundations of behavioral confirmation. In M. P. Zanna (Ed.), *Advances in experimental social psychology* (Vol. 25, pp. 67-114). San Diego, CA: Academic Press.

Snyder, N., & Miene, P. K. (1994). Stereotyping of the elderly: A functional approach. *British Journal of Social Psychology, 33*(1), 63-82.

Sobral, J., Arce, R., & Farina, F. (1989). Aspectos psicosociales de las decisiones judiciales revision y lectura diferenciada [Psychosocial aspects of judicial decisions: Revision and differentiated reading]. *Boletin de Psicologia, 25,* 49-74.

Solomon, R. P. (1992). *Forging a separatist culture.* Albany: State University of New York Press.

Solomos, J., & Wrench, J. (1993). *Racism and migration in Western Europe.* Oxford, UK: Berg.

Sorensen, J. R., & Wallace, D. H. (1995). Capital punishment in Missouri: Examining the issue of racial disparity. *Behavioral Sciences and the Law, 13*(1), 61-80.

Spencer, S., Steele, C. M., & Quinn, D. (1997). *Under suspicion of inability: Stereotype threat and women's math performance.* Manuscript submitted for publication.

Spohn, C. (1994). Crime and the social control of blacks: Offender-victim race and the sentencing of violent offenders. In G. S. Bridges & M. A. Myers (Eds.), *Inequality, crime, and social control* (pp. 249-268). Boulder, CO: Westview.

State of Louisiana ex. rel. Frank Plaia v. Louisiana State Board of Health, 296 So.2d 809 (1974).

State v. Kimber, 3 Ohio Dec. 197 (1959).

Statistikah pelilit. (1992). Jerusalem, Israel: Lishkah ha-merkazit li-statistika.

Steele, C. M. (1975). Name-calling and compliance. *Journal of Personality and Social Psychology, 31,* 361-369.

Steele, C. M. (1988). The psychology of self-affirmation: Sustaining the integrity of the self. In L. Berkowitz (Ed.), *Advances in experimental social psychology* (Vol. 21, pp. 261-302). New York: Academic Press.

Steele, C. M. (1992, April). Race and the schooling of Black Americans. *The Atlantic Monthly,* pp. 68-78.

Steele, C. M., & Aronson, J. (1995). Stereotype threat and the intellectual test performance of African Americans. *Journal of Personality and Social Psychology, 69,* 797-811.

Steele, S. (1990). *The content of our character.* New York: St. Martin's Press.

Steeth, C., & Schuman, H. (1991). Changes in racial attitudes among young white adults, 1984-1990. *American Journal of Sociology, 96,* 340-367.

Stepan, N. (1982). *The idea of race in science: Great Britain 1800-1960.* Hamden, UK: Archon.

Stephan, W. G. (1985). Intergroup relations. In G. Lindzey & E. Aronson (Eds.), *Handbook of social psychology* (3rd ed., Vol. 2, pp. 599-658). New York: Random House.

Stephan, W. G. (1987). The contact hypothesis in intergroup relations. In C. Hendrick (Ed.), *Review of personality and social psychology: Vol. 9. Processes and intergroup relations* (pp. 13-40). Newbury Park, CA: Sage.

Stephan, W. G., & Stephan, C. W. (1985). Intergroup anxiety. *Journal of Social Issues, 41*(3), 157-175.

Stephan, W. G., Ybarra, O., & Bachman, G. (1996). *A threat model of prejudice: The case of immigrants.* Manuscript submitted for publication.

Stephan, W. G., Ybarra, O., Martinez, C. M., Schwarzwald, J., & Tur-Kaspa, M. (1996). *Prejudice toward immigrants to Spain and Israel: An integrated threat theory analysis.* Manuscript submitted for publication.

Stephenson, G. T. (1969). *Race distinctions in American law.* New York: AMS Press. (Original work published in 1910)

Stevens, L. E., & Fiske, S. T. (1996). *Forming motivated impressions of a powerholder: Misperception under evaluative dependency.* Unpublished manuscript, University of Massachusetts at Amherst.

Stevenson, H. C., Jr. (1993). Validation of the scale of racial socialization for African American adolescents: A preliminary analysis. *Psych Discourse, 24*(12), 7-12.

Stewart, J. E. (1980). Defendant's attractiveness as a factor in the outcome of criminal trials: An observational study. *Journal of Applied Social Psychology, 10,* 348-361.

Stewart, J. E. (1985). Appearance and punishment: The attraction-leniency effect in the courtroom. *Journal of Social Psychology, 125,* 373-378.

Strenta, A. C., Elliott, R., Adair, R., Scott, J., & Matier, M. (1993). *Choosing and leaving science in highly selective institutions.* Unpublished report to the Alfred P. Sloan Foundation.

Sunseri v. Cassagne, 191 La. 209 (1938).

Sutherland, E. H. (1940). White-collar criminality. *American Sociological Review, 5,* 1-12.

Swann, W. B., & Ely, R. M. (1984). A battle of self wills: Self-verification versus behavioral conformation. *Journal of Personality and Social Psychology, 46* 1287-1302.

Swann, W. B., Jr., & Read, S. J. (1981a). Acquiring self-knowledge: The search for feedback that fits. *Journal of Personality and Social Psychology, 41,* 1119-1128.

Swann, W. B., Jr., & Read, S. J. (1981b). Self-verification processes: How we sustain our self-conceptions. *Journal of Experimental Social Psychology, 17,* 351-370.

Sweeney, L. T., & Haney, C. (1992). The influence of race on sentencing: A meta-analytic review of experimental studies. *Behavioral Sciences and the Law, 10,* 179-195.

Tajfel, H. (1978). Social categorization, social identity, and social comparison. In H. Tajfel (Ed.), *Differentiation between social groups: Studies in the social psychology of intergroup relations* (pp. 61-76). New York: Academic Press.

Tajfel, H. (1981). *Human groups and social categories: Studies in social psychology.* Cambridge, UK: Cambridge University Press.

Tajfel, H. (Ed.). (1982). *Social identity and intergroup relations.* Cambridge, UK: Cambridge University Press.

Tajfel, H., & Turner, J. C. (1979). An integrative theory of intergroup conflict. In W. G. Austin and S. Worchel (Eds.), *The social psychology of intergroup relations* (pp. 33-48). Monterey, CA: Brooks/Cole.

Tajfel, H., & Turner, J. C. (1986). The social identity theory of intergroup behavior. In S. Worchel & W. G. Austin (Eds.), *Psychology of intergroup relations* (pp. 7-24). Chicago: Nelson-Hall.

Taylor, J. (1980). Dimensionalization of racialism and the black experience: The Pittsburgh project. In R. L. Jones (Ed.), *Black psychology* (2nd ed., pp. 384-400. New York: Russell Sage.

Taylor, J. (1990). Relationships between internalized racism and marital satisfaction. *Journal of Black Psychology, 16*(2), 45-53.

Taylor, J. (in press). Cultural conversion experiences: Implications for mental health research and treatment. In R. L. Jones (Ed.), *Advances in black psychology.* Berkeley, CA: Cobb & Henry.

Taylor, J., & Franklin, A. (in press). Psychological analysis of black teenage pregnancies: Implications for public cultural policies. *Policy Studies Journal.*

Taylor, J., & Grundy, C. (in press). Measuring black internalization of white stereotypes about blacks: The Nadanolitization Scale. In R. L. Jones (Ed.), *Test and measurements for black populations.* Berkeley, CA: Cobb & Henry.

Taylor, J., Henderson, D., & Jackson, B. B. (1991). A holistic model for understanding and predicting depression in African American women. *Journal of Community Psychology, 19,* 306-320.

Taylor, J., & Jackson, B. (1990a). Factors affecting alcohol consumption in black women: Part I. *International Journal of the Addictions, 25,* 1287-1300.

Taylor, J., & Jackson, B. (1990b). Factors affecting alcohol consumption in black women: Part II. *International Journal of the Addictions, 25,* 1415-1427.

Taylor, J., & Jackson, B. (in press). Evaluation of a holistic model of mental health symptoms in African American women. *Journal of Black Psychology.*

Taylor, J., & Rogers, J. (1993). Relationship between cultural identity and exchange disposition. *British Journal of Social Psychology, 19,* 248-265.

Taylor, J., Underwood, C., Thomas, L., & Zhang, X. (1990). Effects of dysphoria on maternal exchange dispositions. *Journal of Psychology, 124,* 685-697.

Taylor, J., & Zhang, X. (1990). Cultural identity in martially distressed and nondistressed black couples. *Western Journal of Black Studies, 14,* 205-213.

Taylor, R. J., Jackson, J. S., & Quick, A. D. (1982). The frequency of social support among black Americans. *Urban Research Review, 8*(2), 1-4.

Taylor, R. L. (1979). Black ethnicity and the persistence of ethnogenesis. *American Journal of Sociology, 84,* 1401-1423.

Taylor, S. E., Fiske, S. T., Etcoff, N. L., & Ruderman, A. J. (1978). Categorization and contextual bases of person memory and stereotyping. *Journal of Personality and Social Psychology, 36,* 778-793.

Taylor, S. E., Repetti, R. L., & Seeman, T. (1997). Health psychology: What is an unhealthy environment and how does it get under the skin? *Annual review of psychology, 48,* 411-447. Palo Alto, CA: Annual Reviews.

Teahan, J. E. (1975a). A longitudinal study of attitude shifts among black and white police officers. *Journal of Social Issues, 31*(1), 47-56.

Teahan, J. E. (1975b). Role playing and group experience to facilitate attitude and value changes among black and white police officers. *Journal of Social Issues, 31*(1), 35-45.

Terrell, F., & Taylor, J. (1980). The development of an inventory to measure certain aspects of black nationalist ideology. *Psychology, 15*(3), 31-33.

Terrell, F., Taylor, J., & Terrell, S. (1980). Self-concept of juveniles who commit black-on-black crimes. *Corrective and Social Psychiatry, 26*(3), 107-109.

Tesser, A. (1988). Toward a self-evaluation maintenance model of social behavior. In L. Berkowitz (Ed.), *Advances in experimental social psychology* (Vol. 21, pp. 181-227). New York: Academic Press.

Thernstrom, S., Orlov, A., & Handlin, O. (Eds.). (1980). *Harvard encyclopedia of American ethnic groups.* Cambridge, MA: Harvard University Press.

Thibault, J. W., & Kelley, H. H. (1959). *The social psychology of groups.* New York: John Wiley.

Thoits, P. A. (1991). On merging identity theory and stress research. *Social Psychology Quarterly, 54*(2), 101-112.

Thomas, W. I., & Thomas, D. S. (1928). *The child in America: Behavior problems and programs.* New York: Knopf.

Thornberry, T. P. (1973). Race, socioeconomic status, and sentencing in the juvenile justice system. *Journal of Criminal Law and Criminology, 64*(1), 90-98.

Timmerman, H., Bosma, J. J., & Jongman, R. W. (1986). Minderheden voor de rechter. *Tudschrift voor Criminologie, 2,* 57-72.

Towers, T., McGinley, H., & Pasewark, R. A. (1992). Insanity defense: Ethnicity of defendants and mock jurors. *Journal of Psychiatry and Law, 20,* 243-256.

Treisman, U. (1985). *A study of mathematics performance of Black students at the University of California, Berkeley.* Unpublished report.

Triandis, H. C. (1990). Theoretical concepts that are applicable to the analysis of ethnocentrism. In R. W. Brislin (Ed.), *Applied cross-cultural psychology* (pp. 34-55). Newbury Park, CA: Sage.

Turk, A. (1969). *Criminality and the legal order.* Chicago: Rand McNally.

Turner, J. C. (1987). *Rediscovering the social group: A self-categorization theory.* New York: Basil Blackwell.

Turner, J. C., Hogg, M. A., Oakes, P. J., Reicher, S. D., & Wetherell, M. S. (1987). *Rediscovering the social group: A self-categorization theory.* Oxford, UK: Blackwell.

Turner, J. C., Oakes, P. J., Haslam, S. A., & McGarty, C. (1994). Self and collective: Cognition and social context. *Personality and Social Psychology Bulletin, 20,* 454-463.

Turner, M. E., & Pratkanis, A. R. (1994). Affirmative action as help: A review of recipient reactions to preferential selection and affirmative action. *Basic and Applied Social Psychology, 15,* 43-70.

United States Sentencing Commission. (1995). *Special report to the Congress: Cocaine and federal sentencing policy.* Washington, DC: Author.

Unnerver, J. D., & Hembroff, L. A. (1988). The prediction of racial-ethnic sentencing disparities: An expectation states approach. *Journal of Research in Crime and Delinquency, 25*(1), 53-82.

van de Berghe, P. L. (1981). *The ethnic phenomenon.* New York: Elsevier.

Vanneman, R. D., & Pettigrew, T. F. (1972). Race and relative deprivation in the urban United States. *Race, 13,* 461-486.

Vars, F. E., & Bowen, W. G. (1997). *SAT scores, race, and academic performance: New evidence from academically successful colleges.* Unpublished manuscript.

Vidanage, S., & Sears, D. O. (1995, April). *The foundations of public opinion toward immigration policy: Group conflict or symbolic politics?* Paper presented at the annual meeting of the Midwest Political Science Association, Chicago.

Visher, C. A. (1983). Gender, police arrest decisions, and notions of chivalry. *Criminology, 21*(1), 5-28.

Voigt, L., Thornton, W. E., Jr., Barrile, L., & Seaman, J. M. (Eds.). (1994). *Criminology and justice.* New York: McGraw-Hill.

Volckens, J. S. (1996). *Rethinking group threat: German's perceptions of encroachment by Turkish residents.* Unpublished manuscript, University of Michigan, Ann Arbor.

Vold, G. (1979). *Theoretical criminality.* New York: Oxford University Press.

Von Hofer, H., & Tham, H. (1991). Foreign citizens and crime: The Swedish case. *Statistiska Centralbyrån Promemoria, 4.*

Wagner, U., & Zick, A. (1995). The relation of formal education to ethnic prejudice: Its reliability, validity, and explanation. *European Journal of Social Psychology, 25*(1), 41-56.

Walsh, A. (1987). The sexual stratification hypothesis and sexual assault in light of the changing conceptions of race. *Criminology, 25,* 153-173.

Ware, N. C., & Dill, D. (1986, March). *Persistence in science among mathematically able male and female college students with precollege plans for a scientific major.* Paper presented at the annual meeting of the American Educational Research Association, San Francisco.

Ware, N. C., Steckler, N. A., & Leserman, J. (1985). Undergraduate women: Who chooses a science major? *Journal of Higher Education, 56,* 73-84.

Weary, G., Marsh, K. L., Gleicher, F., & Edwards, J. A. (1993). Social-cognitive consequences of depression. In G. Weary, F. Gleicher, & K. L. Marsh (Eds.), *Control motivation and social cognition* (pp. 55-290). New York: Springer-Verlag.

Weber, M. (1961). Ethnic groups. In T. Parsons (Ed.), *Theory of society* (pp. 301-309). New York: Free Press.

Weigel, R. H., & Howes, P. W. (1985). Conceptions of racial prejudice: Symbolic racism reconsidered. *Journal of Social Issues, 41*(3), 117-138.

Weiner, B. (1985). An attributional theory of achievement motivation and emotion. *Psychological Review, 92,* 548-573.

Weisz, J. R., Martin, S. L., Walter, B. R., & Fernandez, G. A. (1991). Differential prediction of young adult arrests for property and personal crimes: Findings of a cohort follow-up study of violent boys from North Carolina's Willie M. Program. *Journal of Child Psychology and Psychiatry and Allied Disciplines, 32,* 783-792.

Welke, B. Y. (1995). *Gendered journeys: A history of injury, public transport, and American law, 1865-1920.* Unpublished doctoral dissertation, University of Chicago.

West Chester & Philadelphia Railroad Co v. Miles, 55 Penn. St. 209 (1867).

Wilbanks, W. (1988). Are elderly felons treated more leniently by the criminal justice system? *International Journal of Aging and Human Development, 26,* 275-288.

Wills, T. A. (1981). Downward comparison principles of social psychology. *Psychological Bulletin, 90,* 245-271.

Wilson, E. O. (1978). The genetic evolution of altruism. In L. Wispe (Ed.), *Altruism, sympathy, and helping* (pp. 11-37). New York: Academic Press.

Wilson, W. J. (1973). *Power, racism, and privilege: Race relations in theoretical and sociohistorical perspectives.* New York: Free Press.

Wilson, W. J. (1987). *The truly disadvantaged.* Chicago: University of Chicago Press.

Wine, J. (1971). Test anxiety and direction of attention. *Psychological Bulletin, 76,* 92-104.

Wittenbrink, B., Judd, C. M., & Park, B. (1995). *Implicit racial stereotypes and prejudice and their relationships with questionnaire measures: What we say is what we think.* Unpublished manuscript, University of Colorado.

Wolfe, C. T., & Crocker, J. (1996). *Basing self-esteem on approval from others: Measurement and data.* Manuscript in preparation, University of Michigan, Ann Arbor.

Word, C., Zanna, M. P., & Cooper, J. (1974). The verbal mediation of self-fulfilling prophecies in interracial interaction. *Journal of Experimental Social Psychology, 10*(2), 109-120.

Wylie, R. (1979). *The self-concept* (Vol. 2). Lincoln: University of Nebraska Press.

Yancy, W., Ericksen, E., & Juliani, R. (1976). Emergent ethnicity: A review and reformulation. *American Sociological Review, 41,* 391-403.

Yanico, B. J., Swanson, J. L., & Tokar, D. M. (1994). A psychometric investigation of the black racial identity attitude scale—Form B. *Journal of Vocational Behavior, 44,* 218-234.

Ybarra, O., & Stephan, W. G. (1994). Perceived threat as a predictor of prejudice and stereotypes: Americans' reactions to Mexican immigrants. *Boletin de Psicologia, 42,* 39-54.

Yee, A. H., Fairchild, H., Weizmann, F., & Wyatt, G. E. (1993). Addressing psychology's problems with race. *American Psychologist, 48,* 1132-1140.

Yinger, J. M. (1985). Ethnicity. *Annual Review of Sociology, 11,* 151-180.

Young, T. J. (1993). Alcohol misuse and criminal violence among Native Americans. *Psychiatric Forum, 16,* 20-26.

Yzerbyt, V., Rocher, S., & Schadron, G. (1997). Stereotypes as explanations. In R. Spears, P. J. Oakes, N. Ellemers, & S. A. Haslam (Eds.), *The social psychology of stereotyping in group life* (pp. 20-50). Oxford, UK: Blackwell.

Zárate, M. A., & Smith, E. R. (1990). Person categorization and stereotyping. *Social Cognition, 8,* 161-185.

Zajonc, R. B. (1980). Feeling and thinking: Preferences need no inferences. *American Psychologist, 35,* 151-175.

Zebrowitz, L. A. (1996). Physical appearance as a basis of stereotyping. In C. N. Macrae, C. Stangor, & M. Hewstone (Eds.), *Stereotypes & stereotyping* (pp. 79-120). New York: Guilford.

Zuckerman, M. (1990). Some dubious premises in research and theory on racial differences. *American Psychologist, 45,* 1297-1303.

Zuwerink, J. R., Devine, P. G., Monteith, M. J., & Cook, D. A. (1996). Prejudice toward blacks: With and without compunction? *Basic and Applied Social Psychology, 18*(4), 131-150.

# Index

# About the Editors

**Jennifer L. Eberhardt** is Assistant Professor of Psychology and African American Studies at Yale University. She received her B.A. from the University of Cincinnati in 1987 and her Ph.D. in psychology from Harvard University in 1993. Her primary research interests include racial stereotyping, prejudice, and stigma. She has conducted a number of studies to delineate the factors influencing black Americans' perceptions of prejudice and discrimination in their interactions with whites. In addition, she is interested in how race affects social interactions for both blacks and whites. In 1994-1995, she was the recipient of an Irvine Postdoctoral Teaching Fellowship, an award given to support the development and improvement of multicultural curricula. Also in 1994-1995, she was the recipient of a National Academy of Education Spencer Postdoctoral Fellowship, which enabled her to pursue research involving black students' perceptions of prejudice and discrimination in the academic setting. She is a member of APA and APS and a research Fellow at Yale's Center for Race, Inequality, and Politics. She has served as a reviewer for *Psychological Bulletin, Psychological Science,* and the *Journal of Experimental Social Psychology.*

**Susan T. Fiske,** Distinguished University Professor of Psychology, joined the University of Massachusetts at Amherst faculty in 1986. A 1978 Harvard Ph.D., she received an honorary doctorate from the Université Catholique de Louvain, Louvain-la-Neuve, Belgium, in 1995. She has authored some 50 journal articles and 35 book chapters; she has edited 7 books and journal special issues. Her graduate text, with Shelley Taylor, *Social Cognition* (1984; 2nd ed., 1991), is viewed as defining the subfield of how people think about and make sense of other people. Her federally funded social cognition research focuses on social structure, motivation, and stereotyping, which led to expert testimony cited by the U.S. Supreme Court in a landmark discrimination case. She won the 1991 American Psychological Association Award for Distinguished Contributions to Psychology in the Public Interest, Early Career, in part for that testimony. She also won, with Peter Glick, the 1995 Gordon Allport Intergroup Relations award from the Society for the Psychological Study of Social Issues. She was 1994 president of the Society for Personality and Social Psychology, and she edited, with Daniel Gilbert and Gardner Lindzey, *The Handbook of Social Psychology* (4th ed., 1998). On campus, she teaches undergraduate courses on social psychology and on racism, and she serves on several diversity and multiculturalism committees.

# About the Contributors

R. Richard Banks, a lawyer and writer, received A.B. and A.M. degrees from Stanford University in 1987. He received his J.D., with honors, from Harvard Law School in 1994. He writes on issues concerning the intersection of race and law. His articles have appeared in a wide range of both popular and scholarly publications, including the *New York Times,* the *Los Angeles Times,* and the *Yale Law Journal.*

Kendrick T. Brown, M.A., is a graduate student in the Social Psychology Program in the Department of Psychology at the University of Michigan. His research interests include the influence of skin tone in the African American community, racial identity, psychological well-being, and survey methodology.

Jennifer Crocker attended Reed College and graduated from Michigan State University. She received her Ph.D. from Harvard University in 1979, where her adviser was Shelley Taylor, and Susan Fiske was a fellow student. From 1979 to 1985, she was Assistant Professor of Psychology at Northwestern University, with the exception of one winter she spent at the University of Minnesota as a visiting assistant professor. In 1982, she spent a summer as a Fellow in the Summer Institute on Stigma and Interpersonal Relations at the Center for Advanced Study in the Behavioral Sciences, where her interest in social stigma began. From 1985 to 1995 she was Associate and then full

Professor at the State University of New York at Buffalo. At SUNY at Buffalo, she began her collaboration with Brenda Major on the consequences of social stigma for self-esteem. She moved to the University of Michigan in 1995, where she is Professor of Psychology, Faculty Associate at the Research Center for Group Dynamics at the Institute for Social Research, and chair of the social psychology area of the Psychology Department. With Brenda Major and Claude Steele, she is the author of a chapter on social stigma in the fourth edition of the *Handbook of Social Psychology.*

**Patricia G. Devine** (Ph.D., Ohio State University) is Professor of Psychology at the University of Wisconsin—Madison and is Chair of the Program in Social and Personality Psychology. Her primary research interests focus on the nature of prejudice and intergroup relations. She has also done research on eyewitness identification, impression formation, social hypothesis testing, dissonance theory, and resistance to persuasion. She edited, with David Hamilton and Thomas Ostrom, *Social Cognition: Impact on Social Psychology.* She is currently Associate Editor of the *Journal of Personality and Social Psychology.* Her research and teaching have been recognized with numerous awards and honors. She is the recipient of the 1990 Gordon Allport Intergroup Relations Prize and the 1994 American Psychological Association's Distinguished Scientific Award for an Early Career Contribution; she is also the recipient of the Robert S. Daniel Distinguished Teaching Award from the American Psychological Association.

**John F. Dovidio** is Charles A. Dana Professor of Psychology and Director of University Studies at Colgate University. He received his B.A. from Dartmouth College and, in 1977, his Ph.D. from the University of Delaware. His research interests are in stereotyping, prejudice, and discrimination; social power and nonverbal communication; and altruism and helping. Among his publications is *Prejudice, Discrimination, and Racism,* a book he coedited with Samuel Gaertner. He has served as Editor of *Personality and Social Psychology Bulletin* and is serving as Associate Editor of *Group Processes and Intergroup Relations.* He is also a member of the editorial boards of the *British Journal of Social Psychology* and of *Social Psychology Quarterly.* He is currently a member of the Executive Committee for the Society for the Psychological Study of Social Issues.

**Samuel L. Gaertner** is Professor of Psychology at the University of Delaware. He received his B.A. from Brooklyn College and his Ph.D. from the City University of New York, Graduate Center, in 1970. He is currently examining a strategy for reducing intergroup bias that involves inducing the members of two groups to conceive of themselves as one, more inclusive group rather than as two completely separate groups. He was awarded the 1985 Gordon Allport Award Prize, shared with John Dovidio, for their work on aversive racism. He is presently a member of the Council for the Society for the Psychological Study of Social Issues as well as the editorial boards of the *Journal of Personality and Social Psychology, Personality and Social Psychology Bulletin,* and *Group Processes and Intergroup Relations.*

**James S. Jackson** (Ph.D. in social psychology from Wayne State University) joined the faculty of the University of Michigan in 1971. He has published widely on issues of race and ethnic relations and African American health and mental health, intergenerational relations, adult development and aging, and political behavior; he holds positions at Michigan in these areas as well. Recently appointed Daniel Katz Distinguished University Professor of Psychology, he is a research scientist at the Institute for Social Research, where he is also Director of the Research Center for Group Dynamics and Director and Founder of the Program for Research on Black Americans; Professor of Health Behavior and Health Education in the School of Public Health; and faculty associate at the Center for Afro-American and African Studies and the Institute of Gerontology. He is a Fellow of the American Psychological Society, American Psychological Association, and the Gerontological Society of America, and a member or past member of several review panels, including the National Cancer Institute Scientific Panel on Black-White Cancer Survival Differences, National Advisory Mental Health Council of National Institute of Mental Health (NIMH), and the European Economic Community Study on Immigration and Racism. He is also past chair of the Association for the Advancement of Psychology and the National Association of Black Psychologists. For 1993-1994 he received a Fogarty Senior Postdoctoral International Fellowship for study in France, where he holds the position of *Chercheur Invité* in the *Groupe d'Etudes et de Recherches sur la Science, Ecole des Hautes Etudes en Sciences Sociales.*

**James M. Jones** earned his B.A. degree from Oberlin College in 1963, an M.A. from Temple University in 1967, and a Ph.D. in experimental social psychology at Yale University in 1970. He has taught at Harvard University, Howard University, and is now Professor of Psychology at the University of Delaware. With the support of a Guggenheim Fellowship, he spent 1973 in

Trinidad studying calypso humor. A second edition of his classic 1972 book, *Prejudice and Racism,* was published in December 1996. He is now at work on a new book, *Cultural Psychology of African Americans.* He is a member of the editorial boards of numerous scientific journals and is a past president of the Society of Experimental Social Psychology. He also currently serves as Director of the Minority Fellowship Program and Affirmative Action Officer at the American Psychological Association.

**Daria C. Kirby** is Assistant Professor of Business Administration in the Katz Graduate School of Business, and an adjunct in the Center for Western European Studies Program at the University of Pittsburgh. She received her doctorate in organizational psychology from the University of Michigan. Her research examines the legal, social, and environmental pressures that influence university affirmative action behavior. In addition, she is examining cultural diversity and the development of public policy legislation in the European Union. She is currently investigating the opinions and employment patterns of ethnic minority expatriates living in Europe, to better design selection, training, career planning, and mentoring programs to meet the needs of this group. She consults with the American Assembly Collegiate Schools of Business on how to address issues of diversity in curriculum thus creating a more diverse learning environment. She also teaches International Human Resource Management in the executive education course Global Alliance for Leadership. Her professional involvement includes membership in the Academy of Management and European Community Studies Association. She has served as a reviewer for Sage Publications, *Academy of Management Review, Psychology of Women Quarterly, Business and Society,* and *Human Resources Management Journal.*

**Shana Levin** received her Ph.D. in social psychology at UCLA in 1996. Her area of specialization includes issues of intergroup relations, stereotyping, and intergroup discrimination. Her doctoral dissertation was titled *A Social Psychological Approach to Understanding Intergroup Attitudes in the United States and Israel.* She is the author of six research articles and book chapters dealing with these topics. She is presently serving as a postdoctoral Fellow in the Department of Psychology at UCLA.

**Audrey J. Murrell** received her B.S. from Howard University, magna cum laude, in 1983. She received her M.S. in 1985 and a Ph.D. in 1987 from the University of Delaware. Her field of study while at Delaware was social psychology. She held an academic position in the psychology department at the University of Pittsburgh before joining the faculty of the Katz Graduate School of Business in 1989. Her research interests focus on how individuals become effective members of groups in society and within organizations. She has published widely on the positive versus negative effects of career mobility and transition, emphasizing factors that impact women in management (e.g., sexual harassment, diversity, mentoring). She consults with organizations concerning teamwork effectiveness, diversity, sexual harassment, and workplace discrimination, and she is coauthor of the forthcoming book *Multicultural Mentoring*. She currently serves on several boards of directors—the Minority Enterprise Corporation of Southwestern PA, Family Services of Southwestern PA, Three Rivers Adoption Council, and the Southwestern Pennsylvania Chapter of the American Red Cross—and volunteers with the American Red Cross within the disaster services unit, as a team leader for the disaster action team, a public affairs specialist, and instructor for disaster specialty and community education courses. She is currently examining how management succession influences the development of business opportunities (particularly for minorities and women).

**Don Operario** received his B.S. (UCLA, 1993) in psychology with a concentration in developmental disabilities. He is currently a Ph.D. candidate in personality-social psychology at the University of Massachusetts at Amherst. His research focuses on power and intergroup relations, specifically addressing how stigma and powerlessness affects people's self-concept and influences their interactions with others. He also studies and advocates for multicultural issues in psychology. His research interests stem from his own experiences as a Filipino American, as well as his constant exposure to ethnic issues while growing up in Los Angeles.

**Thomas F. Pettigrew** is Research Professor of Social Psychology at the University of California, Santa Cruz. He earned his B.A. at the University of Virginia (1952) and his M.A. and Ph.D. at Harvard University (1955, 1956). He has taught at the Universities of North Carolina (1956-1957), Harvard (1957-1980), Amsterdam (1986-1991), and California at Santa Cruz (from 1980 to the present). He has served as president of the Society for the Psychological Study of Social Issues (1967-1968); he was also elected a member of the council of the American Sociological Association (1979-1982). He has received a Guggenheim Fellowship (1967-1968), the Spivack Award for Race Relations Research (1978), the Kurt Lewin Award (1987), (with

Joanne Martin) the Allport Intergroup Relations Research Prize (1988), and Fellowships to the Center for Advanced Study in the Behavioral Sciences (1975-1976), The Netherlands Institute for Advanced Study (1984-1985), and the Bellagio Study Center (1991). Specializing throughout his career in intergroup relations, his books include *A Profile of the Negro American* (1964), *Racially Separate or Together?* (1971), *Racial Discrimination in the U.S.* (1975), *The Sociology of Race Relations* (1980), (with Denice Alston) *Tom Bradley's Campaigns for Governor: The Dilemma of Race and Political Strategies* (1988), and *How to Think Like a Social Scientist* (1996).

**Felicia Pratto** is Associate Professor of Psychology at the University of Connecticut. Her research focuses on prejudice, broadly defined. She has examined automatic and unintended evaluations of social stimuli, the role of ideology and social context in promoting stereotyping and discrimination, and the joint influence of psychological orientations and social context on the interpretation of social stimuli and discriminatory behavior. Along with Jim Sidanius, she is the coauthor of social dominance theory.

**Diane Quinn** is a graduate student in social psychology at the University of Michigan. She received her undergraduate degree from the University of Virginia. Her research interests have focused on the experience of being a member of a stigmatized group. She has looked at the effects of stereotypes about women's mathematical abilities on women's math achievement. Currently, she is examining vulnerability and resiliency factors for the psychological well-being of the overweight.

**David O. Sears** received his undergraduate degree in history from Stanford and his 1962 doctoral degree in social and personality psychology from Yale University. At UCLA since 1961, Sears is Professor of Psychology and Political Science, Director of the Institute for Social Science Research, and Chair of the Program in Political Psychology. He was formerly Dean of Social Sciences at UCLA, president of the Society for the Advancement of Socioeconomics, and president of the International Society of Political Psychology. He is a past Guggenheim Fellow and past Fellow of the Center for Advanced Studies in the Behavioral Sciences and the Brookings Institution. His early research focused on experiments concerning communication and attitude change, but as a result of the Watts riots in 1965, he turned to survey research on ghetto violence, resulting in a 1973 book with McConahay, *The Politics of Violence: The New Urban Blacks and the Watts Riot.* He has conducted much research on white racism in U.S. politics, especially "symbolic racism." He also worked on a more general theory of symbolic politics, which generated a 1982 book with Citrin, *Tax Revolt: Something for Nothing in California.* He is also a coauthor of *Social Psychology, Public Opinion,* and coeditor of *Political Cognition.* He has conducted considerable research on selective exposure in communication, political socialization, the gender gap, the use of college students as experimental subjects, the persistence of political attitudes through the life span, and the person positivity bias. His current work focuses on racism in U.S. politics and on public opinion about multiculturalism.

**Jim Sidanius** received his B.A. in psychology from City College, City University of New York, in 1968 and his Ph.D. in political psychology at the University of Stockholm, Sweden, in 1977, where he also taught for 10 years. Since returning to the United States in 1983, he has taught at several universities, including Carnegie-Mellon University, the University of Texas at Austin, New York University, and Princeton University. He joined the Psychology Department at UCLA in 1988. He is the author of some 70 scientific papers in the fields of political-psychology, sex-gender differences, group conflict, and institutional discrimination. At present he is working on a book, together with Felicia Pratto, titled *Social Dominance: An Intergroup Theory of Social Hierarchy and Oppression.*

**Claude M. Steele** received his B.A. from Hiram College and his 1971 Ph.D. from Ohio State University. He has been Professor of Psychology at Stanford University since 1992, and was previously at the University of Michigan, the University of Washington, and the University of Utah. His research spans three areas: Throughout his career he has studied self-evaluation, in particular how people cope with self-image threat. This work led to a general theory of self-affirmation processes. A second interest, growing out of the first, is a theory of how group stereotypes—by posing an extra self-evaluative and belongingness threat to such groups as African Americans in all academic domains and women in quantitative domains—can influence intellectual performance and academic identities. Third, he has long been interested in addictive behaviors, particularly alcohol addiction, where his work with several colleagues has led to a theory of "alcohol myopia," a theory in which many of alcohol's social and stress-reducing effects—effects that may underlie its addictive capacity—are explained as a consequence of alcohol's narrowing of perceptual and cognitive functioning. He was on the board of directors of the American Psychological Society and president of the Western Psychological Association. He has also served as Chair of the Executive Committee of the Society of Experimental Social Psychology, as a member of the executive committee of Personality and Social Psychology (Division 8, of the APA), and on the editorial boards of numerous journals and study sections at both the National Institute of Mental Health and the National Institute of Alcoholism and Alcohol Abuse. He is a Fellow of the APS and the APA, a member of the American Academy of Arts and Sciences, and the 1996 winner of the Gordon Allport Intergroup Relations Prize.

**Kristin A. Vasquez** is a National Science Foundation predoctoral Fellow at the University of Wisconsin—Madison. She holds master's degrees in psychology and business administration. Her main research interests include prejudice and discrimination, morality, and emotion. Her dissertation research examines the moral foundation of the prejudice reduction process and cross-cultural differences and similarities in that process.